LEGAL WRITING and ANALYSIS
Second Edition

Michael D. Murray
Valparaiso University School of Law
and
Christy H. DeSanctis
The George Washington University Law School

FOUNDATION
PRESS

© 2009 Thomson Reuters/Foundation Press
© 2015 LEG, Inc. d/b/a West Academic
444 Cedar Street, Suite 700
St. Paul, MN 55101
1-877-888-1330

Printed in the United States of America

ISBN: 978-1-60930-245-0

ABOUT THE AUTHORS

Michael D. Murray is Associate Professor of Law at Valparaiso University School of Law. He taught at the University of Illinois College of Law from 2002 to 2008, and Saint Louis University School of Law from 1998-2002. Professor Murray teaches law school, graduate school, and undergraduate courses in Art Law, Civil Procedure, First Amendment and Censorship, International Art and Cultural Heritage, International Civil Liberties: Freedom of Expression, Introduction to Advocacy, Legal Research and Writing, Legal Writing and Analysis, and Professional Responsibility. Professor Murray is the author or coauthor of eighteen books and numerous law review articles on art law, civil procedure, copyright, freedom of expression, law and the health care professions, legal research and writing, and products liability. His casebook, *Art Law: Cases and Materials* (1st ed. 2004, 2d ed. 2010), is one of the most widely adopted casebooks in the field. Professor Murray graduated summa cum laude from Loyola University in Maryland and received a graduate certificate from Fudan University in Shanghai, China. He also graduated from Columbia Law School, where he was a Harlan Fiske Stone Scholar. He was a member of a national champion Jessup International Law Moot Court team at Columbia, and Notes Editor of the *Columbia Journal of Transnational Law*. After law school, he clerked for United States District Judge John F. Nangle of the Eastern District of Missouri and Chair of the Judicial Panel on Multidistrict Litigation. Murray also practiced commercial, intellectual property, and products liability litigation for seven years at Bryan Cave law firm in St. Louis.

Christy H. DeSanctis is Professor of Legal Research and Writing and Director of the Legal Research and Writing Program at the George Washington University Law School. The Program encompasses 1L Legal Research and Writing, and Introduction to Advocacy; the Scholarly Writing and LL.M. Thesis Programs; and an in-house Writing Center. After graduating from NYU School of Law, she clerked for John W. Bissell, the former Chief Judge of the U.S. District Court for the District of New Jersey. Prior to joining the GW faculty, Professor DeSanctis practiced at the Washington, D.C., law firms of Collier Shannon Scott and Steptoe & Johnson. There, she focused on trial and appellate litigation at both the state and federal level, including in the U.S. Supreme Court, and worked on a variety of regulatory and legislative matters before federal agencies and Congress. She also published numerous articles relating to major legislative efforts with which she was directly involved, including terrorism insurance legislation and federal health and financial privacy regulations. Professor DeSanctis began teaching as an adjunct faculty member at GW in 2002; she was appointed to the fulltime faculty and assumed the Directorship of the LRW Program in 2004. In addition to teaching legal research and writing courses, she also teaches Law and Literature. She regularly speaks at conferences on legal writing and rhetoric. Professor DeSanctis also has taught several undergraduate English courses at the University of Maryland, College Park, including: Introduction to the Novel; American Literature after 1865; and Freshman Composition, a persuasive writing course based in part on theories of classical rhetoric. In addition to her J.D., Professor DeSanctis holds a Masters in English language and literature with a minor in rhetoric and composition from the University of Maryland. She is a Ph.D. candidate (ABD) in nineteenth and twentieth century American Literature.

DEDICATION

To Denise, Olivia, and Dennis, who make it fun;

To my sisters, Margaret, Mary, Jeannette, Anne, and Laura, who proved to me that the benefits of a teaching career outweigh all the costs.

M.D.M.
Valparaiso, IN
January 2015

To Michael B. DeSanctis, the best lawyer ever (and I am not biased);.

C.H.D.
Washington, DC
January 2015

ACKNOWLEDGMENTS

This book is a continuation of the LRW Series at Foundation Press that we, the authors, started nine years ago. We have had a great deal of assistance from editors and others at Foundation Press over the past ten years. In particular, we would like to thank Ryan Pfeiffer at Foundation Press for steering the new edition through the process. We thank Tessa Boury and Robb Westawker who steered the last edition from a text-only to an interactive book project at Foundation Press, and Heidi Boe and Bob Temple for their part in making the last edition come to fruition. We continue to thank John Bloomquist, the former Editor-in-Chief and Publisher of Foundation Press, for many dedicated years of helping us through each of the stages of publication, marketing, and sales of our books. And we remember fondly Steve Errick, the former Publisher of Foundation Press, for being the first to latch on to our book proposal and for never giving up on it.

Several other people also are owed our gratitude for their unwavering support of our professional endeavors and participation in the process resulting in this book. Professor Murray would like to single out his research and teaching assistants: Sasha Madlem, Robin Martinez, Tyler Pratt, and Vanessa Sheehan at Valparaiso University School of Law; Lindsay Beyer, Brian George, Aaron Goldberg, and Maurice Holman at the University of Illinois College of Law, and Renee Auderer, Jeannie Bell, Jonathan Blitz, John Challis, and Katalin Raby at Saint Louis University School of Law. Special thanks also are due to Professor Murray's assistants over the last nine years, Kristin Takish at Valparaiso University, and Mary Parsons and Deanna Shumard at the University of Illinois, whose support above and beyond the call of duty is remarkable and much appreciated.

Professor DeSanctis would like to recognize the many classes of GW Law Dean's Fellows and Writing Fellows with whom she has had (and will continue to have) the honor and privilege of working. These students bring enormous energy to the Program and an unceasing desire to make teaching legal research (and even citation!) interesting, rewarding and fun.

The authors thank their legal research and writing colleagues who reviewed and commented on the text: Kenneth Chestek (University of Wyoming); Jane Ginsburg (Columbia Law School); Terri LeClercq (ret., University of Texas School of Law); Pamela Lysaght (University of Detroit Mercy School of Law); Joanna Mossop (Columbia Law School); Suzanne Rowe (University of Oregon School of Law); Ann Davis Shields (Washington University School of Law); Judith Smith (Columbia Law School); Mark Wojcik (John Marshall Law School); and Cliff Zimmerman (Northwestern University School of Law). This book is the better for their kind and generous review and input.

Professor DeSanctis's list of thank you's could be very long because it includes hundreds of colleagues and students (adjunct and FT professors, 1Ls, DFs, WFs) from whom she continues to learn so much about teaching writing. A few people should be singled out specifically. Iselin Gambert is an amazing colleague, teacher, and friend. Her oversight of the GW Law Writing Center and the students who staff it have offered insights to the material contained in this text that are unparalleled; the content would not be as strong otherwise. Other GW colleagues (Karen Thornton, Jessica Clark, and Jill Baisinger) have added considerable value as well. Michael Levine will always be a strange muse (strangely amusing, too). Special thanks are owed to every LRW student Professor DeSanctis has had in the past many years of teaching. Naming them all individually would take pages (!), and singling out any risks detracting from the reality that she has learned so much from all of them. She still wants mention a few for their genuine excitement about the legal writing enterprise: LeighAnn Smith, Rachael-Million-Perez, Lauren Pyle, Warren Samlin, Bryan Nance, Jon Horn (x10), Luis Andrade, Priya Patel, Pat Hogan, Thaddeus Ewald, Genette Gaffney, Kristen Jacobsen, Emily Farmer, Amy Pearlman, Vito Iaya, Sierra Murph, Diana Godana, and Randy Wood ....the complete list is much longer, indeed.

PREFACE to the SECOND EDITION

Welcome to a new edition of Legal Writing and Analysis. Quite a bit has happened since the last edition in 2009. Legal writing hasn't changed much in the last five years, but the legal world and the legal writing market certainly has. Law schools are responding to massive changes in the legal employment market that call for deeper, more intensive, client-centered, and practice-oriented training in legal writing and analysis. Law students and legal employers are demanding practice-ready training in lawyering skills. In response to the changing market for the legal profession, the authors have overhauled their entry-level legal writing text to meet the demands of the new legal market and the requirements for practice-ready training in legal writing and analysis.

It is very likely that many of you, students of the second decade of the twenty-first century, will be reading this text in your first semester of law school, or in the first semester of your LLM or certificate program. The text is designed to reach you where you are. The authors have taught both American J.D. students and international LL.M. students for a combined total of 29 years. We are ready to introduce you to the theory, the vocabulary, the structures, the practices, and the expectations of lawyers working on legal writing and analysis no matter what your undergraduate degree was, no matter where or how you learned to write, and no matter how limited or how extensive is your exposure to the American court system and legal profession. In short, we presume nothing about your experience with complex, professional writing and your exposure to the analysis of difficult material. You all can get there with hard work, an open mind, and dedication to learning a demanding set of professional skills that are both challenging and rewarding. This book is a guide to obtaining the key power of lawyers in the American legal system: to analyze the law, figure out the answers, and communicate your results in a manner that will be accepted and applauded by all who will receive your work. To one and all, we welcome you to the study of legal writing and analysis.

There are many things that are new to *Legal Writing and Analysis—Second Edition*: We have streamlined the chapters leading from analysis of a single case or other authority to the chapter on legal organization by splitting out the material on the analysis of multiple authorities and the formation of rule sections and explanation sections. We have increased the callout boxes, charts, tables, and summaries of the contents. We have culled, replaced, and shortened the length of samples so that we provide two times and sometimes three times as many samples of practitioner writing in each chapter of the book.

With this new edition, we hope to train you, a future lawyer, to be an ethical and professional issue-spotter, analyst, counselor, problem-solver, and communicator working to advance your clients' interests. It is a noble and worthwhile task that we are preparing you for. Welcome to the journey.

M.D.M.
Valparaiso, Indiana

C.H.D.
Washington, D.C.

Table of Contents

LEGAL WRITING and ANALYSIS
Second Edition

CHAPTER 1

Introduction to American Legal Method

I. OVERVIEW OF THE METHODS OF LAW IN THE UNITED STATES

If you are a student in your first semester of legal study in the United States, then you have come to the right book. The authors wrote this book primarily for use in a first semester legal research and writing or "legal methods" course for J.D. and LL.M. students. We crafted the topics and examples for readers who are new to the law and legal study in the United States. We do not presume that you will bring extensive knowledge of American law and the American legal system to your study of this book. You need not have previous experience in logic or legal reasoning and analysis. What is necessary is that you have an open mind and the ability to critically analyze language, arguments, concepts, and complicated writing.

FOOD FOR THOUGHT

Do I have the right stuff to be a lawyer?
Legal method, the work of lawyers, does not require any particular set of skills or experience in life or education for you to do well in law school and in the practice of law. The ability to read comprehensively, to think critically, and to write coherently certainly are assets for lawyers, but these are skills that are possessed or can be developed by a wide variety of people who have studied or worked in a wide variety of disciplines. Our top students over the years have studied acting, art, music, computer science, engineering, religion, or mathematics, as well as philosophy, history, political science, or English as an undergraduate major. That is one reason that American law schools have no specific prerequisites beyond an undergraduate degree. So, count yourself in and expect that the skills and experience you bring are sufficient for the study of this book and the law.

The study of law is not easy, but it does not require one set of experiences or one focus of training leading up to it. You have come to law school with training in diverse disciplines, but law practice requires diverse skills. Close reading, critical thinking, and the understanding and appreciation of historical context may come naturally to humanities majors. But the law also requires considerable skills in logic, scientific proofs, and the application of known authorities to new situations. In short, there is no one set of skills that you need to bring to law school to succeed, and it is safe to say that many people with a skill set just like yours have gone before you and excelled.

Similarly, while entering a legal writing course with strong general writing skills may be an advantage in terms of your ability to organize your thoughts and express your ideas on paper, it is not a towering advantage, because this is a different kind of writing. Legal writing can be mastered as quickly by students with little writing experience as those with vast experience. The objectives and skills taught in this book allow everyone to have a fair chance to express legal information clearly, concisely, and correctly, regardless of her prior background or experience.

II.   WRITING LIKE A LAWYER?

Even in the second decade of the twenty-first century, lawyers still communicate primarily in writing—whether in paper or electronic form. Clients, supervisors, and judges will ask you to explain the intricacies of a legal problem, its factual details, the complex facets of the governing cases and legal rules, and the proper outcome in the context of a *written document*—a letter (or even an email), an office memorandum, or a court brief. Writing thus is unavoidable in the legal profession. However, "writing like a lawyer" does not mean infusing your once clear prose with specialized jargon, excessively complicated grammar, and an overly formal tone.

In fact, you may be asking yourself, "Why should I want to write like a lawyer? Lawyers are terrible writers!" You have a point. Lawyers are held up to popular ridicule for writing that is prolix, overly complex, obfuscatory, and even disingenuous. Indeed, the work product of lawyers constantly is used as an example of what is wrong with modern professional communication. This is unfortunate, because a lawyer's ability to communicate advice on how the law should be applied to a particular factual situation, no matter how intricate, is just as important as the ability to determine an answer in the first instance. Yet, while many lawyers easily recognize the importance of proper research and analysis, they often neglect the importance of good communication. As a result, people admire lawyers for their keen skills in reasoning and problem solving but scratch their heads when it comes to legal writing. The causes of the basic complaints of prolixity, excessive complexity, and dishonesty or obfuscation are many and varied, but the problems can be targeted and eliminated.

DO IT WITH STYLE!

Language of the Law – The Three C's

You may have heard that in law school you must "learn the language of the law." That is true to a certain extent—the law does have a vocabulary of its own, and to practice law you will learn terms that are not used in daily conversation. But learning to write in the law is not about learning to speak Latin or French or the convoluted, impenetrable fog of words known as "legalese." It is not about learning to speak in a fancy way popular centuries ago. It is not even about learning to make your writing sound like the judicial opinions you will read. Good legal writing is like good, professional writing of any kind: it should be **clear** and readily understood, it should be **concise** and tailored to the task at hand and the audience of the work, and it must be **correct**, setting out the facts, legal rules, and legal analysis without error or obfuscation. These **Three C's** of legal writing are the most important elements of the legal writing discourse community that you are joining.

Why are lawyers notoriously wordy? Perhaps one answer is the notion that "more is better": if I write more, it will prove that I know more. Nothing could be further from the truth; in fact, excessive verbosity often correlates to knowing (or being clear about) less. As an entering law student, you may be experiencing a similar influence driving you toward excessive verbosity. That is, for several undergraduate years, you may have been told to meet minimum page expectations of fifteen, twenty, thirty or more pages. You might have explained things four times if you wanted to, inserted many quotes from your sources, and watched the pages fly off the printer. To continue in this manner, however, will be a hindrance in legal contexts.

Complexity is a different animal. No one will tell you the law is uncomplicated. Indeed, you will soon find out how complicated it can be. But your written and oral communication should never mirror the same complexity as the legal issues you are discussing. A great lawyer takes the complex and explains it in a simple, straightforward, and easily understandable manner. Part of this skill comes with knowing what and how much to write about in a given document; part of it comes with mastering a legal topic so well that you can explain it to anyone, lawyer or layperson. Make it clear, make it appropriately simple for the audience at hand, and your writing will be valued more because of it.

APPLY IT!

Good writing requires good editing, so our first exercise is to have you edit and rewrite the following statements to make them more simple and direct. Reduce them to a single sentence that communicates the same meaning.

1. I have aspirations, many of which are dreamlike, pertaining to the treatment of my children. My children are going to be evaluated according to various criteria. An unacceptable criterion is to judge them simply according to the color of their skin. My aspiration of a dreamlike nature is for my children's character to be judged, and by this I mean judging according to content of their character.

2. Switching insurance requires a shift in focus to the merits of a different carrier, and the minimum time required for the evaluation of the merits of a different carrier is a quarter of an hour. However, in that quarter of an hour you often can find that you can save money on the premium. The savings are between 14 and 16 percent in most cases.

3. Visual images—photographs, paintings, drawings and the like—are able to communicate quickly and effectively in ways that satisfactorily replace many hundreds of words. As communicative devices, images have great worth that is at least equal to worth of the tens of hundreds of verbal words that can be replaced by use of the image.

Finally, there is a fine line between the impulse to obfuscate and the impulse to mislead. The latter is unethical, not to mention terrible for your client's case and your reputation. Obfuscation, though, is no less insidious. The lawyer who attempts to cloud or distort the meaning of the law or who piles on complexity with the sole purpose of defeating the reader's ability to grasp and deal with the true issues of a case is achieving the same end as the lawyer who intentionally misleads.

One of our goals is to prevent you from developing these bad habits. We will remind you to write clearly, concisely, and correctly. Admittedly, this is not always easy for even the best writers to do. But instead of worrying about filling up pages—rarely a problem with strict word and page limits and material as complex as the legal rules you will be dealing with—we would rather have you worry about leaving sufficient time to edit and proofread your work. In addition, because legal writing is targeted to a specific audience, and the content, tone, and degree of objectivity with which you present your conclusions will vary according to the persons to whom you are writing, you should always keep in mind *what type of writing you are being asked to do*. This book is part of a legal research and writing series whose titles are divided according to the main division in legal writing types: **objective** (or **predictive**) writing and **advocacy-oriented** (or **persuasive**) writing. The first book, which you are reading now, focuses on objective, informative writing, the prime example of which is an office memorandum. The third book focuses on writing as a partisan and advocate in the American adversarial system, using the examples of trial court briefs and appellate briefs. The second book links the two together by discussing the process of legal research and the analysis of specific types of legal authorities. Oral advocacy in trial and appellate courts is addressed in a separate chapter at the end of the third book.

III. LEGAL METHOD

Among the first things a law student should attempt to grasp are: what is the law, where does the law come from, and what is the lawyer's role in the legal process? These three ideas, discussed in more detail below, necessarily interrelate to form the basis for the phrase that titles this Chapter. "Legal method" is an expression to describe the fact that the practice of law at all levels and in all places of employment requires a *methodology* according to which each participant in the process must properly research the law, interpret the law, explain the law to others, and, if appropriate, to advocate a certain interpretation of the law that may require the law to be modified, revoked, or extended. This process fits within the three general terms of legal method: **research**, **analysis**, and **communication.**

MAKE THE CONNECTION!

Legal method is research, analysis, and communication. A lawyer analyzes facts to determine issues (questions) that must be answered in order to render legal advice, and performs research to find the law—the legal authorities—that define and lead to answers to these issues. The lawyer then analyzes the law and determines how it interacts with the facts and communicates the results of this analysis.

You soon will learn many ways to approach and think about legal problems, but the goal of legal education is to equip you with the skills to find the governing law on *any* given topic and to apply that law in new contexts or situations. Your legal research and writing course typically is the first course to teach the skills necessary to do just that. Accordingly, your assignments in your legal writing class likely will be designed to familiarize you with the processes of **determining legal issues** (legal questions that need to be answered from the facts presented in a given situation); **researching the law** that applies to answer such issues; **analyzing and articulating the law** as you uncover it; **applying the law** to a set of facts; and **writing your conclusions to an audience.**

A. What is the law?

A nutshell definition of "the law" may seem easy to state, but you will spend the better part of your law school career trying to get your arms around this concept. The law is authority—that which we hold to be authoritative in governing, regulating, and adjudicating human interaction in a civilized society. The law also is the body of statutes, ordinances, administrative rules and regulations, treaties, executive orders, judicial opinions, legal principles, and interpretations of all of these sources, that govern human actions and relations. *Black's Law Dictionary* states that the law is "The aggregate of legislation, judicial precedents, and accepted legal principles; the body of authoritative grounds of judicial and administrative action; esp., the body of rules, standards, and principles that the courts of a particular jurisdiction apply in deciding controversies brought before them."

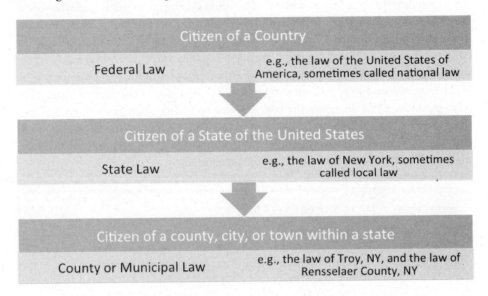

A brief civics lesson may aid this introduction. Recall that as a citizen of a country, the United States for example, you are a citizen of a community—a village, township, city, or other municipal area—and a citizen of a county or parish, and a citizen of a state of the United States, and a citizen of a country, the United States of America. All of these levels of relationship within the United States have a governing body or institution—a government—that can regulate your activities by passing statutes, rules, ordinances, acts, laws, regulations, executive orders, treaties, or international conventions. In addition, these various governmental units have corresponding **legislative entities** (town or county councils; boards of alderman; state, national, or federal legislatures); **executive entities** (mayors, county executives, governors, presidents); **regulatory bodies** (zoning boards, licensing bureaus, housing commissions, or regulatory or administrative agencies); and **judicial entities** (justices of the peace, municipal courts, state and federal courts, administrative law judges, arbitral tribunals). In the United States, all of these entities can contribute to the law by creating it, modifying it, interpreting it in official or advisory capacities, and by applying it to particular persons and situations.

Given the breadth of these definitions and the vast array of entities from which "the law" may emerge, it may seem impossible to answer the question "what is the law?" on any single topic. But reality dictates otherwise. The law is recorded and relatively well organized in only a certain number of sources (albeit a growing number). A solid understanding of what those sources are, how they are searched, and what they are likely to cover will direct your attention (more easily with practice) to the most likely places to find the answers you are looking for.

B. Sources of the law: primary and secondary authority

The three main *primary* sources of the law are:

> ### Legislation - including statutes, ordinances, laws, codes, charters, treaties and other international agreements, and constitutions
>
> • Primary Authority

> ### Administrative rules and regulations - including rules, regulations, decrees, orders, and licenses promulgated by administrative agencies, non-legislative governmental entities, and other regulatory boards and commissions
>
> • Primary Authority

> ### Cases - judicial opinions from legal matters that have come before the courts
>
> • Primary Authority

TAKE NOTE!

Primary Authority

Primary authority is a key concept to learn in this Chapter, so make sure you understand it. Primary authorities are the most important sources that you will look for in your research to find the answers to the issues raised by the facts of a situation. Legislation, administrative rules and regulations, and cases are the only authorities that can control and dictate the answers to legal questions in the United States. Anything short of a primary authority can only be used as a (persuasive) guide that gives advice on the proper way to answer the question. But it is never the answer itself.

In your quest to find an answer to the question "what is the law" on a given topic, you also may refer to commentary and interpretations of the law written by legal scholars, judges, legislators, and legal practitioners in treatises, restatements of the law, hornbooks, law review articles, annotations, encyclopedias, legislative history documents, and other compilations. These are **secondary sources** of the law or **secondary authority.**

> ### Commentary - including treatises, law review articles, encyclopedias, hornbooks, citators, Restatements of the law, practice materials, continuing legal education materials
>
> • Secondary Authority

It is important to get a good grip on these definitions and distinctions. As the name indicates, primary authorities carry much more weight in determining what the law is. Primary authorities will determine the law for every situation where the primary authorities speak to the legal issue, and secondary authorities are only used to explain or supplement them. That said, secondary authorities can be of great assistance to lawyers in interpreting the law in areas where the law is unclear or ambiguous, and this kind of commentary can be very persuasive to lawyers, legislators, and judges. But secondary authorities cannot create law. At most, they can provide guidelines for courts or legislatures to act in areas that are not yet defined by a primary authority or where a change in the law is needed.

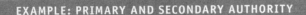

EXAMPLE: PRIMARY AND SECONDARY AUTHORITY

In a certain town, dogs were allowed to run loose and several people were bitten by dogs running wild in public places.

The local legislature passed an ordinance (**legislation - primary authority**) making dog owners responsible for all injuries caused by their dogs who were not kept on a leash.

An administrative agency, the Bureau of Parks and Recreation, passed a **regulation** (**primary authority**) further interpreting the ordinance to require leather or metal chain leashes on dogs.

A lawsuit arose between a dog owner and a person bitten by the owner's dog.

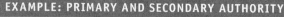

EXAMPLE: PRIMARY AND SECONDARY AUTHORITY

The lawsuit was resolved in a **judicial opinion** (**primary authority**) holding that a dog owner was not responsible when his dog unexpectedly broke free from a strong leather leash and bit someone.

Later, a law professor studied this area of law and wrote a law review article (**secondary authority**) explaining that the referenced judicial opinion interpreted the ordinance and regulation to require a finding of fault on the part of a dog owner before holding him responsible for unleashed dog injuries. He explained that the legislature could have imposed a strict liability standard, but the courts have interpreted the statute to require negligence or fault on the part of the dog owner. The law professor's article explains the effect of the primary authorities, but it does not change what the authorities actually say.

C. The role of the lawyer

The nature of lawyering is to determine what the law is and how it may affect a client in a given situation. The client can be a person or business entity that hires the lawyer, or a private or public entity that employs the lawyer, or a court or judicial body in which the lawyer is employed. A good lawyer in each of these sectors can tell what the current law is, predict how the law will work in various real or hypothetical situations, and offer advice the client on what to do or to avoid doing in those situations.

Rarely will you know what the law is ahead of time. You will know a great deal of legal principles in many areas of the law, and a number of actual legal rules of general and specific application, but these will not be enough to answer even the average question that reaches your desk. What usually happens is that a client or a supervisor will come into your office with a problem that has legal implications. You will listen to the problem, ask questions to gain additional information relating to the problem, and then go to your sources in the library or on-line and attempt to ascertain what will happen based on the law that applies. Occasionally, you will have had this exact issue come up recently, and you will already know what happens and what to do about it. (When this happens, you should enjoy a momentary feeling of great wisdom and power, and then go and double-check yourself by looking it up and making sure you still are the master of this legal information.)

PRACTICE POINTER

When you contemplate stepping into the role of a lawyer, you should realize that a lawyer's job is to analyze problems, most often to render advice to a client about the problem. The basic structure is simple: know the facts, know the rules, and decide how the rules govern the facts.

If your niece and nephew have a simple dispute over a board game ("She can't move there!" "Yes, I can!"), how do you act like a lawyer to help them resolve the dispute?

The answer: Know the facts (What is she trying to do? Or where is she trying to move?), know the rules (What game are they playing? What are the rules of this game?), and decide how the rules govern the facts (At this time, she is allowed to move to that spot because a rule of this game allows that kind of move here).

The process of finding the law—looking it up, finding the proper sources, compiling the information, following up on leads, and using what you have found to find other sources—is the first essential skill of a lawyer, which is referred to as **legal research**. The process of determining what legal issues are implicated by the facts of the problem and what sources should be consulted, reviewing and analyzing what these sources say, and reaching a conclusion about what the law is (or should be), is the second essential skill, referred to as **analysis**. The third part of the process is being able to communicate your findings to a variety of persons—your colleagues where you are working, senior lawyers in your firm, your clients, the courts, your opponents, and various governmental or regulatory bodies. This skill will be referred to as **communication**, and much of the focus of this book will be on communication in writing.

CHAPTER 2

Rules of Law and Legal Reasoning

I. ISSUES, RULES, AND FACTS

As you approach any legal problem, you can think of your task as requiring three basic steps:

Step 1 is determining the **legal issue** you need to address. Step 2 is finding and articulating the applicable **rule of law** governing that issue. And step 3 is determining the **legally significant facts** that will drive your analysis. These three basic factors are the building blocks for all legal analysis, and you should see them as working together. In many cases, determining one depends on the answers to the other two. And in many cases, you will not have all three immediately at your fingertips, but you will need to determine each one before you can proceed.

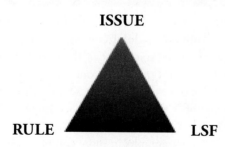

What do these terms mean?

LEGAL ISSUE

An individual legal question implicated by a problem (a set of facts) that needs to be answered in order to render advice concerning the problem.

The **legal issue** is the question you have been asked to address. Sometimes, determining the question is easy because someone has come into your office and stated the issue directly. For example, your boss asks whether a client can make out a case for discrimination against her employer. Or, your legal writing professor asks whether your client has a viable case for intentional infliction of emotional distress.

Very often, the question is not immediately apparent, as in the situation where a non-lawyer client tells you she is being bothered by her supervisor at work and then was accused of stealing office supplies and she asks you, "Can I sue my boss?" and "What can I do about the accusation of theft?" As a lawyer, you would form the issues as asking whether she has a claim for relief or a valid defense to the claim asserted against her.

Each legal issue has a **rule of law** that governs its analysis. You must find the correct rule and apply it to the facts of the problem to answer the legal issue you are analyzing.

> ## RULE OF LAW
> A statement of the legal principles and requirements that govern the analysis of the legal issue at hand.

You should start to think of "**rule of law**" as a group noun—a description of multiple items—because often the statement of the principles and requirements of the law governing an issue requires more than one sentence and includes more than one rule or element. Many of our examples in these early chapters have fairly simple, straightforward statements of the principles and requirements of the law that are presented in a single sentence. But be aware that a statement of the rule or rules may take several sentences or even paragraphs in more complex cases.

Finally, it is not enough simply to gather all the facts of a situation and stop there. You must determine the **legally significant facts** (also called outcome determinative facts), a process that requires paying careful attention to the reasons for previous legal determinations on your issue as well as knowing the facts of your client's situation in detail.

> ## LEGALLY SIGNIFICANT FACTS
> The facts that, if changed or deleted, will affect the outcome of the determination.

This process need not be complicated. In many cases the issues will be simple and straightforward and the significant facts will be few. Finding the correct rule will be the only challenge. Even then, the application of the correct rule to the significant facts may be simple. Consider the following:

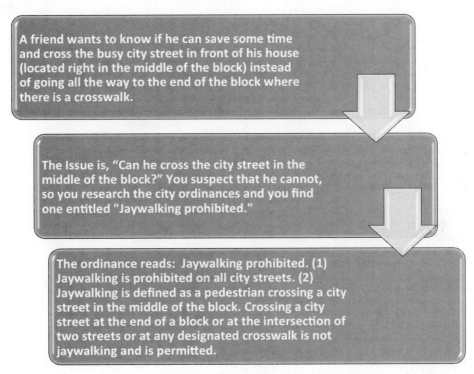

A friend wants to know if he can save some time and cross the busy city street in front of his house (located right in the middle of the block) instead of going all the way to the end of the block where there is a crosswalk.

The Issue is, "Can he cross the city street in the middle of the block?" You suspect that he cannot, so you research the city ordinances and you find one entitled "Jaywalking prohibited."

The ordinance reads: Jaywalking prohibited. (1) Jaywalking is prohibited on all city streets. (2) Jaywalking is defined as a pedestrian crossing a city street in the middle of the block. Crossing a city street at the end of a block or at the intersection of two streets or at any designated crosswalk is not jaywalking and is permitted.

The last box is, of course, the **Rule**. Thus, the **Legally Significant Facts** (your friend wants to cross a city street in the middle of a block) are met with the **Rule of Law** (that prohibits such activity), providing a very clear answer (No) to the **Issue** (can he cross a city street in the middle of a block).

APPLY IT!

Try your hand at the process. Work your way through the following problem:

Your neighbor is a trustee of your subdivision. She wants to repair the diving board at the neighborhood pool, but a county inspector told the trustees that the diving board cannot be repaired or replaced because the pool is only eleven feet deep, which he states is too shallow to meet the requirements of the county recreational safety code. You do some research into the county recreational safety code and find the following provision:

"Diving Boards. Effective January 1, 2007, no diving board shall be built and no existing diving board shall be repaired, replaced, or reconstructed at any public or private swimming, diving, or bathing pool unless the pool is at least thirteen feet deep at the center point or drain of the area used for diving. Effective January 1, 2008, it shall be unlawful to maintain or use any diving board at any public or private swimming, diving, or bathing pool unless the pool is at least thirteen feet deep at the center point or drain of the area used for diving. No exceptions shall be made in either case for diving boards already in existence and in use on either of the two effective dates."

Using this information, state the **Issue**, the **Rule of Law**, and the **Legally Significant Facts**. Then state your **Conclusion** regarding this problem.

II. FINDING, BREAKING DOWN, AND OUTLINING A RULE OF LAW

A. Sources of the law

Rules of law may be found in the various sources we discussed in Chapter 1, both **primary** (legislation, administrative law consisting of administrative rules and regulations, and cases) and **secondary** (commentary on and explanations of the law).

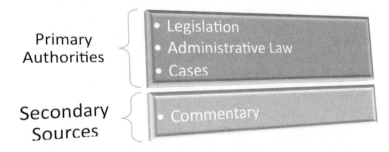

As an example, if a client has a question about dog bite liability—his dog bit a Girl Scout after she rang his door bell and shouted at the dog—you would look for the rule of law that governs liability of dog owners for dog bites. The legal issue is: Will my client be liable for this dog bite injury? To research this issue, you would probably look for a statute or other form of legislation, an administrative rule or regulation, or one or more **cases**—reports of judicial opinions in prior lawsuits and other legal actions—in your state that discuss dog bites and dog owner liability to find the rule.

MAKE THE CONNECTION!

Think back to the board game dispute between your niece and nephew in Chapter 1. The **facts** (What game they are playing, what move is she trying to make) and the **issue** (Can she make that move here?) are the same. To find the **rules**, where do you go? If the rules of the game are fully known to you or are printed inside the box top, the task is as easy as if you were presented with a legal issue whose rules you already knew. But, as in the legal world, accessing the rules of the game may require you to consult a source (*e.g.*, Hoyle's Rules of Games) or to go on-line (*e.g.*, Google) to find them. You would look for the primary authorities first—sources stating the actual rules of the game—rather than a secondary authority—someone's commentary on why the game is a great game, or on how the rules of the game could be improved. You may have to account for local variations of the rules on how the game is played—rules of certain games vary from place to place, and so do laws and legal rules. Once you have the rules, you can analyze how the rules apply in the situation and communicate your conclusions to your niece and nephew.

Let's suppose you are in the State of Apex,[1] and you did not find any legislation or administrative rules or regulations on point, but you came across two cases, Smithy v. Jonesy, 123 W.2d 345, 347 (Apex 1965), and Johnson v. Anderson, 789 W.2d 234, 237 (Apex Ct. App. 1st Dist. 1989),[2] that both say the following about dog bite liability:

> "In Apex, a dog owner is liable for all injuries caused by his dog unless the dog is provoked by the victim."

Assuming you did not find any other authorities on point that add to, change, or articulate a different wording of the rule or a different rule altogether, you have the rule of law that governs this issue.

B. Breaking down a rule of law into its parts

The first thing to do when you find a rule of law is to break it down into its parts, or *elements*. The elements of a rule are those factors that must be present (or conditions satisfied) for the rule to be triggered. If the rule requires the presence of three factors, it has three elements. If you are an advocate in a lawsuit seeking to apply the rule in your client's favor, the elements are the factors that you have to prove for your client to prevail. The opponent in the same lawsuit must try to disprove one or more elements so that she will prevail.

In the example above, the rule as stated in the cases was: **"In Apex, a dog owner is liable for all injuries caused by his dog unless the dog is provoked by the victim."** This rule can be broken down into four requisite elements:

(1) **ownership of the dog by the person from whom the victim seeks recovery,**

(2) **an injury,**

(3) **that is caused by the dog, and**

(4) **a lack of provocation by the victim.**

One thing to note is that **there can be more than one way to break a rule into elements**, because what you really are doing is creating an outline to help you organize your discussion of the rule in writing.

---

1   Fictitious jurisdictions are popular in law school. Apex is our fictitious jurisdiction. You should assume that it is a state of the United States, located between New York and California.

2   Naturally, these two cases do not exist. From time to time we will invent cases to illustrate certain principles of legal analysis and communication. The citations follow proper Bluebook citation form (see Chapter 9), but the actual volume abbreviation ("W." for Western Reporter), page numbers, and dates given in the citations are imaginary. West Group does not publish a "Western" regional reporter as you will learn in the Bluebook or ALWD Manual.

The concept of **elements** is important because elements indicate separate legal questions that must be addressed to fully answer the issue at hand.

The authorities often break down the rule for you; for example, a statute or a line of cases might separate the rule identified above into four elements. In such a case, you should follow what the authorities instruct you to do when you write about it, and address all four parts in your writing.

Even so, you should be aware that certain elements create multiple questions and others rarely present any contested issues for analysis. For example, in a dog bite situation, it may be true that injury and causation almost never are contested issues; no one sues unless they actually have been injured, and, barring some complications of mistaken identity or additional probable causes of the injury, rarely will causation be a serious contested issue in the case. You would therefore not by alarmed to see the elements listed as three: ownership—injury caused by the dog—no provocation of the dog. But if the authorities list it as four parts, so should your outline.

The authorities say:	You prepare to answer:

• A dog owner is liable for all injuries caused by his dog unless the dog is provoked by the victim	• Liability for a dog bite requires
	  • (1) ownership of the dog by the person from whom the victim seeks recovery,
	  • (2) an injury,
	  • (3) the injury is caused by the dog, and
	  • (4) lack of provocation of the dog by the victim.

Some rules are not phrased in a form with one or more required elements. Rules can be stated to require the consideration of a number of factors, not all of which need be present for the rule to be triggered. Other rules are phrased as a balancing test where certain factors are weighed against other factors to determine the outcome. You must read the authorities carefully to determine what form the rule is taking. No matter what the form, it is always possible to break it down into the separate parts that must be considered (or balanced) in the application of the rule.

C. Outlining the parts of a rule

As noted, the parts of a rule often are listed in outline form, the purpose of which is to create an organizational structure for your discussion of the rule in writing. The four required elements for dog bite liability in Apex create four questions to answer that may be outlined briefly as follows:

1. Ownership

2. Injury

3. Caused by the dog

4. No provocation

As stated above, the authorities that provided the rule often do this outlining work for you. For example, *Smithy v. Jonesy* might have expressly stated the rule on dog bite liability as follows: **"To recover, a dog-bite victim must prove the following: (1) defendant owned the dog; (2) plaintiff suffered actual physical injury; (3) the dog caused plaintiff's injury; and (3) plaintiff did not provoke the dog into attacking."**

Other times, where the rule is articulated and discussed as part of a longer narrative, you may have to work a little harder to break it down into workable elements.

If there were a different rule in Apex that incorporated a balancing test, for example, balancing the extent of any provocation against the viciousness of the dog's attack, you might outline the rule as follows:

1. Ownership

2. Injury

3. Caused by the dog

4. The severity of the attack was disproportionate to the provocation.

The outline of the rule still can be stated in four parts even though this rule would work differently than the first because of the balancing equation in the fourth part. There, you would consider whether the dog was provoked into attacking, but even if provoked, the victim might still recover if the attack was disproportionately severe compared to the provocation. For instance, a person might shake a fist at a dog and shout "Down boy!" and receive only a nip from the dog (a proportionate attack), and not recover. But if the person did the same thing and were mauled by the dog, he might recover because the attack was disproportionately severe. If you decide that the analysis of severity and provocation is complicated enough to warrant a further breakdown of the rule into subparts, you might outline the rule as follows:

1. Ownership;

2. Injury;

3. Causation;

4. Balancing of;

    a. the severity of the attack and

    b. the provocation of the dog.

At bottom, **the outline you produce should be an aid to help you with your analysis and explanation of the rule.** There is no need to over-complicate the situation; if the authorities provide a ready-made outline for a rule that accurately states the separate questions needed to answer the issue, the best practice is to use that outline for the convenience of the audience to whom you will communicate your analysis.

D. Use of the outline of parts for structure

Chapter 6 discusses how to create an overall outline for your writing based on the elements or parts of the legal rules involved. As a preview of this, you could outline a memorandum about dog-bite liability in the following way:

Thesis: The Homeowner will be liable for the injuries to the Girl Scout caused by his dog because the Girl Scout did not provoke the attack.

1. Ownership
    Sub-Thesis: It is undisputed that the Homeowner owned the dog.

2. Injury
    Sub-Thesis: It is undisputed that the Girl Scout was injured.

3. Causation
    Sub-Thesis: It is undisputed that the dog caused the injury to the Girl Scout.

4. No provocation
    Sub-Thesis: The Girl Scout did not do anything to provoke the dog within the meaning of this element under the law.

III. LEGAL REASONING

Legal writing requires logical and orderly construction. Your audience consists primarily of lawyers (including judges) and clients who are consumers of properly constructed legal writing. The proper term for this audience is the **legal writing discourse community**. This is a demanding audience because law-trained readers are attuned to look for errors in logic, grammar, and style, as well as inaccurate or improper legal reasoning and analysis.

An explanation of legal principles, whether in an informative memorandum to a client or an advocate's brief to the court, generally requires the use of several types of reasoning:

Rule-based reasoning reflects a simple logical syllogism:

> # Rule-Based Reasoning
>
> The answer is X because the authorities establish the rule that provides an answer (X) to the issue as long as certain facts are present. These facts are present, so the application of the rule to the facts produces X result.

The answer is X if there are certain facts present;

All of the required facts are present;

∴ The answer is X.

The converse also is true:

The answer is X if there are certain facts present;

Not all of the required facts are present;

∴ The answer is not X.

Using our dog-bite example, the syllogism would be:

Rule: The owner will be liable if he owned the dog, the dog caused the injury to the plaintiff, and the plaintiff did not provoke the dog.

Application: The facts indicate that the owner owned the dog, the dog caused the injury to the plaintiff, and the plaintiff did not provoke the dog.

Conclusion: The owner will be liable for his dog's bite.

Rule-based reasoning is the most common form of logical reasoning in legal writing because legal analysis essentially involves applying predetermined rules to a certain set of facts. This process of analysis also is referred to as **deductive reasoning** (the process of reasoning from general proposition to a specific application or conclusion).

The steps denoting this process often are referred to by the acronym **IRAC**. IRAC marks the transition from the **Issue** to the **Rule** that governs the issue, to the **Application** of the rule to the facts of the situation, leading to the **Conclusion.**

The acronym for the organizational framework taught in this book— TREAT—is derived directly from this type of legal reasoning, though it is more sophisticated and therefore an improvement necessary to transition you from exam writing to lawyerly writing in a practical setting. **TREAT** stands for **T**hesis (the answer to the issue), **R**ule (the rule that governs the issue), **E**xplanation of how the rule works in various situations, **A**pplication of the rule to the facts of the present situation, **T**hesis restated as a conclusion. This approach is discussed at greater length in Chapter 6.

FYI

TREAT

TREAT is an acronym. You may also hear acronyms such as IRAC, CREAC (or others), but these are all variations on exactly the same theme—that is, they are all acronyms that mark necessary steps in **the process of deductive reasoning**. You can dislike these acronyms, or find them annoying, and even decide never to mention them out loud. However, you cannot escape what they stand for, because all of these acronyms simply mark necessary steps in the process of explaining to a law-trained audience the conclusions you have reached upon applying new facts to a set of controlling principles in a rule-based environment. For more information on TREAT (and its relationship to IRAC), *see* Chapter 6.

The second type of reasoning is inductive reasoning. The definition of inductive reasoning stated here may sound a little different from your previous encounters with the term **induction** or **inductive reasoning**, but we merely have phrased the definition to match the process as it is used in the law.

Inductive Reasoning

The answer is X because additional principles about how this situation should be resolved can be derived from prior cases and examples and, when these additional rules are applied to the facts, X is the answer.

In inductive reasoning, you are reasoning from specific instances (examples) to general propositions. In legal analysis, the specific instances usually are judicial opinions in cases, and the general propositions are legal rules. The additional rules induced from cases are used to explain or interpret how the primary rules (those used in the rule-based reasoning syllogism) are supposed to be applied in certain situations—namely, the types of situations in the cases from which the rules were derived. The additional rules induced from the cases provide guidance to lawyers in performing the legal analysis of the situation. Inductive reasoning is important to the processes of rule synthesis and explanatory synthesis, discussed later in this book.

INDUCTIVE REASONING EXAMPLE		
ISSUE: HOW DOES THE "PROVOCATION" STANDARD WORK?		
Examples (cases)	What the Example illustrates about the rule of provocation	Principle induced from the four Examples
Smithy v. Jonesy	Yelling at a dog, even an extended period of yelling and cursing, did not constitute provocation of the dog	Provocation within the meaning of the law requires intentional, unintentional, or accidental physical contact with the dog in a manner that injures or threatens injury to the dog.
Chomped v. Fang	Hitting a dog in the head with a plastic whiffle ball bat was provocation	
Chewtoy v. Cujo	Accidental tripping over a dog sleeping in a dark corner, which preceded the dog's biting, was provocation	
Wolf v. R.R. Hood Co.	Dragging a dog with its chain, which caused the dog to trip and fall and be dragged, was provocation	

The third type of legal reasoning you will encounter is **analogical reasoning**. In the law, you often will use **analogical reasoning** to try to link your case to other similar cases in which the outcome was favorable (or to distinguish your case where the outcome was unfavorable). If the court agrees that the cases are similar and that there are no legally significant differences, the court should handle the present case in the same way to produce the same result as in the prior cases. The **converse** of this type of reasoning is used to argue that a certain case should not determine the outcome of the case at hand because there are legally significant differences.

Note that fact patterns in legal writing courses almost never contemplate that you will find a case exactly on point with your purported client's scenario. Rather, you will be required to employ analogical reasoning (and distinctive, or converse analogical reasoning) to compare and contrast your client's circumstances to those that you find in the applicable case law.

Analogical Reasoning
(Reasoning by analogy)

The answer is X because this situation is like the situation in prior cases and in those cases X was the answer.

Converse Analogical Reasoning
(Distinguishing Negative Authority)

Although the result in prior cases was X, the result in this case should not be X because of certain legally significant differences.

Analogical reasoning and converse analogical reasoning can be performed at two levels: One, the simple, more superficial level that compares some basic factual similarities or differences between cases, and the other, a deeper analogy involving policy-based, structural, jurisprudential similarities or differences in the cases.

SURFACE LEVEL SIMILARITIES (or DIFFERENCES)

Similar party, similar situation, similar issue, similar defenses

The Deeper Analogy

POLICY-BASED, STRUCTURAL, JURISPRUDENTIAL SIMILARITIES (or DIFFERENCES)

- Similar public policies underly the cases, and a similar outcome in each case furthers these policies

- The design of the law anticipates situations such as those of the two cases to be determined in a certain manner, and the structure of the law is preserved by the outcome in the cases being the same

- The meaning and coherence of the law depends on the outcomes of each of the cases to be the same

There is nothing wrong with pointing out the surface level similarities between two or more cases. The comparison sometimes can be striking, and as a result, compelling in its suggestion that the two cases are the same and should have the same outcome. Any comparison that can be made communicates the basic idea that similar situations should be handled similarly.

But the deeper analogy shows how completely one precedent should control another, or by noting the fundamental differences, how irrelevant a prior case really is. It is not just coincidence that the cases are similar; the similarity comes from the fabric, design, and meaning of the law itself. If the meaning and coherence of the law depends on cases that implicate fundamental public policies of the law being adjudicated in a similar manner, this is a powerful argument to achieve that outcome.

The basic form of analogical reasoning in legal writing is flexible. You may combine **analogical reasoning** and **converse analogical reasoning**, so as to analogize to the good prior authorities and distinguish the bad:

> Although the result in *Florence v. DeLaurentiis and Ray v. Flay* was X, the result in this case should not be X because of . . . [legally significant differences]. Instead, the court should follow *Batali v. Puck* because of . . . [important similarities]. In *Batali* the result was Y, so Y should be the result in the case at hand.

Of course, what you write in the areas marked by the brackets as the "important similarities" or the "legally significant differences" is what will define whether you are making surface-level comparisons or a deeper analogy or distinction.

Reasoning by analogy is used frequently in legal writing because the American legal system follows the common law tradition where courts follow **precedent**, the record of determinations of similar cases adjudicated from year to year. Precedent can be binding or merely persuasive, but it is a cornerstone of the legal reasoning process. This topic is discussed in greater detail in Chapters 5 and 6.

The legal rules used in the rule-based reasoning syllogism often require explanation and illumination to demonstrate for the reader why your prediction of the outcome is legally sound and likely to occur. **Inductive reasoning and analogical reasoning are used within the rule-based reasoning syllogism** to further the overall discussion by showing how the rule itself or the elements of the rule are supposed to work by discussing and analogizing to or from certain actual circumstances

MAKE THE CONNECTION!

Inductive and analogical reasoning may sound complicated, but in actual practice, the principles are fairly straightforward. Think back to the swimming pool problem earlier in this Chapter. What if the rule from the County Safety Ordinances merely stated: "No pool shall have a diving board unless the pool is thirteen feet deep." Your neighbor wants to repair the existing diving board at her eleven foot deep pool. Through careful research, you find three cases where swimming pools in the county were allowed to repair their existing diving boards or replace parts of their diving boards since the date the ordinance was passed, and in each case the pools were less than thirteen feet deep. From these cases, you can induce the principle (the rule) that there is a "grandfather" effect to the ordinance—existing diving boards can be maintained or repaired after the passage of the ordinance. You can use this newly induced rule to reason that the application of the

ordinance to the facts of your neighbor's case should result in the ability to repair the diving board. In addition, in one of the earlier cases, the pool was exactly eleven feet deep and the trustees were allowed to make the exact type of repair to their diving board that your neighbor's trustee board wants to make to its diving board. You can use **analogical reasoning** to assert that the county should let your neighbor's trustee board repair its board because the county let the earlier swimming pool do it in exactly similar circumstances.

> ## Policy-Based Reasoning
>
> ### The answer should be X because X furthers the policies underlying this particular law or central to this area of law.

(cases) where the rule was applied to produce a certain outcome. The use of inductive and analogical reasoning in the context of an explanation and application section also is discussed in Chapter 6.

Policy-based reasoning most often is used to *buttress* an argument that already is supported by primary authorities. You are arguing that the answer is X not only because the authorities had X result, but also because X result satisfies policies that are important to a particular area of law. Occasionally, when primary sources (cases, statutes, administrative rules) of the law fail you or are nonexistent, and there is no binding authority on point, the only argument you can make is a policy-based argument. The following is an example that we drafted of policy-based reasoning as it might be used in legal writing:

> For centuries, the law has recognized the immorality of executing mentally disabled persons or persons with severe learning disabilities. Robert R. Writter, *The History of Capital Punishment in England and the United States* 234-36 (1978). As early as 1782, in the case *The King v. Smith*, 99 Eng. Rep. 339, 342 (K.B. 1782), the King's Bench court stated that "the marginal satisfaction of blood lust and vengeance secured through the execution of a recognizable [mentally disabled person] is far outweighed by the need for mercy and higher justice." Seventeen states have banned the execution of persons whose multi-phasic intelligence quotient ("IQ") is less than 70, making them borderline to profoundly mentally retarded. R. Randall Peters, *Capital Punishment Mistakes*, 99 Colum. L. Rev. 23, 45 n.76 (1999) (citing state statutes). Although defendant Jones repeatedly has scored a 69 on the multi-phasic IQ test and thus is susceptible to capital punishment at present under the laws of Texas, the court should recognize that Jones's severely limited mental capacity militates against the imposition of the ultimate penalty in this case.

A brief example of the previously discussed forms of argument — **rule-based, inductive, analogical, and policy-based**—together in a discussion that follows the TREAT format of Chapter 6 is the following:

EXAMPLE OF RULE-BASED, INDUCTIVE, ANALOGICAL, AND POLICY-BASED REASONING USED IN LEGAL WRITING

THESIS	**1. Mr. Charles Homeowner is liable for the injuries inflicted on the Girl Scout by his dog because the Scout did not provoke the attack.**
RULE	In Apex, a dog owner is liable for all injuries caused by his dog unless the dog is provoked by the victim. *Smithy v. Jonesy*, 123 W.2d 345, 347 (Apex 1965); *Johnson v. Anderson*, 789 W.2d 234, 237 (Apex Ct. App. 1st Dist. 1989). The elements of a cause of action for dog-bite liability are therefore: (1) ownership of the dog, (2) injuries caused by the dog, and (3) lack of provocation of the dog by the victim. *See Smithy*, 123 W.2d at 347.
EXPLANATION of the rule using inductive reasoning	Provocation requires an active, physical threat to the dog. *See id.* at 348 (finding provocation when boy hit dog's head with stick several times before dog bit him); *Bijou v. Blitzen*, 688 W.2d 12, 15 (Apex Ct. App. 1st Dist. 1981) (finding provocation when paper boy threw rocks at dog before dog bit him); *Buster v. Booboo*, 686 W2d 235, 238 (Apex Ct. App. 1st Dist. 1980) (finding provocation when repairman slapped dog's snout with leather gloves before dog bit him). In contrast, an ordinary, nonthreatening act such as merely walking up to the front of a house and opening the screen door is not provocative within the meaning of the rule. *See Johnson*, 789 W.2d at 239-40 (finding no provocation when dog attacked postal worker who walked up front walk and opened storm door of house to place package inside); *Bruno v. Vic*, 744 W.2d 23, 25 (Apex Ct. App. 1st Dist. 1987) (finding no provocation when UPS worker opened screen door to place package inside); *Cujo v. Chomped*, 729 W.2d 778, 779 (Apex Ct. App. 1st Dist. 1984) (finding no provocation when neighbor opened front door to see if friend was home).
EXPLANATION of the rule, setting up application by using analogical reasoning to a particularly relevant case with very similar facts	In *Johnson*, a postal worker was going about his ordinary duties of delivering mail. He was in the process of opening the outer screen door of a house to place a package inside when the homeowner's dog rushed out and bit him on the arm. The postal worker was engaged in a nonthreatening activity and did not make any threatening movements or gestures toward the dog other than opening the outer door of the home. The homeowner was liable for his dog's injuries because the court found that the postal worker did not provoke the attack. *Johnson*, 789 W.2d at 240.

EXAMPLE OF RULE-BASED, INDUCTIVE, ANALOGICAL, AND POLICY-BASED REASONING USED IN LEGAL WRITING	
EXPLANATION of the rule using policy-based reasoning (and analogical reasoning in comparing livestock and domestic animals)	Allowing persons "attacked by a domesticated animal when acting peaceably and not directly threatening the animal" to recover from the animal's owner for injuries sustained in the attack furthers the policy underlying the Apex rule. *See* Chester A. Scootch, *Apex Animal Laws* 234 (1953). Although Professor Scootch was referring to the Roaming Livestock Damage Act, Apex Rev. Stat. § 222.1234 (1944), there is no practical difference between livestock who are roaming loose on the property and domestic animals, such as dogs, who are encountered on the property. *See Scootch, supra*, at 235. In short, the law provides a remedy for injuries suffered when "the victim is acting peaceably and the dog is not." Mary M. Quitecontrary, *When a Best Friend Bites: Dog Bite Liability in Apex*, 345 U. Apex L. Rev. 100, 122-23 (1979).
APPLICATION of the rule to the facts, and use of analogical reasoning to link the facts to a case with a favorable outcome	Here, there is no dispute that Homeowner's dog attacked and caused injury to the Scout, an eight-year-old girl, when she climbed the front stoop of Homeowner's home and rang the doorbell with the intention of selling Girl Scout cookies. The first two elements of this cause of action are easily established. There is no dispute that the Homeowner owned the dog, and that the Scout suffered injury as a result of the dog bite. The third element is also satisfied because the Scout did nothing to threaten the dog, let alone strike at the dog. Instead, the Scout traversed the walkway leading to the front door of the house to solicit business from Homeowner. These circumstances are similar to those in *Johnson*, where a postal worker was going about her ordinary business of delivering mail and made no threatening movements or gestures toward the dog. Likewise, the Scout was acting in an entirely non-threatening manner. Ringing a doorbell is not a provocative act; indeed, it is less provocative than opening the front door of a house, which *Johnson* determined was not provocative. 789 W.2d at 239-40. Although the postal worker in *Johnson* was acting in the ordinary course of his daily professional duties when he opened the door, whereas here the Scout arguably was not engaged in a regular professional activity, this distinction is not legally significant and thus does not preclude recovery. Furthermore, a finding of liability comports with the underlying policy of providing a remedy for injuries sustained when a victim is acting peaceably and an animal is not. *See* 345 U. Apex L. Rev. at 122-23.
THESIS restated as a CONCLUSION	Therefore, Homeowner must compensate the Scout for her injuries in this case.

As you can see, the first paragraph provides the overall rule-based reasoning framework for the ensuing discussion. The thesis is the heading that precedes the discussion. It functions as the first sentence of the paragraph and is immediately followed by the rule itself. The next two paragraphs explain how the rule works: first, using inductive reasoning; next, establishing the basis for the analogical reasoning that will be completed in the application section; and finally, providing additional support with policy-based reasoning. The application section (the last two paragraphs) completes the analysis by showing how the instant case should be resolved under the rules of provocation induced by the earlier cases, and by showing how the present situation with the Girl Scout is closely analogous to the *Johnson* case, in which the plaintiff prevailed. The last sentence is a conclusion—the same thesis that started the discussion, but here restated as a conclusion—which completes the rule-based reasoning syllogism.

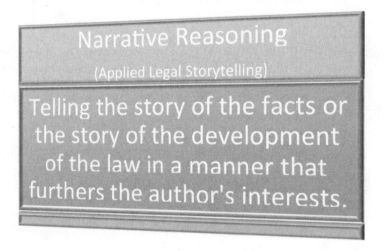

The final type of reasoning used in legal writing—**narrative reasoning**—is commonly used by non-lawyers in communicating facts in the form of a story. The contemporary study of narrative reasoning in the law has a second name, "applied legal storytelling," because it involves the rhetorical action of arranging facts into a story (facts of the situation, the development of the law, or other background information) in such a way that it achieves the author's purpose in the communication. The purpose may be to inform, to draw sympathy, to persuade, or to highlight important lessons. When done skillfully and purposefully, narrative reasoning conveys a thesis, but one that rarely is stated, because the argument is presented as facts or other background information. Most legal writing requires a statement of the facts that are important to the matter at hand. Narrative skills will enable you to make the factual presentation a strong part of your written work product.

To demonstrate the method, we present below a famous pair of statement of facts taken from two United States Supreme Court cases, *Walker v. City of Bir-*

mingham, 388 U.S. 307 (1967), and *Shuttlesworth v. City of Birmingham*, 394 U.S. 147 (1969). These examples reveal the different messages that can be communicated from two narratives of the same event. The event in these cases was the Good Friday March in 1963 during the Birmingham Campaign. The march produced several arrests, including that of the Reverend Martin Luther King, Jr., who wrote his famous "Letter from a Birmingham Jail" while incarcerated in the aftermath of these protests. The two opinions report the same facts, but with narrative reasoning that tells two different versions of the story. Strangely enough, the author of the two opinions is the same: Justice Potter Stewart. Perhaps in the two years between *Walker* and *Shuttlesworth* his thinking on the matter evolved.

Walker and *Shuttlesworth*

Walker, Majority Opinion	*Shuttlesworth*, Majority Opinion
The next afternoon, Good Friday, a large crowd gathered in the vicinity of Sixteenth Street and Sixth Avenue North in Birmingham. A group of about 50 or 60 proceeded to parade along the sidewalk while a crowd of 1,000 to 1,500 onlookers stood by, 'clapping, and hollering, and whooping.' Some of the crowd followed the marchers and spilled out into the street. At least three of the petitioners participated in this march. Meetings sponsored by some of the petitioners were held that night and the following night, where calls for volunteers to 'walk' and go to jail were made. On Easter Sunday, April 14, a crowd of between 1,500 and 2,000 people congregated in the midafternoon in the vicinity of Seventh Avenue and Eleventh Street North in Birmingham. One of the petitioners was seen organizing members of the crowd in formation. A group of about 50, headed by three other petitioners, started down the sidewalk two abreast. At least one other petitioner was among the marchers. Some 300 or 400 people from among the onlookers followed in a crowd that occupied the entire width of the street and overflowed onto the sidewalks. Violence occurred. Members of the crowd threw rocks that injured a newspaperman and damaged a police motorcycle.	On the afternoon of April 12, Good Friday, 1963, 52 people, all Negroes, were led out of a Birmingham church by three Negro ministers, one of whom was the petitioner, Fred L. Shuttlesworth. They walked in orderly fashion, two abreast for the most part, for four blocks. The purpose of their march was to protest the alleged denial of civil rights to Negroes in the city of Birmingham. The marchers stayed on the sidewalks except at street intersections, and they did not interfere with other pedestrians. No automobiles were obstructed, nor were traffic signals disobeyed. The petitioner was with the group for at least part of this time, walking alongside the others, and once moving from the front to the rear. As the marchers moved along, a crowd of spectators fell in behind them at a distance. The spectators at some points spilled out into the street, but the street was not blocked and vehicles were not obstructed. At the end of four blocks the marchers were stopped by the Birmingham police, and were arrested for violating s 1159 of the General Code of Birmingham. . . . The petitioner was convicted for violation of § 1159 and was sentenced to 90 days' imprisonment at hard labor and an additional 48 days at hard labor in default of payment of a $75 fine and $24 costs. . . .

There were two marches referenced in *Walker*, and only the first of these is repeated in *Shuttleworth*. But even this march, on Good Friday, sounds very different in the two accounts. *Walker* describes a "large crowd" of 50-60; *Shuttlesworth* says 52 people. Note the difference in tone and impact of the word "crowd" and the word "people." The group of 52 was orderly in both accounts, but the *Walker* case draws attention to the huge throng of onlookers, and goes out of its way to emphasize their "clapping, and hollering, and whooping." *Shuttlesworth* emphasizes that the crowd left from a church, and was led by ministers; not so with *Walker*. *Shuttlesworth* emphasizes the reason that the people marched was to protest civil rights violations; *Walker* says nothing about their reasons or motivation.

Both *Walker* and *Shuttlesworth* say the spectators following the march spilled out into the street, but only *Shuttlesworth* emphasizes that no traffic was obstructed. *Shuttlesworth* goes immediately into the rather severe punishment of Rev. Shuttlesworth arising from the march; *Walker* mentions nothing of the punishment, and moves on to the Easter Day march in which entire streets were blocked off. Note, too, that the Birmingham police were known for violent acts against protestors, and later in the Birmingham Campaign, they sent police dogs into the marchers, and turned high powered water cannons onto the crowd that included many women and children, in some cases knocking them off their feet and blasting them down the street by water propulsion. But *Walker* massively understates the events with the euphemistic, passive-tense phrase: "Violence occurred." And as to this violence, *Walker* only mentions two injuries—that were caused by the *onlookers*—to a newspaperman and to a police motorcycle.

A second example of applied legal storytelling and the effect of wording and emphasis is taken from two opinions in the Supreme Court case of *National Equipment Rental v. Szukhent*, 375 U.S. 311 (1964).

National Equipment Rental v. Szukhent

Stewart, J., Majority Opinion	Black, J., Dissenting Opinion
The petitioner is a corporation with its principal place of business in New York. It sued the respondents, residents of Michigan, in a New York federal court, claiming that the respondents had defaulted under a farm equipment lease. The only question now before us is whether the person upon whom the summons and complaint were served was 'an agent authorized by appointment' to receive the same, so as to subject the respondents to the jurisdiction of the federal court in New York.	The petitioner, National Equipment Rental, Ltd., is a Delaware corporation with its principal place of business in greater New York City. From that location it does a nationwide equipment rental business. The respondents, Steve and Robert Szukhent, father and son farming in Michigan, leased from National two incubators for their farm, signing in Michigan a lease contract which was a standard printed form obviously prepared by the New York company's lawyers. Included in the 18 paragraphs of fine print was the following provision:
The respondents obtained certain farm equipment from the petitioner under a lease executed in 1961. The lease was on a printed form less than a page and a half in length, and consisted of 18 numbered paragraphs. The last numbered paragraph, appearing just above the respondents' signatures and printed in the same type used in the remainder of the instrument, provided that 'the Lessee hereby designates Florence Weinberg, 47-21 Forty-first Street, Long Island City, N.Y., as agent for the purpose of accepting service of any process within the State of New York.' The respondents were not acquainted with Florence Weinberg.	'* * * the Lessee hereby designates Florence Weinberg, 47-21 Forty-first Street, Long Island City, N.Y., as agent for the purpose of accepting service of any process within the State of New York.'
	The New York company later brought this suit for breach of the lease in the United States District Court for the Eastern District of New York. . . . Process was served on Mrs. Weinberg as 'agent' of the Michigan farmers. She mailed notice of this service to the Szukhents. . . .
In 1962 the petitioner commenced the present action by filing in the federal court in New York a complaint which alleged that the respondents had failed to make any of the periodic payments specified by the lease. The Marshal delivered two copies of the summons and complaint to Florence Weinberg. That same day she mailed the summons and complaint to the respondents, together with a letter stating that the documents had been served upon her as the respondents' agent for the purpose of accepting service of process in New York, in accordance with the agreement contained in the lease. The petitioner itself also notified the respondents by certified mail of the service of process upon Florence Weinberg.	The record on the motion to quash shows that the Szukhents had never had any dealings with Mrs. Weinberg, their supposed agent. They had never met, seen, or heard of her. She did not sign the lease, was not a party to it, received no compensation from the Szukhents, and undertook no obligation to them. In fact, she was handpicked by the New York company to accept service of process in any suits that might thereafter be filed by the company. Only after this suit was brought was it reluctantly revealed that Mrs. Weinberg was in truth the wife of one of the company's officers. The district judge, applying New York law to these facts, held that there had been no effective appointment of Mrs. Weinberg as agent of the Szukhents, that the service on her as their 'agent' was therefore invalid, and that the service should be quashed.

First, note that the two Justices used the same record, the same facts, with which to tell two different stories. The difference is in the wording and in what facts the two authors chose to emphasize.

Starting with Justice Stewart's opinion: he is very business-like, perhaps "clinical," about the underlying facts of the parties, who they are, and what they do. Petitioner is located in "New York," meaning somewhere in New York State. Respondents are just "residents of Michigan," and the items leased were "certain farm equipment." Stewart interjects a reminder that the "only question now before" the Court is whether the agent was authorized to receive service. The reader is not invited to dwell on whether this seems like a good system for giving notice, nor on whether the notice sounds sufficient. Stewart's account seems calculated to remind the reader not to be seduced by certain irregularities of the case—such as the ones Justice Black strives to point out. Stewart spends time on the actual contract terms: "a printed form *less than a page and a half in length*, and consisted of *18 numbered paragraphs*. The last numbered paragraph, *appearing just above the respondents' signatures and printed in the same type used in the remainder of the instrument*" contained the appointment of the agent for service of process.

Justice Stewart obviously anticipated and sought to head off the rhetorical emphasis placed on the contract terms by Justice Black—particularly the "18 paragraphs of fine print" criticism—by pointing out that the entire agreement was only 18 paragraphs, displayed in the same font size, and—most importantly—that the provision for appointment of an agent appeared right above the farmers' signatures. Justices circulate drafts of the majority and other opinions before publication, and sometimes comment on what the majority or the dissent has to say in the separate opinions. Stewart rounds off the discussion by noting that the agent sent out notice to the farmers promptly, and that the petitioner itself sent out duplicate notice to the farmers.

Justice Black is offended by the agency arrangement in this case. He shows it in certain subtle ways. First, Black wants the reader to think of the petitioner as a New York City company—even though apparently we must look to the suburbs of Long Island or Westchester County for the location, referred to as "Greater New York City." Why New York City? Perhaps to emphasize the disparity of size, power, and money between the parties, or perhaps to play on whatever latent prejudices against New York City might be present in the reader. The respondents are treated to a description of being solid, down-home on the farm, toilers of the soil, using "incubators"—devices in which new life gets its start. Farm and farming are mentioned multiple times in Black's account.

We previously noted Black's smear campaign against the contract—"standard printed form *obviously prepared by the New York* company's lawyers . . . [with] *18 paragraphs of fine print*." Was it small print or not? Neither author gives us a reference, such as a font size. Stewart says it was a short contract; Black says it was in fine print. Black spends more time dismissing the agency of Ms. Weinberg—he denigrates her as a "supposed agent" and each time the word "agent" is mentioned by Black, he places it in quotes, as if to suggest the term "so-called agent." Black elaborates on the farmer's unfamiliarity with Weinberg: they "never had any dealings with Mrs. Weinberg, their supposed agent. They had never met, seen, or heard of her." Black goes out of his way to spill the beans about Mrs. Weinberg being the wife of one of the petitioner's officers—further illuminating why she was "handpicked" by this "New York" company. The implication that this whole arrangement was underhanded dealing is evident.

A statement of facts is not supposed to be directly argumentative, so a thesis sentence is not customarily included. But with good story-telling skills, the message of the fact statement will be clear because the reader will draw helpful inferences and conclusions from your narrative presentation.

Compare the following statements of the facts in the Girl Scout dog bite case:

> **Statement #1** On April 7, 1999, the Girl Scout walked up to Homeowner's house and rang the doorbell. Homeowner's dog approached her and bit her three times on the arm, causing injury.

> **Statement #2** Sally Peterson is an eight year old girl, weighing only fifty-five pounds and standing four feet, six inches tall. She is a member of the Girl Scouts of America. For the last two years, Sally has sold Girl Scout cookies in Homeowner's neighborhood. On April 7, 1999, at 11:30 a.m., Sally was walking with her mother, Janice Peterson, on Homeowner's street, going door to door selling cookies. She was wearing her regulation Girl Scout uniform. As she reached each house on the street, Sally would let go of her mother's hand and walk from the public sidewalk up the front walkway and front stoop to ring the doorbell. At the door, she would call out, "Girl Scout cookies!" She followed this practice at Homeowner's door. Homeowner's Doberman Pinscher was not in sight when Sally rang the doorbell, but the dog immediately came tearing around the corner of the house, leaped on top of Sally and sank its teeth several times into her arm. Her mother responded to Sally's screams as quickly as she could, but she could not pry the dog off Sally. A neighbor, Ralph Jones, was driving by at the time of the attack and heard Sally's and her mother's screams. He stopped his car and ran up to the front door, where he was able to rescue Sally from the dog's jaws. Sally had deep cuts in three places on her right arm and received 150 stitches at the Dayton County Hospital emergency room. She was bruised and scarred all along her right arm and shoulder and had to wear her right arm in a sling for three weeks. Her injuries prevented her from attending the annual Girl Scout camp-out and precluded her from playing soccer for the last four weeks of the season and the play-offs.

The second statement of facts is not simply more detailed than the first, it communicates a distinct message to the reader—a theme—without overtly stating it. The message is that Sally was a non-threatening person, acting peacefully, and using public walkways, and that the dog reacted viciously, without any threat or provocation, severely injuring Sally. Other details, such as her small size, the Girl Scout uniform, the breed of dog, and the fact that she screamed, was taken to the emergency room, and received severe and long-lasting injuries, all go toward painting a sympathetic picture of Sally for the reader. Example #2 uses narrative reasoning to drive home the author's message. It is clear that the author of #2 is someone who is on Sally's side, and the intended audience might be someone who has to decide whether Sally should recover for her injuries.

In other contexts and with other audiences, it would not be necessary or proper to include the same details. Certainly, if we represented the dog owner, we would draft this statement differently. For example:

> On the morning of April 7, 1999, Sally Peterson was walking door-to-door in Mrs. Jones's neighborhood, attempting to sell cookies to the residents. She rang the doorbell of every house on the street and shouted, "Girl Scout cookies!" at the front door. Her behavior attracted the attention of the Jones family dog, Benji. When Sally approached Mrs. Jones's door, Benji approached her. Sally yelled "Girl Scout cookies!" right at the dog, and apparently swung a basket of cookie boxes in the direction of Benji's head. Benji responded according to his training, and acted to restrain Sally in the only way available to a dog, by fixing its mouth around Sally's arm. Sally's mother thereafter tackled Benji and began screaming, attracting the attention of a passerby. A considerable melee ensued in which Benji and Sally were wrestled back and forth. In the skirmish, Sally received several cuts on her arm. Benji also was injured, receiving cuts above his left eye and around the corners of its mouth. Both Sally and Benji required stitches for their injuries.

Here, the reader's attention is directed away from Sally, and the narrative attempts to cast the dog in a more sympathetic light (also notice that we used the Homeowner's name in this example, which humanizes the party against whom the claim is asserted). The statement emphasizes Sally's shouting and notes the presence of the basket, which could have been perceived as threatening to the dog. We intentionally used the phrase "On the morning of . . . ." It may have been 11:30 a.m., but if the reader gets the idea that Sally was disturbing an otherwise peaceful morning, that could work in the dog owner's favor. We also included the dog's name, because the particular name in this case ("Benji") calls up the image of a friendly family pet, rather than a fierce attack dog. Of course, this tactic would not work if the dog's actual name had been "Killer," "Psycho," or "Cujo." (Along the same lines, notice that the previous statement specified the dog's breed—Doberman Pinscher—whereas this statement omitted that detail). In addition, the dog in Example #2 is portrayed as acting predictably. We included the fact that the dog had training (likely to protect the house) and acted in accordance with that training. In reality, your client may not have these facts going for her, and under no circumstances can you include what is not true. However, you should always look for the kind of factual details that will help your version of events. As long as you are not being disingenuous about or deceptive with the facts, you can (and should) spin the story in your client's favor.

As a final matter, notice that we emphasized the dog's injuries in Example #2. This is a bit of a gamble, because you don't want to anger your reader with a perceived attempt to trivialize injuries to a human being and exaggerate injuries to an animal. (Even this we say with caution, as we are avid animal-lovers). We took the risk here because we wanted to show that the "melee" was rough-and-tumble, and to suggest that Sally's injuries may have been more the result of the fray than of the dog unilaterally "attacking" her. Getting the reader at least to consider alternative causes of Sally's injuries will help the dog owner.

CHAPTER 3

The Life of a Case, State and Federal Court Systems, and Jurisdiction

A great deal of the research and analysis that you will perform in the first semester of law school will involve **case law**. Cases are the reported opinions of courts at various stages of a lawsuit or other legal action. An understanding of the life of a case, the differences between the state and federal locations where cases are filed, and the three uses of the term "jurisdiction," is essential to understanding the system of precedent and the concepts of controlling and persuasive authority. These concepts will be of paramount importance in all of your first year classes, including in your legal research and writing class.

This Chapter overlaps with the material covered in first-year civil procedure courses, but it should not replace that material. Our aim is only to give a broad foundation and to teach key concepts that are necessary for your analysis of cases and the precedential effect of judicial opinions at different stages of a lawsuit. If your civil procedure professor uses different words or places different emphasis on matters discussed in this Chapter, remember to follow your civil procedure professor's instruction for purposes of that course and final exam.

I.   THE LIFE OF A CASE IN CIVIL LITIGATION[1]

The **plaintiff** is the person who brings the case. A case may have more than one plaintiff, and the plaintiff need not be a human being. Corporations and municipalities, for example, also can be plaintiffs.

Plaintiffs initiate a case by filing a **petition** or **complaint** in a court. The petition or complaint presents allegations against the party sued, called the **defendant**. The level of court where lawsuits are initiated is known as the trial court. Trial court personnel (**trial judges** and their staffs) administer the lawsuit. When formal requests (motions) are made by the parties to the court (the verb is **to move** the court), or disputes and other matters arise in the course of the lawsuit, a trial judge handles them.

---

1   Our examples throughout this chapter will refer to civil litigation, not criminal litigation.

Plaintiff's complaint or petition asserts one or more **claims** (also known as **causes of action**) against the defendant. A claim or cause of action is a legal term for the facts and circumstances that give a person a right to demand legal relief of some kind from another person or entity. Plaintiff alleges a set of facts and circumstances in one or more **counts**, each count representing a separate claim, and then makes a **demand for relief** (also known as a **prayer for relief**). The relief or remedy sought can take the form, among other things, of monetary damages, the doing or refraining from doing of some act, or a demand to turn something over or give something back.

Defendant has several options in responding to the complaint or petition at the outset of the litigation. Defendant may file: (1) an **answer**; (2) an answer and a counterclaim against the plaintiff; or (3) a motion to dismiss the petition or complaint. A **counterclaim** asserts one or more claims against the plaintiff. If the defendant prevails on the counterclaim, the relief he obtains, if any, will offset the plaintiff's recovery. A **motion to dismiss** asserts that the complaint is improper in some manner (for example, the court lacks jurisdiction over the case or the parties, service of process was improper, the complaint does not state a cognizable claim, or there is some other defect in the pleadings). A successful motion to dismiss on all claims promptly ends the litigation before it gets off the ground.

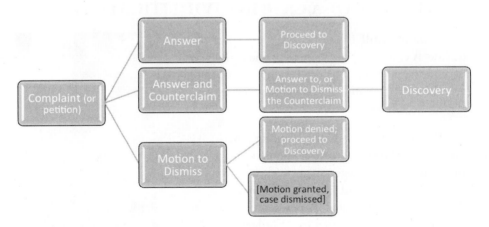

In response, Plaintiff generally may file: (1) an answer to defendant's counterclaim if one was filed; or (2) an **opposition** or **response** to the motion to dismiss. In some courts, the Plaintiff may file a **reply** to defendant's answer (or an **amended complaint** to cure a defect). If there is more than one defendant, the matter can get complicated quickly. One defendant may answer, while another moves to dismiss, and a third answers and files a counterclaim. Plaintiff will respond separately to what each defendant did.

If a motion to dismiss was filed by a defendant, and an opposition or response was filed by the plaintiff, the defendant in most (but not all) courts is entitled to file a **reply** to the opposition or response. Thereafter, the court will rule, or issue a decision, on the motion. If the motion is denied, then the defendant must answer, with or without a counterclaim, as discussed above. After this initial back-and-forth, a party will have the opportunity to bring additional motions or start the process of **discovery** of facts from the other parties.

As mentioned above, a **motion** is a formal request by a party for the court to do something. For example, a party may ask the court to dismiss the plaintiff's complaint, to grant additional time to do something, to allow the party to file something that normally is not filed, to submit a document in a form that requires permission, or to grant the party judgment prior to trial.

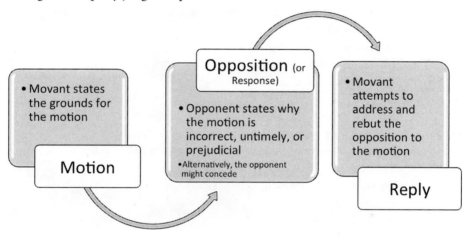

MOTION PRACTICE

Following is the pattern of a typical motion brought in a trial court:

a.   The party bringing the motion is called the **movant**. The motion sets out the grounds (legal and factual) that support the court's granting of the relief sought.

b.   The party against whom the motion is brought is called the **opponent** or **the non-moving party**. The opponent files an **opposition** or **response** to the motion. The opposition lays out the reasons why the motion should not be granted.

c.   The movant can file a **reply** to the opposition or response, which attempts to address and rebut the grounds asserted in the opposition.

d. The opponent might try to file additional responses—for example, a **surreply** to the reply. This rarely is attempted, and in many courts the trial judge must grant **leave** to file a surreply. If leave is granted, the surreply may only address the new issues, arguments, or authorities raised in the reply. In the event that a surreply is allowed, the movant might try to file a **rebuttal** (sometimes called a **sursurreply**). This almost certainly will require leave from the trial judge to file, and the judge undoubtedly will be annoyed with the request. The rebuttal may only address the new issues, arguments, or authorities raised in the surreply. Though rare, the process might continue like a game of hot potato.

e. When the briefing is completed, the court must **dispose** of the motion (reach a **disposition**). In many courts, motions are ruled on after **oral argument**. In some jurisdictions, the court automatically sets a date for motion arguments, but in other places a party (usually the **movant**) **"notices up"** a hearing. This simply means that the party selects a date and time for the hearing by signing up with the court on its calendar, and sends the court and all the other parties a **notice of hearing**, which describes the motion and sets out the date and time for the hearing. At a motion hearing, the parties **appear** before the court and **argue** the motion.  Sometimes, the trial judge will rule on the motion right then and there. The court either will **grant** the motion (sometimes called **sustaining** the motion), or **deny** it (sometimes called **overruling** the motion), or it may **grant it in part, and deny it in part**, which means the movant is awarded some, but not all, of the relief sought.

f. Other courts do not regularly hear oral argument on motions or motions that do not dispose of the claims at issue. In these circumstances, the court rules "on the papers" filed with the court (the motion, memoranda in support, oppositions, replies, etc.). Even in these circumstances, a party can request that oral argument be held on a particular motion, but these requests routinely are denied.

You can only learn so much about the facts of your case from your client and third parties. You also must obtain your opponent's version of the events. Fortunately, there is an orderly process by which the parties in civil litigation learn information about the case from each other, called discovery. This is generally how discovery works:

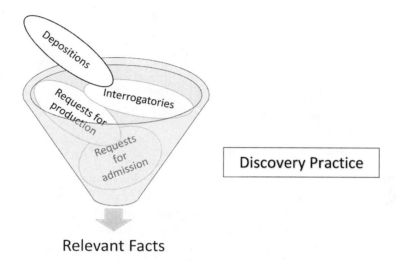

Discovery Practice

Relevant Facts

a.   The parties ask each other specific questions in writing that require a sworn answer. These are called **interrogatories**.

b.   The parties ask each other for documents and data, files, objects, and any other items they think have something to do with the case. These are called **requests for production** or simply **document requests** (often called "RFPs").

c.   The parties ask each other to admit or deny certain information. These are called **requests for admission**. If a party admits something, the other parties can rely on that admission as an established fact in the case without doing anything more to prove that fact (barring some extraordinary occurrence in which the court allows the party to withdraw the admission).

d.   The parties can take **depositions** of the opposing parties, or the parties' representatives if it is a corporation or business entity, and any **witnesses** (people who know something about the facts of the case or the transactions and occurrences from which the case arises). In complicated cases, **expert witnesses** may be involved. These are people—such as economists, medical professionals, scientists, and linguists—whose testimony is sought by a party to explain technical aspects of a case, or any relevant matter requiring specialized knowledge or expertise. The verb is **"to de-**

pose" a witness. The parties take the live witness to a conference room and ask the witness anything and everything that has any connection or relevance whatsoever to the case. The witness is placed under oath, typically represented by an attorney (his own or one of the parties'), and a **court reporter** transcribes all of the questions and the answers, creating a **record** of the deposition. If you do not want something to be taken down, you must go **off the record**. A written **transcript** of the deposition is produced, which can be searched or read like a book. Sometimes, depositions are video-recorded for reference or use later at trial.

e. If a party thinks another party is holding back information or not cooperating, the party can bring a **motion to compel** and request the court's assistance in getting the information it thinks is being withheld. The court will either **compel the production** of the information or deny the request.

At the close of discovery, the parties typically will evaluate whether to move for **summary judgment**. A summary judgment motion argues that the **material facts** in the case (those facts necessary to the court's determination of the claims on which the movant is seeking judgment) are not in dispute, and based on these undisputed facts, the movant is entitled to judgment as a matter of law.

The rules allow a summary judgment motion to be brought at any time in the case, but many such motions are filed once discovery is completed (at that point all of the facts should have been vetted). The movant must prove that there is no genuine issue of "material fact" warranting a **trial**. The concept of (and standard for) summary judgment can be difficult to get your head around, and many lawyers do not understand it until they are immersed in practice.

If no one wins on summary judgment, the case proceeds to **trial**. A trial involves the following:

a. **Jury trial.** In a jury trial, a **jury** of your peers hears the evidence, determines the facts (the jury is the **finder of fact**), and applies the law to those facts to determine the outcome.

The jury is instructed in the law by the trial court in its **jury instructions.**

b.   **Bench trial.** If the court itself (the trial judge) hears the evidence and determines the facts (so, the trial judge is the finder of fact), and then applies the law to the facts to determine the outcome, this is called a **bench-tried case, bench trial,** or **non-jury trial.**

c.   **Evidence** is taken during the trial. Evidence is something that is offered as a fact or something that makes the existence of a fact more or less likely. It **proves** or **disproves** a fact at issue in the case. Evidence consists of the **testimony** of live witnesses, **deposition testimony** (taken from a transcript of the deposition), documents, exhibits and things, admissions of the parties, charts, photographs, maps, drawings, diagrams, movies, tapes (audio and video), and any other means devised by the attorneys for proving or disproving a fact. The **rules of evidence** provide the criteria for the trial court to determine what comes in (and is considered by the finder of fact) and what stays out.

d.   In a jury trial, the jury enters a **verdict** in favor of one side and against the other, and the trial judge enters a **judgment** that follows the direction of the verdict, unless the party against whom the jury rendered its verdict files a **post-trial motion.** A **post-trial motion** posits that the jury erred in its application of the law, made improper determinations of fact, or both. Such a motion also may assert other errors in the trial (e.g., legal errors based on the court's rulings on interim motions), and asks

the court to disregard the verdict. If the verdict is thrown out, the trial judge can either order a **new trial** or enter a **judgment notwithstanding the verdict** in favor of the moving party. In Latin, this phrase appears as **judgment non obstante veredicto**, giving us the initials **judgment NOV, or JNOV,** to refer to the procedure (although in federal courts, this is now referred to as **judgment as a matter of law or JAMOL**). After sorting out all of these **post-trial motions for new trial or for judgment NOV or judgment as a matter of law**, the trial court enters a **judgment** in the case. When a judgment is entered that resolves all the claims of all the parties in the case, it is referred to as a **final judgment**.

The loser at trial in a civil case can **appeal** to the **intermediate level appellate court** (if one exists in that jurisdiction). The party who brings the appeal usually is called the **appellant** or petitioner. The appellant assigns **"errors"** to the court's rulings on the law (including on evidentiary or procedural matters), to factual findings, and to anything prejudicial that occurred during the litigation. The appellant files an **appellant's brief** or **opening brief**. The opponent is called the **appellee** or **respondent**. The appellee files an **appellee's brief** (or **answering brief or opposition brief**). In some courts, the appellant is entitled to a **reply brief**. At present, **oral argument** is available in most appeals, but some appellate courts are moving away from this practice and requiring the parties to make a special demand for it.

If unsuccessful on appeal, the appellant may attempt to seek review by the highest level appellate court, the **court of last resort** in the state or federal system. Such appeals often are not automatic. Instead, these higher courts usually have the right to pick and choose the cases they take, so this level of review is not guaranteed. In other words, you generally only get one appeal "of right," and if you want additional appeals, you must obtain permission to pursue them. If you make it to the highest court in the jurisdiction, the titles of the parties may change (for example, from appellant to **petitioner** and appellee to **respondent**).

The appellate court (at the intermediate or highest level) has several options for addressing a case that comes before it. If the court agrees with the decision below, it will **affirm** the lower court's ruling. If it disagrees, the court will **reverse**–and either: (a) enter judgment for the appellant (and likely issue an opinion correcting the lower court's errors); or (b) identify the procedural errors and **remand** the case back to the trial court for further proceedings consistent with the appellate court decision.

II. FEDERAL, STATE, AND LOCAL COURT SYSTEMS

As noted in Chapter 1, every person in this country is governed by the laws of the nation, state, county or parish, and community (city or town) in which she lives. Citizens of the United States thus are subject to several "sovereigns"—national (also known as federal), state, and local authorities. The laws of the United States, referred to as federal laws, govern everyone living in the United States, while the laws of Illinois only govern people who are living or conducting business in Illinois, and the laws of McLean County in Illinois only apply to people who are living or conducting business in McLean County. Similarly, the ordinances of Normal or Bloomington, Illinois only apply to persons living or conducting business in those towns.[2]

---

2   Map of Illinois-McLean-Bloomington/Normal provided by U.S. Department of Transportation - Federal Highway Administration, http://www.tfhrc.gov/ pubrds/06mar/images/fork7.gif.

Each sovereign has its own court system, meaning that it has separate trial level courts and a court of last resort. The federal system and most states also have an intermediate level appellate court. The court system of each state enforces the laws of that state. The federal court system operates across the United States. There are federal courts physically located across the nation to enforce the federal laws of the United States that are applicable in every state.

Often, however, the coverage of the laws and even the court systems of the nation and the states overlap. Depending on who you are (for example, a citizen of a state), and the subject matter of your action (what you did, or what was done to you—discussed below under the topic of **subject matter jurisdiction**), you may become involved in a state action or a federal action, or both.

For example, on occasion, the same conduct may provide grounds for a legal action in both a state court and the federal court that sits in your state. If you are in Montana and rob a bank with a gun, and in your escape you shoot two people who were blocking your way as you ran to your getaway car, you might be prosecuted in a Montana state court for murder or felony murder and also prosecuted in the United States District Court for the District of Montana (a trial level court in the federal court system, located in Montana) for bank robbery and use of a firearm in connection with a bank robbery, both of which are federal crimes. If you are a citizen and resident of Nevada and you have been swindled out of $100,000 by a Wisconsin citizen and resident, you might sue that person for fraud in state court in Wisconsin or, alternatively, in the United States District Court for the Eastern District of Wisconsin (a federal trial level court) because your state citizenship is "diverse."

WHAT'S THAT?

Federal, State, and Local Laws and Court Systems
If government relations has been a special area of study in your life, the concepts of federal laws, state laws, and local laws, and federal courts, state courts, and local courts may be quite familiar to you. For the rest of us, the concepts can be confusing. It is easiest to start with the idea of territory—the actual physical place in which we live. The United States of America is a physical place that has its own laws, "federal laws," intended to be applied and enforced within its boundaries. The United States has its own system of courts to enforce and adjudicate its laws—the United States courts or federal courts. These courts are found across the nation, which is divided into districts; there is at least one and oftentimes more than one federal district in each state of the nation. But the "district" is not part of the state it sits in, it simply is located there. The process is repeated for small divisions of territory known as states, counties (or parishes), cities, towns, or villages.

The territory of the United States is divided into fifty states and one District of Columbia (leaving aside other territories and protectorates, such as Puerto Rico, Guam, etc.). Each of the states and districts has laws that only apply within these individual states and districts, i.e., within the State of Oregon, or the Commonwealth of Virginia, or the District of Columbia. And each place has a court system to enforce those laws, *e.g.*, the Kentucky courts enforce Kentucky laws applicable within the State of Kentucky. And the process is repeated again for places within a state, such as counties or parishes, and again for places within a county or parish, such as cities and towns and villages. So, you may be standing in the town of Des Peres, Missouri, and at that moment you would be subject to Des Peres's ordinances, St. Louis County laws, Missouri laws, and United States laws each of which might be adjudicated in a different court system.

Different states have different names for their courts, while the federal system uses the same terminology wherever the courts are located across the United States. For example, compare the terms used in the federal system and in the states of California, New York, and Texas:

A. The Federal System

As discussed above, the federal government maintains a court system that operates in each state of the union. The organization of the courts in the federal system is uniform throughout the United States. The federal trial level courts are called the **United States District Courts**. Each of the fifty states (and some U.S. territories) has one or more **districts**, which correspond to a specific geographic region. For example, North, South, East, West, Middle, or Central. Federal trial courts in states with **one district** are called the United States District Court for the District of [State]; for example, the United States District Court for the District of Maryland and the United States District Court for the District of Kansas. The District of Columbia is one district, and the court there is called the United States District Court for the District of Columbia (a cumbersome title). Often, singularly districted courts are located in different **vicinages**, such as the United States District Court for the District of New Jersey, which is comprised of judges sitting in three locations (Newark, Trenton, and Camden). Federal trial courts in states with **multiple districts** are identified as the United States District Court for the [geographic region] District of [State]; for example, the United States District Court for the Eastern District of Missouri, the United States District Court for the Southern District of New York, the United States District Court for the Central District of California, and the United States District Court for the Middle District of Pennsylvania.

Each federal district court is subdivided into courts identified by a number, letter, or the judge's name (or initials). These courts are presided over by a **United States District Judge or a United States Magistrate Judge**. On a tier below the district courts are the federal trial level courts with more limited jurisdiction—the **United States Bankruptcy Court and the United States Tax Court**.

The intermediate level appellate courts in the federal system are known as the **United States Courts of Appeals**. The United States Courts of Appeals are located in thirteen circuits, eleven of which encompass the fifty states. The remaining two are the United States Court of Appeals for the District of Columbia Circuit, which hears appeals from the United States District Court for the District of Columbia (and many cases involving appeals from federal agencies); and the United States Court of Appeals for the Federal Circuit, which has nationwide jurisdiction over appeals based on subject matter (arising from the United States Court of Federal Claims, the United States Court of International Trade, and appeals from the district courts in patent cases).

The federal districts and circuits are broken down as follows[3]

---

3   Circuit map provided by the U.S. Courts page of the Administrative Office of the U.S. Courts, http://www.uscourts.gov/courtlinks/.

1st Circuit Court of Appeals	Maine, Massachusetts, New Hampshire, Puerto Rico, and Rhode Island
2nd Circuit Court of Appeals	New York, Vermont, and Connecticut
3rd Circuit Court of Appeals	Pennsylvania, New Jersey, Delaware, and the Virgin Islands
4th Circuit Court of Appeals	Maryland, North Carolina, South Carolina, Virginia, and West Virginia
5th Circuit Court of Appeals	Louisiana, Texas, and Mississippi
6th Circuit Court of Appeals	Michigan, Ohio, Kentucky, and Tennessee
7th Circuit Court of Appeals	Illinois, Indiana, and Wisconsin
8th Circuit Court of Appeals	North and South Dakota, Minnesota, Nebraska, Iowa, Missouri, and Arkansas
9th Circuit Court of Appeals	California, Oregon, Washington, Arizona, Montana, Idaho, Nevada, Alaska, Hawaii, Guam, and the Northern Mariana Islands
10th Circuit Court of Appeals	Colorado, Kansas, New Mexico, Oklahoma, Utah, and Wyoming, plus those portions of the Yellowstone National Park extending into Montana and Idaho
11th Circuit Court of Appeals	Alabama, Georgia, and Florida
District of Columbia Circuit Court of Appeals	The United States District Court for the District of Columbia, the United States Tax Court, and appeals from many administrative agencies of the federal government
Federal Circuit Court of Appeals	The U.S. Court of International Trade, U.S. Court of Federal Claims, the Court of Veterans' Appeals, and most patent appeals

The court of last resort in the federal system is the **United States Supreme Court** with its nine **justices**, all of whom sit to hear each appeal.

B. The State System

Each state is also a separate sovereign with its own system of courts. Some states have more complex systems than others. When you practice in a particular state, you will learn that state's court system inside and out (if it doesn't happen in law school, then the learning process will begin when you study for the bar exam of the state or states you select). Obviously, we cannot cover all of them here. To give you a flavor for how the structure and vocabulary differ from state to state, we will briefly cover the court systems of three states—California, New York, and Texas— all of which use different terminology.

1. California

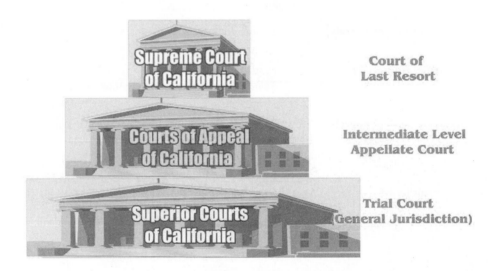

Of the three states we will mention, California has the most typical structure to its court system. The trial level courts of general jurisdiction where cases commence are called the **Superior Courts of California**. There is a superior court for each county (for example, the Superior Court, San Mateo County). The courts are divided into **departments** where the superior court judges are assigned; for example, the Superior Court, Los Angeles County, Department 23.

There is an intermediate level appellate court in California called the **Court of Appeal of California**. Note that the word "appeal" is singular—that is unusual to see because most jurisdictions use the plural. The court of appeal is divided into six appellate districts, numbered First Appellate District through Sixth Appellate District, and two of the larger districts (the First District in the area of San Francisco and the Second District in the area of Los Angeles) are subdivided into multiple divisions. Accordingly, you might find your case in the Court of Appeal, First Appellate District, Division 3. The court of appeal hears appeals from superior courts in panels of three **justices**. Superior court judges have some appellate duties. Appeals in "limited civil cases" (in California, where $25,000 or less is at issue) and misdemeanor cases are heard by the **appellate division of the superior court**, where superior court judges sit on three judge panels. When a small claims case is appealed, a superior court judge decides it. Another exception to the rule that all appeals from the superior court go to the court of appeal is in death penalty cases (appealed directly from the superior court to the Supreme Court of California).

The court of last resort in California is called the **Supreme Court of California**. There are seven **justices** on the Supreme Court of California who sit together to hear each appeal, which is called sitting **en banc**.

2. New York

New York is quite different from other court systems in its terminology. The state trial level court of general jurisdiction in New York is called the **New York Supreme Court**. That is not a misprint. Each trial judge is called a justice. And there is a supreme court for each county. The supreme courts are divided into parts where the justices sit. At the county level, there also are lower courts with more specific subject matter jurisdiction, called the **County Court**, the **Family Court**, and the **Surrogate's Court.** Outside New York City, there is a third tier of limited jurisdiction courts called the **City Courts, District Courts** (on Long Island), **Town Courts** and

Village Courts. In New York City, the second tier of trial courts below the supreme court is divided between the **Civil Courts** and **Criminal Courts**.

The intermediate level appellate court in New York is called the **New York Supreme Court Appellate Division.** It is divided into four numbered **departments**. Appellate division **justices** sit in panels of three and hear civil and criminal appeals from the supreme courts. Appeals from second tier trial level courts in the First and Second Departments go to the **Supreme Court Appellate Term**.

The court of last resort is called the **New York Court of Appeals**, and there are seven **judges** who sit **en banc** on this court. Thus a judge (of the Court of Appeals) may overturn the opinion of a justice (of the Supreme Court) in New York.

3. Texas

Texas also has a fairly complicated court system. The state trial level courts are called District Courts of Texas, and although they correspond to a county, they are numbered (for example, the 238th District Court of Midland County, Texas). Many counties have more than one numbered district. For example, Collin County, Texas has the 219th, 296th, and 366th District Courts. There is one judge in each district. Below the district courts are courts of more limited jurisdiction, also associated with a county, called the County Courts, County Courts at Law, and the Probate Courts. Some counties are large enough to have more than one of these limited jurisdiction courts; for example, Probate Court No. 2, Dallas County, Texas. Even lower are courts at the local level, cities and townships, called the Municipal Courts and Justice of Peace Courts.

The intermediate level appellate court in Texas is called the **Court of Appeals of Texas**. There are fourteen courts of appeals that are numbered and identified by the city where they sit; for example, Third Court of Appeals, Austin. Houston has two—the First and the Fourteenth Courts of Appeals. The court of appeals hears civil and criminal appeals from the district courts and county courts in panels of three **justices**.

There are two courts of last resort in Texas — one for civil appeals, called the **Supreme Court of Texas**, and one for criminal appeals, called the **Court of Criminal Appeals of Texas**. The Supreme Court of Texas has nine **justices** and the Court of Criminal Appeals of Texas has nine **judges**. Both courts hear cases **en banc**.

III. HIERARCHY OF JUDICIAL AUTHORITY

One of the key concepts to master in legal analysis concerns the weight that is afforded to different judicial decisions based on the level of the court that issued the opinion. The basic structure of the court systems described above—trial level court → intermediate level appellate court (if any) → court of last resort—is known as a **hierarchy of judicial authority**. It refers to the power of courts higher up *in the same system* to **reverse** or **affirm** the decisions of the courts below. It also refers to the principle that the **decisions of the courts higher up in the hierarchy are controlling authority for any courts directly below the court in the same system**.

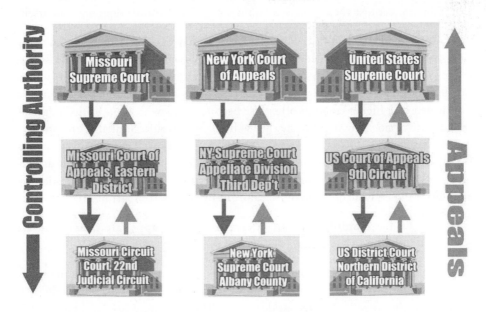

If you think of an appeal as climbing the hierarchy of judicial authority, then the hierarchy of controlling authority uses the same path in reverse. Appeals climb the hierarchy, while controlling authority descends it.

Following are several important principles to keep in mind concerning the ability of one court to control the decisions of another. These are important principles to remember while researching, because they will help you sort your findings into the categories of mandatory (controlling, or binding) versus persuasive authority.

- **Courts on the same tier do not bind each other.**

If a court is on the *same tier* with another court, it does not control the decisions of that court. Thus, a trial court of general jurisdiction in a state will not control the decisions of another trial court of general jurisdiction in the same state. (Nor does it bind any court of *another state* on the same tier, or even on a higher tier, because two different states are two different systems). In the above chart, the decisions of judges of the Missouri Circuit Court, 22nd Judicial Circuit, St. Louis City, are not binding on the judges of the Missouri Circuit Court, 21st Judicial Circuit, St. Louis County. That said, many courts on the same level will look to other decisions from courts on that same level as **persuasive** authority, but not binding authority.

- **Judges on the same court do not bind each other.**

Even the decisions of judges sitting on the same court are not binding on other judges of the court because the judges are all working on the same tier of the hierarchy. For example, the decisions of one judge of the New York Supreme Court, Albany County, are not binding on the other judges of the New York Supreme Court, Albany County, because these courts are on the same tier. A court does not bind itself.

Individual trial courts and appellate courts may decide—per their own court rules—to deviate from this general principle. A trial court may initiate a rule (sometimes referred to as a "bench rule") that requires all judges on the court to follow the decisions of all other judges on the court unless and until those decisions are overturned by a higher court or otherwise become bad law. It is up to the judges of the court to decide how strenuously they will follow this rule. Similarly, an appellate court may adopt a rule (sometimes referred to as a "panel rule") that any decision of a three judge panel of the appellate court must be followed by all subsequently assembled panels of the court unless the decision is overturned or called into question by an intervening en banc decision of the court or by the court of last resort.

- **En banc opinions of an intermediate level appellate court bind all judges on that court**

An exception to the general rule that a court does not bind itself is the situation of an intermediate level appellate court that sits **en banc** (all available judges on the court sitting together) to reconsider a case. These opinions are binding on each judge and subsequently assembled panel of judges of the intermediate level appellate court. The same is not true of courts of last resort, because the judges or justices of these courts often sit en banc to hear every case that comes before them. Thus, an en banc decision of the United States Court of Appeals for the Ninth Circuit binds each subsequently assembled three-judge panel of the Ninth Circuit, but an en banc decision of the United States Supreme Court, which always sits en banc to hear each case, does not bind future decisions of the United States Supreme Court.

- **Courts that are not in the direct line of appeal do not bind lower courts.**

The general rule is that a court must be in the *direct line of appeal* in a hierarchy to bind a court on a lower tier, even if the two courts belong to the same state or federal court system. So, for example, if there are multiple divisions of an intermediate level appellate court in the same jurisdiction, as was the case in all of the state court systems discussed above, only the division that hears appeals from the state trial level court will bind that court with controlling authority. Consider the following examples:

- **The Missouri Court of Appeals, Eastern District hears appeals from the Missouri Circuit Court, 22nd Judicial Circuit, St. Louis City. Accordingly, it binds the judges of that court as well as all of the other Missouri Circuit Courts located in territory of the Eastern District. However, the Missouri Court of Appeals, Western District and the Missouri Court of Appeals, Southern District do not bind the Missouri Circuit Court, 22nd Judicial Circuit, St. Louis City or any other circuit court found within the territory of the Eastern District.**

- **The United States Court of Appeals for the Ninth Circuit controls the decisions of all of the United States District Courts located in the territory of the Ninth Circuit, such as the United States District Court for the District of Oregon or the United States District Court for the Central District of California. However, it does not bind any district court located outside of the Ninth Circuit, such as the United States District Court for the Middle District of Georgia or the United States District Court for the District of Maryland.**

Once again, states may decide to deviate from this rule and adopt a rule that all opinions of the intermediate level appellate courts are binding on all trial level courts wherever they are located within the state. Illinois is one such state that has adopted this rule.[4]

- **Courts of last resort control all courts in the same hierarchy.**

---

4   *See State Farm Fire and Cas. Co. v. Yapejian*, 605 N.E.2d 539 (Ill. 1992) (decisions of one appellate district are not binding on other appellate districts but are binding on all circuit courts across the state).

The highest court in any hierarchy controls all courts below it in the same hierarchy. The Illinois Supreme Court controls the decisions of each district of the Illinois Appellate Court and all of the Illinois Circuit Courts, because all of these courts are below it in the same hierarchy. The United States Supreme Court controls the decisions of the United States Courts of Appeals for each circuit and all of the United States District Courts, because all of these courts are below it in the same hierarchy.

- **Courts of one hierarchy do not bind courts of another hierarchy, but the court of last resort of one hierarchy can bind courts of a second hierarchy *if the first hierarchy's law is being applied by the courts of the second hierarchy.***

This principle is trickier because it requires an understanding not only of *who* decided a case, but of *what* was decided (*i.e.*, which law was applied). Recall that decisions of a court higher up in one hierarchy are not necessarily controlling in courts outside that hierarchy, even if the courts outside are on a lower tier. Thus, courts in the Minnesota state system generally do not bind courts in the Wisconsin state system, nor those in the federal court system, nor the federal courts that sit within the jurisdictional territory of Minnesota.

The exception takes hold when a court of one state is applying another state's law, when a federal court is applying state law, or when a state court is applying federal law (in sum, when a court of one hierarchy is applying the law of another hierarchy).[5]

In these instances, the *court of last resort* of the hierarchy whose law is being applied controls the decisions of a court in another hierarchy. Decisions of lower tiered courts of the hierarchy whose law is being applied do not have this power. For example:

- **The Wisconsin Supreme Court does not control the decisions of any Mississippi court or federal court unless the non-Wisconsin court is applying Wisconsin law in the case it is adjudicating. However, if the Mississippi court is applying Wisconsin law on a particular issue, it must follow the decisions of the Wisconsin Supreme Court. However, the decisions of the Wisconsin Court of Appeals (an intermediate level appellate court) will not bind a Mississippi court even if the court is applying Wisconsin law.**

It is important to note here something that might sound counterintuitive. That is, the United States Supreme Court does not automatically control the decisions of state courts, because they are outside the federal court hierarchy. Of course, if the issue that concerns the state court is a matter of federal law, such as a decision interpret-

---

5   The reasons why courts are called upon to apply the law of another jurisdiction in various instances are the subject of complicated areas of the law known as conflicts of law and choice of law, which are taught in second semester or advanced civil procedure and conflict of law courses. Suffice to say that courts are, on occasion, required to apply the law of another jurisdiction, be it another state, or federal law, or the law of another nation.

ing the U.S. Constitution, then the U.S. Supreme Court's decision is binding. Although the U.S. Supreme Court is popularly referred to as the "highest court in the land," it is only the highest court of the federal hierarchy, not the highest court of every hierarchy in the United States. This concept is discussed further in Chapter 5.

TAKE NOTE!

The Hierarchy of Judicial Authority

Is the hierarchy of judicial authority important? Yes! It is critically important, absolutely essential that you learn the concept of the hierarchy of judicial authority because it is the most important factor that determines whether a court opinion is merely useful or interesting or whether it is a controlling, mandatory authority that, along with other controlling, mandatory authorities, will determine the answer to the legal issue you've been asked to address. If your issue is governed by Idaho law, the decisions of the Idaho Supreme Court on your topic are controlling authority, while the decisions of any court of Washington, Oregon, Nevada, or Utah, or any federal court including the United States Supreme Court, cannot be controlling, mandatory authority. These opinions may be brilliantly written, powerfully persuasive, and a wonder of rhetoric and legal analysis, but they cannot control your issue because they are opinions from the wrong hierarchy of judicial authority. Only cases from Idaho's hierarchy of judicial authority can control issues of Idaho law.

IV. JURISDICTION

The term "jurisdiction" is used in three different ways in legal parlance. The root of the word means "to speak the law," and all of the uses of the word deal in some way with an entity's (typically a court's) ability to exercise power over something or someone. Jurisdiction is the power to apply and enforce the law: (1) in a given location (jurisdiction as a place); (2) with regard to certain persons and entities (personal jurisdiction); or (3) with regard to certain kinds of claims and legal actions (subject matter jurisdiction).

A. Jurisdiction as a place

The first use of the term jurisdiction is a geographic description of a place where an identifiable set of laws and rules applies (and some entity has the power to enforce those laws within that geographical area). The term refers to the limits and boundaries of the area where that entity has this power. The State of New Jersey is a jurisdiction in which New Jersey laws and rules apply, and the government and courts of the state can enforce them. The United States is a jurisdiction where federal law can be applied and enforced. Similarly, a police department has a jurisdiction, which means that it has power within its defined area but not outside of it. This sense of "jurisdiction" is invoked when you say, "He was escorted out of the jurisdiction," or "Another jurisdiction's law applies to this case."

Venue is a companion term that refers to an individual court's power to adjudicate cases in a certain geographic area. Jurisdiction most often is defined and limited by the constitution of a state or nation, whereas venue most often is defined and limited by statute. A state may ordain in its constitution that all trial level courts of the state have the power (jurisdiction) to hear all cases arising in the state, but the legislature may carve up the state into smaller "venues" where an individual court has the right to hear cases that arise in its particular county or other defined location. For example, the Missouri Circuit Court for the 22nd Judicial Circuit has jurisdiction to adjudicate cases that arise anywhere in the State of Missouri, but the venue of the court is limited to cases that arise in St. Louis City, not St. Louis County, or any other county in the state. The Missouri Constitution gives each Missouri Circuit Court the power (jurisdiction) to hear cases arising in the State of Missouri, but further legislation defines the venue of the Missouri Circuit Court for the 22nd Judicial Circuit to comprise case arising in St. Louis City. The fact that the Missouri Circuit Court for the 22nd Judicial Circuit has appropriate jurisdiction over cases that arise anywhere in the State of Missouri means that if a case is *transferred* to that court from another Missouri Circuit Court, for reasons of prejudice or improper venue,[6] the court has the power to adjudicate the transferred case even though initially it would not have been the proper venue for the case.

B. Personal jurisdiction

The second use of the term jurisdiction pertains to power over the parties, or **personal jurisdiction**. A court must have personal jurisdiction over a party to a case for the court to render an enforceable judgment against it. Generally, a party must have some notice that the court is exercising power over it, which is effectuated by **service of process**. Service of process merely *perfects the potential power* that the court already had with regard to that party—if the court has no power over someone, service of process will be of no avail.

The three main sources of a court's power to issue process and thus perfect its power to render judgment against a party, are:

1. **Presence**—If a party (individual, corporation, or another type of entity) is *present* within the jurisdiction and venue of the court, the court can exert power over it. The party is said to be "found" within the jurisdiction. States have inherent power (sovereignty) over their own physical territory, so if a person is present there, the state has power to adjudicate claims concerning that person. In simple terms, a citizen and resident of a jurisdiction, whether it be a human being who has decided to settle there indefinitely, or a corporation or business entity that has its headquarters

---

6   This often is seen in criminal cases that obtain a great deal of publicity in the location where the crime occurred before the trial of the case. The criminal defendant may feel he has been tried in the local press before getting his day in court and may seek to have a change of venue to a different court in a different part of the state where his case did not receive as much or any attention in the local media.

or its principal place of business within a jurisdiction or constantly does business there, will be subject to the power of the courts of that jurisdiction. Beyond that, the boundaries of "presence" within a state or other jurisdiction is a remarkably complicated legal concept, which will be addressed in greater detail in your civil procedure course.

2. **"Gotcha" service**—As of the publication date of this book, service of process on a person who is *temporarily* found within a state or other jurisdiction is still sufficient for a court to obtain power over that person. Some authorities have questioned the viability of this doctrine under the modern requirements of the Due Process Clause (discussed in the section below), but the doctrine is still alive. Thus, if you are served with process while passing through a state, even if you only are there for a few seconds, you are subject to the power of the courts of that state.

3. **Long Arm jurisdiction**—In modern times (post-1900), the above sources of power over individuals and corporations began to be perceived as too limited, and the concept of "long arm" jurisdiction thus was born. The name is derived from the phrase, "the long arm of the law," and refers to a court's power to issue process against an entity that is outside the physical boundaries of the jurisdiction if that entity performed acts that had an effect in the state and if that entity has some minimal connection (called a **nexus**) to the state. If the requirements for the issuance of process are met, and service of process is accomplished according to the laws of the place where the entity is found, then the entity can be hauled into the court. Two requirements must be met for the exercise of jurisdiction to be proper:

    a. **Statutory Requirement**—The action must arise from an activity in the state (or one having an effect in the state). Many states define the kinds of activities that trigger the exercise of extraterritorial jurisdiction in a **Long Arm Statute**. Typically, activities include: (1) doing business in the state; (2) making a contract in the state; (3) committing a tort causing injury in the state; (4) owning or possessing property in the state; or (5) conceiving a child in the state. The lawsuit must *arise from* the entity's contact with the state, while engaging in a defined activity. In states that use a defined list of activities, it is not enough for a person to have done something in the state at one time if the lawsuit has nothing to do with that singular contact. For example, a defendant may have conceived a child in the state, but if the lawsuit is a property dispute that has nothing to do with the child, jurisdiction generally will not exist. Other states have a Long Arm Statute or a body of state law that allows the exercise of extraterritorial jurisdiction in the state to the full extent of the Due Process Clause (discussed below). Even in these states, the lawsuit must arise from a contacts with the state for the exercise of jurisdiction to be appropriate.

b. **Due Process Requirement**—The exercise of Long Arm jurisdiction also must satisfy the requirements of the Due Process Clause of the 14th Amendment of the United States Constitution. The Due Process Clause requires that:

> (1) The entity has certain "minimum contacts" with the state. These contacts must not be "random and fortuitous," but instead must show a "purposeful availment" of the benefits and protections of the laws of the state; and

> (2) The exercise of Long Arm jurisdiction is "reasonable" and does not offend "traditional notions of fair play and substantial justice." Courts look to see if the defendant's actions in the state were such that she reasonably should have anticipated being subject to suit in that state.

These topics are a major source of study in civil procedure courses, and you should refer to your learning there to understand just what these requirements mean.

C. Subject matter jurisdiction

The final use of the term jurisdiction refers to **subject matter jurisdiction**. Courts may be limited in the subject matter of the cases that they can adjudicate. Subject matter jurisdiction is a creature of statutory and (state or federal) constitutional law.

State trial courts often have **unlimited** (or **universal**, or **general**) **jurisdiction** over matters that arise in the state, which means that any action properly brought in that state not within the exclusive subject matter jurisdiction of another court is fair game to be filed in that court.

All federal courts are courts of **limited jurisdiction**, meaning that the subject matter of cases they can hear is limited by the U.S. Constitution and federal statutes. If your case does not meet one of the limited criteria for federal jurisdiction, it cannot be brought in federal court.

Exclusive jurisdiction may be granted to a certain court by statute; for example, a federal statute may state that all cases arising under that statute must be brought in the United States District Courts. The opposite of this is **concurrent jurisdiction**, whereby the same type of action can be brought either in federal or state court.

Appellate courts, particularly courts of last resort, most often have limited jurisdiction whereby parties seeking to have a case heard in these courts must **request**

a transfer to the court or **petition** the court for the issuance of a **writ of certiorari, or writ of mandamus**, or other writ, to allow the case to be heard.

Federal subject matter jurisdiction is limited to **federal question and diversity jurisdiction. Federal question jurisdiction** requires that a claim in the case arise under a federal statute or a federal administrative rule or regulation. There is a **"well pleaded complaint" rule**, meaning that the federal nature of the action must appear from the plaintiff's pleadings; it is not enough that the defendant can assert a **defense** that arises under a federal statute. If the federal nature of the claim is not apparent from the complaint, the case cannot be removed to federal court.

Diversity jurisdiction exists where the parties are diverse and the amount in controversy is *in excess* of $75,000 (*i.e.*, is at least $75,000.01). **Diverse parties** means that all plaintiffs must be "citizens" of different states from all defendants. All plaintiffs need not be from the same state, nor do all defendants need to be from the same state, as long as there is no plaintiff who is from the same state as any defendant. The **amount in controversy** is met if the damages that the plaintiff lawfully seeks, the value of the property at stake, the amount owed under a contract, or any other lawful calculation of the amount one party might gain and the other might lose, adds up to at least $75,000.01. If the criteria of diverse parties and the amount in controversy are met, the case properly can be adjudicated by a federal court even though the case involves a state law claim that could very well have been brought in a state court.

Preemption is a term referring to the situation where a federal law is drafted so as to supplant all state law on that topic. The power to preempt is found in the Supremacy Clause of the U.S. Constitution, art. 6, cl. 2. If an area is preempted, no state can maintain and enforce its own law in that area, and if a state court hears such a claim, it must apply and follow the federal law on the topic. If the preemptive law is also drafted with exclusive jurisdiction in federal court over claims arising within the area, then an action that is filed in state court may be removed to federal court. Examples of areas of the law that have been preempted by federal law are: copyright; patents; employee retirement income and security plans; and the labeling of insecticides, fungicides, and rodenticides.

An action brought in state court that could have been brought in federal court may be removed from the state court to the United States District Court of the state and district where the state court is located. This is known as **removal jurisdiction**. In diversity cases, only an out-of-state defendant (someone not a citizen or resident of the state in which the action is filed) may remove the case to federal court. There were historical reasons for this practice, based on the perception that out-of-state defendants got a raw deal in state courts and were better treated by the distinguished federal judges across the street. At present, the perception of prejudice is fading away, but removal jurisdiction lingers on, perhaps driven by the defense bar who sees that jury verdicts generally are larger in state courts (especially in large cities) than in the federal courts sitting in the same locale. The right to remove a case on diversity grounds is further limited by time—if the case lingers in state court for one year, the right to remove vanishes. And if the removal was technically improper at the time of removal, then the federal court can **remand** the case back to state court.

CHAPTER 4

Determining the Rule from a Single Authority: Cases, Statutes, and Administrative Law

To begin analyzing a legal issue, you must identify the governing rule of law. Articulating the legal rule is, of course, the point of the "Rule" section of your discussion.

This Chapter discusses primary sources in the order of: case law, then statutes and constitutions, then administrative regulations. While not proceeding by authoritativeness, we begin with cases because rules can be quite difficult to extract from them. In contrast, with constitutions, statutes, and regulations, determining the rule often is more straightforward because these sources are themselves rules. If on point, the terms of such sources state the rule—or at least provide the starting point for interpretation. Of course, determining the *meaning* of those terms (through the process of statutory interpretation) thereafter can be tricky; we address this in Section III.

Determining the rule(s) applied by a court in its decision is not a simple feat. Sections I and II of this Chapter discuss how to read and analyze a court order or opinion for this purpose. The rule, which is part of the **holding** of the case, represents the **precedent** for which the case stands. In conjunction with the rules from other sources you select, such precedent constitutes the governing law you will use to analyze a legal issue in a given jurisdiction.

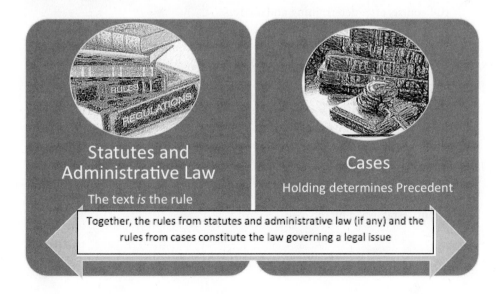

Statutes and Administrative Law

The text *is* the rule

Cases

Holding determines Precedent

Together, the rules from statutes and administrative law (if any) and the rules from cases constitute the law governing a legal issue

I.   FINDING THE RULE(S) IN A SINGLE CASE

Judges are not charged with the official task of *making* law. Rather, their primary task is to find, interpret, and apply the law to adjudicate disputes that come before them. As you will learn, judges are often criticized for "judicial legislating" and "judicial activism"—terms referring to some judges' tendency to go out of their way to establish a certain rule in a case, thereby taking on the normative role traditionally assigned to lawmakers. Judicial activists tend to be the exception among jurists.

Nonetheless, judicial opinions are a *primary* source of the law, and judges can create, modify, or abandon rules of law. In most circumstances, rules are made or modified as a by-product of the judge's adjudicatory functions. The description of this process leads neatly into a discussion of what to consider in determining the rule(s) that a case stands for and the **precedent** it establishes.

A. The legal method of judges

A judge is in a similar position to a lawyer when it comes to the methodology used to solve the problems that reach her desk. Judges receive a set of "problems" in the form of a lawsuit; when they have to make a decision concerning one of these problems, they turn to the same sources of law as the attorneys who appear before them. Yes, the court has the benefit of legal briefs from the parties on both sides of the dispute, but it is atypical for a judge (or law clerk) not to check it out for herself.

Of course, after determining and analyzing the law, judges also have the opportunity and obligation to apply the rule(s) to real persons in concrete situations; when they do this they have created a precedent for how the rule works in a specific set of circumstances.

Judges at the trial level report their decisions in the form of a written **order** (also called a **memorandum and order, order and memorandum**, or **order and judgment**), and at the appellate level, in a written **opinion**. Through these orders and opinions new law is made, most often in small, incremental steps, as the judge explains what the law is, what it means, and how it works in the situation at hand. This brings us to the topics of the "**Borrowed Rule**" and the "**Applied Rule**" and the "**Precedent**" established by the case.

FYI

The terms **Borrowed Rule** and **Applied Rule** describe concepts that are familiar to all lawyers and legal academics. The terms themselves, however, likely will not be familiar to them. Legal writing professors have chosen different terms for the same concepts over the years, and there is little uniformity in the choices. Accordingly, do not presume that anyone who has not read this book will understand these terms until you explain the concepts for which they stand. In contrast, the terms **"precedent"** and **"holding"** have uniform meanings commonly understood in the legal community.

B. The "Borrowed" Rule

Because judges follow the same methodology as practitioners in determining what the law is on an issue, they often include in their writing a statement of the applicable rule found in earlier authorities. Thus, the court "borrows" or adopts a prior statement of a rule as the basis for its own opinion. We refer to this reiteration as the **borrowed rule**.

The borrowed rule may be the precise rule articulated and applied by the court in its decision, thus becoming part of the **holding**. If so, the case becomes one more precedent informing the meaning and application of that rule.

However, the borrowed rule *is not necessarily the rule actually applied by the court* and, thus, it is not necessarily part of the holding and established precedent. In fact, the borrowed rule is part of the holding only when the court does nothing in its discussion to alter or further interpret the borrowed rule. If the court does not discuss or explain what the borrowed rule means, and simply applies it to the facts at hand, then the borrowed rule is the rule from the case that is part of the holding, and the case is one more precedent in its lineage. Thus, there are two options:

- **the court applies the borrowed rule without modification or interpretation, and the borrowed rule is part of the holding and precedent;**

or

- **the court modifies, interprets, or abandons the borrowed rule, and creates a different rule** (the **"applied" rule**, described in the next section), **and the applied rule becomes part of the holding and precedent.**

For example, presume Case 1 in the hierarchy establishes the rule that "the sky is blue on sunny days." If Case 2 in the same hierarchy applies this rule exactly and determines that because the sky was not blue, the day was not sunny, then Case 2 is further embedding the borrowed rule in the line of precedent. If, in contrast, the court in Case 3 adds that "if there is less than 25 percent cloud cover, the sky is still blue" under the rule, then the rule has been altered.

Why does this matter? There may be more than one version of a rule on a given issue in a given jurisdiction. The two articulations may compete; one version may have more or different requirements than the other. In these situations, it is important to know *which* version of the rule you are tracing (because one may be more favorable than another).

C. The "Applied" Rule

Typically, a court will explain the borrowed rule and how it works in a new situation. This discussion may modify the rule, and an attorney can use the judge's opinion as a source not only for the wording of the rule, but also for the meaning and interpretation of its specific terms. This may cast a new light on the terms of the borrowed rule or alter the rule's application.

Expanding on the points above, the court, in analyzing a case and applying the borrowed rule(s) may:

Apply the borrowed rule as is, without interpretation or change—As discussed above, in this instance the borrowed rule is the applied rule; the new decision is one more precedent for the borrowed rule.

Interpret the borrowed rule—The court may offer a new interpretation of the rule. The borrowed rule may remain the same, but the court may apply the rule or an element in such a way that its effect is changed in a legally significant way.

Modify the borrowed rule—The court may redefine or even reword a rule or an element so as to alter its effect. The court may add an element or factor or take one away. In this case, the court has created a new rule—the applied rule.

Abandon (Strike, Abrogate, or **Overturn)** the borrowed rule or part of it, and **Replace** the rule—The borrowed rule is gone; the court has created a new rule—the applied rule. This practice is much more common with courts of last resort that have the last word on the law in a given jurisdiction. With respect to statutory law, a court usually will only strike a statute down because of a state or federal constitutional defect in the law or because the law clashes with federal or international law under the Supremacy Clause of the United States Constitution.

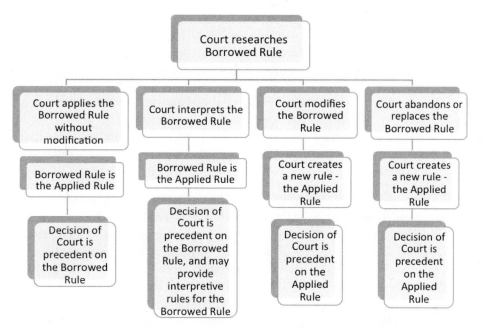

Following are examples of what can happen to a borrowed rule.

Example 1

The first situation is a court that inherits a rule and does nothing to interpret, modify, or change the rule in a legally significant way:

> The Borrowed Rule in the Apex case you are reading, *Astro v. Scooby*, 887 W.2d 234, 236 (Apex 1996), states:

> To prevail on a claim for injuries caused by a dog, a plaintiff must plead and prove: (1) ownership of the dog by the defendant; (2) causation of the injury by the dog; and (3) lack of provocation of the dog. *Lassie v. Benji*, 667 W.2d 234, 236 (Apex 1993).

> The judge applies the rule—"The defendant owned the dog, the defendant's dog bit the plaintiff, and the plaintiff did nothing to provoke the dog. The plaintiff wins."

This case applies the borrowed rule to the case as it found it. *Astro* becomes one more precedent on the borrowed rule laid down in *Lassie*.

Example 2

The second example is a case that writes new rules—in this case, interpretive rules—on certain elements of the borrowed rule:

> The borrowed rule in the Apex case you are reading, *Snout v. Roscoe*, 987 W.2d 134, 136 (Apex 1998), states:

To prevail on a claim for injuries caused by a dog, a plaintiff must plead and prove: (1) ownership of the dog by the defendant; (2) causation of the injury by the dog; and (3) lack of provocation of the dog. *Blue v. Bingo*, 667 W.2d 234, 236 (Apex 1993).

But this judge goes on to state: "The concept of 'ownership' of the dog is not limited to a person having actual possession of title to the animal, but includes a person who harbors or has control over a dog." Later, the judge states: "Provocation requires an actual physical attack on the dog; verbal attacks do not count."

We now know two things about the rule on dog bite liability in Apex that we did not know from a reading of the borrowed rule: ownership is not limited to title and includes harboring and controlling a dog; and provocation requires a physical attack, while verbal attacks are excluded. The borrowed rule has been modified. In the one instance, "ownership" has been expanded; in the other instance, "provocation" has been limited.

Example 3

Occasionally, a judge will reject or abandon certain terms of the rule, as in the following example:

The borrowed rule in the case *Garfield v. Marley*, 777 W.2d 333, 335 (Apex 1989), is presented as follows:

The rule in Apex on liability for damages caused by a domestic cat has traditionally been phrased to require proof that: (1) the defendant owned and controlled the cat; (2) the injury was caused by the cat; (3) the plaintiff did not provoke the cat; and (4) the cat weighed more than eight pounds at the time of the attack. *Piper v. Daisy Mae*, 456 W.2d 654, 658 (Apex 1956).

The court then states: "The last requirement concerning the weight of the cat has never been applied by any court in Apex as a basis for granting or denying relief to any plaintiff. The requirement is a dead letter, and the Court will give it no consideration in this matter."

We now know that the court in question will only apply the first three elements of the cat bite rule, and this opinion will be authority for the argument that the cat bite rule only has three elements in Apex.

Example 4

The court may add to the requirements of the rule, as follows:

The borrowed rule in the case *Haley v. Toonces*, 676 W.2d 545, 548 (Apex Ct. App. 1st Dist. 1985), is stated as follows:

The rule from *In re Morris*, 345 W.2d 987 (Apex. Ct. App. 1st Dist. 1965), was that "a party wishing to exercise the option of waiving the right to a trial by jury must give notice of this decision to the other party in the matter." *Id.* at 988.

The court goes on to say: "In addition, the party must not only give notice of the exercise of the option to her opponent, but must do so promptly, at the earliest opportunity in the case."

The rule has been altered by adding an additional requirement. Attorneys should look at the requirements of the rule differently because of this opinion. When the court is finished, it will apply the rule as modified to the facts of the case to determine the outcome. It is the modified version of the rule actually used to determine the outcome of the case that is most important to the analysis. We will call this the "applied rule" (part of the "**precedent**") set by the case. By this definition, the **precedent** is equivalent to the **holding** of the case, and the holding of the case determines the precedential value of the case.

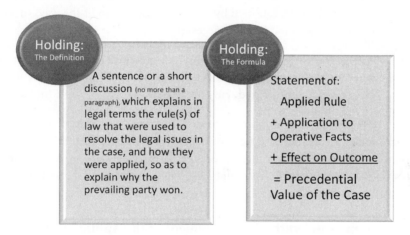

D. How do you phrase the Applied Rule?

The applied rule is the rule you will use in drafting the **R**ule section of your discussion.

You have two choices for how to phrase it: you can articulate the borrowed rule in text followed by an explanation of its modification(s) over time (typically producing a few sentences or a paragraph), or you can **synthesize** one or more cases into a single, revised version of the rule—thus, revealing the applied rule in one or two sentences. Which option you take depends on the complexity of the rule (its historical status and iterations), as well as on your own ability to explain its iterations in as straightforward but accurate a manner as possible.

There are some guidelines to follow:

- **Never change the wording of rules from constitutions, statutes, and administrative regulations.**

If a case modifies a rule taken from a constitution, statute, or administrative regulation, write the modification separately, after you have laid out the specific wording of the primary source. In other words: do not paraphrase or rephrase the terms of a statute or regulation in the first instance of use.

- **Do not change the wording of a much-cited historical rule. Write the rule first, and any modifications second.**

A borrowed rule from case law is sometimes so commonly stated in one phrasing that it is tantamount to a statute. *I.e.*, if a multitude of cases in a jurisdiction cite the same borrowed rule as *the* rule on the issue, and the rule always is phrased using the same language—same terms, same number of elements—then you should adopt the same phrasing. Respect the authorities by starting with the same (traditional, historical version) of the rule, followed by a separate discussion of the ways in which the borrowed rule has been modified, if necessary.

- **Synthesize the applied rule if you can generate a clear, succinct, and coherent statement. Do not synthesize the rule if you must write a long, overly complicated, run-on sentence.**

In some instances, it is appropriate to modify the wording of the borrowed rule when you present it in writing. For example, the court in Example 4 above added a new requirement that affected one of its existing elements. The rule and modification are short and simple enough that when we present the applied rule, we would go add the change:

Example 4: Synthesized Statement of the Applied Rule

A party seeking to waive the right to a trial by jury must give notice of this decision to the other party in the matter promptly, at the earliest opportunity in the case. *See Haley v. Toonces*, 676 W.2d 545, 548 (Apex Ct. App. 1st Dist. 1985); *accord In re Morris*, 345 W.2d 987, 988 (Apex Ct. App. 1st Dist. 1965) (notice required).

FOOD FOR THOUGHT

When it is more accurate to present a current, synthesized version of a rule created over time by a string of cases (frequently true with common law rules), then you should **synthesize** the authorities in your rule section. But when the rule comes from a statute or administrative rule or regulation, or is the product of a single, well-known, and controlling case, then it makes sense to present the rule first and the modifications second. Readers familiar with the well-known version of the rule will be educated by your history of the subsequent modifications and will not be put off by first seeing an unfamiliar synthesized rule.

In re Morris was the source of the borrowed rule, and *Haley* added to it, so both cases should be mentioned. There are no quotation marks around the rule because the exact wording presented does not appear in either of the cited sources, although the meaning of the rule would be apparent to anyone reading the two cases (the reason to use the signal "*See*").

Example 2 is different. The terms of the borrowed rule have not been altered directly, but we now know a lot more about what two of those terms mean. If we were presenting the applied rule in a rule section, we would not try to cobble together the two sources into a single statement. Do not produce something like the following:

DO NOT WRITE A RULE SECTION LIKE THIS:

To prevail on a claim for injuries caused by a dog, a plaintiff must plead and prove: (1) ownership of the dog by the defendant, which is not limited to a person having actual possession of title to the animal, but includes a person who harbors or has control over a dog; (2) causation of the injury by the dog; and (3) lack of provocation of the dog, meaning lack of an actual physical attack on the dog, because verbal attacks do not count. *Astro v. Scooby*, 887 W.2d 234, 236 (Apex 1996); *Lassie v. Benji*, 667 W.2d 234, 236 (Apex 1993).

Simply cobbling the two together makes a long and cumbersome rule that is too wordy to be useful in the application of the law to the facts. Judges and other audiences will not trust your synthesis of the two authorities if the end product looks like a Frankenstein monster (metaphorically speaking). Instead, put these interpretative sub-rules where they belong—in the sub-sections of the discussion that handle these elements of the rule (referred to in Chapter 6 as "sub-TREAT" sections):

Rule on Main Issue:

To prevail on a claim for injuries caused by a dog, a plaintiff must plead and prove: (1) ownership of the dog by the defendant; (2) causation of the injury by the dog; and (3) lack of provocation of the dog. *Astro v. Scooby*, 887 W.2d 234, 236 (Apex 1996); *Lassie v. Benji*, 667 W.2d 234, 236 (Apex 1993).

Sub-Rule on Ownership
(from the sub-TREAT on Ownership):

The concept of "ownership" of the dog is not limited to a person having actual possession of title to the animal, but includes a person who harbors or has control over a dog." *Astro*, 887 W.2d at 236.

Sub-Rule on Provocation
(from the Sub-TREAT on Provocation):

Provocation requires an actual physical attack on the dog; verbal attacks do not count. *Id.*

Example 3 eliminated the fourth element of the borrowed rule. In expressing this change, do not simply rewrite the rule with the last element missing. Instead, give notice to the reader that there was a fourth element, but it is no longer applicable:

The rule in Apex on liability for damages caused by a domestic cat has traditionally been phrased to require proof that: (1) the defendant owned and controlled the cat; (2) the injury was caused by the cat; (3) the plaintiff did not provoke the cat; and (4) the cat weighed more than eight pounds at the time of the attack. *Piper v. Daisy Mae*, 456 W.2d 654, 658 (Apex 1956). The fourth element, the weight of the cat, has fallen out of favor with courts in Apex, and no longer is applied. *See Garfield v. Marley*, 777 W.2d 333, 335 (Apex 1989).

By presenting the borrowed rule first followed by the modification, the reader is given the correct rule, but she will not be surprised if she goes and reads cases that still list four elements to the rule.

E. The holding of the case and dicta

Remember, the definition of and formula for holding is:

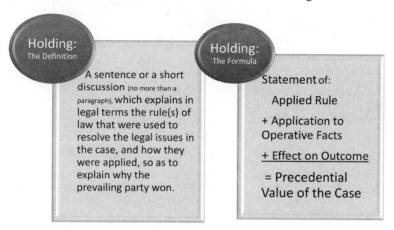

The holding is a combination of the applied rules and a discussion of how they were applied to the legally significant facts in the case to produce the result. A proper description of the holding would discuss all three of these things—the applied rules, legally significant facts, and how the rules were applied to the facts to produce the result in the case.

There should be a separate holding on each issue raised by the parties in support of their demands for relief. An appellate opinion typically takes up and resolves a number of independent issues, each of which is offered by the appellant as a ground for reversal of the judgment below, and each of which produces a separate holding.

Dicta is a legal discussion in the case that is not part of the holding. Sometimes it is difficult to determine what is dicta as opposed to the holding. Consider the following definition and factors regarding dicta:

DICTA - The Definition

What is Dicta?

Dicta is anything in a case (any statement about the law, legal analysis, discussion of an element or factor) that is unnecessary to the outcome of the case. If the discussion of the law you are considering has no impact on the outcome of the case (the decision of the court as to who won and lost and why), then it is dicta.

DICTA - The Formula

Factors Establishing Dicta:

• Did the court make its decision halfway through the case, and announce it, but went on to discuss several elements, items, or factors anyway? If so, the items discussed after the court announced its decision are probably dicta.

• Did the court say that it was not reaching certain issues? This is a dead giveaway that any discussion of these issues is dicta.

• Did the court predict an outcome for a future case if the facts or circumstances were different? That kind of prediction is dicta.

• If you simply dropped the issue or the discussion of the issue from the case—removed every mention of it— would it still be possible to:

a. Discern why the prevailing party prevailed?
b. State the factors, policies and considerations that brought about the decision?
c. Explain the rule(s) or element(s) that were analyzed and applied to determine the outcome?
d. State the facts that the court found to be important to the decision?

If you answer YES to a, b, c, and d, you have dicta.

Dicta is not irrelevant; to the contrary, it can be important. As you will see in the chapters that follow, lawyers and judges often will be very curious to find out what other courts have said in previous cases, especially cases from a higher court in the appropriate hierarchy, no matter if the statements are holding or dicta. Dicta can be a useful predictor of what a court will do in a future case where the issue discussed in dicta is finally reached and resolved. The important distinction is that a lower court is not bound by dicta, while it is bound by the holding.

II. DETERMINING THE RULE FROM CONSTITUTIONS, STATUTES, OR ADMINISTRATIVE REGULATIONS

In contrast to case law, *identifying* the rule of law in a constitution, statute, or administrative regulation typically is straightforward: the constitution, statute, or regulation is itself the rule on the legal issues described in the title and text of the provision. Of course, it may not be easy to locate the correct provision: you must research and analyze the law of your jurisdiction to determine which provision(s) actually speak to the issue at hand. Once you find the correct sections, though, you have identified the rule. Thereafter, the process of statutory interpretation (Section III below) becomes relevant for determining what the terms of the provision(s) mean—and that alone can be challenging.

When presenting this type of rule in writing, you should *quote the exact terms of the constitution, statute, or regulation* on point. These are referred to as **operative**, **pertinent**, or **applicable terms** of the statute or regulation. It is generally not correct to paraphrase the terms of a constitution, statute, or regulation. The terms are important on their own.

For example:

Your client has waited four years after a car accident to decide she wants to sue the other driver. She asks you if it is too late to sue. You understand her cause of action to be for negligence, and you correctly deduce that the answer to the timing issue will be covered by a statute, which in this case is called a "statute of limitations." You find the following statute in Apex:

Apex Rev. Stat. § 300.2–102.
Limitations on Tort and Contract Actions.

All actions of libel, slander, intentional torts, negligence, fraud, negligent misrepresentation, and for breach of contract (except contracts for the provision or payment of money, which are covered by section 300.2-101), shall be brought within five years of the date the cause of action accrued.

You have the rule, no question, and would write it up—the first time you mention it in the main part of your analysis—as follows:

"All actions of . . . negligence . . . shall be brought within five years of the date the cause of action accrued." Apex Rev. Stat. § 300.2–102 (1997).

Quoting only these terms is helpful for the reader, because the rest of the statute is irrelevant to the legal issue you are researching. Remember to use ellipses (". . . ") to show where you took information out of the statute.

DO IT WITH STYLE!

Ellipses are used to mark text that has been removed. Three ellipsis dots are used if the removal was in the middle of a sentence ("John fell . . . and broke his leg."). Four ellipsis dots are used if the material was taken at the end of a sentence ("John fell into a hole . . . . Marsha came to rescue him."). Additional rules on ellipses are presented in Appendix B, Section II(C).

There are, of course, interpretive issues raised by this rule: What does "accrued" mean, and when did this action accrue? There will be cases interpreting and applying this and other language in the rule, which should be addressed in your paper. But the starting point in the rule section is the language of the statute quoted above.

The reason why you should not paraphrase the operative provisions of a constitution, statute, or regulation (at least at first mention) is because that language represents the *official* language of a rule of law created by those charged with making laws and regulations—i.e., legislators and agencies. Courts, in contrast, are not charged with making law, but wind up creating law in the form of legal precedent as a by-product of their adjudicatory function. Because constitutions, statutes, and regulations are the official versions of rules, you must give them priority in your discussion by quoting them—and, not incidentally, by quoting them **first** in the **R**ule section of your analysis. Other primary authorities (cases) and secondary authorities (law review articles, treatises, scholarly commentary, etc.) may interpret the official language and affect its meaning, but the official language itself should take the lead.

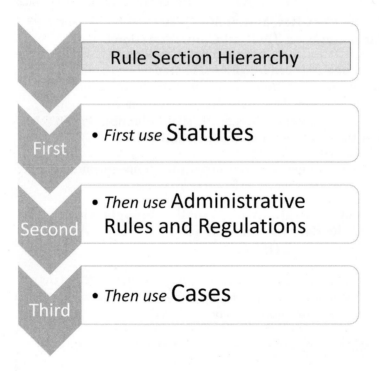

III. STATUTORY INTERPRETATION

As we have discussed, a statute or regulation is itself a rule, and therefore its text should be the starting point for your "**R**ule" section. Typically, however, the bare terms of a statute require additional explanation. Such explanation engages the process of statutory interpretation.

MAKE THE CONNECTION!

We are focusing here on drafting a rule section. The first step is to quote the pertinent terms of the statute (or constitution or regulation). The process of statutory interpretation may produce additional information that might be added to the rule section thereafter.

The process of statutory interpretation is complicated—though fascinating—and can be the subject of an entire course in law school. The following discussion is not intended to replace this course of study. Instead, we cover in outline form important steps in the process—from textual analysis, to contextual analysis, to secondary sources of interpretation—because you likely will be asked to engage in statutory analysis in connection with at least one of your legal writing problems in your first year of law school.

The chart on the next page depicts the process of statutory interpretation. Interpretation always begins with the text; thus, the first step is referred to as the "textual" part of the analysis. The second step typically involves a "contextual" analysis. This step involves looking to the context of the relevant statutory section—other provisions of the statute or code— to find interpretive support. A textual or contextual analysis may be assisted by the application of principles of interpretation called "canons of construction." These canons enable lawyers and judges to make more uniform and predictable interpretations of statutory language in certain specific contexts described in the canons.

FOOD FOR THOUGHT!

If you are interested in seeing how the canons are applied in action, check out the U.S. Supreme Court's opinion in *Bailey v. United States*, 516 U.S. 137 (1995).

Legislative history also provides evidence of contemporaneous constructions of statutory terms. Although not part of the statute, and thus not primary authority, legislative history is typically considered more authoritative than secondary authority that merely comments on the statute after it has been passed into law. As discussed below, when the text and context and the general principles of interpretation fail to identify a conclusive meaning of statutory terms, legislative history can be the next best step in proving that your own interpretation is the correct one.

Secondary authority, in the form of treatises, law review and journal articles, etc., is also useful in supporting an interpretation of statutory terms. Rarely would such commentary swing the vote of your audience by itself, but it can invoked to buttress a textual, contextual, or historical interpretation.

The process of interpretation described here refers to the determination of the meaning of the terms of the statute on the day that it was passed into law. The next step is to consider how the statute has been changed by later authorities, namely statutory amendments and case law.

THE PROCESS OF STATUTORY INTERPRETATION[1]

	Interpretive Aid	Uniform Statute and Rule Construction Act	Nature of the Authority
TEXT	**Text** Text of the statutory provision Definitions in the statute	Sections 1, 2, 19	Primary
CONTEXT	**Context** Definitions in other parts of the code Usage of similar terms in other parts of the code Common or technical meaning of terms Meaning derived from provisions in the same title of the code Meaning derived from the purpose of the act or regime that created the provision	Section 2	Primary

---

1   This section of this chapter is largely derived from the Uniform Statute and Rule Construction Act (ULA 1995) ("USRCA"), which is itself a revision of the Model Statutory Construction Act (ULA 1965, rev'd 1975).

PRINCIPLES OF INTERPRETATION	**Principles of Interpretation and Construction**		
	Baseline definitions in USRCA §§ 3-7 (if adopted in your jurisdiction); Federal Dictionary Act, 1 U.S.C. §§ 1-7	Sections 3-7	Neither [These are rules for how to read text and context]
	Prospective operation of statutes (vs. retrospective operation)	Section 8	
	Severability of invalid provisions	Section 9	
	Irreconcilable statutes or provisions— Later statutes prevail Comprehensive revision eliminates prior inconsistent laws	Section 10	
	Enrolled bill text controls over errors in codified version and later publications	Section 11	
	Incorporation by reference rules	Section 12	
	Headings and titles are not used unless they were drafted by the legislature and included in the enrolled bill passed by the legislature	Section 13	
	Rules concerning repeal of statutes and repeal of repealing statutes	Sections 14-16	
	General rules (maxims) of construction	Sections 18, 20	
JUDICIAL CONSTRUCTION	**Judicial Construction of the Statute** (in cases applying the statute)		
	Courts have the power to interpret and apply the law, and may change the meaning and effect of the statute as a by-product of this power	Section 20	Primary

	Legislative History		
LEGISLATIVE HISTORY	**Legislative History** Contemporaneous constructions in House, Senate, and Conference committee reports Amendments and changes in the bill, in committee or on the floor of the chamber Answers to specific questions in floor debate and committee reports	Section 20(b), (c) Section 20(c), (d) Section 20(c), (d)	Although not primary, these aids are more authoritative and persuasive than the secondary sources discussed below
COMMENTARY	**Commentary** Official commentary on the statute General commentary in treatises, law reviews and other second authorities		Secondary
SIMILAR STATUTES	**Similar Statutes** Uniform Laws Construction of similar statutes in other jurisdictions, using text, context, judicial decisions, legislative history, and commentary	Section 20(b)	Primary, but not controlling, and used in a way that simulates secondary authority

GENERAL PRINCIPLES OF STATUTORY INTERPRETATION

Reading the text of a statute may sound simple, but as will become readily apparent, words do not always mean what a layperson thinks they mean at first glance. This is especially true of statutory terms. Following are some general principles of statutory interpretation—also called canons of construction—applied in the United States:

Principle 1. The text of a statute is the primary, essential source of its meaning

Text is the primary, essential, and often only required source for the meaning of a statute or rule. The Uniform Statute and Rule Construction Act § 19 (ULA 1995) ("USRCA") confirms the general principle that statutory interpretation must begin with the text of the statute or relevant provision. The following guidelines apply:

A. If the statute contains a definition of a word, its meaning is determined by the definition.

If the statute discusses the term "beverage," and the statute also contains a definition for that term as "alcoholic drinks and carbonated sodas," it is proper to construe the term "beverage" as including beer, wine, liquor, cola, root beer, orange soda, and tasteless malt beverages, but it would not be proper to include water and natural fruit juices.

B. If the statute does not contain a definition of a word, its meaning is determined by:

1. Common usage of the terms, including:

a. A meaning obvious to the judge

You do not have to prove to the court the obvious meaning of terms. "Feline" refers to cats and "canine" to dogs. More exotic terms (ursine, equine, or porcine) may require a definition and dictionary citation. When in doubt, provide support for the obvious, but do it clearly and succinctly.

b. Dictionary definitions

Legislators are presumed to know the common dictionary meanings of the words that they use in legislation. If they intend a different meaning or only one of several possible dictionary meanings, they should spell it out clearly in the statute. Still, dictionaries are popular sources for some judges when faced with resolving the meaning of ambiguous language.

c. Use of the same word elsewhere in the same statute

This is straightforward contextual analysis. The applicable statutory provision may not contain definitions of its terms, but the provision may have been passed as part of a larger act that contains definitions. In the absence of contrary evidence, the meaning given to the same terms at the same time by the same legislators is powerful evidence that the terms carry the same meaning.

d. Use in other statutes, legislative materials, and other public documents

A more tenuous position is to point to definitions found in the same code (though not necessarily the same act), even to definitions established years before or after the specific statutory provision at hand. The logic is that legislators are aware of the meaning of all terms used in the code of a jurisdiction, so if they use the same terms later, they are presumed to carry the same meaning as before. Of course, the legislators may want to override this logic by defining the terms to mean what they want them to mean at the time of passage.

e. Common law meaning of a term

Again, in the absence of contrary evidence, if a term has a defined legal meaning in the common law developed by a chain of cases, then legislators are presumed to be aware of it. They are further presumed to have intended the term to have the same meaning when they employed it in the statute. As discussed above, legislators are free to depart from a common law legal meaning of a term by defining it separately.

2. Words that have acquired a technical or particular meaning in a given context

Much like the trade usage concept from contract law, certain words have well known legal meanings when used in a specific context. The word "freight" has a particular meaning in the context of sales of goods (the fee paid for shipping goods with a carrier of goods, such as a trucking company), which is different from the layperson's understanding of "freight," meaning the goods that are being shipped. Legislators are presumed to know these technical meanings, so if they draft sales of goods legislation and use the word "freight," it will be construed to have the same meaning it usually has in sales contexts. If the legislators do not intend the term to carry that regular meaning, they should define the term to remove the presumption.

3. Legal meaning as defined in the Dictionary Act, 1 U.S.C. §§ 1-7

In 1 U.S.C. §§ 1-7, Congress defined some terms that frequently appear in federal legislation. For example, 1 U.S.C. § 1 provides, "words importing the singular include and apply to several persons, parties, or things; words importing the plural include the singular; words importing the masculine gender include the feminine as well; . . . the words 'person' and 'whoever' include corporations, companies, associations, firms, partnerships, societies, and joint stock companies, as well as individuals."

4. Legal meaning as defined by state statute or common law

The USRCA recognizes that certain terms have an established meaning under the common law and state statutory law. For example, "shall" and "must" express a duty, obligation, requirement, or condition precedent. "May" confers a power, authority, privilege, or right. Use of a word of one gender includes corresponding words of the other. Use of a verb in the present tense includes the future tense.

5. The context in which the terms appear

Meaning can be derived from context, as discussed above.

6. The rules of English grammar

Most of us like to believe that English is a precise enough language for the law, but consider the following:

Dog owners shall not bring dogs into the park unless they are leashed.

Is it the dogs that must be leased, or the owners?

And how are we to interpret these phrases:[2]

> The ladies of the church have cast off clothing of every kind, and they may be seen in the church basement Friday.

> This afternoon there will be a meeting in the south and north ends of the church. Children will be baptized at both ends.

> Eight new choir robes are currently needed, due to the addition of several new members and to the deterioration of some older ones.

The moral here is to be careful about the English language letting you down.

Principle 2. Prospective and retrospective operation

A statute operates only prospectively (going forward) unless the statute or its context requires otherwise. This principle is an issue of fairness and due process. Cases operate retrospectively because they involve past events that gave rise to claims. But statutes and regulations define future rights and liabilities. If a statute is passed to prohibit certain behavior, a person is permitted to behave in the proscribed way up to the effective date of the statute. If she ceases her proscribed behavior the moment the statute goes into effect, she will not be punished. For example, if a client was growing marijuana in his basement, but learns that Congress passed a law making the growing of marijuana in basements illegal as of July 1, 2014, the client can throw out plants on June 30 and not suffer any repercussions.

---

2   *See* Church Bulletin Bloopers, http://www.angelfire.com/tx4/BulletinBloopers/ (last visited Oct. 23, 2014).

However, some statutes operate retrospectively, as in situations where the statute regulates activities, events, rights, or duties that happened in the past. For example, a statute providing for the distribution of reparations for victims of the September 11, 2001, terrorist attack necessarily operates retrospectively to regulate rights that arose in the past. Most procedural and jurisdictional statutes operate without regard to when the events of a particular lawsuit occurred, so the terms retroactive and prospective do not have an impact on their operation.

Principle 3. Severability of invalid provisions

If a provision of a statute or its application to any person or circumstance is invalidated, that should not affect other provisions or applications of the statute that can be given effect regardless. This means that the statutory provisions are severable. One bad provision does not destroy the operation of the rest of the statute as long as one can make sense of the requirements of the remaining provisions without reference to or use of the stricken terms.

Principle 4. Statutes whose terms conflict

If statutes enacted into law in the same jurisdiction appear to conflict, they should be construed, if possible, to give effect to each. If the conflict is irreconcilable, the later enacted statute governs. *I.e.*, Legislators are presumed to have known of the conflict and are understood to have passed a law that changed the rules of the earlier statute even if they did not specifically repeal the earlier one. However, an earlier enacted specific, special, or local statute prevails over a later enacted general statute unless the context of the later one indicates otherwise. Statutes with particular subject matter (for example, licensing of bicycles), as opposed to general legislation (for example, regulation of all vehicles) may be interpreted as surviving the passage of the later, generally worded statute unless it is clear that the legislators intended to change the rules for all moving vehicles including bicycles. If the general statute has provisions that address bicycles, then the intent of the legislators to regulate bicycles is made clear.

Principle 5. Comprehensive revisions of the law

If a statute proposes to be a comprehensive revision of the law on a subject, it prevails over prior statutes regulating the same subject matter whether or not the revision and the prior statutes conflict irreconcilably. From time to time, legislators pass into law a new statutory regime that is intended to regulate all aspects of certain legal subject matter.

For example, in 1973, Congress passed the Employee Retirement Income Security Act (ERISA), which was intended to establish a new legal regime governing all aspects of employee benefit and retirement plans. The sweeping nature of the legislation was clear from the language of the act. Therefore, any federal laws governing aspects of employee benefits and retirement income plans on the books prior to 1973 were deemed supplanted by ERISA—unless Congress indicated otherwise.

Principle 6. Statutes incorporating another statute of the same jurisdiction

A statute that incorporates by reference another statute of the same jurisdiction is deemed to incorporate a later amendment of the other. If a state's sales of artwork statute incorporates by reference a definition or regulation of the payment of freight from the Uniform Commercial Code enacted in the same state, and the definition or regulation of freight is later updated, the newer, updated version of the freight provision is deemed to be incorporated into the sales of artwork statute unless the legislators indicate something to the contrary.

Principle 7. Use of headings and titles

Headings and titles should not be used in construing a statute unless they are contained in the enrolled or final version. This principle points to the possibility that the legislators themselves did not draft the headings or titles of the codified statute. Other government agencies, such as the Congressional Office of Law Revision Counsel, take the laws that are passed and assign them to subject matter classifications within the body of a jurisdiction's laws, and these entities may have been responsible for creating a heading or title when they inserted it into the code. If Congress or the state or local legislature is not responsible (which would be revealed by looking at the final version of the statute that was voted on and passed into law), then the heading or title should have no impact on the provision's interpretation. If the heading or title was drafted by the legislature, it simply is part of the terms of the statute, and can be used for interpretation.

Principle 8. Revisions to statutes

A statute that is revised, whether by amendment or by repeal and reenactment, is a continuation of the previous statute and not a new enactment to the extent that it contains substantially the same language. i.e., the coverage of the law does not skip a beat while a new amendment has passed but has not yet gone into effect.

Principle 9. Repeal of a repealing statute

The repeal of a repealing statute does not revive the statute originally repealed or impair the effect of a savings clause in the original repealing statute. If the legislature intends this effect, it must expressly state it in the new legislation.

Principle 10. Effect of amendment or repeal of civil statutes on civil claims

Except as to procedural provisions, an amendment or repeal of a civil statute does not affect a pending action or right accrued before the amendment or repeal takes effect. A pending civil action or proceeding may be completed, and a right that has already accrued may be enforced through new litigation as if the statute had not been amended or repealed.

For example, if you had the right to sue a health care provider for strict liability for implanting a defective heart valve at the time the valve was found to be defective, you still can pursue a legal action for strict liability against the health care provider even if the legislature passes a law that forbids strict liability claims against health care providers. You had the right, and the new law does not take it away. This follows the general principle that statutes only operate prospectively. However, if your valve was installed and found to be defective after the legislation was passed, your right to sue for strict liability is extinguished, or more accurately stated, it never accrued.

Procedural provisions—rules that regulate the conduct of litigation rather than the substantive rights of the parties—are not subject to this principle. Therefore, if the procedural rules on the requirements for the filing of summary judgment motions change while your law suit is pending, you must follow the new rules.

This general principle applies to civil (non-criminal) statutes. A different rule applies to certain criminal statutes, as discussed below.

Principle 11. Effect of amendment of criminal sentencing provisions on pending criminal actions

If a penalty for a violation of a statute is reduced by an amendment, the penalty, if not already imposed, must be imposed under the statute as amended. This principle is based on concepts of due process and freedom from cruel and unusual punishment. If the public opinion as to the proper sentence for a crime is lessened, the criminal should get the benefit of the lesser sentence.

Principle 12. General avoidance of interpretations that doom a statute to fail

The law has come to recognize general rules of thumb of what to avoid when attempting to find the proper interpretation of a statute. These principles suggest that an interpretation should not end in declaring a statute unenforceable. *I.e.*, legislators are presumed not to have intended to pass futile and ineffective laws doomed to fail. Therefore, **a statute is construed so as to:**

    A.   avoid an unconstitutional result;

    B.   avoid a result that violates international law or an international treaty;

C. avoid extraterritorial effect;

D. avoid an absurd result;

E. avoid an unachievable result;

F. have uniform nationwide or statewide application;

G. give effect, if possible, to its entire text;

H. give effect, if possible, to its objective and purpose; and

I. give effect to any carefully crafted compromises embodied in the statute.

Principle 13. "Ejusdem generis" maxim

Latin-phrased statutory maxims are an exception to the general rule to avoid using such terms in your writing. On occasion, they have great effect. "Ejusdem generis" is a latin phrase still regularly used. The principle takes two forms in the construction of a statute:

A. the meaning of a word is limited by the series of words or phrases of which it is a part;

B. the meaning of a general word or phrase following two or more specific words or phrases is limited to the category or class established by the specific words or phrases.

For example, if a park regulation allows "household pets" to run free from noon to 4:00 p.m., and the regulation itself repeatedly refers to "dogs and cats" in application, it is a good argument that the regulation was intended to be limited to common, domestic pets, and not to exotic pets, such as wolves or tigers.

If a bankruptcy law provision allows a debtor to keep "televisions, refrigerators, washers, dryers, dishwashers, microwaves, ranges, ovens, and *other common household goods*" free from execution as part of the homestead exception, it is a good argument that this exception was not meant to cover extremely valuable artwork or an elaborate collection of antique beer brewing equipment. Even though these items may be found in the same home, they are not of the same class or category as the goods specifically mentioned in the section.

Principle 14. Statutes on the same subject

Statutes on the same subject should be construed as a whole even if they were enacted or adopted at different times. This general rule is useful and practical, especially when entities such as the Congressional Office of Law Revision Counsel take statutes that were passed at different times and group them into the same section of the code because of their subject matter.

Principle 15. Language excluded from supplanting legislation

If language of an earlier statute on the same subject is excluded from a later statute that replaces it, the excluded language should not be presumed included in the supplanting statute. If the legislature intended the earlier language to be included, it should not have omitted it from the later legislation.

Principle 16. Interpretation of definitions of crimes

Definitions of crimes are interpreted narrowly to give the benefit of the doubt to the accused. Our system of justice and due process affords many protections to the accused, and this principle is one of them.

Principle 17. Statutes in derogation of the common law

The rule that a civil statute in derogation of the common law is construed strictly does not apply to statutes enacted in the twentieth century. This reflects the fact that our society is well along the way to one in which laws are defined by statutes and administrative rules and regulations. So there is no need to apply an old maxim of interpretation that had meaning when the law was defined by the common law.

Principle 18. Additional aids to construction

If, after considering the text and context of a statute in light of the above rules, the meaning of a term remains uncertain, the following aids to construction may be considered:

A.   a settled judicial construction of a statute in another jurisdiction as of the time of the borrowing of that statute from the other jurisdiction;

B.   a previous statute, or the common law, on the same subject;

C.   related statutes;

D.   a judicial construction of the same or similar statute;

E.   an administrative construction of the same or similar statute;

F.   the circumstances that prompted the enactment or adoption of the statute, the "mischief" that the statute was meant to correct;

G.   the purpose of a statute as determined from the legislative or administrative history of the statute;

H.   the historical development of other legislation on the same subject;

I.   whether the legislature reenacted a statute or an administrative agency readopted a rule without changing the pertinent language after a court or agency construed the statute; and

J.   treatises and articles by leading experts on the subject.

Principle 19: Legislative history

Although listed last here, legislative history is not the least used tool of statutory interpretation. Not all lawyers and judges agree on the weight that should be afforded to it. That said, many courts often give considerable weight to the contemporaneous interpretations of the terms of statutes that are reported by the very legislators who later voted the statute into law. The most authoritative sources of these constructions are **house and senate committee reports**. These reports frequently are used to confirm the interpretation given by application of principles 1 to 18 above, and they may be used to resolve an ambiguity left after applying these principles.

Federal legislative history usually is more thoroughly documented and almost always more accessible than the legislative history of state or local legislative bodies. To the extent that the information is available, you also may use other legislative materials, including:

A. **proposed or adopted amendments, preambles, statements of intent or purpose, findings of fact, notes indicating source, contemporaneous documents prepared as a part of the legislative or rulemaking process, fiscal notes, and committee reports; and**

B. **the record of legislative or administrative agency debates and hearings.**

When ascribing weight to evidence of meaning of this kind, the greatest is given to materials that: are shown to have been considered by the legislature before passage or adoption (or were available to the legislature at the time); formed the basis for the language in the statute; and were not revised after they were considered.

These considerations should strike you as obvious; however, not all statutory interpretation is an exercise in rote logic. To the contrary, the interpretation of a given statute can be a wonderful and at times complex journey through a vast collection of sources of meaning and theories of interpretation.

GO ONLINE!

We have presented a good introduction to statutory interpretation in this section, but the topic is broader than we can cover here. You can go online to further your education. A logical next step would be to consult Jim Chen, *Statutory interpretation: a rudimentary reading list,* http://jurisdynamics.blogspot.com/2006/08/statutory-interpretation-rudimentary. html (Aug. 8, 2006) (last visited Oct. 23, 2014).

CHAPTER 5

Determining the Applicable Rules: Analysis of Multiple Authorities

This Chapter discusses how to read and analyze multiple authorities (including statutes, rules and regulations, and case law), to determine the rule that applies to an issue in a given jurisdiction. To formulate a rule, you must build on what you already have learned:

- You must know which of your sources are primary authorities and which are secondary (Chapter 1).

- You must understand the priority of statutes and regulations and how to integrate subsequent interpretations by courts and legal commentators (Chapters 4 and 5).

- You must understand the hierarchy of judicial authority in your jurisdiction so that you can properly rank the cases you have found, both controlling and persuasive authorities (Chapters 3 and 5).

- You must understand the holdings of the cases and their applied rules to determine their place as precedent in the body of law you are constructing on the issue (Chapter 4).

Formulating the rule:

Taking all of the fruits of your research,

Sorting primary from secondary authorities,

Sorting controlling from persuasive authorities,

Sorting holding from dicta,

Produces the authorities used in the rule section.

- You must understand what was dicta in these cases, so that you can include that with the persuasive authority on the issue (Chapter 4).

Your goal is to construct an accurate and coherent statement of the rules that govern the issue supported by appropriate legal authority (Chapters 1-5).

A collection of legal sources must be ordered in terms of priority. You must understand which authorities are primary versus secondary. Among the primary authorities, you must understand which are controlling (binding) versus persuasive. Finally, you must analyze the precedents from each of the authorities and attempt to reconcile them so that you can articulate one coherent version of the rule.

I.   SORTING MULTIPLE AUTHORITIES

At this point, you have conducted research on the issue(s) you've been asked to address, and now the question is: **How do I formulate the operative legal rule for each issue?**

We assume that your research has produced multiple authorities; you might have a whole pile of cases, statutes, and other materials that potentially govern the outcome of your issue. The question becomes: how do you *order those authorities*? Which ones should be given more or less weight? Which ones should you use to start your analysis? It may be useful to remember that we are focused here primarily on the "R" (Rule) section and only secondarily on the "E" (Explanation) section of the "TREAT" paradigm.

Sorting Step 1: On Point vs. Inapposite

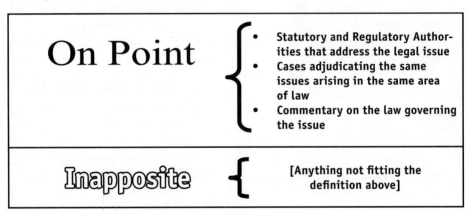

On Point	{	• Statutory and Regulatory Authorities that address the legal issue • Cases adjudicating the same issues arising in the same area of law • Commentary on the law governing the issue
Inapposite	{	[Anything not fitting the definition above]

Most research efforts will produce many more sources than you need to incorporate or rely on. While searching, you should first determine which authorities are on point, and which are not. Any authorities (primary or secondary) that address the issue in question are on point. Though not all will be necessary for your analysis, the first step is to determine what will not be useful at all. Discard those sources.

Sorting Step 2: Primary and Secondary Authority

PRIMARY	Legislation Administrative Law Cases
Secondary	**Commentary** and **interpretations** of the law

Recall from Chapter 1 that **primary authorities** include: **legislation** (constitutions, statutes, ordinances, laws, codes, treaties, and charters), **administrative rules and regulations** (the rules, regulations, decrees, orders, licenses, and interpretations promulgated by administrative agencies, non-legislative governmental entities, and other regulatory boards and commissions), and **case law** (judicial orders and opinions).

Secondary authorities encompass commentary on and interpretations of the law written by legal scholars, judges, legislators, and legal practitioners in treatises, restatements of the law, hornbooks, law review articles, annotations, encyclopedias, legislative history documents, and other publications. Secondary authorities summarize, explain, illustrate, interpret, and organize the law. Sometimes they criticize the law and recommend changes. Secondary authorities may be used as persuasive authorities, but they are never controlling. They are secondary in name and secondary in importance; they should be used to **support** a discussion or an argument about the law that is made with primary authority.

Sorting Step 3: Controlling Authority and Persuasive Authority

The next sorting step concerns **controlling authority** (also known as **binding** or **mandatory authority**) and **persuasive authority**. Controlling authority is authority that **must** be followed; it *binds* lower courts and practitioners and literally *controls* the rule that determines the outcome of the issue at hand.

Persuasive authority is everything else. It does not have to be particularly persuasive to keep its name. Persuasive authority is a generic term to refer to all authority that is not controlling. A court might follow persuasive authority if the court finds it useful, but the court is not bound by it. In that persuasive authority will be followed if it is convincing and as long as it does not contradict controlling authority, attorneys must be well-versed in the merits of its use.

You may have deduced from this discussion that only primary authorities can be controlling; however, not every primary authority is even potentially so.

MAKE THE CONNECTION!

Controlling, potentially controlling, persuasive . . . these can be frustrating concepts to master at this early stage of your legal education. A lot of thought will go into determining which authorities truly speak to the issue you have been asked to address. When you find on-point cases, you should first understand their weight (and thus their value). You should prioritize for your articulation of a rule the primary sources that *must* be followed. Once identified, these will constitute your go-to sources. Everything else will be – at best – material that supports your interpretation of those sources.

A. Determining Potentially Controlling Authority

Determining what authority is controlling begins with a determination of which authorities have even the potential of being so. Below are a series of principles that should aid in that determination.

Principle 1: Know what jurisdiction's law applies. Only primary authorities from that jurisdiction have the potential to be controlling.

Every issue is governed by a certain set of laws (state, federal, perhaps international). "Issue" is not the same as "lawsuit;" thus, it may well be the case that different issues in a single suit are, in fact, governed by the laws of different jurisdictions.

Determining what law properly applies to each issue is a topic generally covered in an entire course, usually called "**conflicts of law**" or "**choice of law.**" You might study **choice of law rules** in your first year civil procedure course or in an advanced course on procedure or the dedicated courses mentioned. For present purposes, your legal writing teacher likely will tell you to assume that a certain state's law applies, and you will research and analyze the law with that assumption in mind.

Only primary authorities from the jurisdiction whose law applies to your case have the potential to be controlling. Whether they actually are controlling depends on the factors discussed below. If they are not controlling, they should be relegated to the "persuasive authority" pile. Within that stack, you will have to assess their order of "persuasiveness."

Principle 2: Constitutions, statutes, and administrative rules and regulations from the applicable jurisdiction that are on point are *always* controlling.

If a constitution, statute, or administrative rule or regulation from your jurisdiction is on point—*i.e.*, it concerns the subject matter of your issue—then it is controlling. There is no guesswork involved. In addition, because constitutions, laws, and administrative rules and regulations are created by the persons charged with law-making in our country, you also must give these sources priority in your construction and eventual presentation of the rule on the issue.

Principle 3: If a constitution, statute, or administrative rule or regulation is on point, you should begin your "Rule" section by quoting the relevant language.

If a constitution, statute, or administrative rule or regulation is on point, you should begin your "Rule" section *by actually quoting the relevant language*. You need not quote an entire provision if only a few terms are at issue. You should apply logic here to determine how much additional language it makes sense to include for context, and you should use ellipses for omitted terms.

For example, 18 U.S.C. § 924(c)(1)(A) provides:

> Except to the extent that a greater minimum sentence is otherwise provided by this subsection or by any other provision of law, any person who, during and in relation to any crime of violence or drug trafficking crime (including a crime of violence or drug trafficking crime that provides for an enhanced punishment if committed by the use of a deadly or dangerous weapon or device) for which the person may be prosecuted in a court of the United States, uses or carries a firearm, or who, in furtherance of any such crime, possesses a firearm, shall, in addition to the punishment provided for such crime of violence or drug trafficking crime--
>
> (i) be sentenced to a term of imprisonment of not less than 5 years;
>
> (ii) if the firearm is brandished, be sentenced to a term of imprisonment of not less than 7 years; and
>
> (iii) if the firearm is discharged, be sentenced to a term of imprisonment of not less than 10 years.

If you were asked to evaluate whether your client can be convicted of an enhanced drug trafficking offense under this rule, you might begin your Rule section with the following statement:

> A person will receive an enhanced sentence under 18 U.S.C. § 924(c)(1)(A) (2012) if he:
>
> "uses" a firearm "during and in relation" to a drug trafficking crime; "carries" a firearm "during and in relation" to a drug trafficking crime; or "possesses" a firearm "in furtherance" of a drug trafficking crime.
>
> Satisfaction of any one of these elements triggers the enhanced penalty provision of § 924(c). This memorandum addresses each of these statutory conditions (use, carry, and possess) with regard to both firearms found on the premises.

As you can see, enough of the statutory language is quoted to guide the reader, but the language is selected with the specific question in mind (*i.e.*, not all of the statute needs to be quoted but only those portions that the issue implicates). This is just one example of how the Rule section might begin; we can imagine a number of other ways in which the same information might be presented just as effectively.

Principle 4: If you have a statute and one or more regulations on point, present and discuss the statute first, followed thereafter by the regulations.

If you have a statute and one or more regulations on point, present and discuss the statute first, followed thereafter by the regulations. For example, if your issue involves securities law, and arises under the Securities Exchange Act of 1934 (the statute) and Rule 10b-5 (an administrative regulation), you would present the relevant terms of the statute first, followed by the relevant terms of the regulation.

Timing is an important consideration with constitutions, statutes, and regulations. You must find and use the most recent version of the provision, and the most recent amendments. After that, you can get into the cases that interpret them.

Principle 5: Cases interpret and modify constitutions, statutes, and regulations.

We switch gears a bit here and look at legislation and administrative law differently. A mature view of legislation and administrative law in a common law-influenced system such as the United States' requires attention to the effect of case law. Although constitutions, statutes, and regulations are given priority in the discussion of a rule, cases decided subsequent to enactment of the provision necessarily interpret and often change the effect of the language standing alone.

Courts cannot repeal a statute, but they can take the guts out of it by construing it in such a way that it no longer has any practical application. In addition, courts can nullify a statute on federal or state constitutional grounds. If the legislature does not like what the courts are doing when the courts interpret a statute, it can amend the statute to make it clear how it should work.

Principle 6: Cases are potentially controlling authority if they are:

- issued by a higher court

- in the direct hierarchy of judicial authority in the applicable jurisdiction

Potentially controlling cases are actually controlling if:

- the holding of the case discusses and resolves the issue at hand (in other words, the case is **"on point"**)

- the case still is good law

- the case has not been replaced or superseded by more recent controlling authority

We looked at the concept of the hierarchy of judicial authority in Chapter 3. The hierarchy of judicial authority for the jurisdiction whose law applies determines which cases are potentially controlling no matter what the actual forum of the case is. Thus, if a case is governed by a state's law, even if the case is filed in a federal court, the federal court should follow the hierarchy of judicial authority of the state whose law applies, not the federal hierarchy. It is the applicable law and not the forum that determines what cases are potentially controlling.

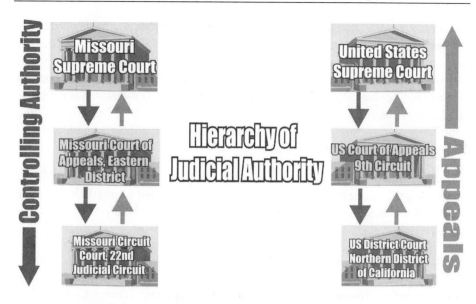

1. Federal law issues in federal court

Example: Federal issue filed in the United States District Court for the Northern District of California

Our first example of how the system of hierarchy of judicial authority and applicable law works concerns an issue governed by federal law (a "federal question") arising in a suit filed in a federal court. In the federal system in a federal question case, the U.S. Supreme Court controls all of the U.S. Courts of Appeals and U.S.

District Courts. Each circuit of the U.S. Court of Appeals controls the district courts within that circuit, but it cannot bind the other circuits, and it cannot bind district courts in other circuits. A decision from one three-judge panel of a Court of Appeals does not bind the other panels within the same circuit, but an **en banc** opinion of all the judges on the circuit court controls each subsequently assembled three-judge panel in that circuit. A U.S. District Court's opinions bind no other districts, and do not even bind the other judges within the same district, although these opinions should be regarded as highly persuasive.

Therefore, the U.S. District Court for the Northern District of California adjudicating an issue of federal (United States) law is bound by the U.S. Supreme Court and the U.S. Court of Appeals for the Ninth Circuit, but not by any other state or federal court.

2. State law issues in state court

Example: Missouri law issue filed in the Missouri Circuit Court, 22nd Judicial Circuit

Our second example is an issue governed by state law arising in a court of the state whose law applies. As to state law issues, the highest court within the state whose law is being applied is the highest authority on that state's law. The U.S. Supreme Court's opinions on that state's law (if any) are *not binding*. The opinions of any federal court or other states' courts likewise are not binding on the courts of the state whose law is being applied.

For example, the Missouri Supreme Court controls all of the courts is the highest court in the state of Missouri. The Missouri Court of Appeals, Eastern District controls all of the trial level courts within the territory of the Eastern District, including the Missouri Circuit Court, 22nd Judicial Circuit. The Missouri Circuit Courts (trial level courts) do not control any other Missouri courts, but their opinions should be regarded as highly persuasive.

3. Federal law issues in state court

Example: Federal law issue filed in the Missouri Circuit Court, 22nd Judicial Circuit

Our first mismatch issue is a situation where an issue is governed by federal law, but the issue arises in a case that is filed in a state court. On such an issue, the state court is applying the law of another jurisdiction—federal law represents a separate jurisdiction from any one state's law. A state court applying another jurisdiction's law must determine how the other jurisdiction's courts would interpret and apply that law in the situation before it.

The court will look to the legislature and the court of last resort in the applicable jurisdiction for compelling evidence of what that jurisdiction's law entails. Intermediate level appellate courts' opinions will be regarded as highly persuasive evidence of the jurisdiction's law, but not controlling authority. As always, trial level opinions will be regarded as persuasive at best.

Thus, in the case of a Missouri Circuit Court applying federal law, including the United States Code and the United States Constitution, the court must follow the U.S. Supreme Court's opinions as controlling authority. The court will not be controlled by the opinions of the U.S. Court of Appeals for the Eighth Circuit or any other circuit of the federal court of appeals. However, these opinions will not be ignored; they will be considered as highly persuasive. There is no way to predict that a Missouri state court judge will give any higher regard to the Eighth Circuit's opinions as opposed to other federal circuit courts, even if her federal colleagues down the street in the U.S. District Court for the Eastern District of Missouri would be compelled to follow them.

In the same way, state appellate court decisions on federal law (if any), whether they are from the same state or another state, are not binding on a state court applying federal law. Nor are trial court opinions from the federal or state system. These opinions will be regarded as persuasive at best, although a well-written federal trial level opinion probably will be considered more persuasive than a state court's opinion, but less persuasive than an equally well-written federal circuit court opinion on federal law.

4. State law issues in federal court

Example: Missouri state law issue filed in the U.S. District Court for the Northern District of California

Mismatch #2 is an issue governed by state law that arises in a lawsuit filed in federal court.

This scenario is common given federal court diversity jurisdiction, but sometimes in cases presenting federal questions there also arise issues governed by state law. A federal court applying state law to an issue will look to the applicable state's legislature and the state's court of last resort as controlling authority on the state's law. Thus, the United States District Court for the Northern District of California applying Missouri law to the case before it should consider itself bound by decisions of the Missouri Supreme Court. Decisions of the Missouri Court of Appeals will be regarded as highly persuasive, but not controlling. The court is not bound by decisions of the U.S. Court of Appeals for the Ninth Circuit or the U.S. Supreme Court even if they are applying Missouri law. However, as a practical matter, if there are any decisions of these courts on Missouri law, they may be considered persuasive. Trial level opinions will be considered persuasive at best.

B. Determining if "potentially controlling" authorities are actually controlling

Throughout this Chapter, we have been discussing potentially controlling authority and non-controlling authority (**persuasive authority**). The applicable law and its associated hierarchy of judicial authority determines what cases are potentially controlling, but not all of them necessarily are so. To determine if a given case is actually controlling, consider the following:

1. Facts and issues of the case: legally significant?

Legally significant facts are those facts that are integral to the holding of a case. Some facts will be provided purely for background or context. Legally significant facts, however, are those that are necessary to the particular outcome a court reaches.

The **facts** and **issues** of the case under examination will determine whether it ultimately controls your client's case. The more similar the facts, the more likely it is to control. If there are legally significant differences, however, the case may either be inapposite or will require distinction in analysis.

It does not matter if the case you are examining raises all of the same issues; in fact, some of the issues it addresses likely may be very different than those involved in your case. **The only issues that really matter are the ones governed by the applied rule that you have determined applies in your client's case.**

Be especially sensitive to claims that may *sound the same* but really raise distinct legal issues. For example, the discussion of the breach of a lease in a bankruptcy proceeding is not necessarily going to control a breach of contract case. On the other hand, be aware that certain claims and causes of action might bear different names but still refer to the same right. *E.g.*, certain jurisdictions refer to the rights regarding the unauthorized use of a person's name, image, or likeness as a "right of privacy" claim, while others use the term "right of publicity." Within the latter jurisdictions, a right of privacy claim may exist, but it will refer to the vindication of other rights, such as preventing invasions of privacy and intrusions into private affairs. In the federal system, publicity rights would be vindicated in a Lanham Act claim for false endorsement, false designation of origin, or unfair trade practices. Be sensitive to the fact that the same claims may be packaged with different labels but still be authoritative.

Also be careful to match apples to apples with the facts and issues of prior cases. For example, if a potentially controlling dog-bite case involved a dog with rabies who bit a person and gave him rabies, and your client's case has no rabid dog in it, the earlier case probably will not be controlling on every issue. There are bound to be legally significant differences between issues concerning provocation and the reasonableness of the response of a rabid dog on the one hand and provocation and response of a healthy dog on the other.

You should make sure to confirm whether the case is controlling by doing additional research to check if other courts have equated rabid dogs with regular dogs or whether courts have distinguished them. Assuming no other authority has made the connection one way or the other, you can assert that there is a legally significant difference so as to distinguish the rabid dog case (or, alternatively, posit an argument that the two instances are not distinguishable).

2. "Good" and "Bad" Cases for determining the rule

In other contexts, we describe a process of distinguishing "**bad**" cases—those that do not support your thesis—from "**good**" cases that do support it. Here, in contrast, the process is slightly different—we are talking about which cases to include in the formulation of the rule. Here, the terms mean **"Good—the authority still is good law,"** and **"Bad—the authority no longer is good law."** The cases that are on point will be used in formulating the rule whether or not the outcome of the cases goes the way of your client.

FYI

"Good" and "Bad" Authorities
When it comes to describing authorities, the terms "good" and "bad" can mean different things depending on context. Typically, these terms refer to the legal status of an authority – *i.e.*, whether it is still "good law." However, once you formulate a rule about a client's situation, these terms tend to refer to the usefulness of an authority – *i.e.*, whether it supports your answer. "Bad" authorities in this context are not necessarily ones that are no longer good law, but ones that are difficult to reconcile with your thesis.

Once you have formed a thesis, you still must account for negative, or difficult authorities. You cannot just discard them. Instead, you must distinguish them or work them into your analysis. The most effective way to do so is to find legally significant differences in either the facts or the issues or both. (The same technique should be applied for cases that appear to come out in your favor so that you know what an opponent may argue against you.)

3. What causes cases to go bad?

There are several reasons why a case may become "bad" law. Most obviously, if on appeal a decision is reversed or vacated, the opinion and holding below is no longer good law. More subtly, a later case may discuss the case you were considering and reject its reasoning or precedential value. The same thing may happen more indirectly. A later case may come out differently on the same legal issue without mentioning the earlier one on which you were hoping to rely.

It matters significantly, of course, what court is launching the attack on your authority. If the later case is from your jurisdiction, you must pay close attention to it. A more recent opinion of the same or a higher court supersedes and replaces any earlier, inconsistent opinion.

If the later case is from a different jurisdiction, the rejection will not control—though it is nevertheless important to understand why the later case rejected the earlier one.

PRACTICE POINTER

Red Flags and Yellow Flags

If you are researching on WestlawNext or Lexis Advance and you find a case marked with a yellow cautionary flag or other yellow symbol, do not assume automatically that the case is suspect for the point for which you want to use it. Indeed, any disagreement by a later court tends to be reflected with cautionary flags or remarks. The disagreement often has no effect or bearing on your issue.

If the criticism comes from outside the hierarchy, from a court in other state, then there is little need to panic. For whatever reason, WestlawNext or Lexis Advance will mark a case with a yellow flag even if an out-of-jurisdiction case determines not to follow the case. The out-of-jurisdiction opinion is merely one more piece of persuasive authority that goes the other way from the earlier case; it cannot overrule or abrogate an opinion from another jurisdiction.

Red flagged cases on WestlawNext and Lexis Advance, on the other hand, should be approached with caution: some part of the case may have been overruled or vacated, rendering it no longer controlling. But even here, it is imperative that you investigate the matter further to determine whether the whole case, or just some part of it, is "bad law." Oftentimes, even red flagged cases can be cited, but you need to know exactly what you are up against.

4. Has the case been superseded by more recent, equally authoritative cases, statutes, or rules?

Even later cases from the same hierarchy of judicial authority do not overrule or severely criticize an earlier opinion, it may be simply that the earlier case is out of date, and there are newer, fresher cases on the same point of law that should be used in formulating the rule.

Later cases can replace the authority you are looking at by restating the same rule or advancing it further through modification and adaptation, not necessarily by stating a new rule on the same legal issue. In those circumstances, the more recent cases are better authority, and you should use them to formulate the rule in your jurisdiction.

> Q: What happens if an *intermediate* level appellate court that is controlling to a lower court changes the law stated in the last opinion of the court of last resort?

> A: The newer, controlling authority controls. It is subject to correction by the court of last resort but, until that happens, the intermediate decision controls.

A similar result occurs when a statute or regulation supersedes an existing line of cases and establishes a new rule of law. In these circumstances, the statute or regulation replaces the cases. If one or more parts of the rule is untouched by the statute or regulation, then that part may survive. This process—the effect of a later enacted statute on an earlier line of cases—is often the subject of commentary in secondary authorities. As always, keep an eye out for such clues in the course of your research.

Once a statute is passed or a regulation is promulgated, case law steps in to assist in interpretation. Thus, while the legislature can "overrule" a line of cases by passing a new statute on the same topic, the courts have the last word in interpreting statutory meaning. Especially for a complicated statute of national importance, it may take many years for the dust to settle.

C. Determining the relative weight of controlling authorities

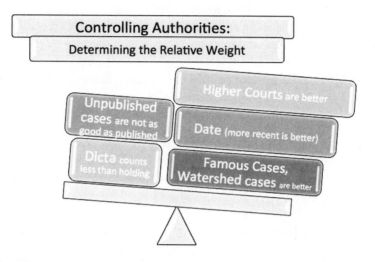

Once you have performed the analytical steps discussed above, you will know which of your authorities, if any, are actually controlling for your legal issue. But you still need to evaluate the relative *weight* of each controlling authority: all controlling authorities are not created equal.

Ordered by weight:

1. Level of Court: Higher authorities are better

Of course, **higher controlling authorities** count more than lower ones when you are looking at them in their relationship to their own jurisdiction and **hierarchy of authority**. Statutes are weightier and have priority over administrative law, which has priority over cases. As to cases, a controlling case of the court of last resort on the law of that jurisdiction has priority over a controlling case of the intermediate level appellate court, which in turn is weightier than any trial-level court opinion.

2. Date: Recent authorities are better

Recent controlling authorities are better than older ones. At least in theory, the more recent authorities have had the chance to survey the older ones and comment on, change, and add to them. Simply stated, you should look for the most recent and complete statements of the law on the topic. That said, there is nothing inherently wrong with an old case, as long as there are no newer cases on the same issue of law from the same or a higher court.

An earlier case actually may be on all fours with (or more analogous to) the facts of your case, more so than a recent opinion. The factual similarity may make the older case more valuable to you for explanation of the rule—and, as well, for use in application—than the more recent opinion. Still, the most recent opinions are likely to appear in the Rule section.

3. Fame: Watershed cases, famous cases, famous judges are better

There is an exception to the general rule of newer is better: certain cases are more valuable because of their fame. You may decide to invoke an older case written by a famous judge or justice over more recent ones written by lesser luminaries. Similarly, an earlier case may be a **"watershed case"** that is constantly recited and followed by later opinions, giving it a special status in the formulation of the rule on the issue.

4. Dicta from controlling cases

In some respects, this category should come under the "persuasive authority" heading. We are including it here, however, because the *best* persuasive authority is dicta from a controlling authority. As previously explained, only the **holding** of a case is actually binding, but trial courts are loathe to pretend that a court higher up in the chain has not gone on record by saying that the law should be a certain way or that the outcome of a case would be different if different facts were present. Today's dicta is tomorrow's binding law, and courts are alerted to that by carefully considering the dicta written by their superiors. If the courts are paying attention, you should, too.

5. Unpublished opinions

Unpublished opinions can present a special headache. First, "unpublished" is a misnomer; it means simply that the case was not published in an official reporter. Unpublished cases are widely available through computer assisted legal research and from most court websites directly.

Courts have various reasons for not publishing an opinion in an official reporter. Especially for lower-level courts, the decision to publish often turns on whether the case has precedential value. Sometimes a decision is "unpublished" because it is redundant of other established cases and adds nothing to the jurisprudence of the jurisdiction on the issue of law. On other occasions, you might find an unpublished opinion that is the *only* opinion available on a given issue.

TAKE NOTE!

Important Note about Unpublished Opinions

In 2006, the U.S. Supreme Court issued a new rule about unpublished opinions, stating that federal courts can no longer prohibit lawyers from citing to them. However, circuits are still permitted to give varying precedential weight to unpublished opinions. The local rules of the courts where you are practicing must be consulted. They will indicate the extent to which the court will rely on unpublished decisions (sometimes, they will look more favorably on unpublished decisions of the same court). Unless the local rules specifically state that unpublished opinions will be accorded the same weight as published opinions, unpublished opinions should fall to the bottom of your controlling authority pile. Their facts may raise them back up a notch, but the specter of "unpublished" still remains hard to exorcize. *See* discussion at http://www.nytimes.com/2015/02/03/us/justice-clarence-thomas-court-decisions-that-set-no-precedent.html?_r=1.

The five factors identified above are themselves ordered by weight: level of court is more important than date, date is more important than fame, and so on.

D. Determining primary persuasive authority

You now have ranked your controlling authorities and, in many instances, have enough to formulate your rule. Assuming that there are at least some gaps in your coverage of the law based on the issue you are analyzing, however, it is appropriate to consider using some persuasive authorities in your Rule section to flesh it out.

Do not lose sight of the importance of controlling authority. No matter how wonderfully written and close to your client's facts a persuasive authority may be, it cannot replace or supersede even the least weighty of your controlling authorities. Persuasive authority fills in the gaps when controlling authority is absent, or it can be used effectively to help explain how the controlling authority should be interpreted and applied. Persuasive authority thus can play a critical role in your legal analysis of the issue, but it is always secondary to controlling authority.

First, let's consider cases as persuasive authorities. Even though statutes and rules are very important in your own jurisdiction, the same authorities from other jurisdictions have more limited application.

Just to remind you: if a statute, rule, or administrative regulation is on point and from the applicable jurisdiction, it is always controlling. Here, we are talking about statutes or regulations from other jurisdictions.

As with controlling authorities, some persuasive authority is better than others.

1. Relative weight of primary persuasive authorities

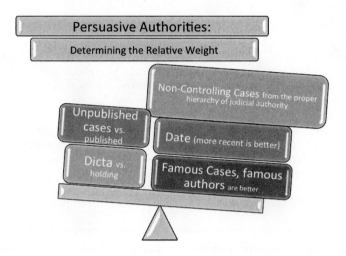

Persuasive Authorities:

Determining the Relative Weight

Non-Controlling Cases from the proper hierarchy of judicial authority

Unpublished cases vs. published

Date (more recent is better)

Dicta vs. holding

Famous Cases, famous authors are better

a. Non-controlling cases from the jurisdiction whose law applies

The best kind of persuasive authority is a non-controlling case from the jurisdiction whose law applies. For example, if your client's case would be filed in the United States District Court for the District of Massachusetts, then only U.S. Supreme Court and First Circuit cases actually control the outcome. However, cases from other U.S. Courts of Appeal are highly persuasive on issues of federal law. Other U.S. District Court cases are less so, but still worth considering—especially if factually similar.

In many jurisdictions in the state system, the intermediate level appellate court is divided into districts or circuits, only one of which will hear appeals from a particular lower court. Thus, in most state systems, only one district or circuit—the district or circuit that would actually hear the appeal—can issue controlling authority for your client's case. However, cases from the other districts or circuits of the same intermediate level appellate court also are valuable, because these courts have day-to-day experience applying the law of the applicable jurisdiction.

For example, if your case is controlled by the Florida First District Court of Appeal, you should consider the opinions of the Second, Third, Fourth, and Fifth Districts of the Court of Appeal to be highly persuasive. Decisions from the trial level courts in Florida are less persuasive but still important to consider.

One practical tip is that, regardless of whether a case is actually controlling, a trial court is very interested in following the opinions and recommendations of courts in the same court system. Therefore, the opinions of these courts should be given great persuasive weight—more weight than any of the categories of cases described below.

b. Date: More recent is better

Next in importance is date. More recent persuasive authority is better than older persuasive authority.

c. Fame: Famous cases and famous authors are better

From time to time, a non-controlling authority of another jurisdiction gains a great deal of notoriety, so much so that it might rise to a level of prominence in your rule section.

For example, for many years, the establishment of personal jurisdiction based on contacts occurring over the Internet was governed by a trial court case in the federal system: *Zippo Manufacturing Co. v. Zippo Dot Com, Inc.*, 952 F. Supp. 1119 (W.D. Pa. 1997). Though not controlling in any subsequent analysis, the case and its "sliding scale" test became so popular and widely used, than any case involving the Internet and personal jurisdiction tended to include *Zippo* in its briefs. Similarly, courts of all levels frequently referred to it in their opinions. Eventually, higher authorities adopted the "*Zippo* sliding scale" test and made it part of the law of their hierarchy, so the test subsequently became properly attributed to controlling authorities and not just the *Zippo* case itself.

Similarly, judges sometimes achieve a level of notoriety that exceeds the level of court from which they write. District court judges such as Learned Hand of the U.S. District Court for the Southern District of New York (later, of the Second Circuit), and Jack Weinstein of the U.S. District Court for the Eastern District of New York, achieved prominence because the quality of their judicial opinions and extra-judicial writings. Some local heroes of one jurisdiction become national heroes—especially on certain issues (*e.g.*, Justice Roger J. Traynor of the California Supreme Court in products liability cases), making their out-of-jurisdiction cases more weighty and valuable as persuasive authority.

d. Holdings of persuasive and out-of-jurisdiction cases v. dicta

Once you have exhausted cases from your jurisdiction and its hierarchy of judicial authority and cases from the same jurisdiction but a parallel hierarchy, you can look to other jurisdictions to see what their courts have said about the law in the area you are examining.

Cases from these sources are far less persuasive than those discussed above, either because the law is not the same or, if it is, the court does not have expertise applying it. Even if the law is manifestly similar—e.g., two different state courts applying the same provision from the Restatement of Torts—your court will be free to disregard the out-of-jurisdiction authority.

Try to rely only on the actual *holdings* of persuasive and out-of-jurisdiction cases. Dicta from an out-of-jurisdiction case is weaker than dicta from a controlling case. At this point, we are already far down the ladder of persuasiveness; thus, it is probably not relevant to use at all in formulating your rule unless there is nothing else out there.

If you pursue its use, the most advantageous way to do so is to *buttress* an argument that you have already supported with weightier authorities. Here, we are talking about *explaining* the legal rule, not justifying its existence. For example, you might argue: "Not only does New York, employ this rule, but Vermont and Connecticut and Rhode Island do, too [citing cases]." If nothing else, these cases can be a good reality check.

A second viable use for out-of-state authority involves a situation where the facts are closer to your client's than the facts of any case from the applicable jurisdiction. In that situation, you can demonstrate that your formulation of the rule is correct and that the outcome you advocate (presumably favorable to your client) is supported.

Use of cases to buttress or support an argument or outcome almost always will come in the explanation section of your work. Only if there is little or no controlling authority on point should such cases be used to formulate the rule.

e. Geographic Proximity?

The opinions of neighboring States (in a state court case) and sister districts in the same Circuit (in a federal case) are no more persuasive as a result of proximity. This is a popular myth, but there is no legal foundation to support it. You should look to other criteria, such as the facts of the case, the quality of the research and analysis evidenced in the opinion, and the similarity of the law of the jurisdiction to the applicable jurisdiction's law.

PRACTICE POINTER

Will a New York judge ever listen to a California judge? Or vice versa? Will a federal judge in Minnesota ever be persuaded by the opinions of the Ninth Circuit or the Second Circuit thousands of miles away? Do southern judges only listen to other southern judges? Questions like these may be fun for cocktail parties, but persuasive value is much more related to other criteria—the factors we have been discussing.

f. Out-of-jurisdiction statutes and regulations

At the rule formulation stage, out-of-jurisdiction statutes and regulations may be useful as a check; other than that, they do not carry much value. You may attempt to show that the statutory law of another jurisdiction is virtually the same as yours (perhaps a "uniform law" has been adopted by both), thus arguably enhancing the persuasive value of the other jurisdiction's case law. For example, the version of the Uniform Commercial Code (UCC) enacted many jurisdictions is identical. Cases from jurisdictions where the law is phrased exactly the same are of greater value than those from jurisdictions where the law differs. Still, we are far down the ladder of overall persuasiveness.

g. Boosts to and detractions from persuasive authority

On some occasions, a persuasive authority stays in your research pile because there truly was nothing else out there on the issue you are analyzing. This might be the case with an extremely new, cutting edge legal topic, or an area of law so undeveloped that there is a dearth of authority of any kind on point in the United States. Here are some tips to keep in mind:

Facts are *always* important: strongly analogous cases are of far better use than tangentially analogous ones.

Some courts are known to have special expertise in certain subject matter areas. An opinion from a New York court or Second Circuit panel on securities law is most likely stronger than a Montana securities law case. It's not that the judges in Montana cannot understand securities law, but this may be the first securities law opinion they have rendered in several years, whereas the New York and Second Circuit courts handle dozens of such cases every year. The United States District Court for the Southern District of New York and the United States Court of Appeals for the Second Circuit used to be famous for their opinions on copyright law because the major music, theater, art, and publishing industries of the United States were located in that district and circuit and the vast majority of copyright cases were resolved there. Today, these industries are more decentralized, but this reputation for excellence lives on in some litigants' and judges' minds. Similarly, the D.C. Court of Appeals is highly regarded on administrative law issues (even if the specific law in question is governed by a different circuit).

The contents of the opinion itself should *never* be neglected. If you compare what the court says and what it actually does and find a mismatch, that is a bad situation for the case. Well-reasoned, thorough opinions are better than poorly reasoned and cursory ones.

For appellate cases, the number of judges who joined the opinion may affect its value to some degree. *En banc* opinions without dissenters are the best; a full panel opinion is better than a split panel. A clear majority opinion (5-4) is much better than a plurality opinion where there is no numeric majority and different reasons for agreeing on the holding.

Concurring opinions should be cited with explanation and, even so, should come from a justice on the highest court in the jurisdiction. Concurring opinions at the intermediate level appellate court level do not carry much weight. Dissenting opinions have little to no value, unless they have been taken up by other authorities in some respect. (Or, if you are advocating for a change in the law.)

Finally: certain trends in the law can affect the weight of opinions. An example from two decades or so ago was the shift from the concepts of contributory negligence and assumption of risk in negligence law to comparative negligence and comparative fault. Cases that picked up on the comparative fault trend began to gain more and more credibility as the trend spread and the jurisdictions adopting the trend grew in number. On the other hand, if a case is catching a wave that is brand new, it is best to avoid until the trend turns to a "widespread development."

II.   SECONDARY AUTHORITY

What about all the law review articles, ALRs, and encyclopedia entries that you found in your research?

Remember that this Chapter has been focusing on forming the rules in the **Rule section** of your writing. Secondary authority should *rarely* be used in the actual formulation of the rule on an issue. If there absolutely is **no** controlling authority, and the persuasive authority from the applicable jurisdiction is sparse or weak, only then you might turn to secondary authorities for rule formulation.

That said, secondary authorities are great sources of legal principles and instructions for how to interpret legal rules. Save them for the development of the **Explanation section**.

Occasionally, a court **adopts** a secondary authority as the applicable rule for the jurisdiction. If a primary controlling authority adopts a secondary authority, then secondary authority is bootstrapped into prominence. The secondary authority may be elevated to become the centerpiece of your discussion, but only because a primary controlling authority did the elevating. For example, if in the *Smithy* case, a controlling authority adopted section 43 of the Restatement (Second) of Contracts, you would present the rule as coming from *Smithy*, and then explain that *Smithy* got it from the Restatement.

When evaluating the weight of secondary authorities, the name of the game is prestige—the prestige of the author(s) or the prestige of the work (the treatise, the hornbook, the law review article, the Restatement). Certain works are as good as gold, and courts find these sources to be extremely persuasive. Wright and Miller's Federal Practice and Procedure and Moore's Federal Practice are this kind of source, as are the Restatement of Contracts and the Restatement of Torts. In addition, Devitt and Blackmar's Federal Jury Practice and Instructions is regarded as the bible on jury instructions in federal court.

TAKE NOTE!

Keeping Restatements and Model Codes in Their Place
Some students come away from their first-year classes with the impression that the Restatement of Contracts, the Restatement of Torts, the Uniform Commercial Code (U.C.C.), and the Model Penal Code are the best authorities on the law of their respective areas. Not so in practice. Secondary authorities control no court's decision; their power is only the power of persuasion. As a general rule, do not discuss secondary authority before primary authority, certainly not if the primary authority is controlling. Secondary authority may be discussed before primary persuasive authorities from other jurisdictions—but only if the secondary authority is strong enough. Secondary authority can add a great deal of credence to your rule formulation and rule explanation if an important treatise or other weighty authority comes to the same conclusions that you reach. But there is no substitute for primary controlling authority.

Pay attention to the author of the secondary source. Certain authors are legendary in their field, and will command a great deal of respect; thus, they are more persuasive. Examples include: Prosser on Torts, Weinstein on Evidence, Nimmer on Copyright, Newberg on Class Actions, Farnsworth, Williston, and Corbin on Contracts (individually, not as a team), Miller and Wright on Federal Practice and Procedure, and McCormick on Evidence and Federal Procedure. This list is far from exhaustive, but we will leave it to your own law school professors to tell you who their dream dates are.

Similarly, certain authors are local heroes, and will be highly persuasive in the jurisdiction where they are famous. For example, Judge Weinstein and Professors Korn and Smit are local experts on the New York Civil Practice Laws and Regulations, and Judge Traynor's writings and opinions on California law are given special weight. Some judges reach the status of national heroes: Holmes, Cardozo, John Marshall, Brandeis, and Learned Hand certainly qualify in this category.

Up-to-date, timely secondary sources are better than old ones, all else being the same. If you are working with a crusty old treatise or a law review article that is decades old on a topic of the law that sees frequent development (securities law, intellectual property law, and employment law as compared to the more static topics of contracts or torts), then try to find more recent secondary authorities. If the area of law you are researching has undergone a major revolution through the passage of groundbreaking legislation, any article or treatise chapter written on that topic prior to the revolution is useless. For example, any article or treatise written on employee benefits and retirement plans prior to the passage of ERISA will be highly suspect.

The next section discusses the actual writing of the Rule section. Before we turn to that topic, we present a summary of the lessons learned in sorting your authorities.

Summary: Sorting Your Authorities
Controlling vs. Persuasive vs. No Authority

Sorting Step	Reason	Controlling Pile	Persuasive Pile	"No Authority" Pile
Applicable Law	Determines the applicable hierarchy of judicial authority	Only authorities from the applicable hierarchy can be controlling	Authorities outside the hierarchy are persuasive	
Primary vs. Secondary Authority	Only primary authorities can be controlling	**Primary authorities are ranked: Const. 1st, Statutes 2nd, Regs 3rd; Cases 4th**	All secondary authorities are persuasive	
Good Law vs. Bad Law	Check to see if the authorities are good law	**Statutes** that have not been amended, struck down, or superseded; **cases** that have not been reversed, overruled, abrogated, or criticized by the same or a higher court *on the issue you are researching*		If an authority is not good law it is NO authority at all

Sorting Step	Reason	Controlling Pile	Persuasive Pile	"No Authority" Pile
Court where case is filed (or will be filed), and does it match the applicable law	**Matches:** If state law applies and case is filed in a state court of the hierarchy; or fed. law applies and case is filed in fed. court:	Court of last resort <u>and</u> intermediate app. court cases of the applicable hierarchy control	Trial level cases of the hierarchy are persuasive	
	Mismatches: If state law applies but case is filed in fed. court; or if fed. law applies and case is filed in state court:	Only court of last resort cases of the applicable hierarchy control	Trial level and intermed. app. court opinions of the hierarchy are persuasive	
Level of Court	Courts of last resort are better	Among controlling cases, sort last resort from intermed. app. court cases	Among persuasive cases, sort last resort from intermed. app. and trial court cases	
Date	All else being equal, more recent authority is better	Sort controlling cases by date	Sort persuasive authorities by date	Don't leave out old cases!
"Watershed" and other famous cases	Look for famous cases constantly cited in the jurisdiction	Watershed cases should be given priority in drafting the rule section	Some out of jurisdiction cases may have achieved fame in your jurisdiction	

Sorting Step	Reason	Controlling Pile	Persuasive Pile	"No Authority" Pile
Holding vs. Dicta	All else being equal, it is better to rely on holding	Only the holding of a case can bind other courts	You have to relegate a controlling authority to this pile if it states dicta	
Famous authors and legal superstars	Look for judges and commentators who are highly regarded	Opinions written by a star of the hierarchy's courts are noteworthy	With out of jurisdiction cases and secondary authorities, reputation of the author can make a huge difference in weighing the authority	
Facts	All else being equal, facts that are closer to your client's situation are better	You may have to distinguish cases based on facts	Out of jurisdiction cases that are closer to the client's facts are much better	Once in a while, a non-controlling case will be so off the facts that you will drop it
Published vs. unpublished	If local rules allow you to cite unpublished cases, rank them lower than published		If local rules forbid citation to unpublished cases, they are non-authority	

III. RULE SYNTHESIS: DRAFTING THE RULE IN A RULE SECTION BY RECONCILING, SYNTHESIZING, AND HARMONIZING THE VARIOUS AUTHORITIES

Finally, we have come to the *writing* stage. So far, this Chapter has focused on research and analysis—how to sort and order the authorities that you have uncovered.

Once you have compiled your authorities, you must analyze them together to determine the applicable rule in your jurisdiction. The next task is to capture them in writing in a manner acceptable to the legal writing discourse community. The process of combining, reconciling, and harmonizing the various authorities is called

Rule Synthesis. This process has several steps depicted in the following chart, each of which will be explained more completely below:

Rule Synthesis (Formulate the rule and draft the Rule section)	
1. Start with the highest and most recent controlling authority	◆ If you have a statute (or regulation), start with the statute. ◆ If you have a watershed case that is controlling, start with that. ◆ If your best authority is from the court of last resort, take the most recent opinion from that court, and start with that. ◆ If these first three criteria do not apply, start with the most recent actual controlling authority that is on point. ◆ Only if none of the above applies would you consider turning to non-controlling authority—primary or secondary. ◆ Don't expect to use all of your authorities.
2. Reconcile differing statements or phrasings of the rule from controlling authorities, and attempt to synthesize the rule into one coherent statement of the legal principles that govern the issue	◆ DON'T change the wording of or paraphrase rules from statutes, administrative rules and regs, and watershed cases. ◆ Unless a processed applied rule can be written smoothly and effectively in one sentence or phrase, write the rule first with modifications second.
3. Write the rule first, interpretative rules second, and exceptions to the rule third	◆ Write interpretive sub-rules on elements of the rule in the section or sub-TREAT discussion that discusses that element of the rule. Write exceptions to the sub-rules after you lay out the sub-rules themselves.
4. Do not write a rule with inherent contradictions	◆ Check for ambiguity in the terms you have used to formulate the rule (even if some of these terms came from the authorities).
5. Do accept the remote possibility that two competing rules on the same issue might exist in the same jurisdiction	◆ When this happens, you may have to analyze the facts under both competing sets of rules.

How to interpret what this chart tells you about drafting the Rule section:

1. Start with constitutions, statutes, or regulations.

With constitutions, statutes, or regulations (from a controlling jurisdiction), start with the relevant terms and finish with subsequent authorities that add to, delete from, modify, or clarify the rule (or its parts) through discussion and interpretation.

2. Otherwise, start with a watershed opinion.

If there are no constitutional, statutory, or regulatory provisions on point, start with a much-cited opinion that is used by virtually every authority you have read on the topic. We refer to these as watershed cases. Subsequent authorities will modify the rule, and you will have to decide how to present the watershed case's rule and the key (three or four) subsequent authorities that have changed the rule in some way. Refer back to Examples 1-3 from Chapter 4.

3. Do not change the contents or order of elements of an established rule.

A well-established rule (frequently borrowed or from a watershed case) almost always will be presented the same way in the authorities you find on the topic. Do not change the order or wording of the elements **when you first present it as the rule in your writing**. Do not cause the reader to wonder: did this person miss something, or did she copy this down wrong?

That said, you may *discuss the elements* in a different order if there is a reason to do so (*e.g.*, if one element is the central one in contention). If you do discusses elements in a way that makes better sense, announce to your reader that you are going out of order (perhaps in a roadmap).

In your presentation of the rule, you may add an element to the three or four traditional elements of the rule, giving proper recognition to the traditional sources of the rule and the authority that has added the element (see Example 3 from Chapter 4). In most circumstances, however, it is best to present the rule in the traditional manner first. Then write additional sentences showing any changes given the authorities on which you are relying. (*See* the discussion of Rule Synthesis below.)

4. Reconcile your authorities; do not formulate a rule with inherent contradictions.

Courts are not always tidy about the rules they apply to resolve the cases before them. You should strive to be neater. If a controlling case sticks out—*e.g.*, it bucks the trend—consider addressing it in the Explanation section (to follow). If this cannot be done, try to reconcile the opinion with the rest of your authorities. Is the holding really contradictory? Can you present the rule in a different way that takes into account all of the controlling cases? If you are having a hard time harmonizing the case, you might simply have to present two rules—the rule from the other authorities and the rule from the individual case.

5. List interpretive rules and exceptions after the main rule.

A handful of your cases may borrow the traditional rule, but they might go on to state interpretive rules or exceptions. In these circumstances, you should present the traditional rule first, and then list the interpretive rules and exceptions afterwards.

An **interpretive rule** provides criteria to aid in the interpretation and application of the rule itself. For example:

> **[Rule:]** Fraud requires proof of (1) a representation; (2) its falsity; (3) its materiality; (4) the speaker's knowledge of the falsity or his ignorance of the truth; (5) the hearer's reliance on the representation; (6) the hearer's ignorance of the falsity; (7) the hearer's right to rely; (8) the reasonableness of the hearer's reliance; and (9) proximately caused damages from the reliance. *Coyote v. Road Runner*, 345 W.2d 258, 259 (Apex 1978). **[Interpretive Rules:]** Fraud is a disfavored cause of action. *Id.* Fraud will never be presumed. *Rocky v. Walter*, 788 W.2d 890, 894 (Apex Ct. App. 1st Dist. 1990). Plaintiff must prove each element with clear and convincing evidence. *Id.*

These interpretive rules modify the way lawyers should look at the rule in its entirety. Fraud is not the average cause of action; it is harder to prove than most claims. Refer to the following example, based on Example 1 from Chapter 4:

> **[Rule:]** To prevail on a claim for injuries caused by a dog, a plaintiff must plead and prove: (1) ownership of the dog by the defendant; (2) causation of the injury by the dog; and (3) lack of provocation of the dog. *Billy v. Tilly*, 887 W.2d 234, 236 (Apex 1996); *Lori v. Benji*, 667 W.2d 234, 236 (Apex 1993). **[Interpretive Rule:]** Dog bite liability is rooted in the area of negligence, and, as such, a comparative negligence analysis applies in calculating the responsibility for a dog's attack. *Id.* at 569.

This interpretive rule tells us that dog bite liability is not based on strict liability or other theories of tort liability. It is a negligence-type claim, which informs lawyers that they can prove it and defend against it with the common tools used in negligence actions. Interpretive rules reflect that the cases discussing the overall rule have thrown in extra rules that modify how we all should interpret and apply the borrowed rule.

An **exception** to the rule is just that; the opinion carves out a set of facts or circumstances and states that rule will not cover them or will work a different way when they are present. For example:

> **[Rule:]** To prevail on a claim for injuries caused by a dog, a plaintiff must plead and prove: (1) ownership of the dog by the defendant; (2) causation

of the injury by the dog; and (3) lack of provocation of the dog. *Billy v. Tilly*, 887 W.2d 234, 236 (Apex 1996); *Lori v. Benji*, 667 W.2d 234, 236 (Apex 1993).[**Exception:**] The rule does not apply to police dogs when these dogs are acting in their ordinary law enforcement capacity. *City of Dogpatch v. Mauledguy*, 786 W.2d 345, 348 (Apex Ct. App. 1st Dist. 1996).

6. List sub-rules on elements of the rule in the "TREATment" of the individual element

Interpretive rules are distinguishable from "sub-rules" that provide criteria for the interpretation and application of one element. For example, we learn the following from Example 1 from Chapter 4:

> [**Rule:**] To prevail on a claim for injuries caused by a dog, a plaintiff must plead and prove: (1) ownership of the dog by the defendant; (2) causation of the injury by the dog; and (3) lack of provocation of the dog. *Billy v. Tilly*, 887 W.2d 234, 236 (Apex 1996); *Lori v. Benji*, 667 W.2d 234, 236 (Apex 1993).
>
> . . .
>
> [**Sub-rule on Ownership Element, from a later section of the document:**] "The concept of 'ownership' of the dog is not limited to a person having actual possession of title to the animal, but includes a person who harbors or has control over a dog." *Billy*, 887 W.2d at 236.
>
> . . .
>
> [**Sub-rule on Provocation Element, from an even later section of the document:**] "Provocation requires an actual physical attack on the dog; verbal attacks do not count." *Billy*, 887 W.2d at 236. [**Interpretive Rule of Sub-rule:**] The burden of proof on plaintiff to show lack of provocation is a high one, and substantial evidence must be brought forth in order to bear the burden. *Lefty v. Smartz*, 553 W.2d 567, 568 (Apex 1987).

If the authority states a sub-rule on a single element, and that element presents an issue that is sufficiently detailed so as to require a separate TREATment, then save the sub-rule for the rule section on that element. Do not include it in the rule section on the major (overarching) issue.

In the first example above, if you were going to do a separate TREAT on the ownership element, you would state the sub-rule on ownership from *Billy* ("The concept of 'ownership' of the dog is not limited to a person having actual possession of title to the animal, but includes a person who harbors or has control over a dog.") in the rule section of your analysis of the ownership element (not in the rule section of the overall issue).

A partial outline here may be useful (NOTE: this structure is discussed further in Chapter 6):

T: Thesis on overall ("big") Issue: Dog Bite Liability

R: Rule on Dog Bite Liability = (1) Ownership; (2) Causation; (3) Lack of Provocation.

> t(1) thesis on ownership
> r(1) sub-rule on ownership: from *Billy*
> e(1) explanation of ownership sub-rule from case law
> a(1) application to facts of case at hand
> t(1) conclusion on sub-rule of ownership

Whether the other elements of the "big" Rule (dog bite liability) require similarly separate sub-TREATs depends on what the authorities tell you. If so, you would follow the "mini"-treat identified above with similar mini (sub) TREATs on each element.

> t(2) thesis on causation
> r(2) sub-rule on causation
> e(2) explanation of causation sub-rule from case law
> a(2) application to facts of case at hand
> t(2) conclusion on sub-rule of causation

If not, you might incorporate what you have to say about those elements into the Rule and Explanation of the overall, "big" Rule.

7. Accept the possibility that competing rules might exist.

On occasion, two rules coexist and compete at the same time in the same jurisdiction. This situation is unusual enough that you should reexamine your authorities to be sure.

> a. If the rules appear to be inconsistent, reexamine the facts of each case in the competing lines of authority. Can you reconcile the competing lines as being a single rule with an exception to the rule for a particular fact pattern?
>
> b. Consider whether there are different public policies at work in the competing lines of authority. If so, then you might have to refine your understanding of the issue. If a particular set of facts drives the application of one set of policies and a different set of facts drives the application of the other, you should be able to determine the correct policies and rule to apply to your client's situation.

If neither situation applies, then you have found the rare situation of two competing rules defined and applied in controlling authority of the same jurisdiction.

When this happens, you must do your best to present both rules, and to analyze the law and apply both rules to your client's facts to predict the most likely outcome under each competing version.

IV. ILLUSTRATION OF A PROPERLY SYNTHESIZED RULE SECTION

Before you read further, please understand three things.

First: Rule synthesis is one of the most important skills you can acquire and is the centerpiece of the TREAT paradigm.

Second: We will address Rule Synthesis within the context of the TREAT paradigm in Chapter 6 and in the examples in Chapter 7.

Third: Whether a Rule section should be highly synthesized is a matter of preference for law-trained readers. It is not a requirement. As with Explanation sections (see Chapters 6 and 7), some supervisors and employers may prefer a less synthesized approach. We offer our suggestions below, but pay attention to the local rules and preferences where you work.

The information below constitutes an initial effort at illustrating the culmination of the process we have been describing in this Chapter. The goal is to illustrate the benefits of rule synthesis.

The examples discussed thus far in this Chapter establish the basic criteria for rule formulation.

If you have a statute or regulation that provides the exact wording of the rule on your issue, you should present that wording first in your rule section. This articulation should be followed by any further statements (from other authorities) that explain, modify, or supplement the elements of the rule. The same principle applies when there is standard rule wording—the version established by a watershed case and used consistently by the authorities in your jurisdiction. Present the traditional wording of the rule first, followed by any further explanation and modification of the rule found in later authorities.

When you have multiple controlling authorities that *do not agree* on the precise wording of the applicable rule, you should try to synthesize the precedents into a coherent statement of the rule and its elements. Supporting discussion and commentary about the rule can be presented separately, but the actual statement of the required elements of the rule should be presented as cohesively as possible. An unsynthesized presentation of the rule can be confusing.

Assume for example that you have three authorities on money had and received in Apex, which state the following in relevant part:

> "The core of the claim of money had and received is a transfer of funds to the defendant, caused by the mistake of the plaintiff, and the defendant's retention of the funds is unjust. The historical origins of this claim were an action at law for assumpsit. In essence, it is a claim of restitution for unjust enrichment in the particular context of money transfers." *First Federal Bank and Trust Co. v. Stevens*, 678 W.2d 234, 237 (Apex 1988).

> "Apex law of money had and received requires a transfer to the defendant and an unjust retention of the funds. It is permitted for the transferor to have made a mistake of fact, but not a mistake of law, in sending the funds to the defendant. If the defendant caused or contributed to the transferor's mistake of fact, this will mitigate in favor of a finding that the defendant's retention of the funds is unjust." *Green Cross and Red Shield of Apex v. Carson*, 688 W.2d 564, 566 (Apex Ct. App. 1st Dist. 1991).

> "Historically, money had and received was a legal, not an equitable action, but the modern claim borrows the elements of unjust enrichment—an enrichment by transfer of funds, and that the enrichment is unjust. If the defendant is lawfully entitled to the amount of the transfer by virtue of a prior debt or account from the transferor, the retention of the funds is not unjust. It does not matter if the transferor did not plan to pay the debt or account until a later date, so long as the debt was due and owing." *ATI Transnational Credit Corp. v. Adam's Asphalt Co.*, 778 W.2d 42, 44-45 (Apex Ct. App. 1st Dist. 1994).

An unsynthesized presentation of the rule based on these three authorities might look something like this:

UNSYNTHESIZED RULE SECTION

Money had and received is a transfer of funds to the defendant, caused by the mistake of the plaintiff, and the defendant's retention of the funds is unjust. *First Federal Bank and Trust Co. v. Stevens*, 678 W.2d 234, 237 (Apex 1988). It is permitted for the transferor to have made a mistake of fact, but not a mistake of law, in sending the funds to the defendant. *Green Cross and Red Shield of Apex v. Carson*, 688 W.2d 564, 566 (Apex Ct. App. 1st Dist. 1991). If the defendant caused or contributed to the transferor's mistake of fact, this will mitigate in favor of a finding that the defendant's retention of the funds is unjust. *Id.*

If the defendant is lawfully entitled to the amount of the transfer by virtue of a prior debt or account from the transferor, the retention of the funds is not unjust. *ATI Transnational Credit Corp. v. Adam's Asphalt Co.*, 778 W.2d 42, 44-45 (Apex Ct. App. 1st Dist. 1994). It does not matter if the transferor did not plan to pay the debt or account until a later date, so long as the debt was due at the time of the transfer. *Id.*

Historically, money had and received was a legal, not an equitable action. *Id.* The origins of this claim were an action at law for assumpsit. *First Federal Bank*, 678 W.2d at 237. In essence, it is a claim of restitution for unjust enrichment in the particular context of money transfers—namely, an enrichment by transfer of funds, and that the enrichment is unjust. *Id.; ATI*, 778 W.2d at 45.

Without question, this example accurately reports the law, but it is presented in undigested form. It may be the *safest* way to state the rule—certainly, no one can accuse you of misstating the law. And, some readers might think it is the most *accurate* way to present it, because you did not change anything from what the authorities said. But "safest" and "closest to the wording of the sources" is not always the best policy in rule formulation.

Instead, think about the potential contribution of *your analysis*—the "value added" that comes from your considerable research and diligent sorting of various authorities in the process.

Your task is not only to reiterate the law, but *to explain it* – to present it to the reader in the most concise and understandable way. You do not want your reader to have to do the work of rule synthesis; rather, you were tasked with doing it when you were assigned the case or issue. In addition, you need the reader to understand the rule that you are applying when you get to the facts.

The above unsynthesized example commits several errors. First, it is too wordy. Second, it does not help the reader understand the law any better than if you simply handed her photocopies of the three cases. Even if the photocopies are highlighted. **This is critical!** You should always ask yourself whether you are synthesizing the authorities or just listing them—and thereby telling your reader to synthesize them for you.

A more helpful "rule synthesis" will take the rather rambling statements of the law listed above and present a cohesive whole, making the necessary connections and combinations of required elements so that the reader gains a broader understanding of the rule in much less time (and fewer words) than if she pulled the cases and read the pages cited. This is a worthy goal.

The following example shows a synthesis of the authorities, which makes the presentation of the rule more helpful to the reader:

SYNTHESIZED RULE SECTION

To prevail on a claim of money had and received, a plaintiff must prove: (1) a transfer of funds to the defendant, (2) that is the result of a mistake of fact but not of law, and (3) that has caused an unjust enrichment of the defendant. *See First Federal Bank and Trust Co. v. Stevens*, 678 W.2d 234, 237 (Apex 1988); *ATI Transnational Credit Corp. v. Adam's Asphalt Co.*, 778 W.2d 42, 44-45 (Apex Ct. App. 1st Dist. 1994); *Green Cross and Red Shield of Apex v. Carson*, 688 W.2d 564, 566 (Apex Ct. App. 1st Dist. 1991). A defendant's contribution to the transferor's mistake of fact will mitigate in favor of a finding that the defendant's retention of the funds is unjust. *Green Cross and Red Shield*, 688 W.2d at 566. However, if the defendant is lawfully entitled to the amount of the transfer by virtue of a debt or account from the transferor that is due, the retention of the funds is not unjust. *ATI*, 778 W.2d at 44-45.

The above example is not only shorter, more concise and direct, but it has made connections—*in writing*—and has linked the authorities together in a way that the rote recitation of cases in the first example did not do. The second example helps the reader grasp the meaning of the rule faster and more completely than the first.

(Note that "*See*" was used as a signal for the authorities on the synthesized rule; no one case is the source of the exact wording and phrasing you used for the elements of the rule, so a signal is necessary, but the authorities directly support the synthesized rule developed, so "*See*" is the proper signal.)

Rule synthesis also can be employed in the situation where a standard wording of the rule exists (from a statute, rule, or landmark case), but later authorities have restated, redefined, illuminated, or supplemented its. Remember that in these circumstances, the original version should be stated first, followed by a synthesis of the later authorities. In this way, the law is presented to the reader in the most efficient package.

Now that you understand the key principles involved in determining and articulating a rule from either single or multiple authorities, you are ready to complete the analytical process by applying the rule to the relevant facts to reach a conclusion on each legal issue (or sub-issue) you have been asked to address. In Chapter 6, we turn to this process and present an organizational framework that will guide you as you put your analysis into writing.

CHAPTER 6

Organizing Legal Writing: The T-R-E-A-T Method

This Chapter teaches you to write your analysis of a legal issue in a cohesive format for an audience of law-trained readers. It emphasizes structure, especially where legal style requires a certain presentation. Our goal is to teach you how to make *conscious choices* at every step of the process, so that in the long run you will also know how to veer from our proposed structure and find places where your own style choices can shine through.

First, we discuss the presentation of a single legal issue. Of course, many projects will require analysis of more than one legal issue or of separate sub-issues, such as where a rule involves multiple elements. For example, even if your sole assignment is to determine whether your client has a viable claim for negligence, your discussion necessarily will involve analysis of the separate elements of this tort (duty, breach, causation, harm). Accordingly, we also will discuss how to duplicate the proposed organizational format for each individual issue or sub-issue you are analyzing.

I. MOVING FROM ISSUES TO ANSWERS AND *IRAC* TO *TREAT*

A. Simple IRAC

A legal issue presents a question for a lawyer to answer, the answer to which depends on the identification of a legal rule and the application of the rule to legally significant facts. Many of our examples thus far have involved very simple issues—with only one question to address and an answer that requires considering a single rule requiring little or no explanation.

> **Question:** Is Claudia Client's tort claim based on events that occurred eighteen months ago timely given the statute of limitations in New Mexico?
>
> **The statute of limitations for a tort in New Mexico is governed by N.M. Stat. § 23-45-8 (2005), which states: "The following causes of action have a five-year limitations period: . . . all actions of . . . tort . . . ."**
>
> **Claudia Client seeks to bring a claim for negligence based on a car accident in which she injured her neck. Client's negligence claim is a tort action, which in New Mexico, has a five-year statute of limitations. Because the accident is based on events that happened eighteen months ago, her claim is timely.**

This analysis is short and uncomplicated. Given the straightforward nature of both the question and the rule, the answer actually does cover all the necessary analytical steps.

The short answer presents the issue, the applicable rule, the relevant facts, and a conclusion. It generally follows the structure of a rule-based reasoning **syllogism**.[1]

PRACTICE POINTER

IRAC on EXAMS

The IRAC formula can work well on law school exams, when you have only three or four hours to address a multitude of issues in essay form.

The more sophisticated structural paradigm that we discuss in detail below—called "TREAT"—is geared more toward legal writing in practice. Yes, the two structures have much in common, because they both emanate from the syllogistic reasoning construct identified above. Indeed, these paradigms—and others like them—constitute methods of presenting logical arguments in a rule-based environment.

The simpler, IRAC version works well when you are under time pressure and, for example, need not work to craft strong thesis statements or thorough explanations of how a rule operates in like situations. In practice, however, the opposite is true: you want to be as helpful to your readers as possible when issue-spotting is not the primary task at hand.

B. Moving from IRAC to TREAT

Legal analysis is rarely as simple as applying a clear rule—*e.g.*, the statute of limitations for a tort claim in New Mexico—to a straightforward set of factual circumstances.

The structural method employed in this book—TREAT—is designed to accommodate greater analytical complexity and improve IRAC in at least two key respects. First, the T encourages you to provide answers to issues up front in a manner more useful to practitioners than simply identifying the legal issue (which is presumably already known to the attorney who asked for your analysis of it). Second, the E indicates the need to explain the applicable rule to your readers in way that foreshadows your Application of the rule, employing inductive reasoning in the process.

The following chart shows the relationship between the two acronyms and what they represent:

---

1   Rule-Based Reasoning Syllogism: The answer is X because [Major Premise:] the authorities establish the rule that governs this situation, and the rule requires certain facts to be present, and [Minor Premise:] these facts are present, so [Conclusion:] the application of the rule to the facts produces X result.] This structure is the **I-R-A-C** formula in its simplest form: state the Issue, state the Rule that answers the issue, Apply the rule to the facts, and draw your Conclusion.

IRAC TERMINOLOGY	TREAT TERMINOLOGY
Issue—Identifies the issue for the reader	**Thesis**—Identifies the issue for the reader and states the answer up front, where it helps the reader the most. A good T sentence also will indicate (briefly) the primary basis for your conclusion.
Rule Section—States the legal principles that govern the issue	**Rule Statement**—Identifies the legal rule (and its required elements) that governs the issue at hand.
	Explanation Section—Explains and illustrates how the rule works in actual, prior situations, thus providing greater clarity and context for the conclusion and predictions of the memorandum.[2]
Application Section—Applies the rule to the facts of the case at hand	**Application Section**—Applies the rule to the facts of the case at hand.
Conclusion—States the conclusion on the issue	**Thesis restated as conclusion**—Restates the conclusion on the issue to reinforce the answer and bring closure to the discussion.

---

2   A good lawyer using IRAC will explain the rule, too, but our method uses a rigorous explanation formulation (explanatory synthesis) that employs inductive and analogical reasoning to illustrate how the rule works. This is above and beyond "simple IRAC," and it is much more useful to a busy, law-trained reader.

FYI

Where did TREAT come from?

Before becoming law professors, both authors were litigators at large, nationwide law firms and, prior to that, each clerked in federal district courts. They practiced in areas such as, for one, financial services, energy, health care, and privacy regulation; the other, complex commercial litigation, intellectual property, and products liability. These experiences presented numerous opportunities for them to review—and write!—briefs and office memoranda of the kind that law firm partners and judges considered excellent examples. Both authors were taught IRAC in law school, and both quickly recognized its limitations in practice.

That said, each recognized that one could not escape IRAC completely because, as noted above, IRAC is simply marking steps in the process of deductive reasoning. *All* of the acronyms in widespread use do just that, and there are several IRAC progeny to choose from: **CREAC** (Conclusion, Rule, Explanation, Application, Conclusion) and **CIRAC** (Conclusion, Issue, Rule, Application, Conclusion) are popular choices. More recent is **BARAC** (Brief Answer, Rule, Application, Conclusion), which seems to be missing a K . . . .

They ultimately agreed on **TREAT** for the reasons already stated. Of course, they would be remiss if they didn't also note that, unlike its sister acronyms, TREAT is an actual English word, both a noun and a verb no less. Fortuitously, its primary meanings also relate to what it attempts to convey. As a verb, "treat" means "to deal with in a certain way," which is *exactly* what it encourages as an analytical structure. As a noun . . . "an event that gives great pleasure" . . . perhaps this is purely aspirational.

A single "TREAT" is the format for the discussion of a single issue; execution of each of its steps is discussed in detail below.

Most legal problems, however, involve analysis of more than one legal issue. *Each legal issue* under consideration requires its own TREAT. For example, if you have been asked to analyze whether Daisy Dogwalker is liable for either dog bite liability or for negligence, then you need to formulate two separate TREATs, one for each legal issue.

As well, most rules involve multiple parts (elements or factors). For example, your analysis of the first issue (dog bite liability) requires a discussion of the three elements of this cause of action in Apex: ownership, causation, provocation. Accordingly, your TREAT for that legal issue entails three sub-TREATs—one for each element of the claim. If any one element is assumed—does not require discussion—you should note that at the outset, take it off the table, and proceed with remaining sub-TREATs in question.

Let's briefly outline an analysis of the two claims that Daisy Dogwalker (DD) faces. Assume for purposes of this analysis and both claims that causation and injury are not disputed (*i.e.*, Duke the Doberman actually did bite Piper Patterson's (PP) arm, causing it to bleed).

An initial outline of your analysis is as follows:

1. **T:** DD is/is not liable for dog bite liability because . . . .

    R: Dog bite liability entails proof of (1) ownership, (n/a) causation, (2) lack of provocation. Causation is assumed.

    E/A(1):   **t:** Ownership of Duke?
    r/e: what various precedents state about ownership.
    a: application to facts at hand.
    t: conclusion on this sub-issue.

    E/A(2):   **t:** Provocation by PP?
    r/e: what various precedents state about provocation.
    a: application to facts at hand.
    t: conclusion on this sub-issue.

    T: Final conclusion on dog bite liability.

2. **T:** DD is/is not liable for negligence because . . . .

    R: Negligence entails proof of (1) duty, (2) breach, (n/a) causation, (n/a) harm. The latter two elements are assumed.

    E/A(1):   **t:** DD's duty toward PP?
    r/e: what various precedents state about dogwalker duty.
    a: application to facts at hand.
    t: conclusion on this sub-issue.

    E/A(2):   **t:** DD's breach?
    r/e: what various precedents state about breach.
    a: application to facts at hand.
    t: conclusion on this sub-issue.

    T: Final conclusion on negligence.

What we have produced is almost mathematical in nature. Keep this Big TREAT / small treat structure in mind as we move forward with more details about what each step in the process entails. Once you learn the structure, it will become second nature. An important upside is that you will rarely be confused about where each piece of your analysis should appear.

II.   THESIS HEADINGS

A. Drafting a Thesis Statement

Your engagement with the TREAT paradigm begins when you have completed your research and analysis of an issue and are ready to report your conclusions in writing. Your discussion of each issue (or sub-issue) should begins with your **position** on that issue—your answer—which we call your **thesis**. The thesis almost always is written in one sentence; it should articulate the legal issue and how that issue is resolved.

Presenting your thesis brings to the forefront of your discussion your answer to the question posed. Making it into a point heading highlights this critical information for the reader. **Point headings** also operate as guideposts for your readers, orienting them and literally guiding them through the key points of your analysis. Strong and informative point headings enable even the busiest readers to follow your analysis, almost at a glance.

FOOD FOR THOUGHT

Thesis headings, and the "because . . . " part
Helping busy readers, highlighting information for their benefit—that is what you are aiming for. The TREAT format makes it easy for readers to access your writing and appreciate its structural efficiency. It is an audience-friendly writing format.

Point headings are especially useful. We recommend writing your conclusion—your Thesis—in each heading, along with a short statement capturing the reasons for your conclusion. The easiest way to accomplish this is to include a "because clause." Instead of writing simply, "Dogwalker will not be liable for dog bite liability," include the why: "because Patterson's attempt to kick the dog in the head constitutes sufficient provocation."

In the examples presented earlier in this text, we studied the situation of a client who owned a Doberman Pinscher. The dog encountered a girl selling Girl Scout cookies and became agitated when the girl swung her bag of cookies at his head. The dog apparently thought the girl was threatening him and reacted by clamping his jaw around her arm. Unfortunately, a skirmish ensued during which the girl received several deep cuts on her arm. The case was analyzed under the mythical law of Apex.

For purposes of this Chapter, let's assume that Texas law applies. (Note that the examples below nevertheless employ fictitious cases.) Let's also assume that the client's name is Dennis Dogman, and the girl's name is Sarah Scout. After completing your research and analyzing the matter under Texas law, your conclusion is that your client, the dog owner, will be liable for the injuries inflicted on the girl's arm by the dog. Your Thesis might be,

"The dog owner is liable for plaintiff's injuries."

At a minimum, the Thesis should reveal the issue—liability for dog bite injuries—and the answer to the question—yes, the client will be liable. An additional component to consider is a short explanation *why*. To accomplish this, we recommend using a **"because clause"** that captures in a nutshell the basis for your prediction:

> **"Dogman is liable for Scout's injuries because Scout's act of swinging a bag near the dog's head does not constitute sufficient provocation."**

This statement accomplishes three things that help the reader: it identifies the issue, answers the question, and provides a brief explanation for the prediction.

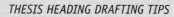

DO IT WITH STYLE!

THESIS HEADING DRAFTING TIPS

1. Should the Thesis use the parties' names, or are party designations sufficient?

Legal readers generally prefer when you use the parties' names rather than generic titles such as plaintiff and defendant. (We have previously used party titles in this book for simplicity's sake when we were not focusing on thesis drafting tips.) You are better served using actual names, unless you consciously decide to do otherwise. For example, some litigators prefer calling the opposing party by title as a way to "depersonalize" the other side. In some areas of practice, the parties' *roles* in the action are more commonly used. For example, in tax practice, the convention is often to use the terms "Taxpayer" and "Service" (IRS); in government contracts practice, you often see "Contractor" and "Government."

2. Should the Thesis use all caps, sentence case, or title case capitalization?

There is no single right answer to this question. You should defer to you instructor's preference for font, formatting, and capitalization standards. Going forward, you should check the preferences of your place of employment or, in litigation, the Local Rules for the court and jurisdiction in which you are filing. Basic, default guidelines are used in the memo examples in Chapter 7.

You want to be careful not to include *too much* information in a Thesis heading, or it risks becoming unwieldy. How much is too much? It is challenging to provide a formula that works for every situation. Logic and readability have a lot to do with it, and experience will improve your judgment.

An over-length Thesis would be:

> "Dogman is liable for Scout's injuries because Scout can prove ownership of the dog by Dogman, her lawful and peaceful presence at his home, and lack of provocation because her actions in swinging a bag of cookies near the dog's head is insufficient provocation under Texas law."

Despite the fact that the previous statement incorporates all of the key elements of the rule, it is probably better separated into three theses—one prediction per each element, assuming all three elements are in dispute.

Also over-length, though less so and limited to a single element might be:

> "Dogman is liable for the injuries to Scout's arm that were caused by the dog when it felt threatened by the bag she swung near its head because her actions were insufficient to constitute provocation under Texas law."

The point is to try to boil down the explanation to only the most essential nuggets. Most likely—though not always—your Thesis will be focused on one rule or aspect thereof. So a good tip is to make sure your Thesis speaks only to the actual point in controversy. And, not unlike legal writing in general, be especially conscious of the use of active versus passive voice when constructing Thesis statements. Overly passive constructions will almost always make your Thesis statements too long and less reader-friendly.

B. Thesis Heading Placement

Thesis statements typically appear as the heading of a particular section or sub-section of your discussion of a legal issue. The paragraph immediately following the heading should state the applicable rule. Consider the following example:

1. Dogman is liable for Scout's injuries because Scout's act of swinging a bag near the dog's head does not constitute sufficient provocation.

[T] Dogman is liable for Scout's injuries because Scout's act of swinging a bag near the dog's head does not constitute sufficient provocation. [R] In Texas, a dog owner is liable for all injuries caused by his dog unless the dog is provoked by the victim. *Smithy v. Jonesy*, 123 S.W.2d 345, 347 (Tex. 1965); *Johnson v. Anderson*, 789 S.W.2d 234, 237 (Tex. App. 1989). The elements of a cause of action for dog-bite liability are: (1) defendant's ownership of the dog, (2) injuries caused by the dog, and (3) lack of provocation of the dog by the plaintiff. *See Smithy*, 123 S.W.2d at 347.

POINT-COUNTERPOINT

Should you repeat the Thesis heading as the first line of text?
Repeating the Thesis heading as the first sentence of text (or rephrasing it) is a matter of discretion and personal choice. Rephrasing the Thesis headings allows you to write slightly shorter headings, saving some of the important information for the first line of text. Doing so also preserves the information for readers who tend to skip over point headings. Even if you do not repeat or rephrase it, you should nevertheless put all of the relevant information into the heading (the issue, answer, and "because clause"). Doing so provides a useful summary for readers who do the opposite of what we just said— those who skim the discussion section reading only the Thesis headings to get the gist of your predictions. This is a style point on which reasonable law-trained writers legitimately differ. You should employ the technique that best suits your writing and/or the directions of your professor or supervisor.

III. RULE STATEMENT OR RULE SECTION

A. Statement of legal principles and requirements that govern the issue

The Rule section follows the Thesis. It states the rule(s) that govern the legal issue under analysis. Recall from Chapter 4 that a rule of law is a statement of the legal principles and requirements that govern the analysis of a legal issue. Sometimes there is one clear rule that is followed by all the authorities in your jurisdiction. In many instances, however, various authorities state the rule differently, perhaps just using different language, but sometimes illuminating or adding a new factor.

The previous two chapters discussed at length the process of finding and analyzing the authorities that define the rule of law governing the legal issue in question. We referenced the process of **synthesizing** various accounts of a rule into one coherent presentation. There is much more to say on this topic, discussed below.

> Note: Here, we are still focused on articulating the **R**ule itself; we are not quite at the point of **R**ule **E**xplanation.

There are three basic scenarios for the kind of rule statement you need to draft. The simplest form is a rule that comes from a **single source**. Often, this source is a statute, constitutional provision, or administrative regulation. The rule in this case has not been modified by later authorities. For example:

> **The statute of limitations for a tort in New Mexico is governed by N.M. Stat. § 23-45-8 (2005), which states: "The following causes of action have a five year limitations period: . . . all actions of . . . tort . . . ."**

This sentence might be the *entire* "rule section" if there is nothing else relevant to add.

But, more often than not, the rule has undergone some development over time. This leads to the second formulation. Perhaps the rule started with a statute and then was modified by cases:

> **The Illinois statute pertaining to liability of an owner of a dog attacking or injuring persons provides:**
>
> > **If a dog or other animal without provocation, attacks or injures any person who is peacefully conducting himself in any place where he may lawfully be, the owner of such dog or other animal is liable in damages to such person for the full amount of the injury sustained.**
>
> **Ill. Rev. Stat. ch. 8, par. 366 (1973).**
>
> **Under this statute Illinois courts have found that there are four elements that must be proved: injury caused by a dog owned or harbored by the defendant; lack of provocation; peaceable conduct of the person injured; and the presence of the person injured in a place where he has a legal right to be. *Siewerth v. Charleston*, 231 N.E.2d 644, 646 (Ill. App. Ct. 1967); *Messa v. Sullivan*, 209 N.E.2d 872, 873 (Ill. App. Ct. 1965); *Beckert v. Risberg*, 199 N.E.2d 811, 815 (Ill. App. Ct. 1964), *rev'd on other grounds*, 210 N.E.2d 207 (Ill. 1965).**

Most common of all is the third scenario, where a rule has developed over time with both modifications and interpretations in later authorities that affect its meaning:

> **Under U.S. copyright law, a work using copyrighted material of another author may be protected from copyright infringement prosecution if it is found to be a "fair use." The U.S. Copyright Act reads, in pertinent part,**
>
> > **The fair use of a copyrighted work . . . for purposes such as criticism [and] comment . . . is not an infringement of copyright. In determining whether the use made of a work in any particular case is a fair use the factors to be considered shall include—(1) the purpose and character of the use, including whether such use is of a commercial nature; . . . (2) the nature of the copyrighted work; (3) the amount and substantiality of the portion used in relation to the copyrighted work as a whole; and (4) the effect of the use upon the potential market for or value of the copyrighted work . . . .**
>
> **17 U.S.C. § 107.**

In applying this law, courts have rejected the use of bright line rules, calling instead for a case-by-case analysis that considers all four of the fair use factors. *Campbell*, 473 U.S. at 577-78. Significantly for the principal case, parody may be considered a fair use, qualifying as such under the first factor, "purpose and character of the use." *Id.* at 579.

Parody, qualifying as fair use, is a work that (1) targets the borrowed original work and, at least in part, makes comment on it, and (2) is transformative of the original work, rather than simply superseding it. *Id.* at 579-80. It has additionally been found to be immaterial whether the alleged parody is in good or bad taste, *id.* at 582, whether the work is labeled as a parody, *id.* at 583, or whether the copyright owner would endorse or prohibit the work. *Leibovitz*, 980 F.2d at 115.

The following chart (from Chapter 5) should refresh your recollection about how to go about "synthesizing" a rule section from multiple authorities. We are still focusing on the Rule statement or Rule section. The process of "explanatory synthesis" has yet to be introduced:

RULE SYNTHESIS (Formulate the rule and draft the rule section)	
1. Start with the highest and most recent controlling authority.	◆ If you have a statute (or regulation), start with the statute. ◆ If you have a watershed case that is controlling, start with that. ◆ If your best authority is from the court of last resort, take the most recent opinion from that court, and start with that. ◆ If these first three criteria do not apply, start with the most recent actual controlling authority that is on point. ◆ Only if none of the above applies should you consider turning to non-controlling authority—primary or secondary. ◆ Don't expect to use all of your authorities.

RULE SYNTHESIS (Formulate the rule and draft the rule section)	
2. Reconcile differing statements or phrasings of the rule from controlling authorities, and attempt to synthesize the rule into one coherent statement of the legal principles that govern the issue.	◆ DON'T change the wording of or paraphrase rules from statutes, administrative rules and regulations, and watershed cases. ◆ Unless a processed applied rule can be written smoothly and effectively in one sentence or phrase, write the rule first with modifications second.
3. Write interpretive sub-rules on elements of the rule in the section or sub-TREAT discussion that discusses that element of the rule. Write exceptions to the sub-rules after you lay out the sub-rules themselves.	◆ Write interpretive sub-rules on elements of the rule in the section or sub-TREAT discussion that discusses that element of the rule. Write exceptions to the sub-rules after you lay out the sub-rules themselves.
4. Do not write a rule with inherent contradictions.	◆ Check for ambiguity in the terms you have used to formulate the rule (even if some of these terms came from the authorities).
5. Do accept the remote possibility that two competing rules on the same issue might exist in the same jurisdiction.	◆ When this happens, you may have to analyze the facts under both competing sets of rules.

DO IT WITH STYLE!

RULE SECTION DRAFTING TIPS
1. What do you mean by rule "statement" or "section"?

We mean simply the space that it takes to articulate the rule(s) governing the issue at hand. You likely will have multiple rule "sections" in a single document because your fact pattern or situation will present multiple questions to answer. We are making a fine distinction for now between the "R" and the "E" in the TREAT paradigm: the Rule is the law that applies; the Explanation (soon to come) will illustrate how the rule(s) operates in actual situations.

2. How long should a rule statement or section be?

The answer varies depending on the rule at issue. Occasionally, a rule section might be a single sentence (or quote) from a single authority, such as a statute. It might be several sentences, or a paragraph, that lists the rule's elements or key interpretations. Again, there is considerable discretion involved, and you will over time develop a better sense of what a reader might need or want to know. Do not ignore the guidance of simple logic: if there is a settled, straightforward rule in your jurisdiction, then you likely need not include the history of how that rule developed or the policies underlying it. In contrast, if a rule has a complicated history in your jurisdiction, then you may need additional support for your articulation of it.

3. To what extent should I cite authorities in the rule section?

Certainly, you want to cite any primary authorities (statutes, regulations, or cases) that themselves articulate or support the rule. Without citations, your reader will not understand where your information is coming from. Whether you actually quote authorities depends on the type of rule involved. Rules from statutes or regulations or watershed cases should be quoted, but rules derived from a longer line of cases might not be. The facts of cases, even key cases, are likely not necessary to include at this juncture. You will have plenty of room to do so in the course of explaining and applying the rule, discussed in more detail below. For now, we are talking exclusively about stating what the rule is.

B. Definitional rules and interpretive rules

Prior chapters mentioned something that must now be made explicit: Rule sections typically contain *two different kinds of rules* that apply to a given legal question. Our discussion thus far has been about the rules that define the governing legal standard. We call these **definitional rules**, or the **main rules** presented in the rule section.

But the rule section also entails **interpretive rules** from primary and secondary authorities. Interpretive rules are statements from legal authorities that offer instruction on a rule's application. They are not elements or factors, and they are not the principles derived from a synthesis of the authorities. Instead, interpretative rules are individual statements from authorities that have discussed and applied the rule in question. They share a kinship with the principles of statutory interpretation presented in Chapter 4. But interpretive rules are crafted by the authors of legal authorities—judges, administrative agencies, sometimes commentators—to guide the application of specific, individual rules (not all legal rules in general).

For example, in the hypothetical problem we have been using, assume that one case from your jurisdiction characterizes the rule on dog bite liability as a "disfavored cause of action," stating that "to prove liability for a dog bite, the plaintiff must prove each element of the claim with clear and convincing evidence." Next, assume that a second case discusses relatively recent developments in the law and explains that dog bite liability has moved from a point where "every dog was entitled to one unprovoked bite," to a point where "each attack by a dog, even the first, may give rise to a valid claim against the dog owner." These interpretative rules belong in the rule section because they are integral to its definition.

The third example above shows the use of interpretive rules in the context of a more complicated rule section:

> **[Definitional Rule:]** Under U.S. copyright law, a work using copyrighted material of another author may be protected from copyright infringement prosecution if it is found to be a "fair use." The U.S. Copyright Act reads, in pertinent part,
>
>> The fair use of a copyrighted work . . . for purposes such as criticism [and] comment . . . is not an infringement of copyright. In determining whether the use made of a work in any particular case is a fair use the factors to be considered shall include—(1) the purpose and character of the use, including whether such use is of a commercial nature; . . . (2) the nature of the copyrighted work; (3) the amount and substantiality of the portion used in relation to the copyrighted work as a whole; and (4) the effect of the use upon the potential market for or value of the copyrighted work . . . .

17 U.S.C. § 107.

> **[Interpretive Rules:]** In applying this law, courts have rejected the use of bright line rules, calling instead for a case-by-case analysis which weighs together a consideration of all four of the included factors. *Campbell*, 473 U.S. at 577-78. Significantly for the issue in the principal case, parody may be considered a fair use, qualifying as such under the first factor, "purpose and character of the use." *Id.* at 579.

> **[Definitional Rule:]** Parody, qualifying as fair use, is a work that (1) targets the borrowed original work and, at least in part, makes comment on it, and (2) is transformative of the original work, rather than simply superseding it. *Id.* at 579-80. **[Interpretive Rules:]** It has additionally been found to be immaterial whether the alleged parody is in good or bad taste, *id.* at 582, whether the work is labeled as a parody, *id.* at 583, or whether the copyright owner would endorse or prohibit the work. *Leibovitz*, 980 F.2d at 115.

In an earlier example, the rule on dog bite liability in Texas was stated the same way in each of the authorities relied on. If, instead, we included the interpretive rules provided in multiple authorities, the rule section might read as follows:

THESIS HEADING AND RULE SECTION

1. Dogman is liable for Scout's injuries because Scout's act of swinging a bag near the dog's head does not constitute sufficient provocation.

[Definitional Rules:] In Texas, a dog owner is liable for all injuries caused by his dog unless the dog is provoked by the victim. *Smithy v. Jonesy*, 123 S.W.2d 345, 347 (Tex. 1965); *Johnson v. Anderson*, 789 S.W.2d 234, 237 (Tex. App. 1989). The elements of a cause of action for dog-bite liability are therefore: (1) defendant's ownership of the dog, (2) injuries caused by the dog, and (3) lack of provocation of the dog by the plaintiff. *See Smithy*, 123 S.W.2d at 347. **[Interpretive Rules:]** The rule on dog bite liability has moved from a point where "every dog was entitled to one unprovoked bite," to a point where "each attack by a dog, even the first, may give rise to a valid claim against the dog owner." *Hawthorne v. Melville*, 999 S.W.2d 17, 20 (Tex. App. 1998). That said, a claim seeking to impose liability for a dog bite is a "disfavored cause of action" in Texas; as such, "the plaintiff must prove each element of the claim with clear and convincing evidence." *Roberts v. Thomas*, 676 S.W.2d 34, 37 (Tex. 1979).

Interpretive rules can and often do come from a single source. The best interpretive rules come from primary controlling authority, but a strong, insightful interpretive rule from a persuasive authority of the jurisdiction whose law applies to the case also is worth citing.

IV. EXPLANATION SECTION

The explanation, or "E" section, is critically important for a comprehensive and sophisticated legal analysis. It is a step that many writers do not make good use of. Indeed, some legal writers confuse Rule Explanation with proving the rules that govern the issue; others confuse it with the task of applying the rule(s) to the facts of the client's situation. The latter is a common pitfall in legal writing—in which key aspects of the rule dribble out almost accidentally when its tenets are applied to the factual circumstances at hand. Finally, many writers sell the "E" section short by masking important legal principles in a case-by-case description of prior applications of the rule. Our goal is to teach you the benefits of explanatory synthesis as a way to enhance your writing.

A. Purpose of the Explanation section

In the Explanation section, you will use the key legal authorities uncovered in your research to explain the rules by showing how they operate in various situations. The goal of Explanation is to teach your readers **how to interpret** (and later apply) the rule(s) in question.

The question may arise: how is this process of explaining the rule(s) different from the presentation of the rule(s) in the rule section? If you are asking this question, you are on the right track and exactly where you should be.

In the Rule section, you articulate the legal standards that govern the issue. From that alone, a sophisticated law-trained reader might be able to guess how those standards will operate in a given factual situation. But it will be just that—a guess. You can facilitate your reader's understanding of how the rule will operate in your case by illustrating and explaining how it has worked in prior situations. Consider the following:

GOALS OF THE EXPLANATION SECTION

The goal is to explain how the rule should be interpreted and applied based on how the authorities have applied it in actual, concrete factual settings, and on how commentators have interpreted it.	◆ You are going beyond what the courts have already said about the rule in Interpretive Rules found in cases.
Two methods are available: (1) inductive reasoning through synthesis of multiple authorities from which you induce principles of how the rule properly is to be interpreted and applied; or (2) direct analogical comparisons of individual cases with the client's case, which would happen in the Application section.	◆ You are presenting principles of interpretation that are supported by a careful reading of the cases and implemented with analogical reasoning.
	◆ You are doing the work of digesting and synthesizing the cases so the reader doesn't have to do it.
	◆ You are following common law principles of stare decisis and the doctrine of precedent.

B. A Critical Tool: Explanatory Synthesis

The two fundamental methods of rule explanation are **explanatory synthesis and case-by-case presentations of explanatory principles**. Each has its place, but there are occasions where one works better than the other. Our goal in this Chapter is to convince you that explanatory synthesis should be your go-to method, because it has several advantages over a case-by-case presentation framework. Explanatory synthesis is a more versatile and powerful tool for an efficient and convincing explanation of how rules work.

1. Explanatory Synthesis Method

Explanatory synthesis is our term for putting together multiple authorities in an efficient and effective manner for the purpose of explaining how a rule works. With case law, the author studies the cases, the policies that seem to connect them, and the outcomes determined by the application of the rules to the different facts of the different cases. Parallels in application and outcome among cases are noted: the application of the rules to certain types of situations allow the plaintiffs to prevail; the application of the rules to other types of situations cause the plaintiffs to lose. The author uses these examples to write principles about how lawyers and judges should properly read, interpret, understand, and apply the rules that govern the issue that is being answered.

Explanatory synthesis does not itself *define* the rule; instead, it *illustrates the rule's operation*. Explanatory synthesis relies on inductive reasoning drawing from multiple authorities both to create knowledge about the meaning and effect of the precedents and to persuade the reader that the author's understanding of how the precedents work supports the predictions, conclusions, and recommendations the author is making in the writing as to the client's case. Parentheticals are used in explanatory synthesis to present and demonstrate the material drawn from each of the multiple authorities that are cited in a string cite to support the proposition induced from these authorities. The author also can insert other kinds of authorities—for example, secondary authorities—into the synthesis to further explain and support the principles of interpretation and application of the rules that the author has induced from the authorities.

The structure of explanatory synthesis has three parts:

Principle—citation—parenthetical

The idea is to extract from a case or series of cases and secondary authorities the key **principles** that animate the courts' conclusions. Those principles—likely from more than one authority—illustrate the rule in operation. These principles should be keyed to the issue at hand; they are not necessarily illustrative in the abstract. Rather, they foreshadow the **A**pplication of the rule to the specific factual circumstances at issue. Accordingly, the construction of these explanatory principles depends on a deep understanding of the legal issue, the legally significant facts, and the overall question on the table.

Citations to authority are necessary to support the principles extracted. **Parentheticals** are used to capture the specific facts from cited authorities that were used to formulate the guiding principles but were omitted when the principle was extracted and generalized. Secondary authorities may be used to further explain or buttress a particular principle or its application.

This narrative may sound more difficult than the technique actually entails. First, consider the structure alone. In text, you would produce the following:

Explanatory Principle induced from Authorities 1, 2, and 3. Cite Authority 1 (offer factual details or public policy rationale supporting the principle); Cite Authority 2 (offer factual details or public policy rationale supporting the principle); Cite Authority 3 (offer factual details or public policy rationale supporting the principle).

(Note: yes, you may have more or fewer than three cases, and yes, your paragraph may be comprised of more than one textual sentence.)

Next, consider several examples of the structure deployed. Following are excerpts from two (real) judicial opinions and two appellate briefs:

Example 1:

A candidate or independent group might not spend money if the direct result of that spending is additional funding to political adversaries. *See, e.g., Green Party of Conn.*, 616 F.3d, at 242 (matching funds impose "a substantial burden on the exercise of First Amendment rights" (internal quotation marks omitted)); *McComish v. Bennett*, 611 F.3d, at 524 (matching funds create "potential chilling effects" and "impose some First Amendment burden"); *Scott v. Roberts*, 612 F.3d 1279, 1290 (11th Cir. 2010) ("we think it is obvious that the [matching funds] subsidy imposes a burden on [privately financed] candidates"); *id.*, at 1291 ("we know of no court that doubts that a [matching funds] subsidy like the one at issue here burdens" the speech of privately financed candidates); *see also Day v. Holahan*, 34 F.3d 1356, 1360 (8th Cir. 1994) (it is "clear" that matching funds provisions infringe on "protected speech because of the chilling effect" they have "on the political speech of the person or group making the [triggering] expenditure" (cited in *Davis, supra*, at 739, 128 S. Ct. 2759)).

Ariz. Free Enter. Club's Freedom Club PAC v. Bennett, __ U.S. __; 131 S. Ct. 2806, 2823–24 (2011) (Roberts, C.J., majority op.) (parentheticals in original; citation form corrected).

Example 1 illustrates synthesis of a single legal proposition: that a candidate or independent group might not spend money if the direct result of that spending is additional funding to political adversaries. Multiple sources are marshaled in support of the proposition, but the author does not merely provide a string of bare citations to supporting authorities. Citations alone might be persuasive if the authorities are controlling and the audience is already familiar with them. Citations alone also may be sufficient for propositions that are straightforward and uncontroversial. The inclusion of **explanatory parentheticals**, however, offers additional information and support for the authorities used. They illustrate the proposition as applied and thus provide the reader with important details about *how and why* the authorities support it. This guidance is often critical for a thorough understanding of the issue. It also demonstrates the depth of the author's analysis and may save the reader from having to read the cases herself.

Parentheticals inform the reader of how the authorities support or illustrate the proposition in combination, not just individually. A string of bare citations must be taken at face value as individual authorities, but when an author provides a parenthetical behind each citation, the author can guide the reader through the synthesis of the multiple authorities. This guidance is often critical to the author's purpose for the discourse and to the reader's understanding and appreciation of the discussion. The author is demonstrating to the reader the level of analysis performed by the author, and potentially saving the reader from having to follow up on a string of bare citations to find the facts or policies or other information concerning the proper interpretation and application of the rules that exist within the cited authorities. Parentheticals allow the author to provide supporting information which may be both necessary and sufficient to achieving the author's logos or pathos purposes in inducing the proposition from the supporting authorities, all in reader-friendly approach that also is likely to bolster the author's ethos-reception with the reader.

Example 2:

> Numerous courts outside Illinois have applied adverse domination tolling with respect to receiver/trustee/conservator claims against third parties regardless of whether the plaintiff states a civil conspiracy claim against the third parties. *See, e.g., Rajala v. Gardner*, Nos. 09-2482-EFM, 10-2243-EFM, 2011 WL 453432, *5–*8 (D. Kan. Feb. 4, 2011) (adverse domination tolling applied to bankruptcy trustee claims against non-directors because it wasn't until wrongdoing directors were removed that claims became "reasonably ascertainable"); *Warfield v. Carnie*, No. 3:04-cv-633-R, 2007 WL 1112591, *15–*17 (N.D. Tex. Apr. 13, 2007) (adverse domination tolling applied to receiver's claims because it would have been impossible for the plaintiffs to have asserted such claims while controlled by the "perpetrators of the Ponzi scheme"); *Quilling v. Cristell*, No. Civ. A. 304CV252, 2006 WL 316981, *6 (W.D.N.C. Feb. 9, 2006) (adverse domination tolling applied to receiver's claims against non-director defendant in connection with a Ponzi scheme because "so long as a corporation remains under the control of wrongdoers, it cannot be expected to take action to vindicate the harms and injustices perpetrated by the wrongdoers").
>
> Br. and Short App. of Plaintiff–Appellant Indep. Trust Corp., *Indep. Trust Corp. v. Stewart Info. Servs. Corp.*, 2011 WL 3283774 at *25–26 (No. 11-2108, 665 F.3d 930, 7th Cir. 2012).

Example 2 demonstrates the potential of explanatory synthesis when discussing non-binding authorities. Readers may skim over citations to non-binding authorities too quickly but for the inclusion of illustrative content from those authorities.

The parentheticals in Example 2 incorporate the policy rationales underlying the cited authorities that make them relevant to the discussion.

Example 3:

> We have declined to find a transformative use when the defendant has done no more than find a new way to exploit the creative virtues of the original work. *See Davis*, 246 F.3d at 174 (use of plaintiff's eyewear in a clothing advertisement not transformative because it was "worn as eye jewelry in the manner it was made to be worn"); *Castle Rock Entm't*, 150 F.3d at 142–43 (quiz book called the "*Seinfeld* Aptitude Test" not transformative when its purpose was "to repackage [the television show] *Seinfeld* to entertain *Seinfeld* viewers"); *Ringgold v. Black Entm't Television, Inc.* 126 F.3d 70, 79 (2d Cir. 1997) (copy of plaintiff's painting used as decoration for a television program's set not transformative because it was used for "the same decorative purpose" as the original).

Blanch v. Koons, 467 F.3d 244, 252 (2d Cir. 2006) (footnote omitted).

Example 3 uses parentheticals in a synthesis of authorities for a different purpose. Here, the parentheticals illustrate the failed storylines of each authority cited (the failure to establish a fair use of the copyrighted material in the case). The three failed storylines establish the legal backdrop to which the facts of the matter under analysis can be compared and contrasted in the Application section.

Example 4:

> Plaintiffs waived their On-Call Policy claims by failing to include them in a single motion for notice. *See* Plaintiffs' ER, at 101:26–28; Plaintiffs' Brief, at pgs. 3–4. As a result, those claims have been dismissed on their merits. *See e.g., Ficken v. Golden*, 696 F. Supp.2d 21, 33–34 (D.D.C. 2010) (holding *res judicata* barred re-filing of claims in prior action that were dismissed due to plaintiffs' failure to comply with order directing them to provide a more definite statement); *Mendoza v. Block*, 27 F.3d 1357, 1363 (9th Cir. 1994) (affirming dismissal of claims that were deemed waived); *Sidhu v. Flecto Co., Inc.*, 279 F.3d 896, 900 (9th Cir. 2002) (prior suit dismissed as untimely was a final judgment on the merits for *res judicata*); *Marin v. Hew, Health Care Financing*, 769 F.2d 590 (9th Cir. 1985) (denial of leave to file second amended complaint based on statutory time bar was a final judgment on the merits for *res judicata*).

Answering Br. of Defs.–Appellees, *Riggio v. Serv. Corp. Int'l*, 2011 WL 3436909 at *10 (No. 11-15696, 476 Fed. Appx., 2012).

Example 4 returns to the basic, but versatile use of explanatory synthesis to present a principle concerning the proper interpretation and application of a rule induced from multiple authorities applying it. The author uses parentheticals to illustrate how the authorities apply the principle being analyzed.

All four examples follow the method and structure of explanatory synthesis because they identify specific situations with concrete facts in which a rule has been applied to produce a concrete outcome. The inductions that they make are intended to guide the disposition of the matter under consideration. These inductions involve extracting key principles from multiple, similar cases based on the common principles of law and policies that unite them. These principles may not be binding, but they are persuasive and reliable. They demonstrate how the law should be interpreted and applied in a given situation based on the deployment of that law in multiple situations in the past.

The chart below attempts to capture the process of explanatory synthesis:

THE PROCESS OF EXPLANATORY SYNTHESIS	
1. Read cases and look for common facts and common outcomes.	◆ Group cases by facts. ◆ Divide groups of cases by outcome.
2. Review the groups to find the factors or public policies that make the difference in the outcome.	◆ Reconcile cases that have different outcomes; what policy or theme or factor determined the outcome in these cases. ◆ Reconcile cases that have the same outcome on different facts; what common policy or theme or factors brought about the same outcome on different facts.
3. Write principles of interpretation that explain your findings.	◆ Phrase your principles of interpretation in language that mimics interpretive rules. ◆ Often you can use interpretive rules as principles that tie together multiple authorities; there is no requirement that you always have to come up with brand new principles.
4. Cite the cases that support your principles of interpretation with parentheticals that provide facts or other information about each cases.	◆ Parentheticals should contain enough information to illustrate how the individual case supports the general principle you have laid out. ◆ Use shorthand and abbreviated phrases to save space.

THE PROCESS OF EXPLANATORY SYNTHESIS	
5. When you draft the application section, apply the principles of interpretation to your own facts; as a general rule, do not apply individual cases to your facts.	◆ Applying principles to facts will make your analysis more convincing; you have spelled out the connections to be made between the authorities and then followed through and showed how the principles learned from a study of the authorities determines the outcome of the case at hand. ◆ The exception to this rule is when you have one or two critically important cases that are worthy of individual attention in the explanation section; discuss them individually in the application section, whether as support or to distinguish them.

Explanatory synthesis is different from rule synthesis in terms of its role and placement in the discussion of a legal issue. Both concepts, though, have the same goal: to explain the rule—its terms and operation—to the reader. The analytical and rhetorical value of the synthesis to guide and persuade the disposition of the present case is based largely on the fact that that guiding principles are drawn from multiple samples of dispositions of similar cases based on the common principles of law and policy that unite the different cases.

2. Case-by-Case Explanatory Presentation

Case-by-case explanatory presentation means discussing a single case in one or more paragraphs for purposes of (later) comparing it to the circumstances of the matter under consideration. And then juxtaposing several such paragraphs from multiple cases as a method of "explaining" a rule. The idea is to describe how the rule worked in one particular situation with concrete facts and a concrete outcome so as to later compare that information to the facts and circumstances under consideration. Sounds relatively easy and reliable? It is to a degree.

You should immediately recognize what we are talking about because casebooks are rife with it. Paragraphs such as the following are common:

> **In *Barnette*, the Jehovah's Witness student refused to salute the flag in his classroom because he believed the salute violated the Biblical prohibition on the worship of graven images. The respondent, West Virginia State Board of Education, asserted that . . .**

> . . .

> *Tinker* **stands for the proposition that students in the public schools do not "shed their constitutional rights to freedom of speech or expression at the schoolhouse gate," 393 U.S. at 506. In** *Tinker,* **a teen-aged high school student and her middle school-aged brother wore black armbands . . .**

These paragraphs build up to a comparison of the facts and circumstances of the case under consideration, either to analogize a client's case to an earlier one, or to distinguish the client's case therefrom:

> **Granger's website could not be accessed from inside any of the class-rooms at Hogwarts High School. The derogatory remarks she made about the Advanced Placement program at Hogwarts and the teaching abilities of her AP course professors could not be viewed at any of the high school terminals or computer labs because the school's filtering software only allowed approved internet content to be displayed from educational sources and Wikipedia. Granger's speech never was broadcasted or displayed in school rooms. This contrasts Granger's situation from both** *Barnette* **and** *Tinker.* **In** *Barnette,* **the Jehovah's Witness student refused to stand up, place his hand out in salute, or recite the words of the pledge of allegiance. And in** *Tinker,* **the petitioners' black arm bands were visible wherever the two students went in their school buildings, and the display of the arm bands was preceded by considerable discussion of the fact that the reason the students were wearing the bands was to protest the Vietnam war. . . .**

Certainly, **analogical reasoning** (comparing/contrasting one case to another on the premise that if X was done in one case, X should be done in the other, similar case) is an important tool in your analytical toolbox. However, it is most effective in the Application section of your analysis (discussed later in this Chapter). Here, we are still talking about how to **explain** a legal rule.

There is nothing wrong with case-by-case reasoning; in fact, especially for watershed cases, you will want to make direct case-to-case comparisons. Indeed, explanatory synthesis and case-by-case presentations both are frequently used in in legal writing, often in the same discussion. Here is a section from a single federal appellate brief that uses both explanatory synthesis and case-by-case presentations in the same section of the brief:

> **The district court had no power to redefine the Greens' beliefs about their own participation in abortion into beliefs about "someone else's" participation in it. [Explanatory Synthesis:] It is settled that courts may not re-draw theological lines.** *See, e.g., Smith,* **494 U.S. at 887 ("[r]epeatedly . . . we have warned that courts must not presume to determine the place of a particular belief in a religion or the plausibility of a religious claim");** *United States v. Lee,* **455 U.S. 252, 256-57 (1982) ("[i]t is not within 'the judicial function and judicial competence' . . . to deter-**

mine whether appellee or the Government has the proper interpretation of the Amish faith"); *Thomas*, 450 U.S. at 715-16 (because Jehovah's Witness "drew a line" against participating in tank manufacturing, "it is not for us to say that the line he drew was an unreasonable one").

[Case-by-Case Presentation:] The Supreme Court's decision in *Thomas* is particularly instructive. There, a Jehovah's Witness lost his job and was denied unemployment benefits because his religious beliefs prohibited him "from participating in the production of war materials," such as tank turrets. *Thomas*, 450 U.S. at 709. He was willing to work in a department producing raw steel, because such work was "sufficiently insulated from producing weapons of war." *Id.* at 715. But he could not participate in fabricating tank turrets, because it would make him a "direct party" to war. *Id.* at 715. The lower court rejected his claim because he "was not able to 'articulate' his belief precisely," and because his beliefs seemed "inconsistent." *Id.* at 707-08, 715.

The Supreme Court reversed, concluding that the lower court was wrong "to dissect [his] religious beliefs." *Id.* Rather, if he believed that "work in the roll foundry [was] sufficiently insulated from producing weapons of war," the Court had to take him at his word. *Id.* As the Court put it, "Thomas drew a line, and it is not for us to say that the line he drew was an unreasonable one." *Id.*

Similar lines are drawn by the Greens' faith. They do not object to paying salaries to employees who may then buy abortifacient [abortion-causing] drugs. But offering those specific drugs in their health plan crosses a moral line. Doing so, the Greens believe, unacceptably entangles them and their business in abortion. JA 14a. *This* is the "exercise of religion" to which the district court should have applied this Circuit's substantial burden test, but it did not do so. Instead, the court acted as an "arbiter[] of scriptural interpretation," *Thomas*, 450 U.S. at 716, and adopted its own interpretation of the Greens' beliefs.

Other courts considering challenges to the Mandate have overwhelmingly rejected this kind of theological line-drawing. In *Korte*, the Seventh Circuit emphasized that "[t]he religious-liberty violation at issue here inheres in the *coerced coverage* of contraception, abortifacients, sterilization, and related services, *not*—or perhaps more precisely, *not only*—in the later purchase or use of contraception or related services." *Korte*, 2012 WL 6757353, at *3. Addressing another business' claim, the Seventh Circuit reiterated that [Explanatory Synthesis:] "the government's minimalist characterization of the burden continues to obscure the substance of the religious-liberty violation asserted." *Grote*, 2013 WL 362725 at *3l; *see also Tyndale*, 2012 WL 5817323, at *15 ("Because it is the coverage, not just the use, of the contraceptives at issue to which the plaintiffs object, it is irrelevant that the use of the contraceptives depends on the independent decisions of third parties."); *see also Legatus*, 2012 WL 5359630, at *6 (deferring to plaintiffs' assertion that Mandate "substantially burdens the observance of the tenets of Catholicism"); *Monaghan*, 2012 WL 6738476, at *4 (same); *Am. Pulverizer*, 2012 WL 6951316, at *4 (rejecting argument that "any causation between the [plaintiffs] and the use of the provided contraceptive services would be broken by the individual's own decision to use the contraceptive services" because "[w]hile the compulsion may be indirect, the infringement upon free exercise is nonetheless substantial") (citation omitted). [Explanatory Synthesis:] Indeed, four of the seven district court decisions which have erroneously redefined business plaintiffs' beliefs have been enjoined on appeal. *See Korte*, 2012 WL 6757353, at *3; *Grote*, 2013 WL 362725 at *3; *O'Brien II*, No. 12-3357 (8th Cir. Nov. 28, 2012); Order, *Annex Medical*, No. 13-1118 (8th Cir. Feb. 1, 2013); *but see* Order, *Conestoga*, No. 13-1144 (3d Cir. Feb. 7, 2013) (denying injunctive relief); Order, *Autocam*, No. 12-2673 (6th Cir. Dec. 28, 2012) (same).

Br. of Appellants, *Hobby Lobby Stores, Inc. v. Sebelius*, 2013 WL 656599 at 29-32 (10th Cir. Feb. 11, 2013) (bracketed designations supplied).

3. When to prefer one method over the other?

In many instances, explanatory synthesis achieves the author's purposes better than a case-by-presentation for two simple reasons:

(1) **Explanatory synthesis always makes its points by drawing from multiple authorities; case-by-case explanatory presentations only use one case at a time to make each point.**

(2) **Explanatory synthesis takes up less room—it is quicker to read a synthesis of 4-5 (or more) authorities than it is to read a minimum of 4-5 paragraphs of text in case-by-case analogical reasoning—so in combination with the above factor, you are making points using more authorities in less space and time.**

To illustrate, consider the case-by-case presentation evident in the following sequence of paragraphs (we have limited the details that the author could have continued on about):

In *Nelson*, a two-year old girl was playing crack-the-whip near a Dalmatian when she accidentally was thrown on top of the dog. Her actions were inadvertent and unintentional. The dog reacted by scratching the girl on her right eye. The dog did not bite the girl; however, the girl did suffer an injury to the tear duct of her eye . . . .

In *Siewerth*, two boys, age six and seven, were playing with a Collie dog on the seven-year old's front porch. The six-year old began hitting the dog on the head with a plastic toy truck. He persisted in hitting the dog on the head until the dog nipped him on the hand. The boy then started punching the dog in the dog's side with his two fists, and the dog reacted by biting the boy on the arm . . . .

In *Messa*, a five year boy accidentally pushed open the wrong door to an apartment on the same floor of the apartment building where he lived, and encountered a German Shepherd. At first the dog only barked at the boy while he tried to back away from the doorway, but after the boy started to run away, the dog pursued him down the hallway. The dog eventually caught up to the boy and . . . .

In *Beckert*, a postal carrier was going house to house delivering the mail. At Beckert's house, the mail carrier opened the outer, screen door to put the mail inside the door, when he found himself face to face with Beckert's Boxer dog. The mail carrier tried to back away from the dog, but the dog followed him. The mail carrier picked up his pace slightly, trying to get away from the dog, and the dog chased him to the sidewalk. The dog then bit the mail carrier on his leg . . . .

Each of these paragraphs might have gone on for several more lines with facts and details from each case. And, there may have been additional, relevant cases that the author wanted to write about. That discussion could have gone on for several pages, and we still would not have not gotten to the key point that that author wanted to make: that one or more of these cases are indicative of how the rule works in various situations that ultimately assist in predicting the outcome of the particular case under examination.

This is not just a point about length and wordiness. Rather, the upshot concerns the reader's reaction. If you take a leisurely stroll through a series of cases, piling on the details as you go, your reader will want to stop you in the hall and say, "But just tell me what the cases mean; how do they affect our outcome?"

Explanatory synthesis anticipates this reaction. It focuses on the **principles** that can be **induced** from the cases, and not on the entire, detailed stories of the cases themselves.

Now consider the following **synthesized explanation** of the same four cases mentioned above. Notice the principles that are extracted from the cases. Notice, too, how many words are used to make each point and how much space is used to draw out the facts and details of the cases and still make the points about how the rules should be interpreted and applied:

The age of the dog bite victim is not determinative of the dog owner's liability. *See Nelson*, **344 N.E.2d at 270 (denying recovery where two-year**

old provoked the dog); *Siewerth*, 231 N.E.2d at 647 (denying recovery where six-year old provoked the dog); *Messa*, 209 N.E.2d at 875 (determining that five-year old was entitled to recover in the absence of provocation); *Beckert*, 199 N.E.2d at 813 (determining that thirty-seven year old postal worker was entitled to recover in the absence of provocation). Even small children acting intentionally or unintentionally can provoke dogs into attacking and forfeit the chance to recover. *See Nelson*, 344 N.E.2d at 269 (finding provocation where two-year old girl unintentionally fell on dog); *Siewerth*, 231 N.E.2d at 647 (finding provocation where six-year old boy hit dog on head). Rather, the cases turn on whether the dog bite victim made hostile physical contact with the dog; those that did were held to have provoked the dog, while those that did not were held not to have provoked the dog. *See Siewerth*, 231 N.E.2d at 647 (finding provocation where victim repeatedly hit dog); *Messa*, 209 N.E.2d at 875 (finding no provocation where victim escaped dog and never touched dog); *Beckert*, 199 N.E.2d at 813 (same). The physical contact need not have been intentional; even accidental contact may give rise to a finding of provocation if sufficiently threatening to the dog. *See Nelson*, 344 N.E.2d at 270-71 (finding provocation where victim was thrown on top of dog).

Our point is not that specific cases are unimportant. To the contrary, notice how we incorporated in text the facts in constructing the principles (or themes) and, as well, in parenthetical information when certain details were especially illuminating.

Of course, there are circumstances where a case-by-case presentation may be superior, as in the situation where only one or two binding cases are relevant to the discussion. The point is to make a conscious decision about which method to use and why.

Use a **case-by-case presentation**:

(1) **When one or more cases is extremely important to the analysis, and you want to examine it in great detail so as to demonstrate how completely it should control your situation (or, alternatively, where you want to carefully distinguish a case to show why it does not control);**

(2) **When a primary or secondary authority is critically important to your analysis of the law or of your client's case, *and* it is too complicated to be reduced to a short phrase or a single sentence in a parenthetical.**

If one or two cases are stunningly similar to your client's case such that they dictate its outcome, then absolutely use the space necessary to explain these cases in depth.

Indeed, an in text discussion is prudent anytime you want to illustrate more fully those cases that are exactly on point. For example, if you are representing a toddler who was pushed into a dog that bit her, you will want to cover the *Nelson* case (above) in sufficient detail.

A general rule of thumb is that the more you plan to rely on a case to draw specific fact-to-fact comparisons or distinctions in your **A**pplication section, the more you likely will want to say about it in your **E**xplanation section. You will have set it up for purposes of **A**pplication, and you can discuss its facts in more detail as required when you get there. For example, if you are representing a postal carrier who opened a screen door and encountered a menacing dog, promptly hitting it on the head with her mail bag, you need to set up the *Beckert* case in a way that foreshadows the factual distinctions you presumably will draw later.

In many instances, however, you will not have a single case (positive or negative) that is exactly on point with your own. You may have a number of helpful cases that establish the legal landscape from which you can predict an outcome, and perhaps some that are not as helpful. In these situations, a synthesis of the authorities will aid the reader far more than a recitation of one case after another. If, instead, you write an unsynthesized explanation, you will not have presented sufficient guiding principles for the reader to determine how the rule really works.

For example, assume you are analyzing whether a burglary has occurred. One of the elements of burglary is "breaking and entering." If you found one case in which the court held that breaking a window counts, and you merely describe those factual circumstances, your explanation of that element will be deficient. It might lead the reader to believe that breaking always means breaking a window. This conclusion is logical, but inaccurate because it is incomplete; many more things count as "breaking."

Stated otherwise, the Explanation section should be much more than a laundry list of cases. It should tell a coherent story of how a rule is properly interpreted and applied. This section is as functional and practical as the rule section—readers learn the rule first, and are further educated about the rule's operation thereafter.

The lessons you illustrate in the **E**xplanation section are directly tied to the issues and sub-issues under analysis. A narrative of the progress of the law can be used to connect the lessons into a coherent statement of how the rules work:

> **The transformative test initially was used in artistic expression cases to measure whether the new work was altered in content and appearance sufficiently to overcome the remaining content and appearance of the original work. [Case 1]; [Case 2]; [Case 3]; [Case 4]; [Case 5]. Later, courts began to focus more on changes to the overall function and purpose of the works, such as changes brought by recontextualization of the work, [Case 6]; [Case 7]; [Case 8], or applications of the content of the work for completely new expressive functions and purposes. [Case 9]; [Case 10].**

If explanatory synthesis is used, the narrative of the law in these ten cases can be presented in an efficient amount of space and reader time.

Case-by-case presentations make the *reader* do most of the analytical work necessary to connect the dots among cases. Details from cases can be exciting, but *the facts themselves do not teach the reader how the rule actually works*. The Explanation section is there to present principles of interpretation that demonstrate to the reader how a rule or sub-rule has worked in prior situations. Accordingly, it should extract the lessons and connect the dots explicitly—it should do the *explaining* that the reader actually wants and needs. Case-by-case presentations eventually may get there, but the case-by-case method requires considerably more patience to complete these tasks.

FYI

What is the difference between showing and telling?
The Rule section tells the reader what the rules are that answer the issue. The Explanation section shows the reader how these rules work, basing its illustration on actual, concrete situations where the rule has worked to produce a fixed outcome. What is the difference between showing and telling? Consider this example:

Your father just bought a new German Shepherd puppy. Several of your father's buddies told him about a county ordinance that states, in its entirety, "All owners of dangerous dogs must register the dog and obtain a permit to keep the dog at the owner's residence in the county." Your father turns to you for advice. Does he need to register and obtain a permit for the puppy? You can tell your father the words of the statute and further tell him that other legal sources have said the following about the rule:

"Dangerous dogs present more than the average risk of injury to persons than ordinary dogs present." "Dangerous dogs are brutal and short-tempered." "Dangerous dogs have a propensity to cause injury beyond the normal propensity of common, domestic dogs."

All of these could be characterized as Interpretive Rules, and they may or may not give your father a better idea about how the rule is applied. But if you research and read all of the dangerous dog cases in the county and find that the dangerous dog cases have certain things in common, you can show your father how the rule works in a way that is far more useful:

The breed of dog matters greatly in dangerous dog cases. The only breeds that courts have found to be dangerous are: Pit Bull Terriers, Doberman Pinschers, and German Shepherds. Dangerous dogs typically are those who have been trained to fight and defend persons and property, as well as those who actually have attacked intruders perceived to threaten the same. No case involving a German Shepherd has found the dog to be dangerous unless it had been trained to guard persons and property and attack intruders; absent that special training, German Shepherds are not considered dangerous.

Your father would probably trust you based on that analysis alone, but a law-trained reader also wants you to cite the cases you used and write brief illustrations (in parentheticals) of how or why the cases support your interpretations. This is the process of explanatory synthesis: you read the cases as examples of situations where the rule produced a certain outcome, you carefully induce the truths from these examples about how the rule is supposed to be interpreted and applied, and you write up the results of this inductive reasoning with illustrations from the cases that concentrate on showing how the rules work—rather than simply summarizing the cases alone.

4. Explanation Sections and the "Deeper Analogy"

Think of **E**xplanation sections as your "value-added" to the rules.

It is where you digest the relevant authorities and derive from them one or more principles of interpretation for purposes of application. These principles are derived from common factual elements, policies, or themes found in the cases and other authorities that are relevant to the interpretation. Ideally, you should strive to identify a policy or theme underlying authorities and resonating with the definition of the applicable rule. As with the concept of the "deeper analogy" that we discussed in Chapter 2, a principle of interpretation derived from the central meaning, common ground, public policy, or theme behind a group of earlier cases where the rule was applied is probative of how the rule properly is to be interpreted and applied in cases going forward. Furthermore, when you apply this principle to the facts of your client's case in the Application section, the results will be more reliable than if you simply were to compare one at a time the earlier case to the facts of your own.

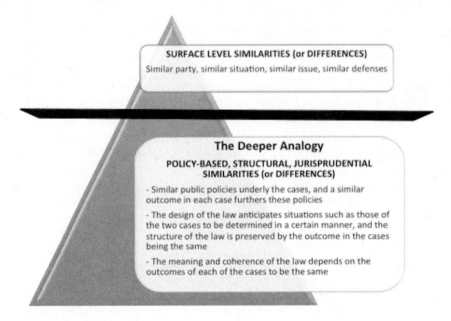

For example, if all the dog bite injury cases in your jurisdiction can be unified with the theme that "the law provides a remedy for injuries suffered when the victim is acting peaceably and the dog is not," then use this as your explanation of the rule, followed by references to examples of how this theme was played out in earlier authorities. (Note: no case may have said this precise phrase; rather, this is your synthesis (value-added) of the relevant authorities). This technique tells the reader how the rule has worked in your jurisdiction in the past, and how it should work again in the future. This is much more useful to the reader than simply writing a paragraph on each case, even if you conclude each paragraph with: "Once again, plaintiff recovered because the victim was acting peaceably, and the dog was not."

Hopefully, it is becoming clear that the goal of the **E**xplanation section is to demonstrate how the law works in relevant, indicative situations without making it appear that each case you cite or discuss is a law unto itself. A **case alone is not a rule**; it is an *example* of a situation where a rule was applied to produce a specific outcome. A line of precedent should not look like an obstacle course to get through before victory can be won.

The cases to use in the **E**xplanation section are those that are most indicative of how the courts have applied the rule to facts that are relevant to the case at hand. The questions to ask yourself when drafting this section are: "Does this case add something new to my explanation of the rule?" and "Will my explanation be weaker if the reader does not know about this case?" If the answer to both questions is "no," leave the case out.

When you explain how the rule works in the various situations represented by your cases, you should bring to the forefront the facts and circumstances that make the ***positive cases*** (decided in the same way as your prediction) sound more like your client's case than the ***negative cases*** (where the result goes the other way from what you predict). This technique is called ***analogizing*** to the positive cases and ***distinguishing*** the negative cases. It is a key technique to employ in the **A**pplication section. Synthesis aids this process because you can link together a number of positive authorities that stand for a proposition that supports your thesis, and you also can link together the negative authorities that do not support your thesis and show a common reason (facts, law, or policy) why each of them should not control the outcome of the instant case. If you do a good job of it, the reader is more likely to agree with you.

5. Comparing unsynthesized and synthesized explanation sections

The citation of multiple authorities, each of which is supported by an explanatory parenthetical, is the hallmark of a well-synthesized explanation. Where the individual facts of authorities you are using are important, **explanatory parentheticals** are the primary option that you can use to present them. In essence, your parentheticals should include the specific facts that you extracted to arrive at the more generalized principles that you present in text.

Consider, for example, our use of parentheticals several pages ago when we discussed the *Nelson, Siewerth, Messa*, and *Beckert* cases. In addition, consider using the ***"compare . . . and . . . with . . . and"*** format of citation to make the kind of connections you need to make to further reinforce how the rule works in various situations. For example:

Actions that might exclude others, such as fence building, do not determine whether a possession is exclusive. *Compare Witt*, 845 S.W.2d at 667 (claimant had fence), *with Conaway*, 972 S.W.2d at 445 (claimant had no fence), *and Grace*, 970 S.W.2d at 55 (same), *and Flowers*, 945 S.W.2d at 470 (claimant built fence, but owners removed it).

The following examples demonstrate the difference between an unsynthesized explanation section and a synthesized section.

Example 1:

One element of adverse possession is "exclusive possession" of the disputed land. Assume that you have already stated the rule for adverse possession, and now you are proceeding to address this particular element (sub-rule) of "exclusive possession," which is at issue in your case.

UNSYNTHESIZED EXPLANATION

In *Flowers*, the claimant cleared a road and cut down trees and used the land for his own purposes for ten years. He even built a fence, but the neighbors who owned the land pulled down the fence. The court held that the possession was exclusive anyway because the neighbors did not move back onto the land to use it after taking down the fence. *Flowers*, 979 S.W.2d at 470.

In *Conaway*, the claimant had no fence. He used the disputed land to build a shed and a horseshoe pit, and he put a little fountain on the land. He cut the grass and maintained the land and the improvement he had put on the land. His neighbor, who actually owned the land, came over and pitched horseshoes from time to time, and may have cut the grass once or twice in ten years, but these visits were sporadic. The claimant was the only one to make use of the land for ten years. The court held this to be exclusive. *Conaway*, 972 S.W.2d at 445.

In *Witt*, the claimant had a fence around the disputed land. Although the true owner of the land testified that he thought he could use the disputed land any time he wanted, the evidence revealed that the claimant was the only person who used the land. *Witt*, 845 S.W.2d at 667. Therefore, the claimant proved that his possession was "exclusive." *Id.*

Now consider how you could present the same information using a ***synthesized*** explanation section:

SYNTHESIZED EXPLANATION

Exclusive possession in Missouri refers to situations where the claimant is the exclusive user of the land rather than to situations where the claimant has taken action to exclude other people from coming on the land. *See Flowers*, 979 S.W.2d at 470 (finding exclusive possession where claimants were only ones to use land for ten year period); *Conaway*, 972 S.W.2d at 445 (finding that claimants were principal users of land because true owner only made sporadic visits); *Witt*, 845 S.W.2d at 667 (same). Exclusive is used as an adjective to mean that the claimant is the principal user, rather than as a verb meaning to exclude. *See generally Flowers*, 979 S.W.2d at 470 (plaintiff was principle user, even though defendant occasionally used the land); *Conaway*, 972 S.W.2d at 445 (same); *Witt*, 845 S.W.2d at 667 (same). Actions that might exclude others, such as fence building, do not determine whether a possession is exclusive. *Compare Witt*, 845 S.W.2d at 667 (claimant had fence), *with Flowers*, 979 S.W.2d at 470 (claimant built fence, but owners removed it), *and Conaway*, 972 S.W.2d at 445 (claimant had no fence). Total exclusion is not necessary, because the true owner can make sporadic visits to the land without defeating an adverse possession claim. *See Conaway*, 972 S.W.2d at 445 (sporadic visits by true owner to play horseshoes and cut grass did not defeat exclusive possession of claimant); *Flowers*, 979 S.W.2d at 470 (owners' tearing down of claimant's fence did not defeat exclusive possession because true owners did not take over parcel for own use).

The difference between the two methods is that in the unsynthesized explanation section the reader learns a lot of interesting details from the cases, but the section did not reach the underlying principles of interpretation that would help the reader apply this element to future situations. The focus of the unsynthesized explanation section is on the cases, not on the principles or themes of interpretation that the cases support. A devoted, law-trained reader may be able to ponder your history of the cases and draw her own conclusions about the categories of situations that will satisfy the rule, but most readers would prefer you to take the time to think this through and present a complete analysis of how this element of the rule works.

The synthesized explanation section, in contrast, focuses the reader's attention on the principles of interpretation and application that can be discerned from the cases. This section resembles a small scale treatise on this particular element of the adverse possession rule. Factual details are presented when they are necessary to draw connections between cases and to distinguish positive cases from negative ones. (In our example, we have used parentheticals to communicate factual details; however, *if a case is particularly relevant, you might include the same information in text and still produce a synthesized explanation.*) A law-trained reader that reads this section will not have to wonder about the categories of situations that satisfy this element of the rule. That's the point.

Example 2:

In Connecticut, the elements of money had and received are: (1) Receipt of money; (2) by mistake; (3) under circumstances that render the retention of the money unjust. Again, assume that you have already stated this rule and have focused attention on the third element, whether retention of the money was unjust:

UNSYNTHESIZED EXPLANATION

In *First Federal Bank*, defendant Stevens received an unexpected wire transfer from the plaintiff Bank. 678 N.E.2d at 237. The court granted summary judgment to Stevens, allowing him to retain the funds, because Stevens was entitled to the mistakenly transferred sum as an offset of a judgment he had obtained against the Bank in an earlier lawsuit. The court held that the prior debt gave just cause for Stevens to retain the funds. *Id.*

In *ATI*, 778 N.E.2d at 44-45, defendant Adams had a potential claim against ATI, but no action had been filed and no judgment entered. Through a fortuitous mistake, Adams received a wire transfer from ATI that was intended for Adams's replacement on a construction project. ATI immediately informed Adams of the mistake, but Adams refused to relinquish the funds. The court held that there was no justification for this retention. *Id.*

Blue Cross, 688 N.E.2d at 566-68, shows the effect of time and laches on the unjust enrichment evaluation. Defendant Carson was a regular beneficiary of payments from Blue Cross for medical expenses. The case arose from a mistaken quarterly payment by Blue Cross of three *years* of benefits to Carson instead of three months. Blue Cross did not notice the mistake until a year later; by then, Carson had spent the money on his medical care and nursing home expenses. The court refused to order Carson to reimburse Blue Cross, because Carson had a valid expectation of indefinite quarterly payments from Blue Cross, and had changed his position drastically in reliance on his good faith belief that he was entitled to whatever payments he received from Blue Cross, no matter if they may have been larger or smaller than the average quarterly payment.

A **synthesized** approach to this explanation section might look like the following:

SYNTHESIZED EXPLANATION

Connecticut case law has demonstrated the importance of a present obligation from the transferor to the transferee in determining whether the transferee's retention of the funds is unjust. *See First Federal Bank*, 678 N.E.2d at 237 (finding no unjust enrichment where transferor had present obligation); *Blue Cross*, 688 N.E.2d at 566-68 (same); *ATI*, 778 N.E.2d at 44-45 (finding unjust enrichment where transferor had no present obligation). If there is an outstanding debt due between the transferor and the transferee, the fact that the transferor did not intend to pay the debt at the time of the transfer does not prevent the transferee from justly retaining the funds it fortuitously received. *See First Federal Bank*, 678 N.E.2d at 237; *ATI*, 778 N.E.2d at 44-45. Even if the funds were not all due at the time of transfer, the expectation of receipt of funds through an existing account or payment scheme can render the retention just. *See Blue Cross*, 688 N.E.2d at 566-67 (finding of unjust enrichment was buttressed by transferor's laches).

As in Example 1, the unsynthesized explanation section above focuses on the cases themselves, while the synthesized explanation section focuses on the principles of interpretation and application that can be derived from the cases.

You may notice that many of the individual facts from the cases are left out of the synthesized explanation section. Facts such as the horseshoe pit and shed in one adverse possession case and the wire transfers in two of the money had and received cases are only relevant if they tell the reader something about how the rule properly is applied and how the facts affected the outcome produced by the application. Because these facts did not affect the application of the rule and the outcome of this application, they were omitted from the synthesized account entirely. The facts about fences in the three adverse possession cases and the facts about debts and current obligations in the three money had and received cases were relevant to an understanding of how the rule works, so these facts were included in parentheticals in the synthesized version. Arguably, that information could have been included in the text, and that may be a valid choice when your own facts are particularly analogous to (or distinguishable from) the factual scenarios raised in the cases.

A synthesized method is shorter in terms of using up fewer pages of your page limit than the unsynthesized method. But this result is only one reason to use explanatory synthesis, not the best reason. It is not just a time and space-saving device; it makes the reader's comprehension of the situation clearer and your analysis and conclusions stronger.

Explanatory synthesis also has a positive effect on the Application section, discussed in section IV, below. If the facts and policies of the cases are synthesized in this way, it makes it easier to compare the client's situation to the category of prior situations that satisfy the rule defined by the authorities. Instead of writing an Application section that says,

> **"As in *Flowers*, our claimant had a partial fence . . . . Unlike in *Witt*, the fence did not go all the way around the disputed parcel; rather . . . ."**

which make it seem like the cases are the rule, rather than the cases standing as individual examples of situations where the rule was applied to produce a certain outcome. Your application section instead might state that,

> **"Claimant and her predecessor in interest were the only persons to use the disputed parcel for fourteen years. Therefore, they will satisfy the exclusive possession requirement."**

Similarly, using the above example on money had and received, it would be easy to write an Application section that states,

> **"In the instant case, there was no outstanding debt or payment scheme to justify the defendant's retention of the funds . . . "**

and, thus, to apply the rule to the client's facts in a short, straightforward manner.

What you are doing in the process of explanatory synthesis is setting up your Application section so that you can apply the principles induced from the cases and to the client's facts, and not applying cases—thus, you avoid perpetuating the myth that cases are rules unto themselves instead of the truth that cases are simply examples of situations where the actual rules applied to produce a concrete outcome.

The cases that you might actually cite or discuss in more detail in the Application section should be ones that are so close to your client's facts that your time spent doing fact-to-fact comparisons is justified.

For a simple fact pattern, you may not have cases of this nature to discuss and, thus, you will not need to cite to any cases in the Application section. However, the more complicated the case under investigation, the more likely that you will have to invoke more specific details in Application (and thus need to cite).

PRACTICE POINTER

Increasing the n of your samples

Scientists and statisticians especially may appreciate this. One huge advantage to explanatory synthesis over other forms of explanation is that you are able to drastically increase the n (the number) of your examples—cases—when you are inducing principles of interpretation and application from the sample group.

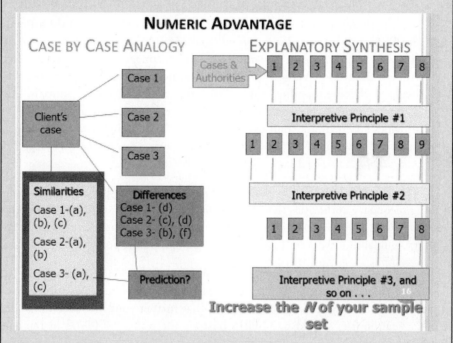

Case-by-case presentations test the patience of your readers such that it is inadvisable to present more than three or four cases in any given Explanation section. That is a very small statistical sample, especially when you consider that an established rule of law may have been applied in scores of cases, all of which are available to you in the sample pool.

Explanatory synthesis is very economical—both in its use of words to state a principle as well as in its use of parentheticals to provide illustrative detail. As a result, you can increase the number of cases from which you derive your principles of interpretation and application. Increasing the number of your examples makes your principles more reliable and persuasive because they are supported by a larger number of authorities.

C. Use of secondary authorities in the Explanation section

The Explanation section also might include discussion of secondary authorities—scholarly works that interpret or explain the law. These authorities cannot control the outcome of your case, but they may persuade the reader that you are on the right track with your thesis. In other words, secondary authorities can be used as support for a principle that you derive from the cases. If you are joined by one or more scholars in drawing the conclusion that there is a relevant underlying theme that ties together most if not all of the prior cases, then reference to the work of these scholars will make your explanation section more persuasive.

An example of the use of secondary sources to explain a rule is demonstrated in the following paragraph:

> The underlying public policy behind the Texas rule is that persons "attacked by a domesticated animal when the person is acting peaceably and not directly threatening the animal" shall recover from the owner of the animals. *See* Chester A. Arthur, *Texas Animal Laws* 234 (1953). Although Professor Arthur was referring to the Roaming Livestock Damage Act, Tex. Agric. Code Ann. § 222.1234 (Vernon 1944), there is no practical difference between livestock that are roaming loose on the property and domestic animals, such as dogs, that are encountered on the property. *See* Arthur at 235. The law provides a remedy for injuries suffered when "the victim is acting peaceably and the dog is not." Mary M. McDermott, *When a Best Friend Bites: Dog Bite Liability in Texas*, 45 Tex. L. Rev. 122-23 (1979).

This paragraph discusses policies that support your thesis. We made a point of using secondary authorities that discuss these policies (rather than just spinning them out of our own minds). It is important to support *every* statement about the law by referring to authority, even if you are talking about public policy.

Given the priority of primary controlling authority in legal analysis, you should discuss the cases from the applicable jurisdiction in your explanation section before you present any secondary authorities that further your interpretations. The secondary authorities should be used to buttress the principles found in the controlling case law, not to supersede them.

V.   APPLICATION SECTION

The **Application section** is critical. It is where you apply the rule to your client's facts and show how the rule will work in that situation. If you are writing an informative, objective work such as an office memorandum, you will explain how you think the client will fare based on your analysis of the law. If you are writing a persuasive piece of advocacy, you will use this opportunity to argue exactly why your client wins when the law is applied to the facts (and the other side loses).

In the Application section, you must make or reject the connection between your client's situation and the situations in the authorities you are relying on in support of your thesis. This section presents the second half of the logical reasoning process that you began in the Explanation; it takes the general principles derived from cases and applies them to a new set of facts. Thus, it connects the fruits of inductive reasoning back to the deductive, rule-based reasoning paradigm. The Application section also continues the process of analogical reasoning: when you have identified one or more cases that are close enough to the client's facts that you must spend some time analogizing to or distinguishing them

If your Explanation section was dominated by a case-by-case presentation, then your application section most likely will look like this:

Application Section Following Case-by-Case Presentation

In the instant case, there is no dispute that the defendant's dog attacked and caused injury to Mrs. Robinson, his neighbor, when she walked out of her apartment and bumped into the dog with her shopping bag. Thus, the first two elements of this cause of action are established. In reference to the third element, lack of provocation, Mrs. Robinson did nothing to present a serious threat to the dog, let alone strike the dog, in contrast to the plaintiff in *Smithy*. Mrs. Robinson may have swung her shopping bag near the dog in a careless manner, but this is a far cry from the beating that the dog in *Smithy* received before it attacked the victim in that case. Like the plaintiff in *Johnson*, Mrs. Robinson was using a public hallway that led to the front door of the apartment building. *See Johnson*, 789 S.W.2d at 237. According to *Johnson*, walking in a hallway is not a provocative action, *id.*, and it certainly is no more provocative than mistakenly opening the wrong door of an apartment where the dog is found, as was the case in *Russell*. *See* 797 S.W.2d at 44.

Although the postman in *Johnson* was acting in the ordinary course of his daily employment duties, whereas Mrs. Robinson was doing something outside of her ordinary employment activities, this should not be viewed as a legally significant difference that precludes recovery. A decision in favor of Mrs. Robinson, moreover, furthers the policy of allowing recovery where the victim was acting peaceably and the dog was not. *See Merriweather*, 90 Apex L. Rev. at 666.

Is this the most effective Application section the author could write? It might well be, especially if there are only a few cases on point, and all of those cases were important to the analysis and prediction of the outcome.

If, however, there were many cases that were on point, and you used *explanatory synthesis* to combine authorities in the Explanation section so as to draw out important *principles* about how the rules ought to be interpreted and applied, then the Application is free to apply the principles of interpretation derived from the common facts or themes of the earlier cases. This method stands in stark contrast to a one-by-one comparison of the facts of the instant case to each earlier case in a series. Instead, you can actually complete your *analysis*. (Think of the **A** as standing for analysis as much as for **a**pplication). You will explain how the common, underlying theme articulated in your **E**xplanation is furthered by your interpretation of how that rule applies your case. Or, in contrast, you will distinguish the earlier cases because of common facts or policies that are not present in the instant case.

Consider the following modified application section that follows a **synthesized** explanation section:

Application Section following a Synthesized Explanation Section

Here, there is no dispute that defendant's dog attacked and caused injury to Mrs. Robinson, his neighbor, when she walked out of her apartment and bumped into the dog with her shopping bag. Thus, the first two elements of this cause of action are established. As for the third element, lack of provocation, case law in Texas suggests that a plaintiff who is peaceably going about her business and is attacked by an aggressive dog will recover, while a plaintiff who picked a fight with the dog and caused injury to the dog first will not recover. Mrs. Robinson did not pick a fight with defendant's dog. She did nothing to present a serious threat to the dog, let alone intentionally strike the dog. Mrs. Robinson may have been careless in swinging her shopping bag near the dog, but that does not rise to the level necessary to constitute provocation. A decision in favor of Mrs. Robinson, moreover, furthers the policy of allowing recovery where the victim was acting peaceably and the dog was not.

This synthesis and application of synthesized principles only works if it is fair to link all of the prior cases together under the theme of "a plaintiff recovers when the plaintiff was acting peaceably and the dog was not." *You cannot invent a common theme that is not present in the earlier cases, nor can you assume common facts that are not discussed.* However, if you can discern a common set of facts and theme or policy that is important to the understanding of how the rule should work, it is enormously useful to your reader to point it out.

A very important point of consideration. The example above does not cite cases. It absolutely could. You might use the "*Compare . . . with . . .* " signal after the third sentence (beginning "As for the third element") and input two cases that are emblematic of the stated parameters. As well, you might include a "*See, e.g.,*" signal after the last sentence regarding policy.

In other words, do not assume that a strong **A**pplication section should not refer to specific cases. Our example above must be considered in light of the stated premise that there were a *multitude* of Texas cases that could be linked together to formulate a cohesive, thematic thread and the further presumption that the **E**xplanation section appropriately synthesized and cited these cases beforehand. Note, too, that this is a relatively simplistic example used to make a point—whereas you typically will be dealing with more complicated legal scenarios.

Indeed, most **Application** sections will require you to use analogical and converse-analogical reasoning that compare and contrast your case to earlier ones on specific, legally significant facts. Accordingly, you more often than not will refer (and cite) to cases in **Application**, as demonstrated below.

Application Section using Analogical and Converse Analogical Reasoning

Johnson and *Beckert* are the two leading cases in Texas addressing dog bites suffered by mail carriers. [Plaintiff] Newman's case is most comparable to *Beckert*, where the mail carrier opened the outer screen door of the dog owner's home and encountered the dog. The dog gave chase and bit the mail carrier while he was trying to escape. Similarly, here, Newman opened the outer storm door of the home to place the parcel inside, protected from the rain. Thereafter, [Defendant] Wiley's dog chased Newman from the front steps of the house to the sidewalk. While Newman was attempting to evade the dog, it bit her on the leg. As in *Beckert*, where the mail carrier stood frozen in fear on the doorstep, Newman did not provoke the dog in any way and, thus, should be able to recover for her injury. *See* 199 N.E.2d at 815. *Johnson*, however, is distinguishable. There, the mail carrier initially used her mailbag as a shield, but then promptly employed it as a weapon with which to hit the dog four times on the head. Still, the dog was not deterred and bit the mail carrier in response. In *Johnson*, the plaintiff mail carrier was denied recovery specifically because he initiated the physical attack, and only thereafter did the dog bite. *See* 789 S.W.2d at 237 (determining that initiating aggressive contact with a dog constitutes provocation). Because Newman did not make any contact with the dog, unwelcome or otherwise, before the bite, she should recover from Wiley for the injuries inflicted.

A few take-away points are worth emphasizing. First, while referencing or citing cases in the application section is acceptable whenever it is necessary or prudent to do so, it sometimes may be ***unnecessary***. If you have presented a cohesive, synthesized **Explanation** on one or more points, you may find opportunities to narrate your **Application** section (or some part of it) in a manner divorced from any specific case but, rather, tailored to the thematic threads established beforehand. In such instances, it is really the extracted principles that should be applied to the client's facts, not the individual cases from which those principles were induced.

Second, it may be unnecessary to re-cite cases that are **Explained** in close proximity to the **Application** section. Even if you invoke the case names in the text of the **Application** section, you may not need to re-cite to them if their details were discussed in text and/or in parentheticals in the paragraph immediately preceding your **Application**.

Third, if you are engaging in direct case-to-case or fact-to-fact comparisons (analogical and converse-analogical reasoning), then it is always best to refer and cite to specific cases. Analogical reasoning is a useful tool especially when you have a more limited number of cases that are close enough to the client's facts to warrant special attention. In addition, if you want to draw your reader's attention to a specific legal authority that supports your thesis, then you should cite to it, whether or not you refer to the authority in the text of your analysis.

Finally, there is some leeway here for professorial (or supervisory) preferences. If your professor or supervisor prefers that you include a citation for every point that you make, then do that. We do not believe that doing so is necessary, but legal writing is an audience-driven endeavor.

One More Example

Before we move on to the last topic of this Chapter, let's look at one more example of an excellent synthesis and application. This example was written by a first-year law student and received a very high score. It is not perfect—for example, in many assignments we would expect students to use and write syntheses with more than three cases—but it achieves everything we have been talking about so far.

The question was whether a particular invasion—involving recordings of workplace activities—was sufficiently "offensive" so as to trigger the California tort of "invasion upon seclusion." What follows here is, first, a great example of explanatory synthesis for this problem and, second, a very sophisticated application section that relies on case-to-case analogical comparisons that are appropriate in light of the small number of relevant cases (three), as discussed above.

EXAMPLE OF EXCELLENT SYNTHESIS:

The setting and degree of invasion are likely to establish offensiveness in Ms. Jefferson's case. The setting and degree of invasion constitute the first of the two most significant elements when determining offensiveness. Intrusions that invade settings the community holds as private or where intimate activities do, or can, take place are regarded as highly offensive. *See Miller v. Tiller*, 187 Cal. App. 3d 1489, 1491 (1982) (finding intrusion into bedroom highly offensive). It is not necessary that the setting be completely sealed from the outside world to render the intrusion "highly offensive," so long as there is a social expectation of limited privacy. *See Sanders v. Am. Broad. Co.*, 20 Cal. 4th 907, 916-17 (Cal. 1999) (reasoning that privacy extends beyond total control of space to include nonpublic zones in public areas, such as office cubicle); *See also Trujillo v. City of Ontario*, 428 F. Supp. 2d 1094, 1105-06 (C.D. Cal. 2006) (determining access by other persons does not necessarily negate offensiveness). The intrudee's efforts to preserve privacy within a nonpublic area can contribute to the offensiveness of an intrusion. *See Sanders*, 20 Cal. 4th, 913 (finding offense where personal topics were recorded in an office cubicle thought to be private). Courts have evaluated offensiveness by the degree of invasion, which takes into account the extent the intrusion can be seen or foreseen. The degree of invasion is intensified by the hidden nature or unforsee-ability of the intrusion. *Compare Sanders*, 20 Cal. 4th, 921 (highlighting offensive nature of hidden and un-anticipatory video intrusion), *with Wilkins v. Nat'l Broad. Co.*, 71 Cal. App. 4th 1066, 1079 (1999) (finding no offense where persons recorded were filmed in crowded, public restaurant).

EXAMPLE OF AN EXCELLENT APPLICATION:

A California court faced with Ms. Jefferson's case will find offense when examined through the context of setting and degree for three reasons: the office cubicle is a socially-held space of limited privacy, Ms. Jefferson took precautions to preserve the privacy of the space, and the hidden and electronic nature of the intrusion makes it unforeseeable. In Ms. Jefferson's case, the intrusion occurred in her office cubicle, which is a nonpublic space. As expressed in *Sanders* and *Trujillo*, there are inherent expectations of privacy endemic to certain "nonpublic" public areas. Society safeguards certain areas predicated upon the assumption that the personal, as well as human dignity, are injured by intrusion into these spaces. *Trujillo*, 428 F. Supp. 2d, 1123. As in *Sanders*, where a non-enclosed office cubicle was deemed one of these spaces of limited privacy in a public area, 20 Cal. 4th, 918-20, here the intrusion occurred in Ms. Jefferson's office cubicle. In Ms. Jefferson's case, offense is further strengthened because her office cubicle is enclosed on all four sides (two sides by permanent walls, two sides by retractable walls). The retractable walls by no means provide any less privacy than permanent ones. The two eight-foot, retractable walls nearly touch the ten-foot ceiling and require great difficulty and strength to move. Ms. Jefferson's office resembles a private suite more than the traditional cubicle. Moreover, in *Sanders*, where court found offense in an office cubicle arranged in a row of many, here Ms. Jefferson's office was secluded in a corner far removed from other persons' working areas. As in *Trujillo*, where other persons and officers besides the plaintiffs had access to the locker room, here a limited number of Ms. Jefferson's co-workers have access to the room in which her office is located. *Trujillo*, 428 F. Supp. 2d, 1100-01. Only six other persons had keys to Ms. Jefferson's office. Unlike in *Wilkins*, where the court found no offense in an intrusion that occurred in a public restaurant, 71 Cal. App. 4th at 1079, here Ms. Jefferson was in a nonpublic place with no other persons around to see her. Also, Ms. Jefferson was in a fully enclosed office that no one could see into. There is history that Ms. Jefferson developed an expectation of privacy that was more similar to someone in the home than in a public restaurant. A California court will note the locational differences between *Wilkins* and Ms. Jefferson's case and find that she had a reasonable expectation of privacy in her office setting.

VI. THESIS RESTATED AS A CONCLUSION

As a general matter, you should complete your discussion of an issue by restating your thesis as a conclusion. This is not the most critical part of the discussion, but we find that it makes a difference to the reader to have that one sentence at the end that brings closure to the issue under discussion.

The conclusion you make can be one sentence, and it can come at the very end of the last paragraph of your **A**pplication section. As an example, the thesis-as-conclusion line of the dog bite example we were working with above with might be as follows:

> **Therefore, defendant Wiley will be required to compensate Newman for her dog bite injuries in this case.**

The thesis-restated-as-conclusion is *not* a throwaway line and should not thought of as such. It may be a single sentence, simply there to note that the section in question is completed. Sometimes it is not necessary at all. If your analysis is either simple enough such that the outcome has already been captured, OR if it is so complex that you have concluded each subsection with mini-conclusions along the way, then a final Thesis may not be necessary—but only because including one would be superfluous.

The point here is that you should conclude each application of your rules and sub-rules with an actual and definitive conclusion. That conclusion may come in separate pieces (by each element, for example), or it may come as a conclusion of the whole. But is should come *somewhere*.

Finally, you should consider using a conclusion sentence (or whole section) to advance your argument one more step, or to make a smooth transition to the next topic. This one is up to you, and you are limited only by your own creativity.

VII. IDENTIFYING MULTIPLE ISSUES FOR T-R-E-A-T-ment

So far in this Chapter, we have been discussing the organization of an individual issue in a client's case. The structure is called **TREAT**, so we have introduced the word, **"TREATment,"** to refer to the act of organizing the discussion of a single legal issue. Some problems do present a single legal question to be answered, leading to a single TREATment of that issue. But it is more often the case that a single issue leads to multiple questions to be answered, each one deserving of its own TREATment.

The dog bite example with which we have been working boiled down to one question: whether the plaintiff provoked the dog. We mentioned in the **R**ule and **A**pplication sections the other elements of dog bite liability, but only so far as to point out that they are not in dispute. If that is the case, then there is no need to have a separate discussion of each element. Yet, we did not ignore them, because you should always plan to cover (*i.e.*, mention) in your written analysis of an issue each required element or factor of the rule that applies. A single sentence may be all that an *undisputed* element requires.

In practice, a single-issue scenario is atypical. More often than not, you will have multiple issues to write about. A client or supervisor will come into your office with a problem, and you will have to identify exactly what issues are implicated by the facts of the situation as you know them. Each problem that reaches your desk likely will raise more than one issue, and each issue will have at least one rule that applies to it. In addition, each rule often will have multiple elements or factors, each of which can present other sub-issues for discussion. An element or factor of a rule can have a sub-rule that has elements or factors, some of which will require separate treatment. It can get fairly complicated quickly, but the TREAT format is flexible enough to accommodate complexity.

To determine the number of issues you have to treat (or "TREAT"), consider the following:

A. What are the separate legal questions you have to answer?

As noted, most client problems will present more than one legal question to answer. If the client literally asks two questions, or one question that involves the discussion of two unrelated legal issues—such as what separate causes of action might the plaintiff bring against the client based on the facts—then each question will constitute a major issue in your discussion. In an outline, the answers (your theses, or conclusions) to these questions will appear as the major headings. In other words, you should plan to state a thesis on each major issue (or element) as a heading of the discussion on that issue.

Client question: Is it too late to file a negligence action in New Mexico to recover for my injury in July 2012?

Analysis: One issue, one rule, one element that applies to the question, means one TREAT

I. Murphy's negligence action arising from her injury in July 2012 is not time barred in New Mexico.

The statute of limitations for a tort in New Mexico is governed by N.M. Stat. § 23-45-8 (2005), which states: "The following causes of action have a five year limitations period: . . . all actions of . . . tort . . . ."

Client was involved in an automobile accident from which her cause of action for negligence arose. Client's negligence action is a tort action that will be governed by New Mexico's five-year statute of limitations for tort actions. Her action arises from an injury in July 2012, and will not be time-barred until July 2017.

In the single question mentioned above on dog bite liability, the major issue was: "Is the dog owner liable for Client's injuries?" We translated this into the thesis heading: "The dog owner will be liable for Client's dog bite injuries because Client did not provoke the dog." If there were two or more possible claims that your client might bring against the dog owner, your writing would have two or more major issues and major theses on these issues. For example,

I.   **The dog owner will be liable to Client under common law dog bite liability standards because the Client did not provoke the dog.**

       [T-R-E-A-T of the issue raised in Roman numeral I]

II.   **The dog owner will be liable to Client under a theory of negligence because the owner had a duty of care to keep Client, an invitee, from harm, and owner breached this duty, causing harm to Client.**

       [T-R-E-A-T of the issue raised in Roman numeral II]

III. **The dog owner will not be strictly liable to Client under the Nevada Pit Bull Control Law because the owner followed the procedures to achieve the "Rescue Dog" exemption from the coverage of the law.**

       [T-R-E-A-T of the issue raised in Roman numeral III]

Each major issue must be handled in a separate TREAT discussion. (See below for a usable, structural example.)

B. Which elements or factors of the rules and sub-rules are at issue?

Often a question leads you to a rule comprised of separate elements, and each of the elements poses a new legal question to be answered. A separate "TREAT" discussion is necessary to address each legal question (issue or sub-issue). This means that each part of the problem—each legal question raised or element in dispute—is really its *own* issue for purposes of the paradigm.

If the rule that governs the issue at hand has one basic requirement, and thus one element, it may be handled in a single discussion of Thesis, Rule, Explanation, Application and Thesis-as-conclusion. Similarly, if the rule has multiple elements or factors, but only one is in dispute, you also may discuss the entire rule in one TREAT discussion, as in our dog bite example above. **But, it is much more likely that the rule in question will present multiple sub-questions.** It thus may require more than one TREAT discussion. For present purposes, where the separate legal questions that must be answered are based on elements or sub-parts of a **single rule**, we will refer to your analysis as a **"sub-TREAT."** This nuance becomes important when you consider how to organize your thoughts and research in writing. The terminology is also important for interpreting the structural TREAT "diagrams" included on the last two pages of this Chapter.

For example, if there was a serious question whether the defendant "owned" the Doberman Pinscher within the meaning of the law— maybe it was a stray that the defendant was feeding each day—then you would have to include some analysis of the ownership element of the overall tort in addition to addressing whether the plaintiff provoked the dog.

I. STARNES IS LIABLE FOR DOG BITE LIABILITY BECAUSE HE OWNED THE DOG THAT INJURED BARNES, AND BARNES DID NOT PROVOKE THE DOG.

In Texas, a defendant is liable for a dog bite injury when (1) the defendant owns or harbors a dog; (2) the dog causes an injury to the plaintiff; and (3) the plaintiff did not provoke the dog. *Hobson v. Lovell*, 787 S.W.2d 23, 25 (Tex. 2006).

In this case, there is no dispute that the dog caused injury to Barnes. This memorandum is limited to the remaining elements: ownership and provocation.

A.   Starnes owned the dog because he fed the dog every day and provided a place for the dog to sleep in his barn.

Ownership of a dog under Texas common law means having some control and . . .

Therefore, by his feeding of the dog over the course of several weeks, and providing a place for the dog to reside, Starnes will be found to have "owned" the dog.

B.   Barnes did not provoke the dog within the meaning of the law because he was an invitee on the Starnes property and did not hit or menace the dog, and instead tried to flee from the dog.

Provocation of a dog requires physical contact with the dog. *Chewtoy v. Cujo*, 887 S.W.2d 34, 37 (Tex. App. 2012). An invitee's presence on property, even property patrolled by a guard dog . . . .

Therefore, Barnes did not provoke the dog into attacking.

In light of Starnes' ownership of the dog that caused injury to Barnes, and the fact that Barnes did not provoke the dog, Starnes will be liable to Barnes for dog bite liability.

Two of the three elements of dog bite liability require discussion; the third (causation) is assumed. Two sub-TREATs—one for each element in dispute—are present (under headings A and B). To focus your attention on structure, we largely excerpted what would have been the content for each of these TREATs in the example above.

That content would contain the following:

Contents of Sub-T-R-E-A-Ts in Example Above

The **Rules** that address ownership (in section A) and provocation (in section B); an **Explanation** of what the rules on ownership mean (in section A) and an **Explanation** of what it means to provoke a dog under the provocation rules (in section B); and an **Application** of the ownership rules to

Starnes' situation (in section A), and an **Application** of the provocation rules to Barnes' actions (in section B), followed by the **Thesis restated as a conclusion** for each of the underlying issues raised by the rule on the main issue. (Note, too, that in the example, the author returned to restate the thesis on the main issue at the very end of the discussion).

The point **is that you must cover every disputed element or factor of a rule in your discussion**. That said, if the element or factor is established without question in your case—either because the person assigning the project tells you to assume it, or because your opponent specifically admits it—that element or factor does not require a full-blown TREAT analysis. One sentence (which we call a ***roadmap sentence***) can convey the required information: for example, you might simply state in conjunction with the rule itself that:

> **"Defendant concedes that he is the owner of the dog that injured the plaintiff and, thus, this element is not in dispute."**

When multiple elements of a rule are in dispute and present separate issues for sub-TREATment, you should consider how you want to present your analysis. Consider which elements are the most important to your analysis. The typical wisdom is to discuss the most important elements first, even if they do not appear first in a court's articulation of the rule. This advice is almost uncontroverted in persuasive writing. In predictive writing, there is more room for debate. Some professors or supervisors may tell you to proceed in the order that the rule presents—in which case, go with that.

For present purposes, we are grouping issues under the main rules that spawned them, meaning that we are attempting to get you to think about each specific question you need to address, whether it is a main legal issue (such as "dog bite liability") or a sub-issue (such as "lack of provocation"). **Each of these matters will necessitate a separate "TREAT" analysis**—in the one case, a main TREAT and in the other a sub-TREAT.

The following two "diagrams" may help you picture how the Discussion section of a full memorandum ultimately will be structured.

DISCUSSION

I.   THESIS on Major Legal Issue I

      RULE on Major Legal Issue I has two elements: A, B

      [E/A broken down by elements as follows:]

   A.   SUB-THESIS on Element A of the rule on Major Issue I
         SUB-RULE on Element A
         EXPLANATION of sub-rule for Element A
         APPLICATION of sub-rule for Element A
         THESIS RESTATED as Conclusion on sub-rule for Element A

   B.   SUB-THESIS on Element B of the rule on the Major Issue
         SUB-RULE on Element B: B has Elements 1, 2, 3

      1.   SUB-SUB-THESIS on Element 1 of sub-rule on Element B
            SUB-SUB-RULE on Element 1 of sub-rule on Element B
            EXPLANATION of sub-sub-rule for Element 1 of sub-rule
              for Element B
            APPLICATION of sub-sub-rule for Element 1 of sub-rule
              for Element B
            THESIS RESTATED as Concl. of sub-sub-rule for Element 1
              of sub-rule for Element B

      2.   [same structure for element 2]

      3.   [same structure for element 3]

      THESIS restated as Conclusion on Major Issue I

II.   THESIS on Major Legal Issue II

      RULE on Major Legal Issue II has three elements: A, B, C

                              Etc., etc.

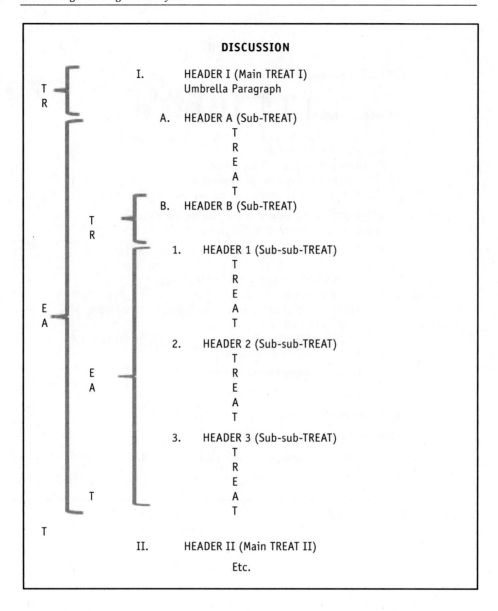

Chapter 7

The Office Memorandum
and the Client Letter

With this Chapter, you are stepping into law practice. In Chapters 4 and 5, we covered the fundamentals of legal analysis through interpretation of single and multiple authorities, respectively. In Chapter 6, we covered how to transform your legal analysis into writing, in a form and style that is acceptable for law practice. Now we are going to cover how to create actual, substantive legal documents used in the practice of law. This Chapter examines the two most common forms of objective (or predictive) legal documents: **office memoranda** and **client letters**.

The **office memorandum** reports your research, analysis, and conclusions about a client problem. The report is made to a law-trained reader, often another lawyer in your own law office, which often means you will be writing to a more senior attorney or your boss or supervisor. The memorandum might make predictions about what will happen in the client's case, or recommendations about how the client or the attorneys on the case should proceed.

FUNCTIONS OF THE OFFICE MEMORANDUM

An office memorandum has three main functions to:

(1) **Report the research, analysis, conclusions, predictions, or recommendations of the author in a form designed for law-trained readers;**
(2) **Memorialize and preserve the research for future use by other attorneys on the case or future attorneys in the law office taking on a similar case with similar issues;**
(3) **Provide a means for the author to make sense of the case through the recursive process of writing.**

Clients sometimes read office memoranda—they pay for them, and often want to see what they paid for—but the client rarely is the primary, intended audience for a true office memorandum. Rather, the same function of reporting research and conclusions often is accomplished by a separate document, a **client letter**. As suggested, the client letter is written for a lay person, not a lawyer. You should always write with your specific audience in mind, including the level of sophistication of your client. If you are certain that the only audience of your work will consist of law-trained readers—for example, in-house counsel—then you can draft the client letter like an office memorandum. But a classic client letter is one that will be read by non-law-trained readers.

FUNCTIONS OF THE CLIENT LETTER

The client letter will report research and analysis, but primarily the client letter is created for two functions to:

    (1) **Communicate the findings and recommendations of the attorney to the client;**

    (2) **Memorialize the legal advice rendered to the client.**

With an office memorandum, the facts and problems of the client about whom you are writing often will be relayed second hand; thus, you will have a static set of facts to work with as you research and draft the memo. One additional benefit of the office memorandum is that it records and reports the facts known and taken into consideration at a certain point in time, which is particularly useful for future attorneys who will read a memorandum with no other information or background on the matter. It also assists the supervisor and other attorneys by revealing what the author determined to be the most important facts of the matter.

I.   FOCUSING ON THE READER OF THE OFFICE MEMO

By definition, an office memo will be read by someone in your law office (or other place of business). Your reader most likely will be a law-trained reader, and so you can presume familiarity with basic legal concepts. However, your reader may or may not be familiar with the particular case about which you are writing or the particular subject matter within the area of law about which you are writing. This information—your reader's degree of familiarity with the case and the issues it raises—is important information for you to have because it should influence your presentation. If you have no access to such information in advance, you should presume *no familiarity*, as that is always the safest course of action.

At the time you are writing, you will have both an **intended (or primary) audience**—the person(s) to whom you are directing your memo—as well as an **unintended (or secondary) audience**. Your unintended audience consists of all of the people who **might** read your work product at some point in the future—for example, other attorneys on the case (now and in the future), or attorneys working on a future case that raises the same or similar legal issues. In other words, all of the readers of your memo may not be known to you at the time you write it. This should drive home the importance of writing with enough detail in the facts and other sections so that your work will be intelligible to many potential readers, regardless of their present familiarity with the case. Even when you modify your work because you know, for example, that your intended audience is already familiar with the facts of the case, your document should still be intelligible standing on its own. In addition, you should remember that what you put in writing in many respects will outlast you. You should always put your best foot forward in every office memorandum you write, because months and years later fellow lawyers and clients of the firm who do not know you very well (or at all) will form an impression of you and your legal skills based on what you wrote. As Woody Allen once said, "You don't get a second chance to make a first impression."

At some point, your memo may be shared with the client. Clients sometimes want to see the work product that they paid for or just want to keep up on how the case is progressing. Always remember that your office memoranda are potential vehicles for transmitting news to clients. Of course, that does not mean that you should draft your office memos with the client as the primary audience (especially where the client is not a law-trained reader). The incidental risk that a non-lawyer client may eventually acquire your memo is insufficient justification to attempt the near impossible task of trying to write the memo so that it is properly detailed and informative for a lawyer and yet easily understandable to a lay person. Instead, the memo later can be accompanied by a client letter. But the main lesson regarding potential secondary audiences is to be judicious, but accurate, as to how you describe the actions, situations, and circumstances of the client. Be professional at all times. If there are detrimental facts, you must convey them honestly and accurately. The office memorandum and client letter will be protected by the ethical confidentiality rule, the attorney-client communication privilege (if the document is transmitted to the client for the purpose of rendering legal advice), and the work product privilege (if the document is prepared in anticipation of litigation). But the fact that these privileges will make it very unlikely that an opponent or the court ever will see the document does not provide you grounds to relax the duty to write professionally and maturely.

FOOD FOR THOUGHT

Attention Levels of the Law-Trained Reader

Even when you know that your work will be read by a law-trained reader, there often is no way to know how much time your reader will devote to your work product. A mid-level associate working on your case might devote a great deal of time to your work, whereas a more senior lawyer might only skim it, presuming that someone will tell her about the most important details in person. Do not despair. One good tip to keep in mind is that **the most important page of your office memorandum is the first page.** Front-load the important information so that even the busiest reader will get something out of your memo by reading only that.

The first page typically presents the **"issues"** (or **"questions presented"**) and your **"conclusions"** (or **"brief answers"**). Together, these sections constitute a kind of executive summary.

You should strive to make these sections concise, yet informative by including relevant facts and details about the elements of the rules, as well as your conclusions about the application of the law to the facts. If an experienced law-trained reader understands the issues you are writing about and is presented with the rules and your conclusions, that reader will be able to grasp your entire report just from the first page. The art of being informative in one page takes practice, and it is something that you will get better at over time as you become more sensitive to the type of information that is important to include. As a general matter, you should strive to limit these sections to one page. The only reason to spill over to a second page is if you have more than one issue to address.

II.   STRUCTURE OF THE OFFICE MEMORANDUM

This section covers the most common format for an "office memorandum." Of course, this format may vary from office to office. The titles for the different sections may vary, as may the overall look of the document itself (including font and style choices). Obviously, you should follow whatever format your place of business prefers. Here we will present the classic form with the section names with which we are the most familiar: Caption, Issues, Conclusions, Statement of Facts, and Discussion.

	PARTS OF THE OFFICE MEMORANDUM AND WHAT THEY LOOK LIKE
CAPTION	**MEMORANDUM** TO: Senior Attorney FROM: Junior Associate DATE: October 31, 2014 RE: Client Name/Client Matter SUBJECT: The important question in client's matter
ISSUES	**ISSUES** 1. The first issue addressed in the memorandum is stated here, generally in a single sentence, but in the form of a Yes-No question, ending in a question mark, see? 2. The second issue addressed in the memorandum is stated here, still a single sentence, still in the form of a Yes-No question, ending in a question mark, see?
CONCLUSIONS	**CONCLUSIONS** 1. Yes, the author's conclusion on the first issue addressed in the memorandum is stated here, and it will start with the answer, Yes or No. The conclusion often will be more than one sentence. It will serve as a summary of the entire discussion of this issue. 2. Yes, the author's conclusion on the second issue addressed in the memorandum is stated here. To be an effective summary, each conclusion will provide the Yes-No answer, a brief statement of the most important facts, a description or summary of the operative parts of the law, and state the author's conclusion on the issue.
STATEMENT OF FACTS	**STATEMENT OF FACTS** In roughly a page, the author will provide the factual information necessary for understanding the situation and the analysis. As mentioned in Chapter 2, the facts section allows the author an opportunity to engage in narrative reasoning to create an effective story of the client's situation and the facts of the matter. You must include the relevant operative facts of the case, including each fact that you will refer to later in the discussion section's application sections.

PARTS OF THE OFFICE MEMORANDUM **AND WHAT THEY LOOK LIKE**	
DISCUSSION	**DISCUSSION** The discussion section presents your legal analysis, delivered using the T-R-E-A-T format. So, this section will feature the TREAT sections that address the issues. **I. Thesis heading on Issue I** 　　　[R] Rule section 　　　[E] Explanation section 　　　[A] Application section 　　　[T] Thesis restated as a conclusion **II. Thesis heading on Issue II** 　　　[R] Rule section 　　　[E] Explanation section 　　　[A] Application section 　　　[T] Thesis restated as a conclusion
[No conclusion at the end]	[You already put your conclusions at the beginning on page 1, so there is no need for a CONCLUSION section at the end.]

In your law office or in your legal writing course, there may be differences to this format. The caption may include slightly different information. Issues section might be called "Questions Presented," and the Conclusions might be called "Brief Answers." Some professors and some employers might require you to draft a separate Conclusion section at the end of the memorandum. Beyond these cosmetic differences, the content of the sections generally does not change—the same requirements will apply regardless of labels.

DO IT WITH STYLE!

Should you include a separate conclusion section?
Our sample above does not include a separate "Conclusion" section at the end. We are generally of the mind that the conclusion belongs at the front and that a separate conclusion section at the end is redundant. However, some people prefer separate conclusion sections—yet another reason to know the memo format that your law office prefers. In addition, there are circumstances where a separate conclusion section may be worthwhile even when the format that you are following does not specifically require one—namely, where you have recommendations for future action either by the client or by the team of lawyers on the case, and you did not spell this out in the discussion section of the memo. For example, perhaps the conclusion that you reach leads you to believe that additional fact witness interviews are necessary, or that an expert witness should be hired. That information may be appropriate for inclusion in a separate Conclusion following the end of the Discussion (though keep in mind that you may want to work any truly critical information into your Brief Answer, or go back and include it in the Discussion itself).

III. DRAFTING THE CAPTION

There is no mystery to the caption. You must identify the recipient(s), the sender(s), and the date of the memo. If there are any "carbon copy" (CC) recipients, they would go in between the TO line and the FROM line. The DATE is very important, because it tells every reader that the research reflected in the memo stopped as of that date. If a reader comes across your memo two years after you wrote it, she should be on notice that the research most likely is out of date, and someone will need to follow up on it. Some formats include the date in the top right corner of the document rather than in the caption.

You should specify the subject matter of the memo in the RE line. In most offices there is also a client/ matter number associated with each case or assignment, and that information often is useful to include in the RE line. In addition, you should include either the name of the case or the client, and a brief statement of what the memo addresses. For example, you might write:

> **RE:**   **Groovin' Records/Jones (12679/57954): Breach of Contract Claim**

Some law offices include both a RE line and a SUBJECT line, splitting up this information (with the client/matter information in the RE line and the subject matter in the SUBJECT line):

> **RE:**   **Groovin' Records/Jones (12679/57954)**

> **SUBJECT:**   **Jones Breach of Contract Claim**

Some offices do not include the client/matter name and number (or include it elsewhere, such as in a header or footer).

As a general matter, the entries in the Caption are single spaced, but each entry is separated from the next by two spaces. In addition, it is common to indent the text of each line item so that all the text lines up neatly. There should be two or more spaces between the bottom of the caption and the beginning of the text that follows (which often will be the heading for the next section of the memo). For example:

M E M O R A N D U M

TO:	Sandra Glib Gabber Xavier A. Bernstein
CC:	A. Barney Stormer Miriam N. Haque
FROM:	Sarah D. Lawyer
DATE:	September 8, 2014
RE:	Groovin' Records/Jones (12679/57954): Breach of Contract Claim arising out of Arista Record Co.'s Cancellation of Sydney Concert

---

IV. DRAFTING THE ISSUES OR QUESTIONS PRESENTED

As with so many other aspects of legal writing, there is an art to drafting a good issue or question presented (we will refer to both of these from here on simply as "QP"). Drafting a QP is not onerous or exceedingly difficult, but you must engage with the material and produce a thoughtful, informative QP that will be useful to the reader. Vague statements of the issue, such as "Should our client prevail?" are not useful (especially when you consider how many readers will rely exclusively on the information you present on the first page of your memo).

We recommend that you include factual information in the QP and that you echo the terminology used in the applicable rule(s). This practice will help you produce more informative QPs and sensitize your reader(s) to operative terminology that she will see again in the Brief Answer and Discussion sections of the memo. However, you should not make the QP so detailed and client-specific that the memo can be used only if another client comes in with the exact same case.

We realize this is abstract advice. As noted, there is an art to drafting good QPs. We offer the following suggestion, which we have found works well.

> **Questions Presented - The Two-Phrase Approach:**
> **[Verb] + [legal issue], [when] + [legally significant facts]**

The best way to write a QP is to draft it in two parts: a phrase that identifies the relevant law and a phrase that identifies the legally significant facts (LSFs).

The most common formulation of the first phrase begins with a verb, such as "Does," "Is," "Can," "Do," or "Will." This phrase should contain key terms from the law that signal to the reader what the legal issue is. The second phrase should begin with "when" (or "where") and provide the most important facts from the case that ultimately will determine which way the issue will come out. Thus, a good QP is structured as:

[Verb] + [legal issue], [when] + [legally significant facts]

Your choice of words matters when you are presenting the key facts. Choose nouns and verbs that are found in the legal standards that you will address later in the Discussion section. In this way, you can introduce the relevant terms from the law in the same phrase as the relevant facts. In addition, consider working into the QP the jurisdiction in which the question arises or under whose law the issue will be addressed. (Alternatively, you can mention the jurisdiction in the Brief Answer or outset of the Discussion section).

> **REQUIREMENTS OF A QUESTION PRESENTED**
> To sum up, the three things you should include in each QP are:
> (1) **A legal question that can be answered Yes or No,**
> (2) **Phrased with reference to the most important (legally significant) facts upon which the issue will turn,**
> (3) **Using key terms borrowed from the legal rules that apply to the issue.**

Compare the following statements of the issue are based on the dog bite hypothetical we have worked with in previous chapters:

> **Example 1** - A useless statement of the issue. It tells the reader nothing:
> **ISSUE**
> Is Mrs. Jones liable?

Example 1 is far too vague. It tells nothing about the actual issue that was researched and answered. It does not even mention that a dog was involved. Avoid this format.

Example 2 - Still no good. It does not have enough details of the facts or the rule:

ISSUE

Is Mrs. Jones liable when her dog bit the plaintiff?

Example 2 is getting better, but this still is too vague. Who is Mrs. Jones? Is she a party to a lawsuit? Who is the plaintiff? What happened? All of these questions could be answered for the benefit of the reader, but you are forcing her to go to the Brief Answer section, or worse, to the Discussion section before the questions will be answered. You can do much better.

Example 3 - A good one:

ISSUE

Is defendant Jones liable under Apex law when the dog she owned bit a Girl Scout selling cookies door-to-door, and the Scout did nothing to provoke the dog prior to the bite?

Example 3 is right on target. We know who is involved, a little of what happened, and "ownership" and "provocation" echo some key terms found in the rule. The QP immediately suggests to the reader that provocation was a major part of the issue you researched. You very well may be able to suggest some improvements to this example, but it is a very solid QP for the matter we've been addressing.

Now compare Example 3 to the following:

Example 4 - This form uses incorrect terminology and distorts the issue:

ISSUE

Is defendant Jones liable under Apex law when the dog she possessed mauled a Girl Scout who was selling cookies at her home and who did not rile up, excite, or anger the dog prior to the mauling?

Example 4 certainly has sufficient detail (arguably too much) and appears to state the issue, but the crucial difference is that the author did not borrow the correct terminology from the rule in presenting the issue. Worse yet, the example sounds like other words are the operative terms for dog bite liability. First of all, we are talking about dog *"bite"* liability, not dog "mauling." The legal standard is "ownership," not "possession" of a dog, and "provocation," not "riling up, exciting, or angering" a dog. Borrow the correct terms when stating the issue so that these terms will resonate later when the reader gets to the rule section.

Also compare Example 3 to the following:

Example 5 - This form goes overboard with details:

ISSUE

Is our client, defendant Martina R. Jones, liable when her Doberman Pinscher bit the plaintiff, a Girl Scout, when the Scout used public sidewalks, climbed up Jones' front stoop, rang the doorbell, and yelled, "Girl Scout cookies," all prior to the dog's attack?

Example 5 contains too much information. While QPs are traditionally one sentence and sometimes can sound a bit cumbersome, this one really goes overboard. It gives the reader no incentive to look at the Brief Answer and may even make the Brief Answer confusing (*e.g.*, what if the use of public sidewalks proves irrelevant?). In addition, it sounds like the memo is tied to a very specific set of facts and thus will not be useful for a future client who has a slightly different set of facts. The reader might have doubts as to the usefulness of the memo if the dog in her case was a St. Bernard, or if the plaintiff crossed the lawn, or knocked on the door, or came to have a petition signed rather than to sell Thin Mints and Samoas.

V.   DRAFTING THE BRIEF ANSWERS OR CONCLUSIONS

Probably the most important part of your office memorandum is the Brief Answer(s) or Conclusion(s) section (we will refer to both of these from here on simply as "BA"). This section follows the QP section, and both together should fit on the first page, if possible. If you have multiple issues to address, your BA section may spill over onto a second page, but we have rarely seen a good QP/BA combination that runs more than about a page and a half.

With its priority in placement, the BA section will receive a lot of attention. As with the QP section, you should strive to make it useful and informative without going overboard (another art that you will get better at over time).

REQUIREMENTS OF A BRIEF ANSWER

The four things you should include in each BA are:

(1) a definite Yes or No answer to the QP,
(2) a brief summary of the law, focusing on the most important disputed elements of the rules,
(3) the most important (legally significant) facts upon which the issue will turn;
(4) your conclusion on the issue.

The required elements of a BA need not appear in the order laid out above, one through four, but all parts should be present in a well-drafted BA.

Because QPs are traditionally drafted as questions, BAs traditionally begin with a "yes" or "no" answer. It is important to give the direct answer first. Later in the BA, you can explain any contingencies or gray areas of the law or facts, but start with a definite Yes or No.

PRACTICE POINTER

What if the answer is maybe?

Law students and junior lawyers tend to equivocate in the BA section. Instead of saying yes or no, you may feel more comfortable saying that something is possible. That's not particularly helpful to your reader; moreover, it is a truism. Of course, any answer is *possible*; otherwise, you would not have been asked to write the memo.

If you cannot answer the question firmly (such as if there are too few authorities on point), then it is better to **explain in the text of the BA the uncertainty** in the facts or the law (and reiterate these reasons in the Discussion). Similarly, you might **qualify your answer** by specifying the precise assumptions on which it rests, and explain any contingencies that affect the answer. But this is information that you can include in the text of the BA and still answer the question yes or no.

Some legal writing professors (and law-trained readers generally) are not bothered by BAs that begin "Probably yes," or "Probably no," but most would rather that you reach a more definite conclusion. That said, if you feel compelled to be equivocal, a "probably" answer is better than a "possibly" answer. If you want to go the "probably" route, make sure (as best you can) that your primary audience will accept that approach.

After your answer to the question, you should include a short statement and summary of the rule as well as the critical facts that will determine the issue. The most efficient way to accomplish this is to discuss the relevant facts in the context of each element at issue in the applicable rule.

SHORT STATEMENT OF FACTS AND SUMMARY OF THE RULE

Discussing the relevant facts in the context of each element at issue in the applicable rule:

The rule on money had and received is: (a) receipt of money (b) under circumstances that render the retention unjust. Defendant received through a mistaken wire transfer money that he did not earn and to which he had no lawful entitlement, rendering his retention of the money unjust.

If you are careful and skillful enough, you may be able to reveal the elements of the rule and the facts together in one sentence (after the yes or no answer).

SHORT STATEMENT OF FACTS AND SUMMARY OF THE RULE

Revealing the elements of the rule and the facts together in one sentence:

Defendant received, through a mistaken wire transfer, money that he did not earn and to which he had no lawful entitlement, rendering his retention of the money unjust.

This kind of writing is not easy, and you may even decide that it is more trouble than it is worth to attempt to reveal the disputed elements and the facts in a single sentence. Though a sentence like the above is very concise, and concision overall is something worth striving for, you should never let concision get in the way of clarity. Especially if the applicable rule is long, you should work on summarizing it and the operative facts as briefly as possible. Do not quote the entire borrowed or applied rule that the reader will find in the Discussion section.

If certain elements are not in dispute or are obviously established, you do not need to summarize these elements in the BA. The facts you will use to present the rule in the BA are those on which the issue turns. This section really is supposed to be "brief," so you have to be selective in what facts to mention.

Finally, the BA should present your legal conclusions. If you have done a good job with the rule and the facts, the conclusion will follow easily. It does not hurt to finish your BA with the same sentence or phrase that you will use as your thesis heading on that issue.

LEGAL CONCLUSIONS

Therefore, Barnes will recover from the dog owner, Starnes, because Starnes' dog reacted viciously and disproportionately to Barnes' bumping into the dog, which will reverse the effect of provocation in the case.

Each BA, however informative, typically should be no longer than one paragraph. Though paragraph lengths vary, a good rule of thumb for the length of *each* BA is approximately three to five sentences and no more than one third of a page. This rule is not set in stone, but it is a good target length.

The Dog Bite example we have been working with might look like this:

QUESTION PRESENTED

Under Apex law, is defendant Jones liable when the dog she owned bit a Girl Scout who was selling cookies door-to-door and who did nothing to provoke the dog prior to the bite?

BRIEF ANSWER

Yes. There is no dispute that Mrs. Jones owned the dog that bit the Girl Scout and caused her injury. Liability for the dog bite will turn on whether the Scout was acting peacefully in a place where she had a lawful right to be, and on whether she provoked the dog. The Scout was walking with her mother on public sidewalks in Mrs. Jones's neighborhood selling cookies door-to-door. The Scout did not strike or threaten the dog, or engage in any behavior to provoke the attack. Therefore, Mrs. Jones will be liable for the injuries caused when her dog bit the plaintiff.

If the issue was liability for money had and received, the Question Presented and Brief Answer might look like this (**notice that we mention the jurisdiction this time in the BA**):

QUESTION PRESENTED

Is defendant Shaw liable for money had and received when he received and retained an unanticipated wire transfer from Western Bank because of the Bank's mistake?

BRIEF ANSWER

Yes. Under Nevada law, liability for money had and received requires a mistaken transfer of money, the receipt of which amounts to an unjust enrichment. Western Bank mistakenly wired $100,000 to Shaw, who was not lawfully entitled to receive and retain any amount of money from Western Bank. Because Shaw received money through a mistaken wire transfer that he did not earn and to which he had no lawful entitlement, his retention of the money is unjust, and thus he is liable for money had and received.

VI. DRAFTING THE STATEMENT OF FACTS

The Statement of Facts is important for at least three reasons: first, it tells the uninformed reader the background of the case and the facts that led to your conclusions. Anyone picking up your memo even years later will know what was going on in your case, and in combination with the law you present, should see why you reached your conclusions.

Similarly, the second reason is that the Statement of Facts shows an informed reader what you, the author, knew at the time you wrote the memo. Very often, in the course of a legal matter, you learn the facts as you go; this is inevitable because of the process of discovery in litigation (or disclosures provided in other contexts). As a result, an office memorandum written early in a case often is based on an incomplete and even erroneous understanding of the facts. If you have taken care to draft a good Statement of Facts, your informed reader later will be able to see the erroneous information you were working with, and can evaluate whether it affects your conclusions.

The third reason is that the Statement of Facts should reveal what you, the author, thought were the most important facts in the case. Your research and analysis of the authorities should educate you as to the most relevant facts in your client's situation; these are the ones the Statement of Facts should highlight. Your readers will expect that you have presented the most relevant facts in the Statement of Facts. If a fact is discussed later in the Discussion section that did not appear in the Statement of Facts, they will either discount that fact's importance (giving you the benefit of the doubt as to why it was left out), or they will discount the Statement of Facts and assume that you have done a less-than thorough job.

With these three priorities in mind, you should draft your Statement of Facts to provide a context for the case and to highlight the facts relevant to your analysis of the issues. Use the narrative reasoning skills we discussed in Chapter 2 to drive home your points by presenting the facts that will determine the outcome of the legal issues.

Recommendations for the Statement of Facts

- Although you should include all relevant facts, it is not time to write a novel. You should strive to limit the Statement of Facts to about one page in a memo of approximately ten pages. In a complicated case, you might come closer to two pages. (Remember here that we are talking about office memos and not briefs, which often have longer fact sections.) In practice, office memoranda do not come with page limits (unless of course your reader specifies one), but you should respect the reader's time and attention span.

- You may face the difficult decision whether to mention a fact that is not relevant to the law but is interesting. If you have the space, by all means include it. You want your memo to be memorable. But do not go overboard; too many interesting tidbits will dilute the truly relevant facts that you need the reader to digest.

We mentioned earlier that one of the audiences for your memo might be the client. If your supervisor intends to circulate your memo to the client, you should draft it with that fact in mind. However, often you will not know ahead of time whether the memo will eventually make its way to the client. A client might read her legal bill and call up your supervisor demanding to see the memorandum that cost her $8,000, and your supervisor may speed it off to her, perhaps without even rereading and revising it to "sanitize" it for the client's eyes. Our advice is to be sympathetic to your client in the statement of facts; do not say anything overtly critical or humorous about the client.

If the client took an action that will produce serious consequences under the law, describe the act and the consequences in a professional way.

Example:

"Allied failed to retain the documents relating to its disposal of Agent Orange even after the special agent requested to see these documents."

"Allied terminated the contract after only six months, which is contrary to the specific provision in section 12(B) of the contract providing for an initial three year term."

Do not say:

"Allied's failure to retain the documents was unbelievably inappropriate under the circumstances. . . ."

"Allied's comptroller, Bill Smith, obviously did not know what he was doing when he terminated the contract after only six months. . . "

The above examples may seem like exaggerations, but we have seen some terribly inappropriate language used in the Statement of Facts. In short, do not editorialize. And do not write anything that you would be embarrassed about if the client read.

Do not bad-mouth the client:

"If you ask me, the client's conduct was insensitive."

"Allied deserves to lose this case for what it tried to pull here."

Being sympathetic does not mean being a cheerleader. Your zeal should be reserved for your writing as an advocate. Remember that the office memorandum should be an objective work, so present the facts as they are, warts and all. If your client did something wrongful or embarrassing *and it is relevant* to your analysis under the law, you should state it. In most instances your office memoranda will not be turned over to the court or to your opponents, so it is generally safe to discuss sensitive matters. In fact, it is extremely problematic to conceal facts from your reader if they bear upon the outcome of the case. Naturally, you should discuss the matters in a serious, professional way.

Do not talk about the law or its elements or the legal standards that govern the case in the Statement of Facts. You have plenty of time for that in the Discussion. As well, leave out legal conclusions from your Statements of Facts. Draw legal conclusions in the Discussion section. (Of course none of this advice is intended to dissuade you from presenting the facts in a targeted manner. Moreover, when you move into persuasive writing, you will see that every section of a brief is an opportunity to cast the facts in a favorable (but truthful) light for your client.)

LEGAL CONCLUSIONS VS. FACTUAL CONCLUSIONS

Legal Conclusions:

Legal conclusions draw a conclusion about the law itself, in particular, a conclusion about the application of the *law* to the facts.

> "The doctor operated **negligently.**"
> "The truck driver was **reckless.**"
> "The transfer **unjustly enriched** Jones."

In contrast, *factual conclusions* are appropriate to include in a memo's Statement of Facts. Factual conclusions include reasonable inferences drawn from the facts that do not involve the application of the *law* to the *facts*.

Factual Conclusions:

"The doctor performed the operation in **less than one third the time** normally allotted for the procedure by the hospital and the Texas Board of Healing Arts."

"The doctor's breath and his demeanor during the operation suggested to three witnesses in the operating room that **he was intoxicated**."

"The truck driver accelerated and attempted to drive around the railway barriers **at a high rate of speed**."

"Jones had no debt or account with the person who transferred the money to Jones when Jones was **not the intended recipient**."

Our example of a Statement of Facts for the Dog Bite case from Chapter 2 could be modified for inclusion in an office memorandum written by one of *defendant's attorneys* as follows:

STATEMENT OF FACTS

On the morning of April 7, 2005, plaintiff Sally Peterson, a Girl Scout, was walking with her mother, Janice Peterson, on defendant Mrs. Jones's street, ringing the doorbells of every house in the neighborhood. When she reached Mrs. Jones's house, Sally walked from the public sidewalk up the front walkway and front stoop of the house. At the door, she rang the doorbell and screamed, "Girl Scout cookies!" in a loud voice at the front door, which was ajar. Defendant's Doberman Pinscher, "Cuddles," was startled by the child's screams, and approached Sally on the front stoop. Having no other means of restraint, and having been trained to protect the house, the dog placed his mouth around plaintiff's arm. Plaintiff's mother was driven into a rage by this act, and tackled the dog with force, striking Cuddles across the eyes and snout with a large pocketbook and an umbrella she was carrying. In spite of this attack and in accordance with its training, Cuddles did not let go of Sally's arm. In the ensuing altercation, Mrs. Peterson pushed and pulled both Sally and Cuddles so much that the dog's teeth were driven into and across Sally's arm repeatedly, causing lacerations. A neighbor, Ralph Bumble, arrived at the scene and forced open Cuddle's jaws, freeing Sally. Both Cuddles and Sally received stitches for the cuts they suffered in the incident.

The money had and received facts might look like this:

STATEMENT OF FACTS

At 9:02 a.m. on March 11, 2005, Western Bank wire transferred $100,000 to an account owned by defendant Hugo Victor. The money was intended to be transferred to an account of co-plaintiff Richard Shaft. Due to a typing error, two digits of the account number were transposed by a clerk of Western Bank, which caused the mistaken transfer. One hour after the transfer, Victor withdrew $100,000 from his account. Six hours after the transfer, the Bank notified Victor of the mistake and requested return of the funds. Victor, who is neither a creditor of the Bank nor of Shaft, refused to return the funds. Victor does not hold an account with the Bank (or Shaft) that would entitle him to the $100,000.

Can you discern the author's client from this statement? Perhaps not; and it is not nearly as important that you be able to do so in a predictive memo. In contrast, it is *always* important in a persuasive piece.

VII. DRAFTING THE DISCUSSION SECTION

Good news! We already discussed the mechanics of drafting a Discussion section in Chapter 6, so you should be well up to speed on this part. The Discussion section is where you apply the "TREAT" paradigm to each issue and sub-issue raised by the rule and its elements and subrules. The examples we gave in Chapter 6 are equally applicable here:

DISCUSSION

I. DEFENDANT STARNES IS LIABLE FOR PLAINTIFF BARNES' DOG BITE INJURIES BECAUSE STARNES OWNED THE DOG AND BARNES ACTED PEACEFULLY IN A LAWFUL PLACE, DOING NOTHING TO PROVOKE THE DOG.

In Apex, to prevail on a cause of action for injuries resulting from the attack of a dog, a plaintiff must prove: (1) defendant owned the dog; (2) plaintiff was conducting herself peacefully at the time of the attack; (3) plaintiff was in a place where he or she had a lawful right to be; and (4) plaintiff did not provoke the dog into attacking. *Timmy v. Lassie*, 567 W.2d 92, 94 (Apex Ct. App. 1st Dist. 1997). Starnes admits that he owned the dog, and therefore this element is not in dispute. This memorandum will address the remaining elements of the tort.

A. Barnes Was Acting Peacefully At All Times During The Event In Question.

In general, acting peacefully means: (a) engaging in a normal day-to-day activity or business; and (b) not behaving in a loud and boisterous manner in close proximity to an unfamiliar dog. *Bobby v. Susie*, 569 W.2d 790,792. . . .

[etc.]

We kept this example short because we present several full-length discussion sections in the sample office memoranda at the end of this Chapter.

There are some additional drafting points to explore here:

- **It is important to use your Theses as headings in the Discussion section.**

If your reader does not have time to read your memo cover to cover, she at least may skim through it and read the headings. If you use your Theses as headings, the reader will get the entire gist of your argument. (In fact, many seasoned attorneys will tell you that in a memo or a brief, the headings should read like a summary of your argument.)

Good Thesis headings (especially in the Roman numerals) contain a conclusion followed by a "because" clause—the facts and legal principles that support the conclusion. A Thesis heading that only states the conclusion is doing half its job.

THESIS HEADINGS–GOOD AND BAD

Not good:	Smith will not be liable under the Illinois Dog Bite Statute for his dog's bite.
Good:	Smith will not be liable under the Illinois Dog Bite Statute for his dog's bite because Jones provoked the dog into attacking.
Not good:	Harris was not unjustly enriched when he received the Union Bank wire transfer by mistake.
Good:	Harris was not unjustly enriched when he received the Union Bank wire transfer by mistake because he had a preexisting debt with Union Bank that exceeded the amount of the transfer.

In each example above, the first thesis heading only states a conclusion; it does not explain the conclusion by providing the facts and key legal principles that support it. The second thesis heading in each pair provides the "because" part, and these headings offer an effective summary of the discussion if the reader merely skims your thesis headings.

POINT-COUNTERPOINT

Should you repeat the Thesis heading as the first line of the text that follows the heading?

The authors differ on whether you should repeat or rephrase your Thesis heading as the first line of text following the heading. This is a style point on which reasonable law-trained writers will differ, and you should employ the technique that best suits your writing (or the preference of the person to whom you are submitting the document).

- **In general, you should order your analysis in the same order that you listed the issues in the Questions Presented or Issues sections, and discuss elements of rules in the order that they are presented in the Rule section.**

One of your most important goals in drafting the Discussion section is to avoid confusing the reader, which easily can happen when you act contrary to reasonable expectations. If you list three Questions Presented, the reader will expect these issues to come up in the Discussion section in the same order, one - two - three. If you list four elements of a rule, the reader is going to expect you to discuss the elements in that order. If you deviate from this order, the reader may become confused and wonder whether she missed something or if you left something out. (You can try to avoid the confusion by using a roadmap, as discussed below).

CAVEAT. In persuasive writing, this principle often is abandoned in favor of one where you lead with your best arguments. That is certainly true in terms of ordering the Issues to be addressed, but it is more risky when it comes to changing the order of a rule's elements. If you want to go in a different order—especially in an objective piece—you should announce your order in the "umbrella paragraph(s)," the paragraph(s) between Roman I and subsection A (or between the Discussion header and Roman I if your Issues need set-up and you are proceeding out of order). This advice leads to our next tip.

- **Use "roadmaps" whenever you think the reader will benefit from a little more direction.**

Your writing will be appreciated by your readers if you keep them on the same page with you. If you simply follow the order in which the issues are presented and discuss the elements of a rule in the order in which they are listed, there is no need to give further directions. A roadmap in these circumstances may be superfluous. But if you proceed out of order (or want to dismiss at the outset one or more issues from consideration), use a **roadmap** sentence or paragraph that will explain the order to the reader ahead of time.

WHAT'S THAT?

What is a "roadmap?"

A roadmap is a common term used in both predictive and persuasive writing—and oral argument—that refers to the writer/speaker's articulation at the outset of a discussion of what she intends to cover, and in what order, in the ensuing discussion. In other words: tell your audience what you plan to do before you do it. Though this may sound boring to those of you that lean more toward creativity (and run counter to your desire to build suspense), rest assured that one of the authors of this text strongly resisted this seemingly banal impulse until several readers of her work had to remind her that she was *not* writing detective fiction.

You can present the roadmap for the entire Discussion section right before your first thesis heading.

Roadmap Example 1 - The first line under DISCUSSION is the **roadmap**:

DISCUSSION

This memorandum first discusses the issue of liability for breach, followed by the issue of the Statute of Frauds, and last, the issue of potential damages for breach.

I. **THORNGREN IS LIABLE FOR BREACH OF THE URSCHEL CONTRACT BECAUSE IT FAILED TO DELIVER GEARS CONFORMING TO THE SPECIFICATIONS OF THE ORDER.**

The same roadmap device is used *within* a TREAT section when you want to skip elements or discuss them in a different order than they are presented in the rule. If you have several not-in-dispute elements to dispose of, you save space by using a roadmap to explain that they are not at issue and will not be discussed. This technique is employed in the example that began this section, and in the example below:

Roadmap Example 2 - The last two lines are the roadmap:

DISCUSSION

This memorandum first discusses the issue of liability for breach, followed by the issue of the Statute of Frauds, and last, the issue of potential damages for breach.

I. **THORNGREN IS LIABLE FOR BREACH OF THE URSCHEL CONTRACT BECAUSE IT FAILED TO DELIVER GEARS CONFORMING TO THE SPECIFICATIONS OF THE CONTRACT.**

A requirements contract may be breached if: (1) non-conforming goods are delivered, and (2) rejected by the buyer within a reasonable time. Apex Statutes § 2-201 (2012). On July 17, 2014, the next day after receipt of the July shipment of gears from Thorngren, Urschel notified Thorngren that 65% of the order was non-conforming to ISO 9023 standards. Thorngren concedes that Urschel's notification was timely—given within a reasonable time. Therefore, this memorandum examines only whether the shipment breached the standards of the contract.

- **Draft the Discussion at an appropriate level of detail for your known audience.**

Your law school professors will teach you principles about many areas of the law, and you will acquire additional information in preparation for the bar exam. How much an average lawyer retains is impossible to predict, but in drafting an office memorandum, you should assume that your reader is familiar with the *basic law* of contracts, torts, property, and civil procedure. Depending on your office, your reader also is probably familiar with basic principles of criminal law, evidence, income tax, constitutional law, and the other classic "bar exam" subjects.

If the people assigning your work are specialists in an area—for example, you are researching a civil procedure issue for litigators or a tax issue for tax lawyers—you can assume additional, specialized knowledge. But no lawyer will know everything, which is why you were asked to do research in the first place.

The point is that you should draft your office memorandum at an appropriate level of detail for your audience. If you are researching a contract issue, there is no need to go back to the first week of contracts class and write about a contract requiring offer, acceptance, and consideration. You don't have to start at day one of torts when you have a negligence issue, either. But you should not assume that a complex area of the law such as securities law is readily understood by anyone other than a securities law expert. It may be necessary to lay a foundation, to provide basic details about the fundamental principles of the area in which your issue resides, before tackling the TREATment of the actual issue you were asked to research. As always: know your primary audience.

- **Discuss collateral issues that have the potential to impact your main issues.**

Very often as you are researching and analyzing your problem, you will stumble on collateral issues, not necessarily tied to the specific issues you were asked to research, but which are discussed in the authorities you are reading. If the issue does not have the potential to impact your analysis of the assigned issues, you have the choice to ignore it or to take it up and resolve it in a separate TREATment. But if the issue has the potential to impact the main issues, you should take up the issue and resolve it.

For example, in a breach of contract problem, you may have been asked to research the issue of whether the defendant had the proper mental capacity to contract in light of his mental illness. But you also may have been told that the defendant disputed that the signature on the contract was his own, even though several witnesses saw the defendant sign the document. The "signature issue" is collateral to the other issue on capacity; nothing about the signature necessarily affects the outcome of your analysis. You have the choice to take up and resolve the issue in your memo to assist the attorneys who assigned the work, but in this instance, there is likely no need to do it. The same does not hold true if the additional issue was that the defendant was using recreational, non-prescription drugs at the time of the contracting. The use of recreational drugs has the potential to affect the person's mental state, making the latent mental illness more or less severe in the circumstances, so this issue certainly should be resolved in the memo. Over time, you will become more sensitive to what does and does not need to be covered.

PRACTICE POINTER

Before you spend a lot of time and the client's money researching and resolving a collateral issue, it is a good idea to inquire of the assigning attorneys whether this issue is being researched and analyzed by someone else, so that you do not duplicate effort. They will be impressed that you thought of it and asked, and the worst thing that will happen is that they will officially assign you the task of researching and writing the analysis of the issue.

VIII. DRAFTING THE CONCLUSION

We addressed above some of the reasons why a formal Conclusion section at the end of an office memorandum may not be necessary. If you have suggestions for further research or recommendations for future action by the client or the lawyers, then you may decide to draft a final Conclusion section. Some audiences simply may want you to restate your main points one more time. Whatever your incentive, remember not to save anything that is critically important to include in a Conclusion at the end. The Conclusion is the last thing people will read, and therefore is the section they are most likely to skip. If it is important, you should work it into the Brief Answer(s) or at least into the Discussion.

IX. LETTER WRITING AND CLIENT LETTERS

A. Writing Letters

Letters are an important tool for every attorney. You should never think of letter drafting as a no-brainer exercise. Occasionally, you can say everything you need to say in a few words drafted in a short time. But the mindset to maintain is that every letter you write is important to someone—your client, your law office, the court, and especially to you. Your letters represent you, and your law firm or law office, just as well and perhaps for a longer period of time than any in-person impressions you make on people.

A little history. Letter writing itself occupies an important narrative form called the "epistolary." Many famous novels have been written in epistolary form, including Bram Stoker's *Dracula*, C. S. Lewis's *The Screwtape Letters*, Mary Shelley's *Frankenstein*, and Alice Walker's *The Color Purple*. If you want to master the craft of letter writing, you can learn a lot from these and other classics of literature that include narrative letter writing and journal entries. Excellent letter writing is a rare art these days, but it is not a lost art. There are some basic approaches to letter writing that you can learn to employ:

Tip 1: Know the Purpose of the Communication

The whole point of professional communication is to fulfill a specific purpose. When we talk about letter writing in the law, we are not talking about issuing a random tweet on what we had for lunch or the latest vine we are watching. Attorney letters have a purpose, and you need to know exactly what you need to achieve.

The purpose will dictate much of the form and most of the contents of the letter. Are you simply sending some files or transmitting a message to someone else? Is the letter simply a cover letter to explain the other document in the envelope? Is it a demand letter—and if so, to whom: your opponent? another lawyer? an agency? Is the letter an engagement letter to a client—if so, you are drafting a contract not a simple letter. Making sure you know the purpose is the first and maybe the most important step of the writing process.

Tip 2: Know your primary audience

Consideration of the audience is critical to all writing. As you probably guessed, a cover letter is written differently than a letter transmitting legal advice to a client, and a demand letter is different from a letter asking for a favor or for some extension of professional courtesy. The contents are different, the tone is different, and the requirements are different. You must know your primary audience.

It is a good idea to try to determine (or at least imagine) the possible secondary audiences. Some will be obvious; if you write a demand letter, there will be a good chance that the letter will end up as an exhibit in litigation, perhaps as your exhibit to a motion to compel, or your opponent's exhibit to a filing concerning your conduct in the case. Therefore, you are writing for the court's eyes as well. The goal is to effectively communicate with the primary audience in a manner that will not be perceived as offensive or unprofessional when viewed by secondary audiences.

Tip 3: Write in a manner that will make you understandable to your primary audience

Many lawyers have a terrible habit of talking over the heads of everyone except other lawyers and judges. This is exactly backwards—lawyers and judges are the only ones who will understand average, complex legal writing. The goal of a letter is to communicate. Do not leave your primary audience in the dark.

Some lawyers write as though they are trying to avoid comprehension; they seem to want the client, or the opponent, or sometimes even the court, to be confused as to what they are saying and what they mean. Confusion is viewed by these lawyers as a shield against being pinned down. It is better, they think, to be able to deny the writing and say, "Oh no, of course I didn't mean it that way." Obfuscation serves no proper purpose in professional communication.

Tip 4: Adopt a tone of respect for your audience

Proper tone is a very important part of professional communication. As a rule of thumb, adopt a respectful tone. Respect often is lacking in lawyer communications. No one wants to be bullied, or talked down to. No one wants to be belittled or patronized. Your communications are not going to be for casual or frivolous reasons. Yet lawyers are caught slinging mud at alarming rates. Rise above the name-calling; respect your audience even if its members are your adversaries.

DO IT WITH STYLE

T-H-I-N-K before you write

The adage T-H-I-N-K before you speak applies equally well in letter writing. Too often, lawyers write in anger or frustration and live to regret this rash approach. The adage isn't simply saying "think" about your writing—it is an acronym standing for:

[T]   Is what you have to say **true**?

[H]   Is it **helpful**?

[I]   Is it **inspiring**?

[N]   Is it **necessary**?

[K]   Is it **kind**?

Some of these considerations obviously apply more readily than others. A lawyer's writing may be low on the "Inspiring" meter. "Is it kind?" might be more properly phrased as is, "Is it respectful and professional?" But the others are 100% on point: State the truth; do not lie or mislead. Write to move your case forward, to help get something done; don't use a letter as a weapon of intimidation. And consider whether the letter is necessary to accomplish what you need to accomplish. Consider, too, whether a face-to-face conversation or at least a telephone call might accomplish your goal faster and more effectively, and at less risk that your words or their tone will be misunderstood.

Tip 5: Say it with candor, frankness, and courage

In professional communications, do not beat around the bush, mince words, or otherwise mix metaphors. Tell it like it is. If it is bad news, express the bad news. Own it. Explain it. Don't make excuses or try to bury it in legalese and other confusion.

Don't mislead. This is not just an ethical rule. The key to credibility with the court, with clients, and with fellow professionals is to tell the truth, the whole truth, and nothing but the truth. In addition to the requirement not to mislead, consider that threats, harassment, or unlawful discrimination also are actionable violations of your ethical duties.

Have the courage of your convictions. You did the research, you have the answer (good or bad).

Don't say "probably yes," or "maybe no." Say YES, or NO, and explain any caveats.

B. Structure of a Client Letter

Letters are typically more free-form in structure than other professional communications. The form of most letters will be dictated by their purpose: a transmittal letter must transmit the information as clearly and concisely as possible. A cover letter describes the other document it covers. Other letters are more substantive. Below we discuss two of the more substantive variety: the **client letter** and the **demand letter**.

A true **"client letter"** within the meaning of this Chapter is a letter that communicates legal advice to a client. A typical structure for this kind of client letter is the following:

Client Letter—Suggested Structure for a letter communicating legal advice

- **Introductory paragraph**—explains or reminds the audience of the assignment, or introduces the purpose and topic of the letter.

- **Thesis**—your answer; your point for the letter. It is a good idea to put it at the end of the intro paragraph.

- **Body**—reviews facts, explains analysis, points, message.

- **Closing** — repeats thesis, communicates further action items, possible follow-up.

The form suggested here will not get in the way of concise writing, but if you take these suggestions, you will meet the objectives of communicating the advice with the most important information first. As we emphasized before: if you perceive a need to deviate for a deliberate purpose, then do so. This is your letter and it must achieve your purposes for the communication.

FYI

Client Letter Content—Q and A

Q. Do you cite legal authority in your client opinion letter?

A. It depends on the sophistication of the client* and her legal training or experience. Usually you will cite very little or no authority. A constitutional provision (the "First Amendment"), a statute (Valparaiso Building Code § 123), or an important case or two might make the cut.

You must adapt to your audience. Whatever you include must be explained to lay-person audiences who don't understand court structure, precedent, or controlling authority.

> *Note that if it is a lawyer client (in-house counsel or otherwise), or a very legally sophisticated client, you could write the letter much like an office research memo. It depends on your understanding of the primary audience for the letter.

Q. Do you write with contingencies or with one coherent answer?

A. Do not structure your letter around contingencies. Write with one coherent message—a firm answer. Do not write "I am not sure of the result. . ." Instead, give a firm answer, then explain contingencies: "CMG will not succeed. . . Even if [contingency A] occurs, then. . . If [contingency B] occurs, then. . ." Do not write "probably yes," or "maybe not. . ." in your communication of legal advice. Many if not most of your clients will dislike seeing this kind of waffling, especially when they get your bill. Instead, write a firm Yes (or No) to legal questions, and then explain your analysis and any caveats.

As noted, a true **client letter** is targeted to a non-lawyer. Because the reader is a non-lawyer, you should take special care to discuss the legal issues in terms that can be understood by a layperson. When a legal term of art is used, such as "estoppel" or "res judicata," take the time to define these words in laymen's terms. Do not use the Black's Law Dictionary definition, because this is a dictionary written for lawyers and other legally-trained readers. If a statute, rule, or regulation is involved, go ahead and cite the applicable terms. But then explain the terms both in laymen's language and as the terms have been interpreted by later authorities.

Your client is going to be most interested in your *conclusions*. You should take special care to present them up front, and to write them clearly and accurately if you know that they are destined for the eyes of a client. Do not hide behind vague or equivocal conclusions. Your client is not paying you to come up with a "probably" or a "maybe yes." If there is significant uncertainty as to the probable outcome, explain the source of the uncertainty, and discuss the most likely outcomes based on the most likely answers to the variables you have identified.

Citation to and use of other types of legal authorities are thorny issues in client letters. Certainly, many clients realize that there are sources for the law other than legislation and the Constitution, and most understand the general concept that a ruling from a court in a lawsuit can control other persons and situations beyond the parties in the lawsuit itself. But, to a non-lawyer, there rarely is a need to cite and explain a multitude of cases in the explanation and application sections of your report on the law. If one or two controlling cases are very close to your client's situation, you might take the time to explain the facts and holding of these cases, but no more than that. Similarly, secondary authority (no matter what its relative weight and prestige) likely will fall on deaf ears with a non-lawyer client.

As indicated above, the format of a client letter is not as formal as an office memorandum. Most letters are drafted without topical or thesis headings, and none would follow the TREAT format, because the client most likely only needs to receive a summary of the rules and your conclusions regarding the application of the rules to the client's facts.

Sample letters are provided after section C below, and after the sample office memoranda presented at the end of the Chapter.

C. Structure of a Demand Letter or other Letter to an Opponent or Opposing Counsel

With a demand letter to opposing counsel, you have two main, practical purposes to achieve: (1) the actual demand; and (2) the record that you made that demand on a certain date. We suggest the following structure for such a letter, but once again, this is only a suggested form, not a mandatory one:

Demand Letter to an Opponent or Opposing Counsel—Suggested Structure

- **Thesis** or **Introductory paragraph**—You might start with your thesis— the main point, meaning the **big request** or **demand**. Often, a direct approach is appropriate.

- *Alternatively*, open by **explaining the purpose and topic** of the letter, and finish the intro with your thesis—the **big request** or **demand**.

- **Body**—explain your points, key facts, your legal position, your requests, and your demands.

- **Closing** —repeats thesis points, communicates further action and items that you request or demand as follow-up.

Naturally, in the above suggestions, the "demand" itself is your thesis, so stating it first is one way to frontload your request. Many attorneys will want to go a little slower with making a demand, and will choose the alternative way to open, explaining the purpose and topic first before getting into the requests or demands. Again, if you perceive a need to deviate for a deliberate purpose, then do so.

We have prepared several examples of client letters at the end of the Chapter, but the following demand letters are worthy of some attention and consideration.

July 12, 2012   VIA EMAIL ONLY

Mr. Patrick Wensink
Louisville, KY
patrickwensink@gmail.com

Re: Mark: **JACK DANIEL'S**
        Subject: Use of Trademarks

Dear Mr. Wensink:

I am an attorney at Jack Daniel's Properties, Inc. ("JDPI") in California. JDPI is the owner of the JACK DANIEL'S trademarks (the "Marks") which have been used extensively and for many years in connection with our well-known Tennessee whiskey product and a wide variety of consumer merchandise.

It has recently come to our attention that the cover of your book *Broken Piano for President*, bears a design that closely mimics the style and distinctive elements of the JACK DANIEL'S trademarks. An image of the cover is set forth below for ease of reference.

We are certainly flattered by your affection for the brand, but while we can appreciate the pop culture appeal of Jack Daniel's, we also have to be diligent to ensure that the Jack Daniel's trademarks are used correctly. Given the brand's popularity, it will probably come as no surprise that we come across designs like this on a regular basis. What may not be so apparent, however, is that if we allow uses like this one, we run the very real risk that our trademark will be weakened. As a fan of the brand, I'm sure that is not something you intended or would want to see happen.

As an author, you can certainly understand our position and the need to contact you. You may even have run into similar problems with your own intellectual property.

In order to resolve this matter, because you are both a Louisville "neighbor" and a fan of the brand, we simply request that you change the cover design when the book is re-printed. If you would be willing to change the design sooner than that (including on the digital version), we would be willing to contribute a reasonable amount towards the costs of doing so. By taking this step, you will help us to ensure that the Jack Daniel's brand will mean as much to future generations as it does today.

We wish you continued success with your writing and we look forward to hearing from you at your earliest convenience. A response by **July 23, 2012** would be appreciated, if possible. In the meantime, if you have any questions or concerns, please do not hesitate to contact me.

Sincerely,

Christy Susman

Christy Susman
Senior Attorney - Trademarks

JACK DANIEL'S PROPERTIES, INC.
4040 CIVIC CENTER DRIVE   •   SUITE 528   •   SAN RAFAEL, CALIFORNIA 94903
TELEPHONE: (415) 446-5225   •   FAX (415) 446-5230

As background, here is the book jacket referred to in the above letter, placed beside the famous Jack Daniel's label trade dress:

In our eyes, Jack Daniels has something to complain about under trademark and unfair trade practices law. But the letter is a genuine surprise.

We are intrigued by this "demand letter," perhaps we might even call it a "Cease and Desist letter," but the quotation marks are used here because it is so downright pleasant and friendly a letter, one could hardly be offended by the attorney's. . . uh. . . demands?—suggestions? Jack Daniels offers to help pay for a reprinting of the jacket. We can only say ". . . !?" when we read that.

Do you think this letter is effective? Consider that every letter has a purpose, and the letter is intentional in its message, so is this a perfect example of the form, contents, and tone of the letter perfectly matching the attorney's purpose?

DO IT WITH STYLE

Contents of Demand Letters and other Letters to Opposing Counsel—Q and A

Q. Do you cite legal authority?

A. As much as you think necessary. But usually not nearly as much as you would cite in an office research memo on the same topic. Always pick your best authorities.

Q. Should you discuss any doubts, contingencies, or uncertainties?

A. Usually, no. If you are working very closely and cooperatively with an opposing counsel, then your writing may be more frank and open, but the rest of the time, be firm, definite, and confident about your legal position and your requests and demands. You are serving your client, not chit chatting. Opponents are not within Attorney-Client Communication or confidentiality protections.

Consider a very different combination of letter and response:

Initial Letter to Counsel:

Gentlemen:

    I am one of your season ticket holders who attends or tries to attend every game. It appears that one of the pastimes of several fans has become the sailing of paper airplanes generally made out of the game program. As you know, there is the risk of serious eye injury and perhaps an ear injury as a result of such airplanes. I am sure that this has been called to your attention and that several of your ushers and policemen witnessed the same.

    Please be advised that since you are in a position to control or terminate such action on the part of fans, I will hold you responsible for any injury sustained by any person in my party attending one of your sporting events. It is hoped that this disrespectful and possibly dangerous activity will be terminated.

                Very truly yours,

                ROETZEL & ANDRESS

                By *[signature]*

                Dale O. Cox

CLEVELAND STADIUM, CORP.
CLEVELAND STADIUM · CLEVELAND, OHIO 44114
Phone: 781-5600

December 21, 1974

Dale O. Cox, Esquire
Roetzel and Andress
20th Floor
One Cascade Plaza
Akron, Ohio 44308

Dear Mr. Cox:

   Attached is a letter that we received on November 19,
1974. I feel that you should be aware that some asshole
is signing your name to stupid letters.

                              Very truly yours,

                              CLEVELAND STADIUM CORP.

                              James N. Bailey,
                              General Counsel

JNB:bjn

cc: Arthur B. Modell

Obviously, you will not see this form of correspondence every week in your practice. We chose it in part because it is famous (and somewhat humorous). It is flip, rude, and unprofessional. But the point of including it here is to consider whether the letter could be (possibly be) effective in achieving the author's purpose.

X.   SAMPLE OFFICE MEMORANDA

The pages that follow contain four complete examples of office memoranda. We have written annotations to explain and comment on the samples.

Please understand that these are *samples of good work, not perfect models.* None of the examples is perfect in all respects. None provides a standard form for drafting an office memorandum. Do not try to cram your own writing into a straight-jacket by trying to copy one of these samples; rather, use these examples as basic guidelines, and listen to your legal writing professor concerning deviations that she or he advises. Note that the citations here are in an abbreviated form approved for the assignments. They do not follow Bluebook or ALWD form.

Our **first sample** is the most uncomplicated. It has no need for a roadmap to explain elements of the law that are not disputed, and thus not discussed in the memorandum. It has a single rule that does not create separate questions that must be addressed in a sub-TREAT; therefore, the whole discussion section is resolved in one main TREAT.

SAMPLE OFFICE MEMORANDUM #1	NOTES
MEMORANDUM **TO:** Michael D. Murray **FROM:** Carol Ng Book **DATE:** October 12, 2011 **RE:** ABC/USA-Online Matter **SUBJECT:** Claim against USA-Online for Erroneous Reporting of Stock Price and Volume of Shares Traded	**Caption**
QUESTION PRESENTED Under New York law, is USA-Online liable to ABC & Co. ("ABC") for erroneous reporting of ABC's stock price and volume of shares traded?	**Question Presented** The QP is short, but states the legal issue ("liability") and facts ("reporting stock price and volume of shares traded") using language from the rules ("erroneous").
BRIEF ANSWER No. There is no indication that USA-Online would be liable to ABC for erroneous reporting of ABC's stock price and volume of shares traded because USA-Online does not owe a duty of care to ABC. In New York, in the absence of a greater duty of care from some fiduciary relationship, the liability of a reporter of stock information requires more than a simple case of getting or printing the wrong numbers. In that erroneous printing is all that can be shown that USA-Online did, ABC has no cause of action against USA-Online.	**Brief Answer** The BA, too, is concise but covers the facts, the law, and the legal conclusion well.

SAMPLE OFFICE MEMORANDUM #1	NOTES

STATEMENT OF FACTS

ABC is one of thousands of companies whose stock information is picked up by USA-Online from Standard and Poor's reporting service and published on USA-Online's "Market Marker" web page. On March 1, 1997, USA-Online erroneously reported that ABC's stock price had dropped to 1/10th of its value and also erroneously reported that the volume of shares traded for the stock had increased tenfold. As a result, there was significant volume of trading in ABC's stock, which pushed its value down even further. When confronted with this information, USA-Online refused to correct the error immediately, but promised to "take care of it within two to three business days," and it corrected the information three days after the erroneous reporting.

DISCUSSION

I.   USA-Online will not be liable to ABC for erroneous reporting of ABC's stock information because USA-Online has no duty to ABC to report information accurately.

To state a claim for negligence or breach of fiduciary duty in the printing of stock information, the defendant must have a duty to the plaintiff to use reasonable care in the performance of its actions. *LeClercq v. Shapo*, 798 N.E.2d 23, 26 (N.Y. 1996). A media outlet, whether it be a newspaper of general circulation or a specialized stock information service, does not owe a duty of care to the general public or to the companies whose stock information it reports to make sure that the information is reported accurately. *Jaillet v. Cashman*, 139 N.E. 714, 716 (N.Y. 1923), *aff'g*, 202 A.D. 805 (1st Dep't 1922), *aff'g*, 115

Notes column:

Facts

The statement of facts delivers the essential facts well. It has a noticeable narrative structure (*i.e.*, story).

Discussion

Main TREAT—Thesis heading: The heading states the Thesis on the sole legal issue.

Rule Section for Main TREAT: Notice that the author does not repeat the heading as the first line of text (which some people prefer). This rule section is short, but the author still has room to articulate the definitional rules and several interpretive rules.

SAMPLE OFFICE MEMORANDUM #1	NOTES

Misc. 383 (N.Y. County 1921); *Daniel v. Dow Jones & Co.*, 137 Misc. 2d 94, 95 (N.Y. County 1987); *Ginsburg v. Agora, Inc.*, 915 F. Supp. 733 (D. Md. 1995). Only a member of a protected class who personally has received information for guidance in a business transaction may assert a claim if the provider gives erroneous information. *Daniel*, 137 Misc. 2d at 95; *see* Restatement (Second) of Torts § 552 (1987).

Rule Section for Main TREAT, continued

A plaintiff will not be able to assert a claim for simple negligence, although he may be able to assert a claim if the news outlet is guilty of libel, defamation, or intentional conduct. *Jaillet*, 139 N.E. at 716 (no action based on simple negligence for misreporting stock numbers; no allegation of defamation, libel, or intentional misconduct); *Daniel*, 137 Misc. 2d at 95 (same); *but see Ginsburg*, 915 F. Supp. at 734 (no cause of action for state or federal securities fraud).

A duty to take care regarding the accuracy of reported financial information arises only if the plaintiff receives particular information from the defendant for his own personal guidance in a business transaction. *See Jaillet*, 139 N.E. at 716 (finding no duty of care in absence of contractual or fiduciary relationship between parties); *Daniel*, 137 Misc. 2d at 95 (same); *accord Gutter v. Dow Jones*, 490 N.E.2d 898 (Ohio 1986) (finding no duty of care owed to mere reader of publication). A duty of care will arise only if there is a contractual or fiduciary relationship between the plaintiff and the defendant. *See Jaillet*, 139 N.E. at 716 (publicly accessible stock ticker service had no duty of care to plaintiff); *Daniel*, 137 Misc. 2d at 95 (plaintiff was not member of protected class of persons to whom specific information was provided for guidance in business transactions); *Ginsburg*, 915 F. Supp. at 734 (publisher had no duty to plaintiff even though he was one of small number of subscribers to the journal, and journal expressly noted its use for making investment decisions); *Gutter*, 490 N.E.2d at 900

Explanation section for Main TREAT: As discussed above, this memorandum has only one issue, and one main TREAT to answer the issue without any need for sub-TREATs. Therefore, this is the explanation section for the entire memorandum. It uses explanatory synthesis to great effect.

SAMPLE OFFICE MEMORANDUM #1	NOTES
(Wall Street Journal lacked duty of care to reader who relied on erroneously reported stock information); Restatement (Second) of Torts § 552. Otherwise, the First Amendment, U.S. Const. amend. I, and the public policy supporting a free and unfettered press favor denying members of the general public the right to sue a news outlet for erroneous publication of stock information. *See Daniel*, 137 Misc. 2d at 95 (on-line service entitled to special protection under the Free Speech and Free Press provisions of U.S. Constitution and the N.Y. Constitution); *Gutter*, 490 N.E.2d at 900 (Dow Jones entitled to First Amendment protections).	*Explanation section for Main TREAT, continued*
In the instant case, ABC had no contractual or fiduciary relationship with USA-Online, and ABC was not a member of a protected class of persons to whom specific information was provided for its guidance in a business transaction. ABC is one of thousands of companies whose stock information is picked up by USA-Online from Standard and Poor's reporting service and published on USA-Online's "Market Marker" web page. There is no allegation that USA-Online's conduct was anything but simple inadvertence or negligence. No allegation is made that USA-Online engaged in libel, defamation, or intentional conduct.	**Application section for the main TREAT** This application section does not contain any citations. They aren't necessary in this case, mainly because the Explanation section was so well synthesized. However, sometimes the analogies and distinctions you make in the Application section will require reference to, discussion of, and citation to cases and other authorities.
Therefore, there is no support for the type of claim ABC wants to bring. No case has suggested that the media has a duty to verify and ensure the correctness of the financial information it reports, and none of the authorities suggests that there is room for an argument that the law should be modified or extended.	**Thesis restated as a Conclusion** This is the thesis restated on the main issue, which is the sole issue for the memorandum.

With sample #2, we move to a more complicated issue governed by a rule with several sub-parts each of which could, potentially, require an entire sub-TREAT to address it. In addition, the problem involves a certain fair use defense, parody, that itself has rules defining and interpreting the defense, again producing the potential need for sub-TREATs to properly handle the questions raised by the rules. See how the author used roadmaps to zero in on the rules, elements, and sub-parts of elements that were in dispute, preserving a select few for actual discussion and analysis in the memorandum.

SAMPLE OFFICE MEMORANDUM #2	NOTES
MEMORANDUM **TO:** Michael D. Murray **FROM:** Student 123 **DATE:** October 14, 2014 **RE:** Friends of Alternative Marriage/National Midnight Star v. FOAM (C1234/00001) **SUBJECT:** Use of Parody Defense in Copyright Infringement Case	**Caption**
ISSUE Will Friends of Alternative Marriage's ("FOAM") poster, which borrowed copyrighted images of celebrities from the National Midnight Star ("NMS") tabloid for the purpose of supporting gay marriage and civil union laws, be protected as fair use parody under 17 U.S.C. § 107 from NMS's copyright infringement claim when FOAM's usage fails to target the original for criticism, but is transformative of the original?	**Issue** This issue is a bit on the long side, but not necessarily too long. It has a lot of information on (1) the legal question, (2) the relevant facts and disputed elements of the law, (3) using language borrowed from the rules.
CONCLUSION No. NMS's original images were created to inform readers of the short-lived marriage exploits of Britney Spears. FOAM used the images borrowed from NMS to produce a poster promoting reforms of state marriage laws. FOAM's efforts were directed to reworking NMS's images in a way that attempted to ridicule religious and socially conservative views of marriage. Although FOAM's poster is transformative of the original as it created from the borrowed images	**Conclusion** This is a thorough, well-drafted conclusion. It is very informative. Note the required parts: (1) the direct answer ("No") at the beginning, (2) a thorough summary of the operative facts, (3) a summary of the disputed elements of the law, and (4) the author's legal conclusion.

SAMPLE OFFICE MEMORANDUM #2	NOTES
content which is of a different character and sends a completely different message than the original, FOAM will not be able to successfully assert that its use of pictures copyrighted by NMS is a fair use parody under 17 U.S.C. § 107. The target of FOAM's work is religious and social conditions and political views that are criticized in an effort to reform prevailing laws on alternative forms of marriage. FOAM has not created a parody of NMS or its work because FOAM does not comment on or criticize the work of NMS, and thus, FOAM does not target the original work for criticism.	*Conclusion, continued*

STATEMENT OF FACTS

In its effort to reform state marriage laws to include gay marriages and civil unions, FOAM created a poster using pictures of pop-star Britney Spears, her husband Jason Alexander, pop-star Jennifer Lopez, and her husband, singer Marc Anthony. The original pictures, used in two images on the poster, were copyrighted by NMS and were used without permission. The first image was the Spears-Alexander marriage license, with a faint image of Spears in the background and a prominent note at the bottom: "Good for 55 hours only." The other work superimposed the faces of Lopez and Anthony on people standing beside bride and groom Spears and Alexander beneath the caption: "Little White Chapel, Las Vegas." The poster was meant to ridicule claims that marriage law reforms such as those endorsed by FOAM would damage the sanctity of marriage. NMS has sued FOAM for copyright infringement in the U.S. District Court for the Southern District of New York.

Facts

The facts section is concise, but it tells enough of a story to inform us of the relevant, operative facts.

SAMPLE OFFICE MEMORANDUM #2	NOTES

DISCUSSION

I. FOAM's use of the copyrighted images will not be protected as parody under the fair use provision of United States copyright law because its commentary does not target the original NMS work for criticism.

Under United States copyright law, a work using copyrighted material of another author may be protected from copyright infringement prosecution if it is found to be a "fair use." The U.S. Copyright Act reads, in pertinent part,

> The fair use of a copyrighted work. . . for purposes such as criticism [and] comment. . . is not an infringement of copyright. In determining whether the use made of a work in any particular case is a fair use the factors to be considered shall include—(1) the purpose and character of the use, including whether such use is of a commercial nature;. . . (2) the nature of the copyrighted work; (3) the amount and substantiality of the portion used in relation to the copyrighted work as a whole; and (4) the effect of the use upon the potential market for or value of the copyrighted work.. . .

17 U.S.C. § 107 (2005). In applying this law, courts have rejected the use of bright line rules, calling instead for a case-by-case analysis which weighs together a consideration of all four of the included factors. *Campbell* at 577-578. **[Remember: This memorandum employs an abbreviated citation form that was approved for this assignment. It does not contain proper Bluebook or ALWD citations and it is not intended to be a reference on citation form.]** Significantly for the issue in the principal case, parody may be considered a fair use, qualifying as such under the first factor, "purpose and character of the use." *Id.* at 579.

Notes column:

Discussion

TREAT I
The **Thesis Heading** is very useful; note the "because" part.

Rule Section—TREAT I

SAMPLE OFFICE MEMORANDUM #2	NOTES
The discussion of FOAM's claim to fair use as parody undertaken below will consider only the first half of element (1), "the purpose and character of use." 17 U.S.C. § 107. The second half of element (1), whether use is of a commercial nature, is not at issue given FOAM's not-for-profit status. Element (2), the nature of the copyrighted work, is also not at issue as the nature of NMS's original work is that it is published, copyrightable work. Element (3), the relation of the substance of the borrowed portion to the whole work, is undisputed as FOAM borrowed the NMS images in their entirety. Finally, element (4), the effect of the use on the potential market for the original, requires fact finding on the effect on the market before it can be considered.	**Roadmap** This is a very involved roadmap. It takes us out of three and a half elements, and sets up the discussion of parody which is the particular "purpose and character" of the use that is at issue in this case.
Parody, qualifying as fair use, is a work that: (1) targets the borrowed original work and, at least in part, makes comment on it, and (2) is transformative of the original work, rather than simply superseding it. *See Campbell* at 579-580. It has additionally been found to be immaterial whether the alleged parody is in good or bad taste, *Id.* at 582, whether the work is labeled as a parody, *Id.* at 583, or whether the copyright owner would endorse or prohibit the work, *Leibovitz* at 115.	The roadmap concludes in a continuation of the rule section to provide the definitional rules for parody.
A. FOAM'S poster does not target and comment on the original work of NMS when it targets a broad social issue, marriage reform.	**Sub-TREAT A–** Thesis Heading
For an alleged parody to satisfy this element it must in some way hold up the original from which it borrowed for comment or ridicule. *Compare Campbell* at 583 (rap group 2 Live Crew's song borrowing from Roy Orbison's "Oh, Pretty Woman" was held to be a fair use parody where its "bawdy" lyrics were found to direct a critique at the "naivete. . . of an earlier day" expressed in Orbison's work), *and Leibovitz*	**Explanation section** Note the use of explanatory synthesis throughout this explanation section.

SAMPLE OFFICE MEMORANDUM #2	NOTES
at 114 (Paramount Picture's movie advertisement, which borrowed from a famous Annie Leibovitz photograph, was held to be a fair use parody where it criticized the "pretentiousness" of the original), *with Dr. Seuss* at 1401 (held that Penguin Books' publication using the famous style of children's author Theodore Geisel to ridicule the O.J. Simpson murder trial was not a fair use parody where the original was the vehicle for but not the target of the comment).	*Explanation section, continued*
Furthermore, satire, which targets some larger aspect of society, only qualifies as fair use parody where it also targets the original. *See Rogers* at 310 (use of copyrighted photo to satirize modern materialism was held not to be a fair use parody where the borrowed work was in no way the object of the satire); *Dr. Seuss* at 1401 (satire of Simpson trial was not a fair use parody where no part of the critique was directed at Geisel's original work); *Steinberg* at 714 (Columbia Picture's use of a copyrighted work of art to satirize a "parochial view of the world" in an advertisement was held not to be a fair use parody where its satire failed to critique the borrowed-from original in any way).	
The bearing of this analysis on the instant case is evident. FOAM's poster clearly falls within Campbell's construction of satire, but not parody. *Campbell* at 580-581.	**Application section**
FOAM's work does not target the borrowed-from original with its critique and commentary. The images of Spears, Alexander, Lopez, and Anthony are used by FOAM to make the satirical comment that traditional marriages already threaten the "sanctity" of marriage. The poster's comment is purely meant to further FOAM's broad social and political goal of marriage reform. The critique does not in any way target NMS or NMS's use of the images that FOAM borrowed. Therefore, it fails to satisfy the first required element of a parody.	**Thesis restated as a conclusion** The last two sentences contain the thesis restated for this sub-TREAT.

SAMPLE OFFICE MEMORANDUM #2	NOTES
B. **FOAM's poster is "transformative" of the original work because it alters the original to create a new meaning for the work.**	**Sub-TREAT B—** Thesis Heading
The second element of parody requires that the work be transformative of the original rather than merely superseding it. *Campbell* at 579. The *Campbell* court went on to define transformative as "add(ing) something new, with a further purpose or different character, altering the first with new expression, meaning or message .. . . " *Id.* The court also notes that the more significant the transformative element, the less significant other factors, such as commercialism for example, become. *Id.*	**Rule section— Sub-TREAT B**
In order to be considered transformative of an original, a work must take the original and create something which clearly alters or goes beyond the original in some substantive way. *Compare Campbell* at 579 (held as fair use parody where the rap song "has an obvious claim to transformative value"), *and Leibovitz* at 114 (held that the reconstituted photo "adds something new" and was a fair use parody), *with Dr. Seuss* at 1401 (held not to be fair use parody where the wholesale borrowing of Geisel's style, despite the alteration in content, did not create any "new expression").	**Explanation section** Note the use of explanatory synthesis in this explanation section.
In the instant case, the substance of form and message in the FOAM poster is clearly new and different from the original. Whatever the NMS tabloid's use of the photos might have been, FOAM's employment of them as a vehicle by which to participate in the ongoing social and political debate over marriage law reform and to offer a critique of traditional marriages undoubtedly does more than merely supersede the original use. By using the photos in this way, the new work is necessarily transformative because it creates of the borrowed photos meaning and purpose separate and	**Application section Thesis restated as a conclusion on Sub-TREAT B –** The last sentence of the paragraph is the Thesis restated on Sub-TREAT B.

SAMPLE OFFICE MEMORANDUM #2	NOTES
apart from that of the original. Thus, FOAM's poster is transformative of the original. As discussed above, FOAM's poster using copyrighted images from NMS does not qualify as a parody for purposes of fair use under 17 U.S.C. § 107 as it fails to target the original.	**Thesis restated as a conclusion— Main Issue** The last sentence of the memorandum is the thesis restated for the main issue. This follows the best practice to finish the main TREAT that you started and bring closure to the entire discussion.

Sample office memorandum #3 is another take on the same assignment used in sample #2.

SAMPLE OFFICE MEMORANDUM #3	NOTES
MEMORANDUM	**Caption**
TO: Michael D. Murray **FROM:** Student 456 **DATE:** October 12, 2014 **RE:** Friends of Alternative Marriage/National Midnight Star v. FOAM (C1234/00002) **SUBJECT:** Use of Parody Defense in Copyright Infringement Case	
ISSUE Does the use and modification of glamorous National Midnight Star ("NMS") photos by Friends of Alternative Marriage ("FOAM") for a serious debate on same sex marriage, allow FOAM to successfully raise a parody defense against NMS' claim of copyright infringement by meeting the transformation and criticism elements required of a parody?	**Issue** This issue, from the same assignment as Sample Memorandum #2, is worded differently but still has a lot of information on (1) the legal question, (2) the relevant facts and disputed elements of the law, (3) using language borrowed from the rules.

SAMPLE OFFICE MEMORANDUM #3	NOTES

CONCLUSION

Yes, FOAM can successfully raise a parody defense against NMS because its work meets the requirements to be considered a parody in the jurisdiction of the United States Court of Appeals for the Second Circuit. A successful parody claim for FOAM requires their work meet two criteria with respect to NMS' copyright claim, a transformation of the original work, and a criticism of the original work. FOAM, through its clever superposition of NMS' works with original material, easily meets the transformative element. In addition, FOAM meets the comment and criticism element by contrasting the glamorous and flippant originals with the serious and principled meaning of FOAM's work.

STATEMENT OF FACTS

As part of an effort to support reformation of state laws regarding gay marriage and civil unions, FOAM developed a poster using several copyrighted images owned by the tabloid magazine National Midnight Star ("NMS"). The images related to Britney Spears' 55 hour marriage to Jason Alexander that started and finished in Las Vegas and to Jennifer Lopez's most recent marriage to Marc Anthony. FOAM did not ask permission to use the images. FOAM modified a marriage license image by adding a faint image of Britney Spears as a background and FOAM added text at the bottom reading: "*Good for 55 hours only." FOAM modified a wedding photograph by superimposing the heads of Marc Anthony and Jennifer Lopez onto the bodies of the unnamed couple appearing next to Spears and Alexander in the photograph, and by adding captioned names for each person: "Marc," "J-Lo," "Britney," and "Jason." FOAM also superimposed the heading "Little White Wedding Chapel, Las Vegas" over the heads of the celebrities in the wedding

Conclusion
This is another thorough, well-drafted conclusion. Note the required parts: (1) the direct answer ("Yes") at the beginning, (2) a thorough summary of the operative facts, (3) a summary of the disputed elements of the law, and (4) the author's legal conclusion.

Facts

The facts section is quite businesslike. It may not read like a bedtime story, but it certainly is reminiscent of a news story—in a good way—by telling us the relevant, operative facts of the case.

SAMPLE OFFICE MEMORANDUM #3	NOTES
photograph. FOAM used portions of NMS's copyrighted images for each of the modifications described above. FOAM used the text "BY ALL MEANS—STOP GAY MARRIAGE DON'T LET IT MAKE MARRIAGE LESS SACRED" to sarcastically highlight the hypocrisy in society and the media regarding the sanctity of marriage and the glamorous portrayal of short and frequent marriages between celebrities. NMS sued FOAM in the United States District Court for the Southern District of New York for copyright infringement.	*Facts, continued*

DISCUSSION

Discussion

I.   **Friends of Alternative Marriage can successfully raise a parody defense against National Midnight Star's claim of copyright infringement because its work both transforms and criticizes the original work, meeting the two part test for parody as a fair use.**

> **TREAT I—**
> **Thesis heading** on main TREAT I—notice the "because" part.

    Parody, as a subset of the fair use doctrine, is set out in the United States Code:

> **Rule section**
> for TREAT I
>
> Note that the author is moving the conversation ahead rapidly by immediately placing "parody" into the overall rule on fair use in copyright law.

> . . . the fair use of a copyrighted work,. . . for purposes such as criticism, comment,. . . is not an infringement of copyright. In determining whether the use made of a work in any particular case is a fair use the factors to be considered shall include—
>
> (1) the purpose and character of the use, including whether such use is of a commercial nature or is for nonprofit educational purposes;
>
> (2) the nature of the copyrighted work;
>
> (3) the amount and substantiality of the portion used in relation to the copyrighted work as a whole; and
>
> (4) the effect of the use upon the potential market for or value of the copyrighted work.

17 U.S.C. § 107 (2005).

SAMPLE OFFICE MEMORANDUM #3	NOTES
Though the four elements delineated above are weighed and considered together in any determination of fair use, *Campbell* at 578, only the first half of element one, the purpose and character of use, will be considered due to the specific requirements of this case. The second half of element one, the commercial nature of the work, is not considered as FOAM is a not-for-profit organization whose motivation is awareness and fundraising. Element two, the nature of the copyrighted work, is not in dispute, as both parties accept the original work as an expressive, publicly-known work that is copyrightable. Element three, the substantiality of the original work used, is also not disputed, with both parties agreeing FOAM used and modified NMS's images in their entirety. Element four, the effect on the market for the original work, will not be considered at this time because sufficient market analysis has not yet been conducted to make a determination on that point.	**Roadmap** This is another extensive roadmap to take the reader out of three and a half elements of the fair use provision, and lead the discussion into the "purpose and character of the use" that is at issue in the case—a parody purpose and character of the use.
In the instant case, the purpose and character of the use must be evaluated using the requirements for a parody. *Campbell* at 574. A defendant can successfully raise a parody defense, as a subset of fair use, if: (1) the work is transformative in nature, and (2) the parody comments on or criticizes the original work. *Campbell* at 579, 580-81.	Again, the roadmap ends in a continuation of the rule section, providing the definitional rule with the two elements of parody. This sets an expectation of two sub-TREATs, A and B.
A. <u>**FOAM's work is inherently transformative because it takes the original work and modifies it to express a new idea.**</u>	**Sub-TREAT A –** Thesis heading with a "because" part.
FOAM's work is transformative because it uses, modifies, and expands upon the original work. All parodies must meet the rule that they transform or modify the original work in some way. *See Campbell* at 579; *Leibovitz* at 113; *Rogers* at 311.	**Rule section** on **Sub-TREAT A**

SAMPLE OFFICE MEMORANDUM #3	NOTES
The general rule of transformation is a broad one, but with the overarching principle that some modification must add to or expand the original work, and the more significant this addition is, the greater the weight the transformative element bears in a fair use balancing test. *See Campbell* at 579 (gradual transformation of an old fashioned love song into a lurid tale of a street walker sufficient for parody); *Leibovitz* at 114 (transforming a seriously-posed nude female photograph into one of a similarly posed female, but superimposed with the head of a smiling male was sufficient for parody). The above ideas are reinforced by the corollary that if a claimed parody is a near wholesale copy of the original, no fair use is found. *See Rogers* at 311 (a sculpture copied a photograph "in toto" with no significant additions to meaning or substance; the claim of parody was rejected); *Steinberg* at 714 (a movie poster copied key portions of the original work without adding significant meaning or substance; the claim of parody was rejected).	**Explanation section** Uses explanatory synthesis.
The principle of transformation is met broadly though FOAM's marriage certificate watermark as well as more bluntly in the "Little White Wedding Chapel" picture editing. In both cases FOAM transforms the original photos from celebrity "fanzine" material into an observation on society's and NMS' views of the sanctity of marriage. The transformative meaning of FOAM's newly modified images is further enhanced by the use of selected quotes regarding the sanctity of marriage offered in stark contrast to the frivolous portrayal of marriage perpetrated by the recreated depictions of celebrities with short-lived marriages. The transformation is dramatic and clear, leaving little room for doubt that FOAM truly added to and expanded on the splashy, celebrity-exploiting meaning of NMS's original work.	**Application**

SAMPLE OFFICE MEMORANDUM #3	NOTES
Therefore, FOAM's work meets the requirements of transformation set out above.	**Thesis restated as a conclusion** on Sub-TREAT A
B. **FOAM's work comments on and criticizes the original work because is contrasts the message of celebrity and marriage depicted in the original work against the sanctity of marriage, and it criticizes the original work as superficial relative to the human rights of people desiring to be married.**	**Sub-TREAT B— Thesis heading**
FOAM's work comments on the original work because it contrasts the celebrity-oriented "glamour" depicted by the original images with a fundamental question of human rights ignored or even belittled by the creator of the original images. To be considered a parody, a work must comment on or criticize the original. *Campbell* at 580-81, 583 (contrasting the ugliness of street life with the naiveté of the original)	**Rule section** for Sub-TREAT B This is a decidedly weak rule section.
Commentary or criticism is established if the work in question is reasonably perceived to target the original work. *See Campbell* at 582 (a lurid tale of a street walker seen as criticizing the romanticism of the original work); *Leibovitz* at 114, 115 (mimicking a seriously posed nude female photograph with one of similarly posed female but superimposed with the head of a smiling male). The above principle is highlighted even more clearly when no commentary exists, or in the case of satire, where the work is a commentary, but not on the original. *See Steinberg* at 714 (a movie poster copying key portions of the original work without commenting on or criticizing the original was not a parody); *Rogers* at 310 (a sculpture copying a photograph with no commentary or criticism of the original was not a parody); *Dr. Seuss Enterprises* at 1400 (a satire of OJ Simpson's trial did not criticize the original Dr. Seuss work and was not a parody).	**Explanation section** Uses explanatory synthesis

SAMPLE OFFICE MEMORANDUM #3	NOTES
Although subtle and sophisticated, the contrast between the original and FOAM's work demonstrates a commentary and a criticism targeting society, the press in general, and even NMS in particular. The original work's consistent failure to depict important issues relating to human rights and the ongoing violation of "the sanctity of marriage" that occurs in heterosexual marriages is highlighted and criticized by FOAM's creative work. NMS's images celebrate celebrities without giving any thought to the issues behind these short-lived marriages; the message targeted by FOAM is that NMS is as careless and thoughtless about the serious civil rights issues tied up with the concept of marriage as are the social and religious conservatives whose words also are skewered by FOAM's work.	**Application section**
Finally, when weighed in *toto* with the extensive addition and transformation apparent in FOAM's work, this depiction easily satisfies the relatively lower bar of criticism required to be considered a parody.	**Thesis restated as a conclusion—** The last sentence of the Application is a thesis restated on Sub-TREAT A.
Considering all of the above factors, FOAM's work is at least in part a criticism of the original work, and by meeting both requirements established for parody, FOAM can successfully raise a parody defense against the copyright challenge from NMS.	**Thesis restated as a conclusion on the main issue –** The last sentence of the memorandum is a thesis restated on the main issue of the memorandum.

Memorandum #4 discusses a different problem from memoranda #2 and #3. The subject matter still is the parody defense in copyright law, but the underlying facts are different.

SAMPLE OFFICE MEMORANDUM #4	NOTES
MEMORANDUM	**Caption**

TO: Michael D. Murray
Carol Ng Book

FROM: Student 789

DATE: October 11, 2014

RE: SpinMag.com/New York Post and New York Daily News v. Spin Mag (C1234/00001)

SUBJECT: Use of Parody Defense in Copyright Infringement Case

ISSUE

Does SpinMag.com's reproduction of the images of the New York Post and the New York Daily News in its fake advertisement of a "Britney Shears" doll constitute fair use under a defense of parody, when SpinMag.com did not transform the original images with a new meaning nor target the original for the purposes of criticism?

Issue

This issue section does a good job stating the legal question in sufficient detail—facts and elements of the law revealed by selecting key words from the language of the rules)—to give us a clear picture of the problem addressed in the memorandum.

CONCLUSION

No. SpinMag.com cannot successfully claim that its reproduction of the copyrighted images of the New York Post and the New York Daily News constitutes fair use under a defense of parody because it does not transform the original's character nor can it be reasonably perceived as targeting the original for commentary. SpinMag.com does not alter the images by any means and leaves their expression unchanged. Also, SpinMag.com does not target these media outlets for criticism, as the fake ad is solely directed to comment on Britney Spears.

Conclusion

This conclusion provides a good summary of the facts, the disputed elements of the law, and the author's legal conclusions after performing her analysis. It all starts with a definite answer to the issue—"No."

SAMPLE OFFICE MEMORANDUM #4	NOTES

STATEMENT OF FACTS

After pop star Britney Spears shaved her head in February of 2007, SpinMag.com ran a fake ad for a "Britney Shears" doll on its website. The ad shows a bald-headed Britney likeness in a straight-jacket, with the front page images of the New York Post ("Post") and the New York Daily News ("Daily") issues covering the incident depicted in the background of the toy's packaging. Both the Post and the Daily did not approve of the use of their copyrighted images within the advertisement. SpinMag.com states that one of its purposes in including these images is to convey a message about how the media exploits celebrities and their personal lives. The newspapers sued SpinMag.com for copyright infringement in the United States District Court for the Southern District of New York.

Facts

The actual events from which this assignment was created took place in 2007, so we will have to strain credibility a bit as to why they would be analyzed in 2014.
This statement of the facts is drafted a bit loosely. It does not have as much narrative coherence as the prior examples in memoranda #1 and #2 above. It reads more like a simple listing of important facts.

DISCUSSION

Discussion

I. **Spinmag.com's use of the Post's and the Daily's images is not protected as fair use under a defense of parody, because its use is not transformative nor can it be reasonably perceived to be targeting the original for criticism.**

Main TREAT I—Main Thesis heading
This heading is useful because of the detail and the "because" part.

When assessing whether the use of a copyrighted work is fair use, 17 U.S.C. § 107 states that:

> reproduction...for purposes such as criticism, comment, news reporting, teaching..., scholarship, or research, is not an infringement of copyright. In determining whether the use made of a work...is fair use the factors to be considered shall include: (1) the purpose and character of the use, including whether such use is of a commercial nature or is for nonprofit educational purposes; (2) the nature of the copyrighted work; (3) the amount and substantiality of the portion used in relation to the copyrighted work as a whole; and (4) the effect of the use upon the potential market for or value of the copyrighted work.

Rule section for Main TREAT I
This section lays out the four fair use factors in copyright law, and immediately goes into interpretive rules, one concerning parody, and the other a more general rule on evaluating the four fair use factors.

SAMPLE OFFICE MEMORANDUM #4	NOTES

17 U.S.C. § 107. Parody, defined as a "literary or artistic work that imitates the characteristic style of an author or work for comic effect or ridicule," may claim fair use under the first part of the first element regarding the purpose and character of the use. *Campbell* at 580. The four elements are to be explored and weighed together in light of copyright's purpose of promoting science and the arts. *Campbell* at 569.

In the instant case, no element other than the "purpose and character of the use" is in dispute. SpinMag. com's use is assumed to be commercial, and the nature of the copyrighted work is met because both newspapers' images are publicly known, expressive works that are copyrightable. SpinMag.com also used the images in their entirety, rendering the third element void. The last element is not ripe for discussion until more fact-finding is conducted on the effect of the fake ad on the market for the original works. Hence, only the "nature and purpose" element remains contested, and thus will be discussed hereafter.

Roadmap
Once again, the roadmap is used to direct the focus to the element of the rule that is disputed, and to explain why the other elements will not be discussed further in the memorandum.

In order for a copied work to be considered parody, the use must (a) be transformative, and (b) target the original for criticism. *Campbell* at 579; *Leibovitz* at 114.

The **roadmap** transitions back to the rule section, providing the rule defining the two elements of parody. These will point to the two sub-TREATs analyzing these elements.

A. SpinMag.com's use of the Post's and the Daily's images is not transformative because it does not alter the expression or purpose of the original.

Sub-TREAT A— Thesis heading

For a copied work to be considered transformative, it must not merely supersede the object in the original creation, but it must alter the original with a new expression, meaning, or message. *Campbell* at 569. Though finding "transformativeness" is not absolutely necessary for a finding of fair use, the more transformative the new work is, the less significant the other elements become in weighing against a finding in fair use. *Id.*

Rule section for Sub-TREAT A

SAMPLE OFFICE MEMORANDUM #4	NOTES
A copied work is considered transformative if it alters the expression or purpose of the original. *See Campbell* at 582 (the use of a song's lyrics was found to be transformative in its shocking degeneration of the overly-sentimental original into a derisive play-on words); *Blanch* at 253 (the defendant's appropriation of a fashion photograph of women's legs against a backdrop of food and landscape in a painting was found to be transformative); *Leibovitz* at 115 (the defendant's use of the aesthetics of an original photograph was found to be transformative by its placement of a smirking male face on top of a serious-minded pregnant female's body). A transformative use must actually change the images evoked by the original work. *See Campbell* at 583 (the usage of a song's lyrics was transformative because it changed the original's romanticized view of streetwalkers into a lewd demand for sex); *Blanch* at 248 (the image created by the defendant's collage painting depicting the sexual, recreational, and physical appetites of the human condition changed the original's image of erotic fashion photography); *Leibovitz* at 114 (finding that an ad using an original photograph was transformative, since the ad transformed the original's image of seriousness to a more whimsical image).	**Explanation section for sub-TREAT A**
In the instant case, SpinMag.com's use is not transformative since it fails to alter the meaning or expression of the front page images of the Post and the Daily. Rather, SpinMag.com merely combines these images and places them in the background of its ad, with their prior meaning unchanged. The images serve the purpose of proving that the incident involving Spears shaving her head had actually happened. The expression of the original images remains unaltered, as SpinMag.com's usage was for the purposes of giving the background story behind the spoof doll.	**Application section for Sub-TREAT A**

SAMPLE OFFICE MEMORANDUM #4	NOTES
Therefore, SpinMag.com's reproduction of the images of the Post and the Daily is not transformative because it does not alter the expression or purpose of the original.	**Thesis restated as conclusion for Sub-TREAT A**
B. SpinMag.com's use of the images of the Post and the Daily does not target the original for criticism because the sole focus of its commentary is on Britney Spears.	**Sub-TREAT B—** Thesis heading
In order for a work to target the original for the purposes of parody, it must be reasonably perceived as commenting on the original. *Leibovitz* at 114. The copied work must be an object of the parody, and not just a part of a larger collective statement. *Rogers* at 310.	**Rule section for Sub-TREAT B**
The target of a parody can be reasonably perceived if the new work adds an unexpected element that contributes to a purpose that is different from the original's aim. *Compare Campbell* at 583 (establishing that the original could be reasonably perceived as the target of a song through the juxtaposition of the tame original lyrics with bawdier, degrading ones), *and Leibovitz* at 114 (where an ad replacing the pregnant female's head with a grinning male's expression was found to target the original in a reasonably perceived manner), *with Dr. Seuss* at 1400 (finding the original could not be reasonably perceived as a target for parody because the copied work merely imitated the style of the original and did not introduce any unexpected elements adding to a new purpose).	**Explanation section for sub-TREAT B**
In the instant case, SpinMag.com does not introduce any unexpected element that contributes toward a new purpose that departs from the aims of the Post and the Daily. Instead, SpinMag.com merely reproduces these images to serve as evidence that the event happened, which coincides	**Application section for Sub-TREAT B**

SAMPLE OFFICE MEMORANDUM #4	NOTES
with the newspapers' purpose in producing these images on their front pages. Also, SpinMag.com's placement of these images in the background of the toy's packaging is indicative of the fact that it can be reasonably perceived to only be targeting the subject found at the forefront: Britney Spears. Finally, it cannot be reasonably perceived that SpinMag.com is commenting on the media's coverage of Spears, as SpinMag.com is an online media outlet itself.	*Application, continued*
SpinMag.com's stated purpose of making a parody out of the Post and the Daily cannot be reasonably perceived as targeting these media outlets for criticism.	**Thesis restated as conclusion for Sub-TREAT B**
Therefore, SpinMag.com's use of the Post's and the Daily's images is not protected as fair use under a defense of parody because its use does not transform the original images and does not target the original for criticism.	**Thesis restated as conclusion for the main TREAT of the memorandum**

The last sample is a bit different. Instead of presenting the complete memorandum, we wanted to let you into the kitchen and see a little bit about how the sausages are made. This last sample is the assignment memorandum and "bench memo" prepared by and for teaching assistants to show the various ways that the parts of the office memoranda responsive to the assignment could be completed.

SAMPLE OFFICE MEMORANDUM #5	NOTES
MEMORANDUM **TO:** Michael D. Murray **FROM:** Carol Ng Book **DATE:** October 11, 2014 **RE:** Thierry Guetta/Elvis Presley Enterprises (C7879/001) **SUBJECT:** Copyright fair use issues— Elvis/Don't Be Cruel	**Caption** This is the caption from the assignment memorandum provided to the teaching assistants and the students. Presumably, most students would copy this caption for their office memoranda.

| SAMPLE OFFICE MEMORANDUM #5 | NOTES |

Our firm needs to analyze the claim of a new client, Thierry Guetta. Guetta received a cease-and-desist letter from Elvis Presley Enterprises relating to Guetta's creation of several works based on a photographic image of Elvis and bearing the Elvis-related series title of "Don't Be Cruel." The letter to Guetta states: "(1) cease and desist all efforts to create or replicate the Elvis/Don't Be Cruel works; (2) cease and desist all efforts to advertise, market, sell, or distribute the Elvis/Don't Be Cruel works; (3) collect and retrieve and turn over to Elvis Presley Enterprises all existing, unsold works from the Elvis/Don't Be Cruel series, including all works placed with galleries or dealers or retailers or other persons or entities who might further sell or distribute the works; (4) prepare an accounting of all the sales of the Elvis/Don't Be Cruel works including customer names, purchase prices, gross and net profits. If you fail to comply with these demands within 45 days [of October 5, 2011], Elvis Presley Enterprises will sue you for copyright infringement in federal court in Memphis, Tennessee."

We have confirmed that Elvis Presley Enterprises does own the photographic image of Elvis Presley used by Guetta to create his works, a promo photograph from the 1957 motion picture, *Loving You*, starring Elvis (seen here, at right). This image prompted Guetta to create a series of images displayed in Guetta's 2008 "Life is Beautiful" exhibition in Los Angeles.

© 1957 Elvis Presley Enterprises, Inc.

Guetta continues to sell and market paintings, prints, silkscreens, and other artworks in this series derived

Facts of the Assignment

Note that this assignment pertains to a real dispute (but one not filed in any court at the time of the assignment). The artist is real, the Guetta artworks are real, and the Elvis photograph used by Guetta is real. You can follow up on the information provided here to get a better understanding of the case. Look for *"Exit through the Gift Shop," "Guetta," "Elvis,"* and *"Don't be Cruel."*

SAMPLE OFFICE MEMORANDUM #5	NOTES

from the Elvis Presley image, such as these three examples:

Please have your students predict Guetta's chances of success in establishing that his use of the image of Elvis Presley owned by Elvis Presley Enterprises is a fair use under United States copyright law. Your students should assume that Guetta's use constitutes copyright infringement if Guetta has no fair use defense.

Comments on the ISSUE section:

The case presents one issue—fair use or not—but it turns out to require a fairly long and detailed statement of the ISSUE because of the four 107-fair use factors that should be touched on in the ISSUE statement plus the usual presentation of some key facts to set the scene of the problem. I do think that the students should present one, longish ISSUE statement, not four. They must have the situation and story suggested through some key facts, and they must borrow language from the rules to "touch on" all of the rules—the statute, the four elements, plus the transformative test. The following sample ISSUE statements all do that.

Issue
These are author Murray's comments to his teaching assistants regarding the issue section the students were to write. You can peek behind the scenes and see the kind of input a professor will give his TAs. Maybe you'll excel in the course and become a TA, too!

ISSUE—Sample 1—This discusses a transformative fair use, and would set up a NO answer.

Is Thierry Guetta's use of a copyrighted image of Elvis Presley a fair use under 17 U.S.C. § 107 (2008), when Guetta marginally transformed the original photograph, a published, artistic, copyrighted work, by altering the media

The TAs provided several samples of possible formulations of the issue, each taking a slightly different approach to the problem. Consider each, and see if you can find strengths or weaknesses in each formulation.

SAMPLE OFFICE MEMORANDUM #5	NOTES

from photograph to graphic arts and adding an image of a toy assault rifle in the final work, Guetta used the original copyrighted image in its entirety, he sold his new images for commercial profit, and he potentially affected the marketability of the original copyrighted photograph?

ISSUE—Sample 2—This also discusses a transformative fair use, but it would set up a YES answer.

Whether Thierry Guetta's use of a copyrighted image of Elvis Presley is a fair use under 17 U.S.C. § 107, when Guetta transformed the original photograph, a published, artistic, copyrighted work, into a new artwork with a new meaning and message about the role of iconic and violent images in society by repeating and emphasizing the iconic value of the Elvis image, using the image in its entirety but combining it with a toy assault rifle, and subsequently sold the new image for commercial profit, and potentially affected the marketability of the original copyrighted photograph?

ISSUE—Sample 3—This discusses a parody or satire fair use and it would set up a YES answer.

Whether Thierry Guetta's use of a copyrighted image of Elvis Presley is a fair use under 17 U.S.C. § 107, when Guetta critiqued the meaning and message of the original, published, artistic photograph of iconic superstar Elvis and its impact on popular culture and transformed the message into a work commenting on modern culture's cruel indifference to violence by repeating and re-emphasizing the iconic value of the Elvis image, used in its entirety, but combining it with a Fisher Price toy assault rifle under a title of "Don't Be Cruel," and subsequently sold the new image for commercial profit, and potentially affected the marketability of the original copyrighted photograph?

SAMPLE OFFICE MEMORANDUM #5	NOTES
Comments on CONCLUSION:	**Conclusion**

Comments on CONCLUSION:

This problem is a close call under the law, so don't get concerned if the students come out one way or the other—what is more important than a Yes or a No answer is the reasoning and rationale—in short, the support—for the answer. A simple "NO, because the work was not transformed" is a poor answer—why wasn't it "transformed" when there were alterations to the original? Similarly, a simple "YES, the work was transformed with a new meaning and message" by itself says nothing—what was the old meaning, and how did Guetta pull off a new meaning and message in the new works? Is the context different (*Blanch* method)? Is the media and genre relevant (goes either way, *Dr. Seuss vs. Blanch*)? Is the "purpose" of the new work that much different from the original—if yes, how is it different?

If the student pursues a parody/satire theory, then the critique should take into account the original work—and it helps if it is a negative critique of the original work and what it stands for. Thus, the question is how did Guetta pull off a negative critique of a 1950's celebrity depiction of Elvis in his work? You can go the *Blanch v. Koons* route, but you've got to do some serious shift in context, purpose, and function to make the critical meaning of the new work obvious enough to succeed. Is this another *Blanch* or *Liebovitz* situation where the original work is turned on its head in function, meaning, and purpose, leading to a fair use, or is it more of a *Gaylord* and *Dr. Seuss* situation where enough of the creative, expressive attributes of the original works shine through in the new works so that the use is not fair.

CONCLUSION—Sample NO answer

No. Under 17 U.S.C. § 107, a work is determined to be fair use based on the purpose and character of the use, the nature of the copyrighted work, the amount of the copyrighted work used, and the effect on the market for or value of the copyrighted work. Guetta changed the work physically (he used the image in a new, more artistic media of silkscreens

Notes column:

Conclusion
Here are author Murray's comments to his teaching assistants regarding the conclusion section the students were to write. Now, you have the inside information. In that this was a real-life problem, the cases and rules referenced here are real-life authorities, but the context of the comments did not require full Bluebook citations.

SAMPLE OFFICE MEMORANDUM #5	NOTES
and paintings), but the same basic copyrighted image of Elvis shines through in the new works. Everyone can look at Guetta's works and see and appreciate the original photograph that still communicates its original meaning and message: a depiction of a great American rock-and-roll hero. The additional paint splattered on and the adding of different props does not change the essential function and purpose of the original depiction in the new works—the old work and the new works still depict Elvis as Elvis. Therefore, Guetta did not sufficiently transform the original photograph, and the purpose and character of the use factor will weigh against a finding of fair use. The negative score on fairness is furthered because Guetta sold his works for commercial profit, he used the entire published, expressive, copyrighted image of Elvis Presley in his works, and the faithful recreation of a depiction of Elvis has the potential to affect the market for other forms of Elvis memorabilia based on the original copyrighted photograph. Therefore, Guetta's Elvis-works do not constitute a fair use under 17 U.S.C. § 107.	
CONCLUSION— Sample Yes answer on Parody/Satire Theme Yes. Guetta's use of a copyrighted image of Elvis Presley is a fair use under 17 U.S.C. § 107, because Guetta critiqued the meaning and message of the original photograph of iconic superstar Elvis and its impact on popular culture and transformed the message into one commenting on modern culture's cruel indifference to violence by repeating and emphasizing the iconic value of the Elvis image and combining it with a Fisher Price toy assault rifle, and reapplied the title, "Don't Be Cruel" to the series of new images	

SAMPLE OFFICE MEMORANDUM #5	NOTES

he produced. The new commentary and critique on repetitive imagery and iconography in modern society expressed by Guetta in his work parallels the work of other influential artists, including Andy Warhol and Jeffrey Koons, and the public policy supporting the copyright fair use clause supports the creation of new, critical expression on existing works and their meaning in new contexts of modern society.

The fact that Guetta sold his works for commercial profit, and used the entire copyrighted image does not deny his fair use defense because the new work has a new meaning, message, and function that does not supersede or unfairly compete with the marketability of true, unaltered Elvis memorabilia, including the original copyrighted photograph of "the King."

Comments on RULES—

Fair use, transformative test, parody/satire

When assessing whether the use of a copyrighted work is fair use, 17 U.S.C. § 107 states that:

> reproduction...for purposes such as criticism, comment, news reporting, teaching..., scholarship, or research, is not an infringement of copyright. In determining whether the use made of a work...is fair use the factors to be considered shall include: (1) the purpose and character of the use, including whether such use is of a commercial nature or is for nonprofit educational purposes; (2) the nature of the copyrighted work; (3) the amount and substantiality of the portion used in relation to the copyrighted work as a whole; and (4) the effect of the use upon the potential market for or value of the copyrighted work.

17 U.S.C. § 107. The four elements are to be explored and weighed together in light of copyright's purpose of promoting science and the arts. *Campbell* at 569.

For a copied work to be considered transformative, it must not merely supersede the object in the original creation,

Rules

The applicable rules repeat many of the rules from the rule sections of the sample memoranda above.

SAMPLE OFFICE MEMORANDUM #5	NOTES

but it must alter the original with a new expression, meaning, or message. *Campbell* at 569. Though finding "transformativeness" is not absolutely necessary for a finding of fair use, the more transformative the new work is, the less significant the other elements become in weighing against a finding in fair use. *Id.*

Parody, defined as a "literary or artistic work that imitates the characteristic style of an author or work for comic effect or ridicule," may claim fair use under the first part of the first element regarding the purpose and character of the use. *Campbell* at 580. In order for a work to target the original for the purposes of parody, it must be reasonably perceived as commenting on the original. *Leibovitz* at 114. The copied work must be an object of the parody, and not just a part of a larger collective statement. *Rogers* at 310.

Comments on the EXPLANATION Sections

Comment on explanation sections: What is important to look for in students' work is: (a) are they using controlling authority correctly, in the right order, for useful principles that the controlling authorities actually speak to; (b) are they pursuing the right theory—they are writing on fair use, they are writing on one or more of the factors of 107, they are writing on aspects of the transformation test, or they are writing on a particular fair use theory such as parody or satire; (c) are they writing useful, detailed, illustrative parentheticals for each case in the synthesis. (I had to add detail to each of your draft parentheticals, so it proves that even you guys need to stay sharp on writing good, detailed, useful parentheticals). Beyond that, comment on the cases the students are using, the order that they cite them in, and the quality and creativity of the principles that they are illustrating. Note that good syntheses have more than three cases—don't let them produce a string of 2-case or 3-case syntheses.

Explanation sections

As you can see, after the general comments from Professor Murray, this section provides actual, sample explanatory syntheses for this problem. The Teaching Assistants drafted, and Professor Murray edited, a significant sampling of potential explanation section syntheses in preparation for receiving and evaluating the student's work.

SAMPLE OFFICE MEMORANDUM #5	NOTES

On Fair Use In General

In evaluating the fair use of a new work, it must be determined if the new work merely supersedes the objects of the original work or adds something new, furthering the purpose or character of use. *Compare Campbell v. Acuff-Rose Music, Inc.,* 510 U.S. 569, 579 (1994) (defendant was a rap group that parodied a well-known song; Court found the parody was fair use because the new song's play on words criticized the naiveté of the original song and gave the new song a new function and purpose, thus transformative), *and Blanch v. Koons*, 467 F.3d 244, 251 (2d Cir. 2006) (defendant changed the color and background of plaintiff's photograph to create a collage commenting on imagery leading to mass consumption in modern society; Court found it was fair use because of its new purpose and meaning, thus transformative), *with Zomba Enterprises, Inc. v. Panorama Records, Inc.,* 491 F.3d 574, 582 (6th Cir. 2007) (defendant recorded and sold karaoke discs; Court found only minimally altered because musicians simply stripped out the lyrics and did not change words or music and added nothing new to the original, thus it was not a fair use), *and Gaylord v. U.S.*, 595 F.3d 1364, 1373-74 (Fed. Cir. 2010) (stamp issued by the government based on a copyrighted work of a war memorial not transformative; altering the appearance of the work by adding snow and muting color does not give the work a new character, the original meaning and purpose of the expression of the original still shined through).

On Transformation—Transformative Test

A work is transformative if it alters the first piece with new expression, meaning, or message. *Compare Campbell,* 510 U.S. at 579 (new work criticized the naïve romance of the original "beautiful woman walking down the street" song by adding new, street-wise lyrics to create an updated,

SAMPLE OFFICE MEMORANDUM #5	NOTES

gritty portrayal of street prostitutes; Court found parody was transformative fair use because it created a new work that shed a new, critical light on the original), *and Blanch*, 467 F.3d at 253 (photograph used for collage to comment on society and mass media; work was given new meaning because it altered the original fashion photo of woman's legs by inverting it, hanging it with other images of woman's legs over junk food and Niagara Falls so as to comment on the images used to create consumer urges in modern society), *with Bridgeport Music, Inc. v. UMG Recordings, Inc.*, 585 F.3d 267, 278 (6th Cir. 2009) (new song was not sufficiently transformative and not a fair use when new musicians copied the original track and let it run intact, audibly discernable in its original form, albeit as a part of a new song with a change of genre and context from funk music to rap and hip-hop), *and Dr. Seuss Enterprises v. Penguin Books U.S.A., Inc.*, 109 F.3d 1394 (9th Cir. 1997) (defendant created a book based on the artwork and literary style of *The Cat in the Hat*; Court found it was not fair use because it did not alter the expression of the images and rhyming structure of the original, allowing these expressive elements of the original to shine through in the second work).

Transformative works are those that contribute their own creative aspects to the original, rather than relying primarily on the creative traits of the original to achieve its purposes. *Compare Campbell*, 510 U.S. at 583 (parody of Roy Orbison song changed the lyrics and genre of the original so as to criticize the naiveté of earlier generations' attitudes towards street life), *and Suntrust Bank v. Houghton Mifflin Co.*, 268 F.3d 1257, 1270 (11th Cir. 2001) (book relied on original characters and plot elements to re-tell the story of "Gone With the Wind" from the perspective of slaves as a commentary on race relations), *with Zomba Enters.*, 491 F.3d at 582 (exact copies of songs reproduced without lyric track

SAMPLE OFFICE MEMORANDUM #5	NOTES
for use on karaoke discs relied exclusively on the creative, expressive elements of the originals and was not a fair use), *and Princeton University. Press v. Michigan Document Services, Inc.*, 99 F.3d 1381, 1389 ("mechanical" copying of 95 pages of a 316 page book for use by students relies on the creativity and expression of the original and contributed no new, creative expression through the copying, and was not a fair use), *and Peter Letterese and Assoc., Inc. v. World Institute of Scientology Enterprises*, 533 F.3d 1287, 1311 (11th Cir. 2008) (sales courses merely emphasized the methods taught in the book, "Big League Sales," without changing the form, meaning, or purpose of the original, and was not a fair use).	
Commercial Use—Amount Taken— Effect on the Market The more work that is taken from a copyright owner, the more their interests are infringed, diminishing the likelihood of a successful fair use defense. *Zomba Enterprises*, 491 F.3d at 583 (defendant recorded and sold karaoke discs; not fair use because defendant copied the plaintiff's entire composition including visual and auditory lyrics); *Princeton University Press*, 99 F.3d at 1389 (defendants reproduced substantial segments of copyrighted work and sold to college students; not fair use because the defendants used as much as 30% of one copyrighted work and no less than 5% of the copyrighted work as a whole); *Elvis Presley Enterprises, Inc. v. Passport Video*, 349 F.3d 622, 630 (9th Cir. 2003) (defendant's use of Elvis clips was not fair use because clips were repeated numerous times which exceeded the biographical purpose, also some clips were only a few seconds long but others played for over a minute).	

SAMPLE OFFICE MEMORANDUM #5	NOTES

If artistic works are sold for profit, they are less likely to be found transformative fair use if the works stand to profit primarily from the entertainment value or appeal of the original. *Compare Campbell*, at 583 (2 Live Crew profited from its display of the banality of the original rather than the original's own entertainment value), *with Zomba Enter., Inc.*, at 582 (karaoke company was profiting primarily from the entertainment value of the original songs themselves), *and Salinger v. Colting*, 607 F.3d 68 (2d Cir. 2010) (author of the "sequel" to "Catcher in the Rye" was profiting from the inherent entertainment value of the original's plot and characters without providing commentary or criticism), *and Elvis Presley Enterprises,* 349 F.3d at 628 (documentary containing unlicensed footage of Elvis sought to profit from the inherent entertainment value of the footage, rather than commentary on the footage).

When determining the effect of the work on the marketability of the original work, courts do not require a demonstration of actual harm, but rather the existence of a meaningful risk of economic harm, especially if the alleged infringement became widespread. *See Sony Corp. of Am. v. University City Studios, Inc.*, 464 U.S. 417, 451-54 (1984) (little to no effect on marketability because no meaningful risk of economic harm from the users of home videotape recorders time-shifting programming); *Princeton University Press*, 99 F.3d at 1387 (significant effect on marketability because a meaningful risk existed that copying textbooks would become widespread and greatly reduce book sales); *Bouchat v. Baltimore Ravens*, 619 F.3d 301, 312-13 (4th Cir. 2010) (existence of market for items with team logo proves the threat of product substitution and establishes an effect on marketability).

XI. SAMPLE CLIENT LETTERS

The final pages of this chapter present two client letters (written to non-lawyers). The first is a sample letter drafted to report the research in the first sample memoranda provided above on liability of a stock news service for erroneous reporting; the second is a sample letter drafted to report the research regarding a problem involving commercial frustration. In general, they are solid examples, but having read the sample memos above, you should evaluate what you like and do not like about these letters, and what you might do differently. These letters merely are samples, not models of perfection.

Sample Client Letter 1—Claim for Erroneous Reporting of Stock Information	Comments
PIPER & PICKWICK, L.L.P. March 14, 2000 Roger Bannister ABC Widgets Corp. 1424 Progress Parkway Seattle, WA 99999 **Re: ABC v. USA-Online** Dear Roger, Thank you for the opportunity to advise you on your recent dispute with USA-Online. I am very sorry to report that there is no indication that USA-Online would be liable to ABC for its erroneous reporting of your stock information earlier this month. The problem is that the law does not impose a duty on USA-Online to get this information right, and ABC therefore does not have a legal claim against USA-Online for their error. There are a number of New York cases with facts that are close to those of ABC, and they uniformly hold that a publicly-traded company generally does not have a valid claim against a stock news reporting service when the service makes a mistake in its reporting. USA-Online will be treated like any other member of the press that reports stock information. A media outlet, whether it be a newspaper of general circulation or a	We like this letter because it gets right to the point without waffling, without obfuscation, without trying to muddy the waters with legalese. The results of the research are definitely bad news for the client, and it takes the courage of your convictions to report the bad news to a good client without flinching. Ultimately, this is the best policy, and your clients will, in the end, appreciate your candor over any cheerleading. The letter goes into the legal issues without talking heavy-duty legal talk like an office memorandum. It should be obvious from this letter that the addressee, Roger Bannister, is not a law-trained reader. But the reader still is well-informed, and at a level appropriate for the audience.

Sample Client Letter 1—Claim for Erroneous Reporting of Stock Information	Comments
specialized stock information service, does not owe a duty of care to the general public or to the companies whose stock information it reports to make sure that the information is reported accurately. Only someone who personally has received information for guidance in a business transaction may assert a claim if the provider gives erroneous information. ABC had no contractual or fiduciary relationship with USA-Online, and ABC did not personally receive stock information from USA-Online for its guidance in a business transaction. Rather, ABC is one of many companies whose stock information is picked up by USA-Online from Standard and Poor's reporting service and published on USA-Online's "Market Marker" web page. We considered a number of theories, but there is nothing in the facts to indicate that USA-Online's conduct was anything but simple inadvertence or negligence, and the law absolves them from liability for simple inadvertence or negligence. In addition, we see no indication that USA-Online engaged in libel or defamation, which would require us to prove that they intentionally or recklessly reported false information about ABC. We do not see any viable claim that ABC could assert against USA-Online. I am sorry not to be reporting better news. Please feel free to call me to discuss this or any other matter. Sincerely yours, *Candace Tewe* Candace Tewe	The letter has a bit of boot-strapping at the end—"We considered a number of theories" —which in this case is appropriate to reassure the client that the attorneys did do a thorough job and still were forced to report bad news. A client's first reaction to this kind of news is likely to be, "Really? The situation is that bad? Are you sure?" and this letter anticipates that reaction and addresses it by affirming, "Yes, we tried hard, and we are sure about these negative results." Note, too, the sympathetic tone of the letter. This is the appropriate, professional way to give a good client bad news.

Sample Client Letter 2—Claim for Commercial Frustration	Comments
MUDD & MOORE, P.C. March 14, 2000 Martina Schenck Tunetaster, Inc. 1517 Martin Luther King Blvd. Santa Bonita, CA 91999 **Re: Tunetaster/InYourFace Contract** Dear Martina, It was a pleasure talking with you last month, though I was sorry to hear about the situation with InYourFace (IYF) and the Justice Department. As I predicted at our meeting, there is very little hope that your entry into the consent decree with the Justice Department will release you from your obligations with IYF. Illinois law does not apply the doctrine of frustration to excuse a party from its contractual obligations where that party contributed to, or had control over, the occurrence of the alleged frustrating event. Our research confirms that your voluntary action to end the Justice Department case with a consent decree cannot be used to escape your obligations under the IYF contract, because doing so is considered voluntary, and the reduction in your customer base will be too drastic. In short, the law does not permit a company to voluntarily cause business loss and then walk away from a contract on the ground that the business loss frustrates its performance. When performance of a contract becomes impossible because governmental laws or regulations thereafter make such performance illegal, the non-performance may be excused. In fact, this is a classic justification for non-performance. However, such illegality must not have come about through the action of either of the parties to the contract.	This letter also gets right to the point without waffling, without obfuscation, without trying to muddy the waters with legalese. The results of the research are bad news for the client, and this letter reports the bad news to the client without flinching. As with the first sample, the attorney author does not write over the head of his client. It seems clear that the addressee is not a law-trained reader, and the letter communicates the analysis of the law at a level that is both professional and appropriate. Even though the answer is negative, the letter has an upbeat tone, and suggests the next steps that should be performed in the case, thus indicating that life goes on, and things will work out.

Sample Client Letter 2—Claim for Commercial Frustration	Comments

In addition, a court will assume that the parties to a contract knew the law at the time of contract; thus, if lack of awareness is the issue, a court will not afford relief to the contracting parties. Stated otherwise, if a contract becomes unprofitable because of the application of laws that existed at the time of contracting, the frustrating event is deemed to have been controllable by the promisor. The law is clear on this point, and we see nothing in the facts that facts that would release you from your obligations to IYF in the contract.

I am sorry that we cannot find a theory that would enable you to void the contract, but we stand by our advice that entry into the consent decree is the best outcome for you in the circumstances. We would like to research your exposure to damages under the contract with IYF if you will approve our moving on to this topic. Please feel free to call me to discuss this matter, and I look forward to seeing you at Thursday's board meeting.

Sincerely yours,

Louis B. Lessis

Louis B. Lessis

CHAPTER 8

Editing and Fine-Tuning Your Writing

I. STYLE ISSUES FOR THE OFFICE MEMORANDUM (AND LEGAL WRITING IN GENERAL)

Your training as a lawyer includes becoming a member of a community of readers and writers called the legal writing discourse community. Membership in this community requires you to follow some conventions that at first might seem unusual or constricting, but these conventions will enable your writing to be appreciated for its worth. Bucking one or more of these conventions from time to time may be done to add special effect to your writing, but the best advice is to follow the rules of style identified below and to practice them until you are comfortable enough with the results. Then, you can think about improvising. Jazz musicians in training play the scales and arpeggios; they do not simply pick up a trumpet one day and start playing improvised jazz. Tennis players practice serving and returning before they start trying to make a tricky drop shot or backhand passing shot. The same goes for legal writers: learn these basics, master the basics, and be patient. Your time for making your own music in writing will come.

> ### DO IT WITH STYLE!
>
> *STYLE? Is that so important?*
> The word "style" has several meanings in English. What we mean here are the rules of grammar and usage and the important conventions of the legal writing discourse community that, if followed, allow your work to be understood and appreciated as legal writing (as opposed to other forms of writing). Learning legal style is critically important to those of you seeking recognition as a good legal writer and membership in this discourse community.

A. Plain English

1. Avoid legalese

By "legal style" we do not mean *legalese*. Law students commonly fall into the trap of absorbing the ancient, old, and relatively dated style choices of the authorities in casebooks. The natural instinct is to try to recreate the stilted, wordy, Latin and French-infested verbiage in your own writing. Our advice: fight the instinct.

The "plain English" revolution finally has overtaken the legal field, and we are happy about it. You should speak and write as plainly as possible, using ordinary words, and omitting the legalese ("said parcel," "the party of the first part," "aforementioned") and Latin and French-inspired phrases *("Est ipsorum legislatorum tanquam viva vox," "Et de ceo se mettent en la pays")* as much as possible. The object of legal writing is not to use words and phrases that could have been learned only in law school; instead, you should explain the issues and rules in common language as plainly as possible.

The exception to this rule is when you must invoke those Latin and French phrases that have been so ingrained in the law that they are now legal terms of art, and there is no way to express the concept they stand for in a concise manner except by using the Latin or French term. Examples: *res ipsa loquitur, res judicata, respondeat superior.* In these instances, use the phrase as the most efficient tool to express a complicated concept, not as a crutch to make your writing sound more lawyerly.

2. Be concise

A less obvious form of legalese is verbosity: a lawyer's tendency to use too many words to express a thought. The goal of using plain English is to be readily understood; to this end, you should strive to write as concisely as possible. Omit needless words in your writing. Rigorously examine each sentence to see if it can be made shorter; look for opportunities to use one word instead of a phrase. Watch especially for "nominalizations"—noun phrases that can be transformed into a single (stronger) verb. For example, instead of saying that the officer "conducted an investigation," say that she "investigated." Break up long sentences with independent clauses into two or three short sentences. As a general rule of thumb, paragraphs should contain no more than five or six sentences and be less than half a page in length (double-spaced).

3. Limit your use of the passive tense

The passive tense or passive voice involves the phrasing of a sentence so that the object of the sentence comes first, followed by a form of the verb "to be" in front of the action verb, with the subject residing last. Examples: "The house was searched by the police." "The plan was enforced by the committee." The active tense has the subject before the verb and the verb before the object, as in: "The police searched the house." "The committee enforced the plan."

The passive tense de-emphasizes the "subject" and often leaves the true subject unnamed. This sentence pattern, especially if overused, can make writing vague and indefinite. Examples: "The house was searched." "The plan was enforced." In each example, the reader does not know the true subject, the actor of the sentence—who searched the house? Who enforced the plan?

The object-verb-subject construction sounds weaker than the active voice. The active tense is punchier and (usually) makes the point more directly. Active voice pushes the reader through the piece more smoothly and efficiently. Furthermore, a subject-verb-object construction tends to correspond more accurately to reader expectations. Readers generally expect sentences to unfold in this fashion, unless there is a good reason to emphasize the object instead of the subject of the sentence.

Sometimes, however, there is a good reason to use the passive voice. If your goal is to de-emphasize or conceal the subject, then the passive voice works well to draw attention **away from** it. For example, if you need to downplay the fact that your client let go of the wheel and sent his car out of control, hitting the plaintiff and sending him flying twenty feet into the air, you might write: "Plaintiff was struck by the car," or, "Defendant's Chevrolet went out of control, and the plaintiff was thrown twenty feet into the air." The reader of this information is less focused on your client as the doer of the action.

Finally, the passive tense is inherently wordier than the active tense. "The police searched the house" is two words shorter than "The house was searched by the police." Not a huge difference, to be sure, but when you are striving to make your writing more concise (and remain within a specified word limit), you can save a handful of words just by rephrasing from passive to active voice.

PRACTICE POINTER

Overuse or unintentional use of the passive tense is a common problem for many lawyers, not just law students. Often the problem is a fear of stating things strongly and forcefully. There are many if's and maybe's in life and legal problems, and gun-shy lawyers may react to uncertainty by writing passively. But passive voice is not a shield to criticism; at best it creates a fog of uncertainty as to the actual actors and their responsibilities for the effects of their actions. Unless you have a reason to de-emphasize or conceal the doer of the action, writing to promote vagueness and uncertainty is always a losing proposition. Try to eliminate the unintentional use of the passive tense as much as possible, and your work and the work you edit will be appreciated by your superiors and your clients.

B. Quotations

Much angst is wasted on the question of whether to quote or not to quote from your sources. We do not think this should be so troublesome for law students and attorneys. There are some obvious boundaries within which you will be safe if you follow a moderate level of quotation. The boundaries are as follows:

1. Never plagiarize

Plagiarism is the act of appropriating the writing or the ideas of another and passing them off as the product of one's own mind. In **practical legal writing** (office memoranda and litigation briefs, for example), it is not so much the borrowing of language and ideas from legal sources that is troubling; rather, the problem is the failure to attribute them by proper citation to the source from which you got them. If language is borrowed, you must cite the source of the language. Failure to cite is not only an offense against ethics and intellectual honesty (and, in some instances, a violation of an author's copyright), it does nothing for persuasion. Unless and until you become a famous authority on the law, few attorneys are going to be interested in what you personally say is the law or ought to be if you fail to cite legal authorities to support your statements. What your readers want to hear is what the sources of the law say; by providing a citation to each authority you rely on in your analysis, you are assuring them that you are communicating this information rather than your own musings.

In **academic legal writing** (such as law review notes and journal articles and the work you write for your law school classes), the mandate against plagiarism is very strict. And in academic settings generally, plagiarism is a concern also because you are being graded on your own work. There may be ample opportunity to copy from other students' papers or from treatises or law review articles and to pass this analysis off as your own. Don't do it. Plagiarism is a serious ethical violation, and you should not gamble your future livelihood on the chance that your professors will not discover the secret sources of your writing. If you copy information directly from a source, use quotation marks and cite the source. There is no substitute for this practice in an academic setting.

2. Do not quote so much that the quotes attempt to replace your own analysis of the issues

Students nervous about getting the law "right" often swing to the other extreme and err by quoting everything possible, so that their paper is a sea of quotation marks. The logic appears to be: "If the courts or the legal scholars explained the rule in a certain way, who am I to differ?" We have seen office memoranda completely extracted from a law review article or practice manual on the topic. Even where the article or manual is cited throughout the paper, however, this is not a smart practice and usually means that important analysis is lacking.

Quotation is most important in the rule section—and, even then, only for those rules derived from constitutions, statutes, regulations, or watershed cases, or if key terms within a rule are at issue. If you find yourself writing nothing but quotes in the explanation section and even in the application section, stop there. It is critical to provide your own legal analysis of the issues in these sections, both to explain the rule and how it works, and to apply it to your client's facts. No matter how great the author of an authority, that author was not looking at the law from your client's exact perspective. Always remember that you are looking at every issue in the context of a particular set of facts and circumstances that will almost never be duplicated in any source that you might find on the law. Therefore, you must do the analysis on your own and only use quotations to highlight critical language from the most important explanations and interpretations of the rule from the best controlling authorities.

3. Use proper quotation technique

In most circumstances, it is proper to quote the applicable or pertinent terms of a rule of law. At times, it is very important to do so. You *should* quote the exact terms of a rule of law when:

A. The judicial orders and opinions from your jurisdiction all use the same wording of the rule;

B. The rule comes from a constitution, statute, or administrative regulation; or

C. The rule contains certain required elements or terms of art that must be identified (for example, "proof beyond a reasonable doubt," "clear and convincing evidence"). **In this last instance, only the terms of art need to be quoted.**

In addition, if a source uses a short or pithy phrase or other language that captures your client's situation exactly, it is appropriate to quote it. We emphasize short and pithy. Beyond that, avoid using excessive and lengthy quotations from cases.

4. When to use quotation marks

As noted above, in law school, use of quotation marks around any quoted material is a necessity. All law professors (not just legal writing professors) are extremely sensitive to plagiarism and will demand that you use quotation marks or highlight a quotation with block indented text (see the next subsection below), and provide a citation.

In practice, you may notice the rules on quotation marks are not quite as rigorous as in academic settings. In many instances in legal practice, if a *rule* is short enough (generally one sentence or less than 50 words long), you can simply re-state the rule directly from a source and provide a citation to the source and page number without using a set of quotation marks. Note: only the *quotation marks* are optional; the citation absolutely is required.

The same is not true for quotes from secondary authorities (treatises, law review articles, encyclopedias, and the like). Whereas the text of rules (in constitutions, statutes, administrative regulations, and judicial opinions) generally is public domain material, the text of secondary authorities almost always is copyright-protected, so *any* quotation from a secondary source must show the quoted words with quotation marks or block quotes in addition to having a cite to the source.

Even in law practice, if you use a phrase from a case verbatim with no paraphrasing of the text whatsoever, of course use quotation marks. Also use them when you want to drive home that a certain court (usually the highest court in the applicable jurisdiction) has said something about the law that is very favorable to your client, and you do not want the reader to miss the fact that these are the court's own words, not yours. If you are quoting more than a single sentence, you definitely use quotation marks or the block quote format discussed in the sub-section below.

If in law practice you are really struggling with a decision whether to use quotation marks, employ the "Seven-Word" rule. This is a useful rule of thumb that says if you use seven of the exact words from a source in a row, you should enclose them in quotation marks. Practical legal writing does not require this, and most attorneys do not follow it, but it can help you resolve your own internal debates on the topic.

5. The mechanics of quotation

Citation rules state that if your quotation is more than 50 words, you should block it off from the rest of the paragraph by double indenting the quoted material, single-spacing it, and omitting the quotation marks. The citation is presented in the next *un-indented* line of the paragraph, immediately following the quotation. If the quotation contains fewer than 50 words, you should leave it in the body of the paragraph, use quotation marks if you have determined to do so, and not alter the spacing of the paragraph or lines containing the quotation; in other words, leave it in the same formatting as the rest of the paragraph in which it appears. Remember, the basic rule for law school is to use quotes around every word that is quoted.

Example:

In their landmark book on legal writing, Professors Murray and DeSanctis stated:

> The ALWD manual and Bluebook advise that if your quotation is more than 50 words, you should block it off from the rest of the paragraph by double indenting the quoted material, single-space it, and eliminate the quotation marks around it. If the quotation is fewer than 50 words, you should leave it in the body of the paragraph, use quotation marks if you have determined to do so, and leave the spacing of the paragraph or lines where the quotation appears unaltered; in other words, leave it in the same formatting as the rest of the paragraph in which it appears.

Michael D. Murray & Christy H. DeSanctis, *Legal Research and Writing* 112 (2005).

Compare:

As Professors Murray and DeSanctis recommend, "If you are struggling with a decision whether to use quotation marks, employ the 'Seven-Word' rule." *Id.* at 111.

Your readers must be able to rely upon your research. This will be true whether the document you are writing is an office memorandum or a court brief. You should always double check the accuracy of your quotes.

You should *edit* your quotations as much as possible to make them substantively and stylistically accurate. Only use the relevant words (or the required terms and standards of the rule) in your quoted material. Use ellipses (. . .) to show where you have omitted irrelevant or unnecessary language from your source. Use brackets [ ] to indicate places where you have changed a word or a letter or punctuation from the quoted material to make it flow and fit the context and syntax of your writing.

Examples: "If [law students] are struggling with . . . whether to use quotation marks, [they should] employ the 'Seven-Word' rule."

"If you [have] struggl[ed] with [the] decision . . . to use quotation marks, employ the 'Seven-Word' rule" in the future."

These two examples above only show what is *possible* not what is *recommended*. If your ellipses and brackets clutter the material so much that it looks like military intelligence officers censored your work, consider phrasing the material the way you would like it to appear, and write it up that way without quotes, providing a correct citation to the source. The law allows this kind of reasonable, freestyle paraphrasing in most instances.

C. Parentheticals

Case parentheticals are designed to provide one or two pieces of information about an authority in as few words as possible. As a general rule, they are not used to write a sentence or two summarizing the authority. Parentheticals often are drafted without reference to ordinary rules of grammar and punctuation; thus, you can say exactly what you want to say in the shortest way possible.

Example: *Martin v. Lewis*, 234 W.2d 456, 458 (Apex Ct. App. 1st Dist. 1958) (summary judgment on fraud claim denied); *Smith v. Wesson*, 568 S.W.2d 345, 347 (Tex. 1978) (police search held unconstitutional).

Citation manuals often advise that you begin your parenthetical with a gerund (an "ing" word, such as "holding that . . . " or "determining that . . ."). This certainly is not bad practice, but we have found that many practitioners do not follow this rule (and that the gerund is not always necessary). Use your own judgment.

The only time a citation is used *inside a parenthetical* is when you are indicating that one case is citing or quoting another, as in:

Example: *Estate of Able v. Cain*, 992 W.2d at 567 (citing *Saul v. David*, 912 W.2d 234, 236 (Apex 1994) (en banc)).

There also are acceptable short cuts that can be used in parentheticals, such as "(same)," which simply means that the fact or information stated in the previous parenthetical apply equally to the next authority you are citing.

Example: *Martin v. Lewis*, 234 W.2d 456, 458 (Apex Ct. App. 1st Dist. 1958) (summary judgment on fraud claim denied); *Rowen v. Martin*, 221 W.2d 578, 581 (Apex Ct. App. 1st Dist. 1954) (same).

Smith v. Wesson, 568 S.W.2d 345, 347 (Tex. 1978) (police search held unconstitutional); *Enfield v. Remington*, 498 S.W.2d 357, 367 (Tex. 1968) (same).

Parentheticals can be used in combination with brackets to make an entire section shorter. Compare the efficiency of the following examples:

Not good: *Smith v. Jones* involved a breach of bailment duties. In *Smith*, the court stated "Roscoe Smith owed a duty of care to Wally Jones when Alex Tuttle took charge of Mr. Jones' property." 12 W.2d at 24. In that case, Roscoe Smith was the plaintiff, Alex Tuttle was his agent, and Wally Jones was the defendant. *Tommy v. Armour* was another breach of bailment duties case, and the court again held that plaintiff owed a duty of care to defendant when plaintiff's agent took charge of defendant's property. 10 W.2d at 45.

Better: The court held that "[plaintiff] owed a duty of care to [defendant] when [plaintiff's agent] took charge of [defendant's] property." *Smith v. Jones*, 12 W.2d at 24 (breach of bailment duties case). *See Tommy v. Armour*, 10 W.2d at 45 (same).

While the "better" wording is acceptable, it borders on distracting because of the four brackets. It would be better still *not to quote*, but to paraphrase the statement so that quotation marks and brackets are unnecessary:

Best: The court held that plaintiff's duty of care toward defendant is established when plaintiff's agent takes charge of defendant's property. *See Smith v. Jones*, 12 W.2d at 24 (breach of bailment duties case); *Tommy v. Armour*, 10 W.2d at 45 (same).

D. Discuss dicta correctly so as not to trick the reader into thinking it is a holding from a case

Dicta from a court opinion, particularly an opinion from a court within the appropriate hierarchy of judicial authority, can be very important to your analysis. However, it is important to remember that dicta is not controlling, and you should not pass it off as a holding when you include it in your office memorandum or other legal writing. The goal is to discuss dicta in such a way that the reader will not be led to believe that what you are talking about is part of the holding.

1. Obvious and not so obvious ways to discuss a court's holding

It might be easiest to look at the ways you would describe a court's holding in a case; then you can try **not** to sound like these when you are referring to dicta.

The following are obvious ways to discuss a court's holding in your writing:

Holding: "The court held that . . ."
"The court concluded that . . ."
"The case stands for the proposition that . . ."
"The plaintiff prevailed because . . ."
"The outcome of the case was . . . because . . ."
"The court found that . . . [legal conclusion]"

In the last example, if what you fill in is a **legal conclusion**, a statement regarding the law, then the sentence communicates that the legal conclusion is part of the holding of the case. If it is true that the court determined something as a factual matter (for example, "The court found that plaintiff had three children"), then the sentence does not really communicate a legal holding but, instead, a factual finding. Because factual findings and legal conclusions can be tricky to differentiate on a quick read-through, you should avoid using the phrase "the court found . . ." except in the instance where the court *held* something (as a matter of law), or where the court was the trier of fact and you are reporting the facts that were found by the court.

In addition, there are some non-obvious ways to say "this is holding." Consider the following:

Holding: All Oregon loggers are required by law to equip their saws with a chain brake. *Lefty v. Stihl Chainsaw Co.*, 114 P.2d 23, 26 (Or. 1962).

This sentence does not use the words "held," "holding," "concluded," "found," etc., but when you state a rule or a principle of law and follow it with a citation without further comment or explanation (or parenthetical), you are telling the reader that the case you are citing held this point.

Another non-obvious discussion of the holding is the following:

Holding: The court discussed the fact that in Oregon, all loggers must equip their saws with a chain brake. *Lefty*, 114 P.2d at 25.

In this example, you used a supposedly neutral word, "discussed," and even incorporated the word "fact," but the sentence says "holding" just as clearly as the other examples. Don't get too hung up on magic words like "discussed" or "mentioned" or "noted," because in the right context they can communicate "holding" as easily as other more direct words.

2. How do you avoid communicating that something is the holding?

To avoid communicating that something from a case actually is the holding when it is really dicta, you must discuss the material in such a way that it is clear that it is dicta, but still has importance—and you should explain the importance. Consider the following expressions:

> "The court stated . . ."
> "The *Finley* case discussed . . ."
> "The Supreme Court in *Jones* noted . . ."
> "Justice Breyer mentioned . . ."
> "The trial court determined . . ."

FYI

The judge that one of the authors clerked for was a big fan of the word "determined" to avoid the notion that the court held something. His logic was that "held" immediately connotes "holding," whereas "determined" is more appropriate for a statement found in dicta, especially if it concerns the facts. "Hold" is indeed a magic word in the law, and you should use it sparingly—only when you are actually referring to the holding. That said, whether you use "determined" or another word should depend on precisely what it is that the court did and how you want to characterize it.

These words (stated, discussed, noted, mentioned, determined) are not magical talismans that automatically dispel the sacrosanct implications of a holding, but they can get you in the right frame of mind to discuss the issue and its importance without packaging it as part of the holding. If you are skating on thin ice (and you know it), include a reference as to why you think this is or may be dicta:

Examples: "Although the case did not turn on this issue, the court found that . . . [your dicta issue]"

"The court noted that . . .[dicta issue], but it did not resolve the dispute on this basis."

"The court recognized the defendant's argument that . . . [your dicta issue], and indicated that this position had merit, but it ultimately decided that it was unnecessary to reach this issue in this case."

3. Avoid using the word dicta

The examples in the sub-section above communicate to the reader that the information is not necessarily part of the holding, but notice that none of them uses the word "dicta." We think it is better to avoid using the term "dicta" in your writing; for example, do not say, "The court, in dicta, stated that . . ." or "The [issue] was discussed in the case, although it was dicta." The reason is that "dicta" tends to have a negative impact on a law-trained reader. Many immediately turn their attention away from an item that is labeled "dicta," even though, if they thought about it, they would realize that the item might still be important.

Some readers also believe that if you single out something in your writing as "dicta," you are intentionally trying to tell them that you think the issue is of no real importance or relevance. One judge of a United States District Court where one of the authors regularly practiced would often correct a party who started to discuss something that she was describing as "dicta" by telling her, "That's not dicta, that's important!"—the implication was that if it really were dicta, it would not be so important. We believe some readers who see the word "dicta" in a section of your work will skip over the whole discussion of the issue. Therefore, avoid turning off these readers, and ban the word "dicta" from your writing by describing such information along the lines suggested above.

E. Formality of language

Legal writing must be professional and should sound that way. You should not be loose with your language and should not attempt to inject humor or "hipness" into your writing by using slang or colloquialisms. There is too much at stake in legal matters to be so cavalier. The following rules apply generally to all legal writing, including office memoranda:

1. Do not use slang and colloquialisms

Slang is unprofessional. There is nothing to be gained by using it in legal writing. Even though many attorneys like to be "folksy" in person, this "folksiness" should not slip over into legal writing. Part of the "in person" level of acceptable folksiness is regional and cultural; if you find yourself practicing law in a place where everyone speaks like Dolly Parton or like Andy Griffith in old *Matlock* reruns, then by all means, join in. But we stand by our advice not to *write* that way. Even the most masterful use of the vernacular in writing probably is wasted on most legal audiences.

In this book, however, you undoubtedly will find examples of colloquial speech. But we used this type of writing deliberately to set a more casual tone for the text. We apologize if this is confusing, but colloquial speech is not appropriate in the work you produce for your clients and colleagues. The following examples, although admittedly extreme, should indicate the kind of language we are talking about.

Bad:	It doesn't sit right under the law. The judge won't get it.
Better:	The position is erroneous, and the judge is not likely to accept it.
Bad:	Defendants went pub-crawling and got plastered.

Better: Defendants went to several pubs and became intoxicated.

Some folksy words almost have a term-of-art status. For example, we would not abandon the term "good old boy" from our legal vocabulary to describe this type of person, especially if someone refers to another person (or to himself) in this way. However, we would probably quote that kind of language rather than simply reproduce it in our own legal writing.

2. Avoid slash constructions unless that is the actual word, phrase, or address that you are quoting or referring to

A common legal shortcut (or shortcoming) is to create new words by placing two words on either side of a slash.

Bad examples: Bob was a teacher/researcher.
                       The scope of the committee is research/analysis.
                       We formed a discovery/deposition/motion-practice team.

This is rather awkward English, and it should be avoided. It does not take up that much more space to use "and" in these circumstances.

The phrase "and/or" is a particular favorite of legal writers, and we are not immune.

Bad examples: The court of appeals will reverse and/or remand the case back to the trial court.

The rule states plagiarism is punishable by death and/or a fine of $50,000.

If the *actual text* you are quoting has the phrase "and/or" in it, then by all means quote it that way. But, in most instances, "and/or" can be replaced by "or," or sometimes by "and," depending on the grammatical meaning of your sentence. In those instances that you believe "or" does not complete the idea, use the construction "_____ or _____ or both." Example: "The rule states that plagiarism is punishable by death or a fine of $50,000 or both." This construction is preferable to the "and/or" phrasing.

3. Avoid contractions, but use shorthand words and phrases

In this book, we have employed contractions. Do not be misled by the implications of our doing so. As noted above, though we are discussing formal legal writing, we are doing so in a more informal, conversational style than you might see in formal writing. Contractions generally are considered improper in actual, legal work product, and you should avoid them.

However, it is perfectly fine to use shorthand words and abbreviations of parties, institutions and agencies, acts and statutes, once you have correctly identified them in your work.

Example: The Securities Exchange Commission ("SEC") refused to apply the Securities Act of 1933 ("'33 Act") to the post-sale use of the Section 14 "red herring" prospectus ("prospectus") by McDonnell Douglas Corporation ("MDC"). The SEC said that MDC satisfied the requirements of the '33 Act by providing an updated prospectus to each buyer.

You need not include the parenthetical translation when it is obvious, for example, if you begin with "Plaintiff Leif Erickson . . . " and you thereafter refer to him as "Erikson" or "Mr. Erikson." Indeed, in our example above, some practitioners might say that you need not include the translation ("SEC") because that is such a common acronym for the Securities and Exchange Commission. Use your judgment in these matters.

4. Do not use symbols except where required

You generally should avoid using symbols (&, @, #) in your writing unless the symbol is part of a rule, statute, the name of a company or firm, or an email address. Examples: 14 U.S.C. § 123, 13 Apex Comp. Stat. Ann. ¶ 3-307, Jenner & Block, farnsworthea@slu.edu. The description of money is a special exception to the rule. If you are referring to a rounded sum, like one hundred dollars, it is appropriate to write "one hundred dollars," or "$100." Do not write the decimal points, "$100.00." If, however, the sum has dollars and cents in it, use numerals and a dollar sign, for example, "$101.32," rather than writing that sum out in words.

If you are drafting a legal document such as a will, a check, a settlement agreement, or a contract, follow the practices of your office. If your office follows the practice of including a word phrase followed by redundant numerals in parentheses, then you should probably follow that practice, too. Example: one hundred one dollars and thirty-two cents ($101.32).

5. Avoid first-person and second-person references

It is common in oral conversations with your colleagues and clients, and even with your opponents, judges, and court personnel, to use first- and second-person references, such as: "We are moving to dismiss." "I have an objection." "I believe . . . ." "Our case is strong." "My research shows that no case controls this issue." "You should settle this case early." Avoid this practice when you are composing formal documents. Do not try to be clever and use "this writer" or "this author;" these substitutes are *still* first-person references. Instead, refer to your side by using your client's name, or by the customary shorthand reference to your client used in your office. As a lawyer, you step into your client's shoes.

Correct: "Boeing can argue . . ."
Incorrect: "We can argue . . ."

Not only is this the preferred phrasing, it actually is more accurate, because **parties** make arguments and take positions and bring motions, not their counsel. When referring to the other party in litigation, use the party designation (plaintiff or defendant), or other shorthand reference, and attribute all actions and statements to the party, not to your opposing counsel.

Correct:	"Defendant W.R. Grace failed to file its answer on time."
Incorrect:	"Ms. Smith failed to file XYZ Corporation's answer on time." [if Ms. Smith is the attorney]

One exception to the "no first or second person references" rule in legal writing, in our experience, is the client letter. The tone of a client letter is more informal than an office memorandum or court brief, and often invites the use of familiar speech. We have found that it is common to use first and second person references such as: "Our research indicates . . . ." "You should not terminate the contract . . . ." "We would like to examine your files on . . . ." and the like.

FOOD FOR THOUGHT

Yes, there certainly are a lot of style points and conventions to bear in mind, but that is because the legal writing community generally takes these matters very seriously. We are spending a lot of time on these conventions to give you the tools to make your writing instantly accepted and appreciated by law-trained readers. The first reaction of the average law-trained reader to a lawyer who repeatedly ignores these conventions is not, "Oh, what a clever author! Such fresh ideas and originality!" but rather, "Who is this person who doesn't know how to write like a lawyer?" Or worse yet, "If this writer cannot follow the conventions of legal writing, what other legal rules is he ignoring?" You should want the first impression created by your legal writing to be that is it solid and reliable, not edgy and rebellious, and you will achieve that goal if you take these conventions to heart and apply them in your writing.

6. Avoid rhetorical questions

It is somewhat mystifying why law students and lawyers alike enjoy rhetorical questions. They are a cheap argumentative device akin to a temporary "straw man" argument that is erected for a moment just so that you can smash it to bits in the next breath. If the point you are making is obvious, simply state it in a concise way and move on. Phrasing a point as a rhetorical question does not make it more obvious. If your reader is inclined to disagree with the point you are making, she will simply answer in the opposite way, and you will have squandered space that you could have used to convince her that you are right.

7. Write out dates

In legal writing, you should write out dates in the American English form of **"Month Day, Year,"** as in "August 31, 1998." Do not write "5/4/98" or "Aug.

31, 1998" or "31 August 1998." Many people outside the United States would read "5/4/98" as "April 5, 1998," not "May 4, 1998." You can avoid this confusion by sticking to the Month Day, Year formulation. Note: *both commas* used in the phrase "On August 31, 1998, Jones went to . . . ." are required. You can omit the commas only if you do not include the day: "In August 1998 Jones went to . . . ." is correct. (Also correct: "In August 1998, Jones went to . . . ").

F. Strive for internal consistency and parallelism

Proper legal writing is internally consistent. It promotes clarity to use the same names or terms to refer to the same parties, persons, and objects throughout your work. For example, compare the following:

Good: The Chevy truck went through the intersection. The truck then ploughed into the Ford station wagon. The station wagon was wrecked.

Bad: The truck went through the intersection. The Chevy then ploughed into the Ford. The vehicle was wrecked.

The principle of parallelism also applies to verb tenses, articles, and pronouns. Verb tenses, articles, and pronouns must match the subject throughout a paragraph and section of a paper. If you have inserted a quotation into a paragraph, you must check to see if the tense and verb endings of your quotation match the tense and subjects of the sentence where the quote appears. As discussed above, use brackets where necessary. For example:

Good: Mr. Cleaver maintained in his deposition that his duty had been fulfilled when he "[took] over Clark Enterprises and [paid] off [his] debt to Wayans." Cleaver Dep. at 13, line 10.

Bad: Mr. Cleaver maintained in his deposition that his duty had been fulfilled when "I am taking over Clark Enterprises and paying off my debt to Wayans." Cleaver Dep. at 13, line 10.

It is easier for readers to follow your writing if the sentence format and order of words also follow parallel forms. Compare the following:

Good: The rule has three criteria. The first criterion to consider is . . . . The second criterion is . . . . Finally, the third criterion is . . . .

Bad: The rule has three criteria. The first part to consider is . . . . Secondly, we have to consider the factor of . . . . As for the last element . . . .

G. Track the language of the authorities when applying the rule to your facts

The principle of "parallelism" also advises that you use any terms of art or key phrasing of factors, elements, and legal standards when applying them to your facts. For example, if the applicable standard is "wrongful abuse," describe the client's situation using the terms "wrongful" and "abuse." If the authorities use the terms "prompt disclosure," describe whether the client was "prompt" in making a "disclosure." Do not use creative synonyms ("improper behavior," "tortious abuse," "rapidly informed," "immediately reported") just to vary your vocabulary. The reader may miss the connection and not understand the point you are making.

H. Avoid sexist language

Women make up at least half the population and half of the graduating classes from law schools. They constitute almost half of the practicing bar and represent a growing percentage of judges and corporate counsel. Accordingly, you should not default to the "generic" pronouns "he" "him" "his" or "himself" in reference to persons and positions. Our own method to avoid sexist language is to use feminine pronouns in reference to unspecified lawyers, judges, and clients as often as it makes sense to do so. Other methods are to use the combinations "he or she," "him or her," "herself or himself" in the construction of your sentences, although this can become tiresome if it appears too frequently. To avoid tiring out the reader with these inclusive combinations, you can simply rephrase your sentences. Instead of saying, "An attorney must carefully account for his or her client's funds," simply say "An attorney must carefully account for client funds." Substituting the indefinite (plural) "their" for the singular "his or her" is grammatically inappropriate; it is better to restate the sentence and leave out the possessive pronoun altogether.

I. Be accurate in references to cases and courts

In your first year of law school and beyond, you will be writing a great deal about judicial orders and opinions. There are special considerations involved in such references to cases and courts that do not always come naturally.

Do not attribute emotions to courts. Courts don't "feel," so do not say, "The court felt that Jones was wrong."

Always use the **past tense** to describe what the court said or did in a case you are using as authority. That case is over; it is in the past. It is not happening right now or in the future, so the past tense is the only appropriate tense. For example, state: "The Jones court held that Smith provoked the dog," not: "The Jones court holds that Smith provoked the dog." **Contrast** this with constitutions, statutes, and regulations, which exist in the present tense. You should state: "U.S. Const. amend XIV provides . . ." not "provided."

Be precise in describing what the court did: the court **granted** or **denied** a motion, **sustained** or **overruled** an objection to evidence, **accepted** or **rejected** an argument or position, **held** an issue of law, and **found** a fact. We have discussed some of this terminology above and in prior chapters.

"Court" is singular, no matter how many judges sat and heard the case or joined in the opinion. The court is a thing, not a person. Therefore, when using a pronoun to refer to the court, use "it" not "they."

There are several ways to refer to the case in which you are currently involved. You might say: "the case at hand," "the instant case," or "the case at bar," but these (rather antiquated) phrases have fallen somewhat out of favor recently. Instead, you should try to use "this case" or, simply, "here"—as long as it is clear that you mean the case currently before the court (or other legal audience). Whichever form you choose, use it consistently throughout your writing.

J. Include citation to authority

1. The Golden Rule of Citation

Chapter 9 of this book is devoted to mechanics of citation. We are not going to talk about the many rules of citation mechanics in this short section. Instead, we only will discuss the "Golden Rule of Citation":

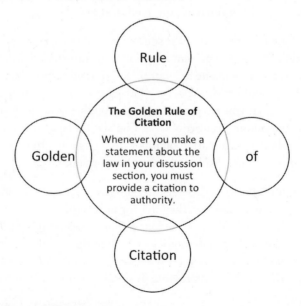

The Golden Rule of Citation is: whenever you make a statement about the law in your discussion section, you must provide a citation to authority. A **legal proposition** is defined as any rule of law, any statement of or about the law, the holding of a case, or any legal principle in your discussion section—whether collateral to your discussion or directly on point—and it ***must*** have a citation to legal authority.

Every time you end a sentence in the discussion section, check to see if it contains a legal proposition (as defined here). If so, include a citation to authority. Our emphasis here on "Discussion section" is not accidental; you do not need citations to authority in your questions presented and brief answers sections. These sections would become too crowded and lengthy if you cited authorities in them. Citation to *factual* sources in your statement of facts, however, is appropriate (and required if you are quoting from factual materials).

2. Jump (pin) cites should be provided

Citations should include the exact page where the material you are citing appears, which is called a "jump cite" or "pinpoint cite" or "pin cite." In the example, *Shorty v. Lefty*, 823 W.2d 234, 237 (Apex 1990), the reference to "237" is the jump cite, meaning that it is the page of the case where the material you are referring to appears. In general, you should provide a jump cite when you are citing an authority for any purpose. Do not be lazy and simply cite the first page of the authority and send your reader off to find the material somewhere in that authority.

One exception is if you are simply pointing out the fact that a case exists (especially if you will go on to discuss it later). *E.g.*, "Only one Supreme Court decision has addressed the question whether a tomato is a fruit or a vegetable." *Nix v. Hedden*, 149 U.S. 304 (1893).

3. Cite all the sources you need, but avoid string cites

Citations should reflect all of the sources you actually used to compose a legal rule or proposition. When you present a legal rule (or sub-rule) that was generated by or in several cases, you should cite to all of them. That said, *do not over-cite*. The only place you generally should construct a long "string cite" of cases (if at all) is in the explanation section, when you are presenting a thorough explanatory synthesis. There is no optimal or maximum number of cases that should be synthesized to induce an important principle of interpretation or application of a rule. In general, when using inductive reasoning through explanatory synthesis, the more cases the better.

String citations (Case 1, Case 2, Case 3, Case 4, etc.; *ad nauseam*) in the rule section generally are unnecessary. They do not necessarily signal to the reader that you did superior research and therefore found more cases than the average attorney; rather, it may indicate that you do not know how to discern the rank and weight of your authorities and did not bother to cite only the very best of them. String citations in a rule section are particularly tiresome to a reader who is going to look up all of the cases you cite.

There are a limited number of circumstances when you should consider using a string of citations in the rule section:

The **first** is when it is critical to demonstrate that a significant number of courts (and cases) have come out in favor of your position. This might be necessary if the position you are asserting is controversial or counterintuitive. It also might be necessary if you are relying on persuasive authority only, and you think the home court reading your argument may have a hard time swallowing it.

The **second** is when you promise the reader that multiple authorities support your proposition. If you state that five states have held the same legal proposition, you now must cite five authorities.

The third is when the second or third citation bolsters the value of the entire string of authorities, such as when you cite an older case from the highest court of the applicable jurisdiction, and you follow it up with one or more cites to more recent controlling cases:

> *Kent v. Olson*, 24 W.2d 237, 246 (Apex 1924). *See also Wayne v. Gordon*, 323 W.2d 776, 779 (Apex 1960); *Powerpuff Girls, Inc. v. Yugio Masters, Inc.*, 989 W.2d 34, 38 (Apex Ct. App. 1st Dist. 2008).

The citation to the 2008 controlling authority tells the reader that this proposition of law still is alive and well in your jurisdiction.

Otherwise, in the rule section, if you have controlling authorities that say the same thing and all are from the same general time period, a good rule of thumb is to cite no more than three of these redundant cases for the point on which they all agree. Of course, pick the three best cases in terms of facts, outcome, and jurisdiction that support your position.

K. Tone: humor and excessive emotion is out; vivid and engaging work is in

The law is too serious of a business for humor. People will win and lose real money and will face potential criminal sentences on the basis of what you do for them. If just one person fails to appreciate your joke (your client, your opponent, the judge, etc.), then you have done a disservice to your client.

That said, we have used humor (or attempted to) frequently in this book and in the classes we teach. A light approach is fine in a textbook or in the classroom. But do not carry this mirthful spirit into your formal writing.

This is not to say that you should leave out all vivid, descriptive, and even clever language from your writing. Clever language used sparingly can be effective. You can turn a clever phrase, but do it to make a point, to drive something home, and to make an impression that might last a bit longer; never do it just to be funny.

We have used the following in actual briefs filed with the court:

Examples: "Defendant is not asking the court to reinvent the deal." [Used in reference to the allegation that the court should rewrite the agreement between the parties].

"Wal-Mart put the brakes on the auto insurance marketing plan."

These examples are not screamingly funny, but we think they were acceptable.

Do not show anger or other excessive emotion in your writing. No one wants to read a lawyer's vicious sniping at the other side, or a long, sorrowful recitation of the equities of the situation. You might lose your cool in person, but you should not do so in writing.

Compare the following:

Bad: "Plaintiff's counsel lies and cheats the court by asserting this farcical position."

Better: "Plaintiff's position is completely erroneous."

Best: "Plaintiff's position is erroneous." or "There is no merit to plaintiff's position."

We are not advocating for writing that is bland. And, certainly, we are not suggesting that you should never be forceful about your position. You can be forthright. You can be direct. You can be passionate. You can show that you feel strongly about the equities. However, do not do so by bleeding your sympathy and sorrow all over the page or burning the very words off the paper with scorching prose. For example (probably exaggerated, but you would be surprised at what we have read):

Bad: "This imprisonment cries out to heaven. Petitioner screams, 'Give me liberty or give me death!' but the Court is deaf to his plea."

Good: "The principles of law and equity demand that petitioner be released. There is no other just result."

II. FINE TUNING WITH MODIFICATIONS OF THE TREAT FORMAT

You should view the TREAT format as versatile enough to cover most situations in which you communicate your findings on the law in writing. The format allows for the TREATment of as many major issues as you need to discuss. Within each TREATment of a major issue, there can be as many sub-TREATs as warranted by the number of subissues (or elements) that your major issues present. The message? **Make TREAT work for you.**

Another way of thinking about this is similar to what we said above regarding style: once you internalize the TREAT paradigm, you earn the right to vary from it—as long as you are making conscious, not random, decisions to do so.

The basic format involves the TREATment of major legal issues one after the other—the first major issue before the second, the second before the third, and so on. Sometimes this structure will prove awkward or ineffective because one major issue encompasses another within its discussion.

One relatively easy-to-comprehend example is when a procedural issue, such as whether or not a motion for preliminary injunction should be granted, also requires analysis of a major substantive issue, such as the likelihood of success on the merits.[1] Instead of TREATing the issue of the right to a preliminary injunction before the substantive issue as you might if you tried to force the TREAT structure, it probably makes more sense to discuss the substantive issue *in the middle* of the TREATment of the preliminary injunction issue.

For example, if the substantive issue was whether the movant will prevail on a claim of money had and received, and the procedural issue was whether the movant can obtain an injunction to prevent the defendant from further transferring the funds, the traditional TREAT organization might look something like this (note: this is just the outline):

I.   Jones Bank will prevail on its claim of money had and received because the mistaken recipient had no right to retain the funds.

> **A. Smith Co. received the funds from Jones Bank.**
>
> **B. The Transfer occurred by mistake.**
>
> **C. It is unjust for Smith Co. to retain the funds.**

II.   Jones Bank will be able to obtain a preliminary injunction against further transfer of the funds by Smith Co.

> **A. As discussed above, Jones Bank will succeed on the merits.**
>
> **B. There is a significant threat of irreparable harm to Jones Bank.**
>
> **C. The balance of hardships between Jones Bank and Smith Co. favors Jones Bank.**
>
> **D. Granting the injunction is in the public interest.**

---

1   The factors considered for the issuance of a preliminary injunction are: (1) the probability that the moving party will succeed on the merits; (2) the threat of irreparable harm to the moving party; (3) the balance of hardships between the moving party and the non-moving party; and (4) the public interest. *See United Indus. Corp. v. Clorox Co.*, 140 F.3d 1175, 1178-79 (8th Cir. 1998); *Dataphase Sys. v. C L Sys., Inc.*, 640 F.2d 109, 114 (8th Cir. 1981) (en banc).

This format can be improved by discussing the substantive issue in the course of addressing the procedural issue:

I.   Jones Bank will be able to obtain a preliminary injunction against further transfer of the funds by Smith Co.

A. Jones Bank will succeed on the merits of its claim of money had and received because Smith Co. received fund by mistake and had no right to retain the funds.

1. Smith Co. received the funds from Jones Bank.

2. The transfer occurred by mistake.

3. It is unjust for Smith Co. to retain the funds because Smith Co. had no prior account or debt from Jones Bank.

B. There is a significant threat of irreparable harm to Jones Bank because the money was intended for a time-sensitive transaction with Swissbank.

C. The balance of hardships between Jones Bank and Smith Co. favors Jones Bank.

D. Granting the injunction is in the public interest.

This alternative format will improve the discussion of a procedural rule that incorporates one or more substantive issues into its analysis; it will not work for procedural rules that merely provide a legal standard for the court to award or deny relief.

In addition to the rule for issuance of a preliminary injunction, the rules for the certification of a class action,[2] and for mandatory joinder of parties,[3] are good candidates for the alternative format, because each of these rules embodies substantive law issues that must be discussed before the outcome of the analysis of the procedural rule can be completed. The same is not true for procedural rules such as the

---

2   One or more members of a class may sue or be sued as representative parties on behalf of all only if: (1) the class is so numerous that joinder of all members is impracticable; (2) there are questions of law or fact common to the class; (3) the claims or defenses of the representative parties are typical of the claims or defenses of the class; and (4) the representative parties will fairly and adequately protect the interests of the class. Fed. R. Civ. P. 23(a).

3   A person who is subject to service of process and whose joinder will not deprive the court of jurisdiction over the subject matter of the action shall be joined as a party in the action if: (1) in the person's absence complete relief cannot be accorded among those already parties; or (2) the person claims an interest relating to the subject of the action and is so situated that the disposition of the action in the person's absence may (i) as a practical matter impair or impede the person's ability to protect that interest or (ii) leave any of the persons already parties subject to a substantial risk of incurring double, multiple, or otherwise inconsistent obligations by reason of the claimed interest . . . .Fed. R Civ. P. 19(a).

rule for the granting of a motion to dismiss for failure to state a claim,[4] or for the award of summary judgment.[5] Even though the discussion of these latter types of motions also involves substantive issues, there is little to be gained by attempting to discuss the substantive issues within the same TREATment of the procedural rule. The procedural rule can be discussed first, followed separately by the substantive issues in the traditional TREAT format. Alternatively, the procedural rule can be combined with the discussion of the substantive issues, as in the following examples:

Example 1: Summary judgment issue combined with substantive law issue:

I. **Jones Bank is entitled to summary judgment on Count III (money had and received) because there is no dispute over the fact that the mistaken recipient had no right to retain the funds.**

    A. **There is no dispute concerning the facts that Smith Co. received the funds as a result of Jones Bank's mistake.**

    B. **Jones Bank is entitled to judgment as a matter of law on Count III because there is no legal or equitable justification for Smith Co. to retain the funds transferred by Jones Bank.**

Example 2: Motion to dismiss issue combined with substantive law issue:

I. **Smith Co.'s motion to dismiss Jones Bank's complaint for failure to state a claim must be denied because the complaint alleges a prima facie case of mistaken transfer.**

    A. **Jones Bank has alleged the requisite elements of money had and received.**

      1. **Notice pleading is sufficient in federal court.**

      2. **Jones Bank alleged a transfer, by mistake, and Smith Co.'s retention is unjust.**

    B. **The factual allegations stated in the complaint are sufficient to state a cause of action upon which relief may be granted.**

4 Under Fed. R. Civ. P. 12(b)(6), a complaint should not be dismissed for failure to state a claim unless it appears beyond doubt that the plaintiff can prove no set of facts in support of his claim which would entitle him to relief. *Conley v. Gibson*, 355 U.S. 41, 45-46 (1957).

5 Summary judgment is appropriate if the pleadings, depositions, answers to interrogatories, and admissions on file, together with the affidavits, if any, show that there is no genuine issue as to any material fact and that the moving party is entitled to a judgment as a matter of law. Fed. R. Civ. P. 56(c).

III. EDITING TIPS

We cannot emphasize enough the importance of editing. The mantra of great authors is that **there is no such thing as good writing, only good rewriting**. If you learn one thing from this Chapter, make it this point: you must edit, rewrite, and proofread your work.

A. Write early, rewrite often

Editing and rewriting takes time, and you cannot do a good job if you do not leave yourself the time to proofread. The mere act of writing forces you to get organized in your thinking and in how to articulate your argument. But when you actually write out a draft of the work, the drafting process will reveal defects, gaps, quirks, and problems in your research or analysis. It may change your mind about your legal conclusions. Leave time for this to occur. The day before the paper (or brief) is due is too late.

Rewrites function similarly: they help get the argument in order, correct mistakes, fill in the gaps, beef up the weak areas, and prune the bushy areas. There is a law of diminishing returns at play here; the eighth rewrite will not fix as many errors as the third, but given that each rewrite can improve the work, it is worth doing as many as you can.

B. Employ more than one editing and proofreading technique

Some of you will reach law school with excellent proofreading skills, and some of you may not, but the one lesson about proofreading that holds true time and time again is that everyone is a better proofreader of *someone else's* work than one's own.

In practice, sometimes you will have the luxury of having another set of (law-trained) eyes proofread your work. In an academic setting, however, oftentimes this practice is discouraged or prohibited. (The "no collaboration" rules imposed by the vast majority of law schools will not allow you to edit and proofread your friends' and classmates' work even if you could find the time to do it.) Regardless, you should learn techniques that enable you to proofread your own work effectively.

You may be thinking, "I'll make my assistant do the proofreading." Even if your future assistants have the skills to proofread well, they may not have the time to do it. Both of the authors worked at top law firms (and have plenty of friends still at top law firms), where it often proved difficult to find another law-trained reader to proofread a document at the precise moment necessary (especially when you are under extreme time pressure to get something out the door). In short, do not put too much stock in the assumption that you will have unlimited, reliable editing and proofreading help when you get into practice. We can offer a ray of hope: when you rise to a certain level in your law practice, you might be able to strong-arm a younger attorney into editing and proofreading your work. Look forward to that day, but for now, learn how to proofread your own work effectively.

There is more than one way to edit and proofread your own work. Simply reading through your work from start to finish is one way, but you probably have observed (as we have in our various readings of the page-proofs of this book) that you are far more likely to miss typographical errors and other spelling, citation, and grammatical errors when reading something you wrote, and when reading it from start to finish. The problem is that your brain becomes accustomed to the passages you have written and skips ahead, saving time but not actually reading each word and sentence.

To avoid your brain's built-in capacity to skim text, try each of the following:

Read your work backwards, word for word and then sentence by sentence. Although this technique is painful, it will succeed in interrupting your brain's inherent text-skipping tendency.

Another technique is to create a "paper mask" that only allows you to see a few words of text at a time. Denying your brain the sight of familiar words in familiar sequence helps to slow it down so that you can look harder at the actual text.

When you are editing and rewriting for general flow and readability, **consider reading the text out loud to yourself**. This often causes you to stumble and trip right over the portions of your text that need clarification or simplification. Reading out loud also forces your brain to look at each word so that you can recite it aloud (reading and recitation are two different activities for your brain, and the latter activity forces your brain to slow down and perform the former activity).

Get your computer to read the text back to you. This takes a little time, but you should be able to hear typos even better than you can read them. We do not recommend this as the only proofreading technique you should employ (it is useless for proofing citations, for example, because they all sound like gibberish when your computer reads them back to you), but it is a good backup that often will catch the last three or four typos in the text that your eyes missed.

GO ONLINE!

Text-to-speech capability has been part of a modern computer's bag of tricks for several years now. There are several programs on the market that allow you to exploit your computer's power to read your documents back to you. The authors have used Sayzme™, a freeware text-to-speech program, and TextAloud™, a text-to-speech program that also will allow you to convert text files into .mp3 files. Just what you want to be listening to at the gym: the brief you drafted.

C. Stay objective

Editing is a good time to test the objectivity of your work. An office memorandum should be an objective, fair treatment of the pros and the cons of the client's situation. You may have gotten carried away with the client's cause and have taken her side too much. Editing is a time to reexamine your work and check this tendency. Your readers (bosses, clients, other colleagues) really do want the right answer, not the answer that you think they want to hear. If you need encouragement in giving the hard, but correct answer, remember your ethical duties to the client, and remember that lawyers get sued for malpractice more and more these days for having provided "popular" but inaccurate advice.

D. Be as definite as you can be

We always tell our students that someone will be counting on them to get the correct answer (and likely is paying a lot of money for this purpose). Do not make it appear as if you gave up halfway through by reporting your answer as a "maybe yes," or "possibly no." The answers that you provide in your work (especially in the Brief Answer, and each Thesis heading or statement) should be as definite as possible. In general, the Brief Answer should start with a yes or no, not a "maybe yes," or "probably no." Take your best shot based on your analysis of the law. If you think there absolutely is no way to give a definitive yes or no answer to the question you wrote in the Question Presented section, then you should go back and rephrase your issue so that you can give a yes or no answer. Otherwise, you should qualify your answer in the text of the Brief Answer or Discussion, explaining any limitations you perceive.

From time to time, your analysis in the application section and your conclusions on an issue will run into the inherent uncertainties of the law. Here, you should try to be as precise as possible in explaining yourself, but where you must express a lack of certainty, pinpoint the **precise source** of the uncertainty. If it is that one case cannot be effectively distinguished, explain that. If a point turns on whether a court will accept or reject a certain argument or make a certain application of the law to your facts, then explain what happens if the court goes each way.

E. Statement of Facts: how much is too much?

When pruning your **statement of facts**, consider this **four-part test:**

  (1) **Am I going to mention this fact again in my discussion section?**
  (2) **Am I going to use this fact to analogize my case to another case or distinguish my case from a contrary authority?**
  (3) **Am I going to use this fact in discussing the application of an element?**
  (4) **Is this fact necessary to explain the client's situation, and if the fact is not present, will the uninformed reader still understand the situation?**

If *none* of the above applies, consider jettisoning the fact entirely.

F. Tips for editing the discussion

1. Side issues, interesting questions

We assume you will not be spending a lot of time (and space) writing about topics that are not part of the assignment. In a legal writing assignment, no one gets extra credit for pointing out the most side issues that may affect the case as a whole in lieu of answering the question at hand.

2. Redundancy is bad

Repeating yourself is a vice. It does not pay to say the same thing two or three times, yet lawyers are prone to redundancy. Many think: "if I say it twice, that is twice as good." This idea may exist because repetition is a good technique in oral advocacy—but save it for that context. You may think you are driving home a point, but more often than not you are driving someone insane. We are not saying that you should not make your point clearly, or that you shouldn't explain yourself fully even if that takes three or four sentences on a single point. You absolutely should explain the same point or the same conclusion in a different way *if* there is something to be revealed through that second exposition. Clarification of legal principles is no easy task; don't make it harder by trying to adhere to a rule of *no* repetitions, ever. But repeating things two or three times is no good if the additional statement shed no new light on the principles you are explaining.

3. Too many authorities?

It does not pay to cite dozens of authorities if you cannot synthesize them properly or discuss any of them in enough detail to make your point. Do not drown out the best controlling and persuasive authorities in a sea of "also rans." If you have strong cases, explain them. If there are many others, cite them once and leave them be—don't try to explain all of them. Use parentheticals to give a few key facts or points from these other cases that support your argument. A fascinated reader will look up these other cases and get the benefit of them if she wants them.

CHAPTER 9

Legal Citation

Citation is not the most riveting topic, but it is a necessary component of legal writing. To communicate legal analysis effectively, you have to cite to authorities. If you cite to them correctly, no one will think twice about your competency. Incorrect citations, however, can cause significant harm for at least two reasons. First, incorrect or missing citations make your work look sloppy and thus less trustworthy. Second, incorrect or missing citations undermine the value and persuasiveness of your writing. That authorities support your legal analysis and conclusions is of utmost importance to a legal audience.

> **FOOD FOR THOUGHT**
>
> *Citation form: it's important*
> You can be the best and most creative writer in the world and still fall short as a lawyer if you do not know at least the basics of legal citation. Most lawyers know at least the basics and will notice when you don't. As stated above, citations contribute to your document's "first impression." Different lawyers and workplaces place different degrees of emphasis on citation. Courts generally care a lot about them. Many law clerks and judges are former law review editors, who certainly will be familiar with correct citation form. Even if you do not become one of them, at the very least, you need to be citation competent.

There are two basic guidebooks for legal citation format: the **ALWD Citation Manual** ("ALWD") and **The Bluebook: A Uniform System of Citation** ("Bluebook" or "BB"). The good news is that *they both use the same citation form.*

There used to be some differences between the two manuals on about a dozen rules, but in its Fifth Edition (Aspen/Wolters Kluwer 2014), the ALWD Manual editors made a concerted effort to eliminate all of the important distinctions between ALWD and the Bluebook. As a result, if you are assigned ALWD as your citation manual, you are going to learn American legal citation the same way as other students who are assigned the Bluebook, no matter what you may hear. We split this Chapter into two parts—so you only have to read half of it!

One important prefatory note. The material in this Chapter concerns citation forms *used in practice-related, practitioner documents,* such those written to a court, in a law office, or in most first-year legal writing programs. This Chapter is *not about law review and law journal citation forms,* which differ in several respects from practice-related citations. Journal forms are not widely different, just different in certain particulars (*e.g.*, italicizing vs. using SMALL CAPS fonts, and other typography differences). Because there are enough differences to be confusing, we elected to focus this Chapter on practice-oriented citation forms, as those are the ones you will use in first-year legal writing.

The **ALWD Citation Manual: A Professional System of Citation** was created in 1999 by the Association of Legal Writing Directors as an alternative to the Bluebook. The ALWD Manual was designed as a "Restatement" of current citation practices and is intended to be the most straightforward method possible for teaching and learning legal citation. As we stated above, in its Fifth Edition, in 2014, the book has moved to harmonize citation form between the Bluebook and the ALWD Manual to a greater extent than ever before.

The Bluebook: A Uniform System of Citation just came out in its Twentieth Edition in March 2015, after this Chapter was already at the last stages of publication. Therefore, this Chapter describes the Nineteenth Edition of the Bluebook. But do not worry. The law review editors of the Columbia Law Review, Harvard Law Review, University of Pennsylvania Law Review, and Yale Law Journal, who are the writers and editors of the Bluebook, rarely make monumental changes from edition to edition. At most, they will tweak the information required in some forms, expand the coverage of foreign and specialty areas of the law, and perhaps add forms for new media.

Much more important than the minute differences between ALWD and the Bluebook is the fact that American legal citation is not practiced with complete uniformity across the United States.

There are local rules and practices too varied to cover here—public domain citation forms, and other state-specific and even court-specific rules and practices do exist. Some law school journals—Chicago and Texas are two examples—use their own variations on the citation rules discussed herein. West Publishing (mainly owned by Thomson Reuters, which includes WestlawNext), West Academic (the casebook business), Lexis Advance, and Shepard's Citations likewise use their own variations on citation forms. Even some law firms and courts (including the United States Supreme Court) deviate from the prescribed rules.

There are two take-aways to keep in mind. First, do not rely on any publisher's or court's citation forms, or anything you see on WestlawNext or Lexis Advance. Second, regardless of whether you learn legal citation via ALWD or the Bluebook, your goal should be to understand legal citation principals in general—and to remember to consult local rules or conventions for specific requirements that neither manual fully addresses.

Part I: The ALWD Citation Manual

GENERAL RULES

This Chapter is not a substitute for reading The ALWD Manual (or the BB); indeed, as is the case with any user manual, you must actually *use* it in order to master it.

In this section, we cover the most important forms, conventions, and requirements for American legal citation. In previous editions of this text, we pointed the various circumstances where ALWD's form did not match the Bluebook's, but as of the latest edition of ALWD (5th ed. 2014), there are no significant distinctions to mention. We note one place where there is an *insignificant* distinction (*see* footnote 2 below).

I.   PLACEMENT OF CITATIONS: CITATION SENTENCES AND CITATION CLAUSES

There are two basic ways to incorporate a citation into a legal document. If the source relates to the entire textual sentence, then the citation should follow as its own "sentence." If the source relates only to part of the sentence, then it will be incorporated as a clause, set off from the text it concerns with commas (ALWD R. 43).

Sentence: Tort liability requires breach of a duty of care. *Injured v. Careless*, 12 S.W.2d 23, 25 (Mo. 2001).

Clause: Tort liability requires breach of a duty of care, *Injured v. Careless*, 12 S.W.2d 23, 25 (Mo. 2001), but the duty varies from claim to claim.

In terms of typeface, most legal citations are presented in a combination of ordinary type and either *italics* or underlining. These typeface apply regardless of the type of practice-related document in which the citation appears (office memorandum, trial brief, appellate brief, court document, or administrative agency filing), and regardless of where the citation appears within that document (in text or in a footnote).[1]

It usually does not matter whether you choose italics or underlining in practice-related documents, though ALWD does appear to express a preference for italics (see ALWD Rules 1, 12). Whichever you choose, be consistent throughout your document! **Do not use a combination of italics and underlining.**

---

[1]   ALWD now has a rule—ALWD Rule 1—that matches the BB rule for law review article citation form, which requires different fonts for different types of documents and placement of sources (see ALWD R. 1; BB R. 2). For practice-related documents, the ALWD rule is the same as the BB rule as described here and in part II of this Chapter.

Appropriate citation material to italicize or underline includes:

- Case names (*e.g.,* ***Haley v. Toonces***)
- Titles of most sources and documents (*e.g.,* ***Report of ALWD Committee on Sales***)
- Introductory signals (*e.g.,* ***See, See also***)
- Internal cross-references (***supra and infra***)
- Prior and subsequent history (***e.g., aff'd, rev'd***)
- The short form ***id.***

You do not italicize other information, such as the reporter or journal abbreviation, the volume and page numbers, the court identifier, and the date.

Incorrect: *12 S.W.2d 23, 25 (Mo. 2001)*

112 Colum. L. Rev. 222, 234 (2012)

A. Citation sentence

A citation sentence is used when you are citing authority after a period that ends a complete sentence. The citation sentence starts with a capital letter, and ends with a period:

> The standard is one of gross negligence. *Hallam v. Scaraggi*, 118 S.W.2d 222, 224 (Mo. 1947).

Multiple cases and other authorities in a citation sentence are separated by semi-colons:

> The standard is one of gross negligence. Mo. Rev. Stat. § 232.12 (1986); *Hallam v. Scaraggi*, 118 S.W.2d 222, 224 (Mo. 1947); *Lowe v. Carmichael*, 446 S.W.2d 333, 335 (Mo. Ct. App. E. Dist. 1987).

B. Citation clauses

When a citation supports only part of a sentence, the citation is inserted in the sentence, set off by commas before and after. This is referred to as a citation clause:

> The Illinois Dog Bite Statute, 510 Ill. Comp. Stat. 5/16 (1996), defines a dog-owner's liability for a dog bite.

Multiple authorities supporting a clause are separated by semicolons, but the whole citation clause is set apart by commas as above. A citation clause does not necessarily start with a capital letter—it only does if you are citing an authority without any introductory phrase, and the authority starts with a capital letter. A sentence citation which supports the second clause can follow at the end of the second clause, after the period that ends the sentence, as in the following example:

Dog bite liability requires a lack of provocation, either intentional or unintentional, *see* 510 Ill. Comp. Stat. 5/16 (1996); *Clark v. Bessler*, 210 N.E.2d 207, 208 (Ill. 1965); *Schooner v. Siegel*, 344 N.E.2d 268, 270 (Ill. App. Ct. 5th Dist. 1976), but provocation can be offset if the dog's attack is particularly vicious and disproportionate to the provocation. *Schooner*, 344 N.E.2d at 271.

As a general matter, within a citation sentence or citation clause, cite the highest and most recent controlling authorities first, followed by lesser and earlier authorities in order of their weight. This order of presentation is important.

Correct: A dog owner is liable for all injuries caused by his dog unless the dog is provoked by the victim. *Vick v. ASPCA*, 123 S.W.2d 345, 347 (Mo. 1965); *Tyson v. United Chicken Protectors, Inc.*, 789 S.W.2d 234, 237 (Mo. Ct. App. E. Dist. 1989); *Willingham v. Terenzoni*, 780 S.W.2d 134, 137 (Mo. Ct. App. E. Dist. 1980).

Incorrect: A dog owner is liable for all injuries caused by his dog unless the dog is provoked by the victim. *Tyson v. United Chicken Protectors, Inc.*, 789 S.W.2d 234, 237 (Mo. Ct. App. E. Dist. 1989); *Willingham v. Terenzoni*, 780 S.W.2d 134, 137 (Mo. Ct. App. E. Dist. 1980); *Vick v. ASPCA*, 123 S.W.2d 345, 347 (Mo. 1965).

In certain circumstances, you will be presenting a large number of authorities that are not controlling and may be of equal importance. When you are in this situation, the order of authorities cited according to ALWD[2] is:

1. Constitutions

2. Statutes

3. Treaties and other international agreements

4. Cases, in the order of:
   a. U.S. Supreme Court
   b. Federal appellate courts
   c. Federal trial courts (including bankruptcy courts)
   d. Judicial Panel on Multidistrict Litigation
   e. Federal claims courts, military courts, tax courts
   f. Administrative agencies
   g. State courts (by state, in alphabetical order, and then by level of court within a state, highest to lowest)
   h. Foreign courts
   i. International courts (ICJ, PCIJ, arbitral panels)

---

2   BB Rule 1.4 specifies a slightly different order. *See* part II of this Chapter. This, in fact, is the only difference we have found in the ALWD and BB rules covered here.

5. Legislative history materials

6. Administrative and executive materials

7. Records, briefs, pleadings of litigants

8. Secondary sources, in the order of:
   a.   Restatements and uniform laws
   b.   Books and treatises
   c.   Law review articles
   d.   Annotations (for example, American Law Reports)
   e.   Magazine and newspaper articles
   f.   Unpublished materials

Within a particular category (for example, federal appellate court or district court cases), the materials should be listed in the order described in ALWD Rule 45.4. The following rules are of particular note:

- U.S. Court of Appeals cases should be ordered first by court (1st, 2d, 3d, etc) and then in reverse chronological order.
- U.S. District Court cases are ordered first alphabetically and then in reverse chronological order.

II.   SIGNALS AND INTRODUCTORY PHRASES (ALWD R. 44)

Either a citation sentence or a citation clause can be preceded by an introductory word or phrase. When the word or phrase begins a citation sentence, it is capitalized. Otherwise it is not.

The entire introductory word or phrase is either underlined or italicized whether or not the source that follows it is underlined or italicized. The signal should be separated from the rest of the citation with one space—do not include any punctuation between the signal and the rest of the citation (ALWD R. 44.6).

Each phrase connotes something different about the authority that follows it:

[No introductory phrase]   Connotes that the authority contains (states) the exact or nearly the exact phrase or sentence for which you are citing the authority (*i.e.*, the words you use are 99% the same as in the source). You may have changed the verb tense or dropped a minor word or two (this, than, the, etc.), but otherwise, one turning to the authority would find that statement in the authority at the page or section to which you are citing. This form is used whether or not you actually put quotation marks around the statement.

If the statement is a legal proposition or conclusion (as opposed to a fact or something other than a statement about the law), this form also connotes that the statement is part of the holding of the case.

See

Connotes that the authority contains the idea and the concept for which you are citing the authority, but the exact words will not be found in the authority. The authority must directly support your statement. You would still cite to a particular page or section of the authority where the idea or concept is stated.

See also

Connotes that the authority contains related or additional information or material that supports the proposition for which the authority is cited, but the exact statement (concept or idea) is not found in the authority. A parenthetical should be used to explain why or how the material supports the proposition.

For example:

> The Erie doctrine confuses the issue of choice of law. *Masters v. Johnson*, 55 Ohio App. 23, 24 (1987); *see also Basinger v. Baldwin*, 766 P.2d 433, 444 (Okla. 1978) (holding that *Erie* confuses most issues of conflict of laws, including forum selection).

Accord

When you have two or more authorities that clearly support the statement or proposition for which you are citing them, but the actual statement only is found in one of the authorities, use *accord* to preface the other citations.

For example:

> A doctor must use reasonably prudent methods to detect viral agents. Mo. Rev. Stat. § 516.132.2 (1999); *accord Smith v. Jones*, 755 S.W.2d 232, 240 (Mo. Ct. App. E. Dist. 1996); *Vogel v. Cosgrove*, 432 N.E.2d 222, 223 (Ill. App. Ct. 5th Dist. 1986).

Cf.

Connotes that the cited authority states a different proposition from the main proposition for which the citation is given, but the second proposition is sufficiently analogous as to lend support to the main proposition. A parenthetical or other explanation should be used to explain the relevance.

For example:

> Architects must take reasonable care to choose a design that will preclude subsidence of the building. *Cf. Murphy v. Cowles*, 239 S.E.2d 235, 237 (S.C. Ct. App. 1st Dist. 1975) (civil engineer required to take reasonable care to choose non-subsiding design); *Beecher v. Stowe*, 236 S.E.2d 457, 459 (S.C. Ct. App. 1st Dist. 1973) (same, building contractor).

Compare . . . [and] . . . with

Used to express that a comparison of one or more cases with one or more other cases will reveal something about the way the law works in this area. Again, a parenthetical explanation should be used to drive the point home even more. Note well that in this citation form commas separate the authorities, not semi-colons.

For example:

> If the damages are nominal, a defamation claim will be dismissed. *Compare Norton v. Cramden*, 432 Vt. 234 (1990) (nominal damages of fifteen dollars, claim dismissed), *and Ricardo v. Mertz*, 335 Vt. 245 (1982) (nominal damages of two dollars, claim dismissed), *with Scooby v. Shaggy*, 553 Vt. 987 (1997) (damages of $150,000, claim not dismissed), *and DeSanctis v. Cheney*, 288 Vt. 256 (1978) (damages of $75,000, claim not dismissed), *and Murray v. Bush*, 228 Vt. 667 (1975) (damages of $55,000, claim not dismissed).

E.g., See, e.g.,

Introduces authorities that support the proposition stated. The concept and general proposition would be found in the cited authorities, but not necessarily the exact word or phrase you are stating. The *E.g.* signal has a comma following it, and if *See* is used, there is a comma after the *See*, too.

For example:

> Many cases in the District of Maryland end in dismissal. *E.g., Dorning v. Morning*, 222 F. Supp. 3d 34 (D. Md. 2014); *Randolph v. Scott*, 111 F. Supp. 3d 309 (D. Md. 2009). Many of these cases are copyright cases. *See, e.g., Spetzel v. Freckle*, 144 F. Supp. 3d 567 (D. Md. 2011); *Redmund v. Dedmund*, 123 F. Supp. 3d 778 (D. Md. 2010).

Unlike *see or see also*, the phrase "*e.g.*" is used if you are stating a rather general legal proposition and wish to suggest that there are many authorities that hold this, and the listed authorities are a representative sample. If the listed authorities actually do not state the exact proposition for which you are citing them, but support it nonetheless, use "*see, e.g.*," instead.

But see (But see, e.g., But cf.)   If you are citing an authority contrary to the proposition stated, you would use *but see* in situations where you would use *see* or no introductory phrase, and *but see, e.g.*, if you are listing several contrary authorities that go against the proposition. Use *but cf.* if the contrary authority is not directly on point, but sufficiently analogous to cause concern. In any of these combinations, a parenthetical should be used to explain the state of things.

For example:

> Most states have adopted the UCC Sales provisions. *But see* La. Rev. Stat. Ann. § 355.1 (West 1988) (only state not to adopt UCC Article 2). In the majority of states, statute of frauds requires contracts for goods over $500 in value to be in writing. *But cf. Delany v. DuBois*, 235 La. 468, 469 (1986) (civil code requires writing only for specific purpose contracts, or for land sales).

See generally   The most nebulous of introductory phrases, *see generally* is used to introduce background or other relevant material—often secondary sources—that are helpful to an understanding of the issues.

III. SHORTHAND DEVICES FOR REPEAT CITATIONS (ALWD R.10 and R.11)

ALWD Rule 11 provides a basic introduction to the concept of "full citations" and "short forms." A full citation includes each component required for the particular source one is citing and gives readers all the information they would need to locate that source in a library. The full citation format for each specific source will require slightly different components, which are identified and discussed in connection with specific source materials later in the manual (ALWD Rules 12-42). The first time a source is cited—in any type of legal document—you must use the full citation format for that kind of source. Thereafter, you may rely on a "short form," which omits some of the required information in a full citation but still enables a reader to identify and locate the source. Acceptable short forms also vary depending on type of source, where the short form occurs in relation to the full citation, and whether the source is cited in text or in a footnote.

Id.   One short form that nearly all legal citations share, however, is "*Id.*," which is short for "idem" and means "the same." *Id.* replaces as much of the immediately preceding citation as is identical with the current one. Of course, a page number or section number might change. For example:

> Red is used for anger. *Boodin v. Zehfuss*, 123 U.S. 234, 238 (1923). Blue is for peace. *Id.* Purple is for sorrow. *Id.* at 239.

> The statute of frauds requires a writing. Mo. Rev. Stat. § 400.2-201 (2013). The writing is necessary if the goods cost $500 or more. *Id.* However, the damages will still be limited to the costs to cover. *Id.* § 400.2-701 *et seq.*

You cannot use *id.* after a citation containing more than one authority. *Id.* can only refer back to a single authority, and you cannot use it to refer back to the authority last cited if that authority was paired with others. (Note, however, that sources identified in explanatory parentheticals, explanatory phrases, or subsequent history are ignored for purposes of this rule (*see* ALWD 11.3(f)). The following examples are ***incorrect:***

> ***Incorrect form:*** *The Erie doctrine confuses the issue of choice of law. Masters v. Johnson, 55 N.E.2d 23, 24 (Ill. 1957); Hill v. Williams, 766 P.2d 433, 444 (Okla. 1978). It also confuses the law of forum selection. Id.*

> **[Cannot use *id.* here because preceding citation sentence had two cases in it. *Id.* cannot be used to refer back to both, nor does it refer back to the last one cited.]**

> **Incorrect form:** *Illinois is a comparative negligence state. Madigan v. Turner, 345 N.E.2d 789, 791 (Ill. 1967); Hodge v. Walpole, 788 N.E.2d 654, 656 (Ill. App. Ct. 1988). Plaintiff's percentage of fault reduces the verdict, even if plaintiff's fault exceeds 50 percent. Hodge, id. at 657.*

> **[Specifying which of the two preceding cases you are referring back to does not help—it still is bad citation form to use *id.* here.]**

Instead, you must use a different short form for the multiple authorities or whichever one of them you want to cite to.

These examples are **CORRECT:**

> The Erie doctrine confuses the issue of choice of law. *Masters v. Johnson*, 55 N.E.2d 23, 24 (Ill. 1957); *Hill v. Williams*, 766 P.2d 433, 444 (Okla. 1978). It also confuses the law of forum selection. *Masters*, 55 N.E.2d at 24; *Hill*, 766 P.2d at 444.

> Illinois is a comparative negligence state. *Ray v. Chuh*, 345 N.E.2d 789, 791 (Ill. 1967); *Levine v. Bauer*, 788 N.E.2d 654, 656 (Ill. App. Ct. 5th Dist. 1988). Plaintiff's percentage of fault reduces the verdict, even if plaintiff's fault exceeds 50 percent. *Levine*, 788 N.E.2d at 657.

Supra, infra

> *Supra* ("above") and *infra* ("below") (ALWD R. 10) are internal cross-references; they are signals that refer readers to other parts of the same document. They most commonly are used in footnotes. They do not refer readers to outside sources. Use *supra* to refer to material that appears earlier in your paper and *infra* to refer to material that will appear later. For example:

> [17] *Supra* note 10.

> [18] *Infra* text accompanying note 50.

> There is also a second use of *supra*—not as an internal cross-reference, but as a short citation for certain types of secondary sources (ALWD R. 11.4). This use of *supra* functions more like *id..* It can only be used after a source has been cited once in full format. But, unlike *id.,* it cannot be used for all sources. It is typically used for sources cited by author name, such as books, law review articles and web sites. Do not use *supra* to refer to cases, statutes, constitutions, regulations and other legislative materi-

als. And, of course, do not use *supra* to refer back to the immediately preceding authority—*id.* is the appropriate short form there.

For example:
> [Full citation on p. 5 of the document] Michael D. Murray, *For the Love of Parentheticals – The Story of Parenthetical Usage in Synthesis, Rhetoric, Economics, and Narrative Reasoning*, 38 U. Dayton L. Rev. 174 (2012).
>
> . . .
>
> [Short citation on p. 7 of the document] *See* Murray, *supra*, at 182.

The example here works if there was only one article cited by Michael D. Murray in the document, or no other article written by someone with the last name "Murray." If, and only if, this is not the case, use more of the author's name or more of the article's name to make the short cite clear: Michael D. Murray, *For the Love, supra*, at 181.

IV. STYLE OF THE CASE (ALWD R. 12)

The names of the first named parties on each side become the style of the case; they are separated by a "v." and underlined or italicized:

Correct: *Belt v. Abyad*
Not: *Belt and Mach v. Abyad and Mayflower Hotel Co.*

A. Certain words are omitted

Omit the parties' first names (unless they are part of a company name):

Correct: *Schechter v. Cheh*

Not: *Roger Schechter v. Mary Cheh*

But *Roger Schechter, Inc. v. Mary Cheh and Co.* is **correct** because these are company names.

Titles, offices, before or after the party's name (for example, Mr., Mrs., Dr., M.D., PhD, Commander, General, Surgeon General of the United States) are omitted unless the person is sued only by her title, and her actual name does not appear in the case style:

Correct:	*Pingree v. Mayor of Sacramento* [if the Mayor is not sued in her own name]
Correct:	*Pingree v. McCheese* [if Mayor McCheese is sued under his own name]
But not:	*Pingree v. McCheese, Mayor of Sacramento*, and not *Dr. Pingree, M.D. v. Mr. McCheese.*

B. Use ALWD standard abbreviations

Abbreviations may be used in legal citations for common sources, such as legal periodicals, case names, and court names. ALWD presents tables of standard abbreviations in Rule 2 and in Appendices 3, 4 and 5. If a word does not appear in one of those tables, it should not be abbreviated.

In general, single capital letters must be grouped together, but any other combination of two or more letters to be set apart from single capitals or other combinations by a space. For example, the following abbreviations are correct:

S.D.N.Y.   E.D. Va.   F. Supp.   Cal. App.

Ordinals, such as 2d and 3d, are treated as one capital letter, and can be grouped together with other single capital letters, as in the following examples:

F.2d

N.Y.3d

But if the ordinal follows a cluster of two or more letters, it must stand alone:

F. Supp. 2d

Cal. Rptr. 4th

Abbreviate company, party, and other names in case styles according to Appendix 3:

Consolidated becomes Consol.

Enterprise becomes Enter.

Industry, industries, industrial become Indus.

South is S.

East is E.

Federal court names are abbreviated according to Appendix 4; state court abbreviations can be developed using a combination of Appendix 1 and Rule 2, or by looking up abbreviations for each individual word in Appendix 3.

Appellate Division is App. Div.

Commonwealth Court is Commw. Ct.

Superior Court is Super. Ct.

When abbreviating state names, follow the rules in Appendix 1. Note that the correct abbreviation for a state is not always the U.S. Postal Service abbreviation. For example:

Ala.   Del.

Miss.   N.M.

Alaska   Iowa

Idaho   Utah

Abbreviations for case history terms are found in ALWD Chart 12.3:

aff'd

rev'd

cert. denied

rev'd on other grounds

As are official terms for actions that are not abbreviated:

appeal denied

vacated

modified

mandamus denied

V.   REQUIRED INFORMATION FOR CASES

Each case citation must tell four pieces of information: (1) the case name; (2) where you find the case; (3) the court; (4) the year of the case. But this information may be conveyed in as many as nine components:

(1) Case name (or style)

(2) Reporter volume

(3) Reporter abbreviation

(4) First page of case

(5) Jump cite (Pinpoint cite or Pin cite) page

(6) Court abbreviation

(7) Date of opinion

(8) Subsequent history designation

(9) Subsequent history citation

Here is an example (the first as it might appear in a legal document, the second broken down to label the nine components listed above:

Gettysburg Morning Post v. Hallam, 144 A.2d 25, 45-46 (Pa. 1966), *rev'd*, 378 U.S. 250 (1967).

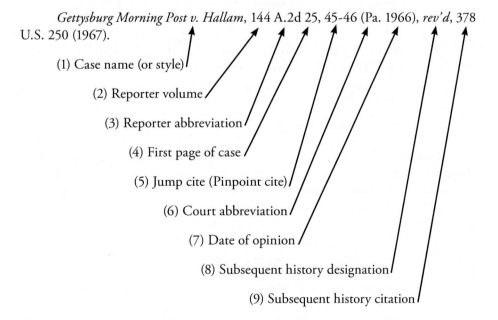

(1) Case name (or style)

(2) Reporter volume

(3) Reporter abbreviation

(4) First page of case

(5) Jump cite (Pinpoint cite)

(6) Court abbreviation

(7) Date of opinion

(8) Subsequent history designation

(9) Subsequent history citation

A. Page spans and jump cites (a/k/a pinpoint cites or pin cites)

If you are referring to a particular part of the case (and you should be in most instances), you must provide a jump cite (also known as a pinpoint cite or pin cite) that refers the reader to the specific page or pages of the opinion that support your proposition. To create a jump cite, put a comma after the page number where the case begins and then cite the page(s) where the material appears. More than one page can be referenced. If the material is on separate pages, cite them separately: 23, 24, 29, 35.

If the material carries over from one page to another, you should indicate the page span. If the page span involves numbers with three or more digits, you must drop repetitive digits and retain two on the right-hand side of the span

125-26   2225-26

If you are referring to material on the first page of a case, you must repeat the first page number:

Shashoua v. Donovan, 833 S.W.2d 222, 222 (Tenn. 1996).

B. Court information

A case citation must include the abbreviation for the court that decided the case (in parentheses preceding the date). Abbreviations are listed in Appendices 1 and 4.

When citing a federal case, information about the state or about the court division is omitted. Thus, it is **incorrect** to write:

(7th Cir. Ill. 1980)

(D.N.J. Newark Div. 1997)

However, when citing a state case, you must include available information about departments, districts or divisions at the appellate or trial court level if the information is relevant or important, and this means the information should be included whenever it assists in the determination of whether or not the cases is controlling or how persuasive a non-controlling authority might be in the case at hand. Appendix 1 of ALWD contains much of the necessary information about the courts of each state and the abbreviations of the various courts.

Capulet v. Montague, 500 N.E.2d 180 (Ill. App. Ct. 1st Dist. 1998).

If the court that wrote the opinion is obvious from one of the reporters you are citing (for example, a reporter with the state's initials is presumed to report the cases of the highest court in the state; a reporter with the state's initials and "App." added on is presumed to report the decisions of the state's intermediate level appellate court), then you need not put the court designation in the parentheses with the year. However, you still need to note the division or department deciding the case. For example:

> *Sheffield v. Vailladolid*, 234 N.Y.2d 245 (1965).

> [Reader knows from the N.Y. reporter citation that the case is from the N.Y. Court of Appeals, the highest court in New York].

> *Irving v. Bissell*, 546 N.Y.S.2d 180 (App. Div. 4th Dept. 1988).

> [Reader knows the case is from New York from the reporter citation, but the citation is not to a case from the state's highest court, and thus the reader requires information about the division of the appellate court that decided the case].

Sometimes an official reporter with the state's initials reports more than just the highest court's cases. If so, you must supply additional information to correct the reader's erroneous presumption, but only as much as is necessary to identify the court:

> *Gore v. Vidal*, 665 Idaho 456, 458 (Ct. App. 1st Dist. 1987).

> **Not:** *Gore v. Vidal*, 665 Idaho 456, 458 (Idaho Ct. App. 1st Dist. 1987).

VI. SUBSEQUENT HISTORY

Subsequent history codes must be used if there is relevant subsequent history to a case (for example, *appeal dismissed, aff'd, rev'd on other grounds, mandamus denied*, etc. *See* ALWD Chart 12.3. For example:

> *Rogers v. Hammerstein*, 388 F.2d 345, 366 (2d Cir. 1958), *aff'd*, 354 U.S. 578 (1959).

The denial of a writ of certiorari (cert. denied) or the denial of other discretionary appeals from a court of last resort with selective jurisdiction should not be included unless the denial occurred less than two years ago or if the denial is "particularly relevant" to your use and citation of the case (*See* ALWD Sidebar 12.5). A citation that has no subsequent history information represents that there have been no relevant legal proceedings in the case occurring after the cited opinion.

If the year of the original opinion is the same as the year of the subsequent opinion(s), you omit the year in the earlier parentheticals and only put the year in the last, latest parenthetical of the citation. In the following example, all of these opinions would be from 1996:

> *Apple Computer, Inc. v. Gates*, 789 P.2d 876, 878 (Wash. App. 1st Dist.), *reh'g denied*, 791 P.2d 345 (Wash. App. 1st Dist.), *appeal dismissed*, 792 P.2d 579 (Wash. 1996).

VII. PARENTHETICALS (ALWD R. 12.11)

Parentheticals are used to provide useful explanatory information that will help the reader understand the significance of a case or the lack thereof. For example, parentheticals can be used for providing some details of the facts that show why you are citing it, or some clarification of the holding if this might not be clear from what preceded the citation, or to clear up a possible misconception about the case not obvious from a naked cite; for example, "Hey reader, this was a plurality opinion, not a majority opinion." Examples:

> *Jones v. Clinton*, 156 F.3d 678, 681 (8th Cir. 1999) (court indicated that defendant lied).

> *Marshall v. Brennan*, 477 U.S. 345 (1969) (per curiam).

Punctuation and complete sentences usually are avoided in parentheticals in order to save space. An exception exists if you actually quote a whole phrase or sentence from the case. Compare this example with the first example above:

> *Jones v. Clinton*, 156 F.3d 678, 681 (8th Cir. 1999) ("We find that the defendant lied to the country.").

If you are citing non-majority opinions, they are noted with their author:

> *Moller v. Texas Horn Co.*, 357 Ark. 456, 468 (1948) (Simpson, J., dissenting).

Multiple parentheticals are possible. Please separate each parenthetical with a space:

> *Marshall v. Brennan*, 477 U.S. 345, 349 (1969) (per curiam) (noting that the "clear and convincing evidence" standard applied).

VIII. SHORT FORMS FOR CASES

The long form of a citation need only be given once in any document; in fact, it is bad form to present it more than once. People will think you are citing a different case and got the citation wrong. In addition to the form used for all authorities (*id.*), with cases, you should use the plaintiff's name (or a short recognizable part of the name if the name is long, as in the case of a corporation) along with the volume-reporter-page number, or one of the other approved forms listed below when you are doing a repeat cite in a situation where *id.* cannot be used:

Full cite:

> *Wickerham v. Brunins*, 432 N.W.2d 356 (Wash. 1988).

Proper short forms (where *id.* does not apply):

> *Wickerham*, 432 N.W.2d at 358-59.

> In *Wickerham*, the court dismissed the suit. 432 N.W.2d at 358-59.

Full cite:

> *Speedy Drydock and Transfer Co., Inc. v. Bosley*, 517 S.W.2d 425 (Mo. App. E. Dist. 1978).

Proper short forms (where *id.* does not apply):

> *Speedy Drydock*, 517 S.W.2d at 426.

> *Speedy Drydock* is the only case to apply the cruel and unusual standard. 517 S.W.2d at 426.

The following forms are **incorrect**:

> *Wickerham* at 358.

> *Speedy Drydock, id.* at 426.

If the plaintiff's name is too common (or shows up too many times in cases you are going to cite), use the defendant's name instead:

> *United States v. Calandra* should be shortened to *Calandra*

> *Smith v. Netanyahu* should be *Netanyahu*

> *Commissioner v. Mitchell* should be *Mitchell*

> *Shalala v. Harris* should be *Harris* [This would be the case if Donna Shalala is the Commissioner of Health and Human Services, and so is a plaintiff in 9 out of the 10 cases you are citing in your Social Security case.]

IX. CITATION FORMS FOR OTHER AUTHORITIES

STATUTES AND CODES

The typical citation to a federal statute contains five or six components, depending on whether the code is official or unofficial (ALWD R. 14).

> (1) Title or volume number where the statute appears;

> (2) Abbreviated name of the code;

> (3) Section symbol;

> (4) The section number of the statute; and

(5) The year the code was published (not the year the statute was enacted or became effective).

When you are citing a statutory section, use the official version of the statute. Do not cite the annotated or other unofficial versions. Of course, if you are citing some commentary or notes or committee reports or interpretative information on the statute that is not found in the official version, certainly cite to the annotated version or wherever the material appears. If you are citing to an unofficial code, then you must include an additional item: the Publisher's name in parentheses prior to the date.

If you never learned how to do a § sign on your computer, write "sec." instead. For example, Mo. Rev. Stat. sec. 400.2-201 (1986). If a ¶ symbol is involved, and you cannot make the ¶ symbol, write "para." instead. More than one section is expressed by §§ or "secs." More than one paragraph is expressed by ¶¶ or "paras."

You are free to use the official or the popular name of the statute in your citation sentence or clause:

Securities Act of 1933, 15 U.S.C. §§ 77a-77aa (1994).

Labor Management Relations (Taft-Hartley) Act § 301(a), 29 U.S.C. § 185(a) (1988).

Note the spacing in the following examples—the § sign stands for the word section so there is a single space before and after the § sign.

Federal:

Official: 30 U.S.C. § 523 (1988).   **Not:** 30 U.S.C. §523 (1988).

Annotated: 30 U.S.C.A. § 523 (West 1995).

Illinois (does not use § symbol):

Official: 510 Ill. Comp. Stat. 5/16 (1996).   **Not:** 510 Ill. Comp. Stat. § 5/16 (1996).

Annotated: 510 Ill. Comp. Stat. Ann. 5/16 (West 1995).

New York:

The annotated versions of the statutes published by McKinney and Consolidated Laws Service are official. A third unannotated form published by Gould also is official; go figure New York would be so lax. The form of the citation is stranger still:

N.Y. [subject matter abbrev.] Law § x (publisher 19xx).

As in: N.Y. Gen. Constr. Law § 456 (McKinney 1989).

N.Y. Mun. Home Rule Law § 77(a) (Consol. 1990).

CONSTITUTIONS

Under ALWD R. 13, a constitution is cited by the abbreviated name of the country or state followed by the word "Const.," followed by the abbreviated name of the section, article, or amendment, and none of it is underlined or italicized. Note, too, where the commas **do** and **do not appear** in these citation forms:

U.S. Const. amend IV.

U.S. Const. art. I, § 8, cl. 8

Ariz. Const. art. 2, § 6.

RULES

Rules of procedure and evidence are abbreviated as shown in ALWD R. 16 and are not underlined:

Fed. R. Evid. 401.

Fed. R. Civ. P. 23.

Fed. R. App. P. 4(a).

Under ALWD R. 18, administrative rules and regulations are cited to the Code of Federal Regulations (CFR), if possible, and to the Federal Register or other source if not found in CFR. A typical citation contains: (1) the volume number; (2) the abbreviation C.F.R.; (3) the section sign and section number (called the pinpoint reference); and (4) the year of publication of the most recent edition of the C.F.R.

28 C.F.R. § 637.7 (1990).

You can add the name of the regulation:

Barge Overnight Locking Regulations, 85 C.F.R. § 251.1 (1990).

RESTATEMENTS, TREATISES, and OTHER BOOKS

ALWD R. 23 states that restatements and model codes are cited without italicization, and without commas separating the parts of the citation:

Restatement (Second) of Contracts § 90 (1981)

Restatement (Third) of Torts: Products Liability § 2 cmt. d (1998).

Restatement of Prop.: Servitudes § 453 illus. 1 (1944).

Other books, treatises and non-periodic materials are governed by Rules 20, 22, 24, (A.L.R.s), 25 (dictionaries) and 26 (encyclopedias), and generally will be cited with: (1) volume number (if more than one volume exists in this authority; (2) author's full name, followed by a comma; (2) title of the book or topic name (italicized or underlined); (3) pinpoint references (including volume, section and page(s) that you are citing); (4) translator (if any); (5) in parentheses, the edition number (if any); and (6) the publisher; and (7) the year of publication. For example:

> 2 E. Allen Farnsworth, *Contracts* § 12, 345, 346-48 (110th ed. 2000).

> Michael D. Murray & Christy H. DeSanctis, *Advanced Legal Writing and Oral Advocacy: Trials, Appeals, and Moot Court* 26 (2d ed. 2014).

Depending on the type of source you want to cite, you should refer to the specific ALWD rule governing it, because some of the information can vary.

LAW REVIEW ARTICLES

Finally, ALWD R. 21 covers legal and other periodicals, such as law reviews. The form is: (1) author's full name, followed by a comma; (2) the title of the article (italicized or underlined), followed by a comma; (3) the volume number of the law review; (4) the abbreviated name of the law review (Appendix 5 for specific abbreviations and spacing); (5) page number where the article begin, followed by the pinpoint page(s) you are citing; and (6) year of publication. If the material to which you are citing appears within a footnote on a certain page, then in the citation itself place the page number and note number in the form "n.#" as in "n.35." For example:

> Christy H. DeSanctis, *Fun Times With Citation*, 99 Colum. L. Rev. 23, 29 n.75 (1999).

This cites to page 29 of Professor DeSanctis's article where the material appears in footnote 75 on that page.

Part II: The Bluebook (A Uniform System of Citation)

GENERAL RULES

The Bluebook ("BB") was created by the law review boards of several Ivy League law schools. The vast majority of the American legal community (including law schools, legal organizations, and courts) currently follows (or accepts) the Bluebook's citation rules, so there is no getting around the arduous task of learning these forms.

PRACTICE POINTER

Why learn Bluebook citation form?
Short answer to the question: Just about everyone practicing law today is competent in Bluebook citation form. You also should note that "to Bluebook" has become a verb form, which means that *whether you learned citation with the ALWD manual or with the Bluebook*, "bluebooking" is a term that tends to encompass both. All it really means is: "can you cite accurately?" No matter which manual you use, the citation form is generally consistent (and fulfills this mandate). If you used ALWD, *you did not learn* a citation format that is different; you simply used a different manual to get to the same place.

Though the Bluebook was created primarily for use in law review articles, the most recent editions go much further toward bridging the citation gap between scholarly publications and documents used by practitioners. The white-colored pages, which comprise the bulk of the book, still provide forms and examples geared toward authors of law review articles. However, several rules specifically explain the difference between law review citations and citations in other legal documents (*see, e.g.,* R.2), which is a helpful new feature of the 18th and 19th editions.

In addition, the Bluebook now includes blue-colored pages at the front that are directed specifically toward authors of legal office memoranda and court briefs. These blue-colored pages—called, appropriately, **the "Bluepages"**—provide an introduction to basic legal citation principles for law students and practicing attorneys. They are a much-expanded version of what were previously known as "Practitioner's Notes" and essentially constitute a summary of the twelve rules most commonly used in legal practice. Following the Bluepages (cited herein as "B#") are two practitioner-directed "Tables." BT.1 suggests abbreviations for words most commonly found in the title of court documents; BT.2 references the "Local Rules" in force in various state and federal courts – which *always* take precedence over the Bluebook. Additional tables containing information about different jurisdictions and publications are found at the back of the manual.

The forms used as examples throughout this section of this Chapter follow the forms noted in the Bluepages and in all respects comply with the Bluebook 19th edition.

A reminder from the outset of this Chapter. There are a variety of **local rules and practices** not covered here. Keep in mind that public domain citation forms, and other state-specific and even court-specific rules and practices do exist.

I.   CITATION SENTENCES AND CITATION CLAUSES

Citations to authority are phrased in two ways: citation clauses and citation sentences. *See* Bluebook Rules B2, BB 1.1 (hereinafter rules will be cited as B___(*e.g.*, B2) for blue-pages rules, and BB___(*e.g.*, BB 1.1) for the white-pages rules).

> Sentence: Tort liability requires breach of a duty of care. *Injured v. Careless*, 12 S.W.2d 23, 25 (Mo. 2001).

> Clause: Tort liability requires breach of a duty of care, *Injured v. Careless*, 12 S.W.2d 23, 25 (Mo. 2001), but the duty varies from claim to claim.

Titles and styles of cases and many other authorities are to be underlined or italicized (but not both). *See* B2 (p. 4). A choice to italicize or underline must be followed consistently in your document; you cannot switch from italicizing to underlining within the same document. Appropriate citation material to italicize or underline includes:

- Case names (*e.g.,* ***Haley v. Toonces***)
- Titles of most sources and documents (*e.g.,* ***Report of ALWD Committee on Sales***)
- Introductory signals (*e.g.,* ***See, See also***)
- Internal cross-references (***supra*** and ***infra***)
- Prior and subsequent history (*e.g.,* ***aff'd, rev'd***)
- The short form ***id.***

You do not italicize other information, such as the reporter or journal abbreviation, the volume and page numbers, the court identifier, and the date.

> **Incorrect:**   *12 S.W.2d 23, 25 (Mo. 2001).*
> *112 Colum. L. Rev. 222, 234 (2012).*

A. Citation sentence

A citation sentence is used when you are citing authority after a period that ends a complete sentence. The citation sentence starts with a capital letter, and ends with a period:

> The standard is one of gross negligence. *Hallam v. Scaraggi*, 118 S.W.2d 222, 224 (Mo. 1947).

Multiple cases and other authorities in a citation sentence are separated by semi-colons:

> The standard is one of gross negligence. Mo. Rev. Stat. § 232.12 (1986); *Hallam v. Scaraggi*, 118 S.W.2d 222, 224 (Mo. 1947); *Lowe v. Carmichael*, 446 S.W.2d 333, 335 (Mo. Ct. App. E. Dist. 1987).

B. Citation clauses

When a citation supports only part of a sentence, the citation is inserted in the sentence, set off by commas before and after. This is referred to as a citation clause:

> The Illinois Dog Bite Statute, 510 Ill. Comp. Stat. 5/16 (1996), defines a dog-owner's liability for a dog bite.

Multiple authorities supporting a clause are separated by semicolons, but the whole citation clause is set apart by commas as above. A citation clause does not necessarily start with a capital letter—it only does if you are citing an authority without any introductory phrase, and the authority starts with a capital letter. A sentence citation which supports the second clause can follow at the end of the second clause, after the period that ends the sentence, as in the following example:

> Dog bite liability requires a lack of provocation, either intentional or unintentional, *see* 510 Ill. Comp. Stat. 5/16 (1996); *Clark v. Bessler*, 210 N.E.2d 207, 208 (Ill. 1965); *Schooner v. Siegel*, 344 N.E.2d 268, 270 (Ill. App. Ct. 5th Dist. 1976), but provocation can be offset if the dog's attack is particularly vicious and disproportionate to the provocation. *Schooner*, 344 N.E.2d at 271.

As a general matter, within a citation sentence or citation clause, cite the highest and most recent controlling authorities first, followed by lesser and earlier authorities in order of their weight. This order of presentation is important.

Correct: A dog owner is liable for all injuries caused by his dog unless the dog is provoked by the victim. *Vick v. ASPCA*, 123 S.W.2d 345, 347 (Mo. 1965); *Tyson v. United Chicken Protectors, Inc.*, 789 S.W.2d 234, 237 (Mo. Ct. App. E. Dist. 1989); *Willingham v. Terenzoni*, 780 S.W.2d 134, 137 (Mo. Ct. App. E. Dist. 1980).

Incorrect: A dog owner is liable for all injuries caused by his dog unless the dog is provoked by the victim. *Tyson v. United Chicken Protectors, Inc.*, 789 S.W.2d 234, 237 (Mo. Ct. App. E. Dist. 1989); *Willingham v. Terenzoni*, 780 S.W.2d 134, 137 (Mo. Ct. App. E. Dist. 1980); *Vick v. ASPCA*, 123 S.W.2d 345, 347 (Mo. 1965).

In certain circumstances, you will be presenting a large number of authorities that are not controlling and may be of equal importance. This happens frequently in law review articles, and remember that the Bluebook was designed primarily as a citation manual for law review articles. When you are in this situation, the order of authorities is as follows:[3]

1. Constitutions and other foundational documents

2. Statutes

3. Treaties and other international agreements

4. Cases, in the order of:

> **Federal Sources**
>
> a. U.S. Supreme Court
>
> b. Courts of Appeals
>
> c. Court of Claims, Court of Customs and Patent Appeals, and bankruptcy appellate panels
>
> d. District courts, Judicial Panel on Multidistrict Litigation, Court of International Trade
>
> e. District bankruptcy courts and Railroad Reorganization Court
>
> f. Court of Federal Claims, Court of Appeals for the Armed Forces, and Tax Court
>
> g. Administrative agencies (alphabetically by agency)
>
> **State Sources**
>
> h. Courts (alphabetically by state, and then by level of court within a state, highest to lowest)
>
> i. Administrative agencies (alphabetically by state and then by agency within each state)
>
> **Foreign Sources**
>
> j. Courts (alphabetically by jurisdiction and then by rank within each jurisdiction)
>
> k. Agencies (alphabetically by jurisdiction and then by agency within each jurisdiction)

---

3   This is the only place within our coverage of the two citation manuals where there appears to be a difference between the two manuals. BB Rule 1.4 specifies a *slightly* different order than ALWD R. 36.3.

International Law Sources

l. International Court of Justice, Permanent Court of International Justice

m. Other international tribunals and arbitral panels (alphabetically by name)

5. Legislative materials

6. Administrative and executive materials

7. Resolutions, regulations, and decisions of intergovernmental organizations

8. Records, briefs, pleadings of litigants

9. Secondary sources, in the order of:

a. Uniform codes, model codes, and restatements

b. Books and pamphlets

c. Law review articles and works in journals

d. Book reviews not written by students

e. Student-written journal articles and book reviews

f. Annotations (for example, American Law Reports)

g. Magazine and newspaper articles

h. Working papers

i. Unpublished materials

j. Electronic sources

Within a category of cases (for example, federal appellate court cases), the materials are listed in reverse chronological order (most recent first, and so on). If the year is the same, then list them in alphabetical order. For some of the other categories (constitutions, statutes) *see* BB 1.4 for the specific ordering rules (which generally follow a federal-state foreign format).

II.   INTRODUCTORY SIGNALS AND PHRASES (BB 1.2)

Both citation sentences and citation clauses can be preceded by an introductory word or phrase. When the word or phrase begins a citation sentence, it is capitalized. Otherwise it is not.

The entire introductory word or phrase is underlined or italicized. Each phrase connotes something different about the authority that follows it:

[No introductory phrase]	Connotes that the authority contains (states) the exact or nearly the exact phrase or sentence for which you are citing the authority (*i.e.*, the words you use are 99% the same as in the source). You may have changed the verb tense or dropped a minor word or two (this, than, the, etc.), but otherwise, one turning to the authority would find that statement in the authority at the page or section to which you are citing. This form is used whether or not you actually put quotation marks around the statement.

If the statement is a legal proposition or conclusion (as opposed to a fact or something other than a statement about the law), this form also connotes that the statement is part of the holding of the case.

See	Connotes that the authority contains the idea and the concept for which you are citing the authority, but the exact words will not be found in the authority. The authority must directly support your statement. You would still cite to a particular page or section of the authority where the idea or concept is stated.
See also	Connotes that the authority contains related or additional information or material that supports the proposition for which the authority is cited, but the exact statement (concept or idea) is not found in the authority. A parenthetical should be used to explain why or how the material supports the proposition.

For example:
The Erie doctrine confuses the issue of choice of law. *Masters v. Johnson*, 55 Ohio App. 23, 24 (1987); *see also Basinger v. Baldwin*, 766 P.2d 433, 444 (Okla. 1978) (holding that *Erie* confuses most issues of conflict of laws, including forum selection).

Accord   When you have two or more authorities that clearly support the statement or proposition for which you are citing them, but the actual statement only is found in one of the authorities, use *accord* to preface the other citations.

For example:

A doctor must use reasonably prudent methods to detect viral agents. Mo. Rev. Stat. § 516.132.2 (1999); *accord Smith v. Jones*, 755 S.W.2d 232, 240 (Mo. Ct. App. E. Dist. 1996); *Vogel v. Cosgrove*, 432 N.E.2d 222, 223 (Ill. App. Ct. 5th Dist. 1986).

Cf.   Connotes that the cited authority states a different proposition from the main proposition for which the citation is given, but the second proposition is sufficiently analogous as to lend support to the main proposition. A parenthetical or other explanation should be used to explain the relevance.

For example:

Architects must take reasonable care to choose a design that will preclude subsidence of the building. *Cf. Murphy v. Cowles*, 239 S.E.2d 235, 237 (S.C. Ct. App. 1st Dist. 1975) (civil engineer required to take reasonable care to choose non-subsiding design); *Beecher v. Stowe*, 236 S.E.2d 457, 459 (S.C. Ct. App. 1st Dist. 1973) (same, building contractor).

Compare . . . [and] . . . with   Used to express that a comparison of one or more cases with one or more other cases will reveal something about the way the law works in this area. Again, a parenthetical explanation should be used to drive the point home even more. Note well that in this citation form commas separate the authorities, not semi-colons.

For example:

> If the damages are nominal, a defamation claim will be dismissed. *Compare Norton v. Cramden*, 432 Vt. 234 (1990) (nominal damages of fifteen dollars, claim dismissed), *and Ricardo v. Mertz*, 335 Vt. 245 (1982) (nominal damages of two dollars, claim dismissed), *with Scooby v. Shaggy*, 553 Vt. 987 (1997) (damages of $150,000, claim not dismissed), *and DeSanctis v. Cheney*, 288 Vt. 256 (1978) (damages of $75,000, claim not dismissed), *and Murray v. Bush*, 228 Vt. 667 (1975) (damages of $55,000, claim not dismissed).

E.g., See, e.g.,   Introduces authorities that support the proposition stated. The concept and general proposition would be found in the cited authorities, but not necessarily the exact word or phrase you are stating. The *E.g.* signal has a comma following it, and if *See* is used, there is a comma after the *See*, too.

For example:

> Many cases in the District of Maryland end in dismissal. *E.g., Dorning v. Morning*, 222 F. Supp. 3d 34 (D. Md. 2014); *Randolph v. Scott*, 111 F. Supp. 3d 309 (D. Md. 2009). Many of these cases are copyright cases. *See, e.g., Spetzel v. Freckle*, 144 F. Supp. 3d 567 (D. Md. 2011); *Redmund v. Dedmund*, 123 F. Supp. 3d 778 (D. Md. 2010).

Unlike *see* or *see also*, the phrase "*e.g.*" is used if you are stating a rather general legal proposition and wish to suggest that there are many authorities that hold this, and the listed authorities are a representative sample. If the listed authorities actually do not state the exact proposition for which you are citing them, but support it nonetheless, use "*see, e.g.,*" instead.

But see,
But see, e.g.,
But cf.

If you are citing an authority contrary to the proposition stated, you would use *but see* in situations where you would use see or no introductory phrase, and *but see, e.g.*, if you are listing several contrary authorities that go against the proposition. Use *but cf.* if the contrary authority is not directly on point, but sufficiently analogous to cause concern. In any of these combinations, a parenthetical should be used to explain the state of things.

For example:

Most states have adopted the UCC Sales provisions. *But see* La. Rev. Stat. Ann. § 355.1 (West 1988) (only state not to adopt UCC Article 2). In the majority of states, statute of frauds requires contracts for goods over $500 in value to be in writing. *But cf. Delany v. DuBois*, 235 La. 468, 469 (1986) (civil code requires writing only for specific purpose contracts, or for land sales).

See generally

The most nebulous of introductory phrases, *see generally* is used to introduce background or other relevant material—often secondary sources—that are helpful to an understanding of the issues.

III. SHORTHAND DEVICES FOR REPEAT CITATIONS (BB 4.1, 4.2 and B4.2, B8.2)

When you cite the same authority more than once, you do not have to keep writing the full citation form (also called the "long form") for the work over and over again. You can use the following to make short work of repeat citations:

Id.

Use as a shorthand to recite the exact same authority that you just previously cited, with no other authorities in between. Of course, a page number or section number might change.

For example:

> Red is used for anger. *Boodin v. Zehfuss*, 123 U.S. 234, 238 (1923). Blue is for peace. *Id.* Purple is for sorrow. *Id.* at 239.

> The statute of frauds requires. Mo. Rev. Stat. § 400.2-201 (2013). The writing is necessary if the goods cost $500 or more. *Id.* However, the damages will still be limited to the costs to cover. *Id.* § 400.2-701 et seq.

You cannot use *id.* after a citation containing more than one authority. *Id.* can only refer back to a single authority, and you cannot use it to refer back to the authority last cited if that authority was paired with others. (Note, however, that sources identified in explanatory parentheticals, explanatory phrases, or subsequent history are ignored for purposes of this rule (*see* BB 4.1)).

The following examples are ***incorrect***:

> ***Incorrect form:*** *The Erie doctrine confuses the issue of choice of law. Masters v. Johnson, 55 N.E.2d 23, 24 (Ill. 1957); Hill v. Williams, 766 P.2d 433, 444 (Okla. 1978). It also confuses the law of forum selection. Id.*

> **[Cannot use *id.* here because preceding citation sentence had two cases in it. *Id.* cannot be used to refer back to both, nor does it refer back to the last one cited.]**

> ***Incorrect form:*** *Illinois is a comparative negligence state. Madigan v. Turner, 345 N.E.2d 789, 791 (Ill. 1967); Hodge v. Walpole, 788 N.E.2d 654, 656 (Ill. App. Ct. 1988). Plaintiff's percentage of fault reduces the verdict, even if plaintiff's fault exceeds 50 percent. Hodge, id. at 657.*

> **[Specifying which of the two preceding cases you are referring back to does not help—it still is bad citation form to use *id.* here.]**

Instead, you must use a different short form for the multiple authorities or whichever one of them you want to cite to.

These examples are **CORRECT:**

> The Erie doctrine confuses the issue of choice of law. *Masters v. Johnson,* 55 N.E.2d 23, 24 (Ill. 1957); *Hill v. Williams,* 766 P.2d 433, 444 (Okla. 1978). It also confuses the law of forum selection. *Masters,* 55 N.E.2d at 24; *Hill,* 766 P.2d at 444.

> Illinois is a comparative negligence state. *Ray v. Chuh,* 345 N.E.2d 789, 791 (Ill. 1967); *Levine v. Bauer,* 788 N.E.2d 654, 656 (Ill. App. Ct. 5th Dist. 1988). Plaintiff's percentage of fault reduces the verdict, even if plaintiff's fault exceeds 50 percent. *Levine,* 788 N.E.2d at 657.

A few wrinkles to the *id.* rule are worth noting. First, when citing cases **in law review footnotes**, the "5 footnote rule" applies to **any short form citation**. This means that a short form (including *id.*) is appropriate only to refer back to a case in one of the **preceding 5 footnotes**. If you are attempting to refer back to a case cited prior to that, you must use a full citation. **The same rule does not apply to citations in practitioners' documents – only to law review footnotes** (BB 10.9(a)).

Second, when *id.* refers to a **different opinion** in the same case, a parenthetical is required. In other words, if you have been citing to a majority opinion for several citations, use of *id.* is appropriate; however, if you then shift to citing a concurring opinion, you must include a parenthetical so indicating (BB 10.9(b)(i)).

Third, for cases in which a parallel citation is required, the *id.* form looks slightly different (to avoid confusion):

> **Initial Citation:** *Terrenzoni v. Cosgrove,* 500 Pa. 105, 110, 240 A.2d 540, 545 (1968).

> **Short Citation:** *Id.* at 111, 240 A.2d at 546.

> ***Supra***   According to BB 4.2(a) and B8.2, *supra* refers to an earlier cited **book, treatise**, or **other volume**, when it is not the immediately preceding authority. (If it is the immediately preceding authority, you use *id.*). In practitioner documents, even when the source was first cited in a footnote, you no longer reference the footnote number with supra in the current edition of the Bluebook (B8.2) because that form only is used in academic writing in law reviews and journals (BB 4.2(a)). For example, if you cited Laurence Tribe's treatise, *Constitutional Law,* earlier in

your office memorandum or appellate brief in footnote 2, you can use the following form to cite it again later on:

> Tribe, *supra*, at 335-36.

> (**not** Tribe, *supra* note 2, at 335-36).

Supra is no longer used to refer to a previously cited case, statute or rule because they each have their own forms.

Infra

Infra is not used as an introductory phrase for citations to legal authority. *Infra* is used to direct attention to sections or footnotes or other portions of the text that come later in the same document. When used in this way, *infra* usually follows the word see.

> *See infra* Part IV.

> *Infra* pp. 10-11.

> *See* sources cited *infra* note 7.

Supra also can be used in this informal way to refer back to a preceding section of the text.

> *See supra* part IV.

> *Supra* pp. 10-11.

IV. STYLE OF THE CASE (BB 10)

The names of the first named parties on each side become the style of the case; they are separated by a "v." and underlined or italicized:

McCoy v. Trump   **not**   *McCoy and Columbo v. Trump, Jones, and Smith*

A. Certain words are omitted

Omit the parties' first names (unless they are part of a company name):

DeSanctis v. Murray   **not**   *Christy DeSanctis v. Michael Murray*

But *Christy H. DeSanctis, Ltd. v. Michael Murray and Co.* is correct because these are company names.

Titles, offices, before or after the party's name (for example, Mr., Mrs., Dr., M.D., PhD, Commander, General, Surgeon General of the United States) are omitted unless the person is sued only by her title, and her actual name does not appear in the case style:

> *Anastasi v. Mayor of Santa Fe* [if the Mayor is not sued in her own name]

> *Anastasi v. Guadeloupe* [if Mayor Guadeloupe is sued under her own name]

> **But not** *Anastasi v. Guadeloupe, Mayor of Santa Fe* **and not** *Anastasi, M.D. v. Ms. Guadeloupe.*

B. Use Bluebook standard abbreviations

The Bluebook requires you to abbreviate certain words in very definite, specified ways. In general, the Bluebook requires single capital letters to be grouped together, but any other combination of two or more letters to be set apart from single capitals or other combinations by a space. For example, the following abbreviations are **correct**:

> S.D.N.Y.

> E.D. Mo.

> F. Supp.

> Ill. App. Ct.

Ordinals, such as 2d and 3d, are treated as one capital letter, and can be grouped together with other single capital letters, as in the following examples:

> F.2d

> N.Y.3d

But if the ordinal follows a cluster of two or more letters, it must stand alone:

> Ill. App. 3d

> F. Supp. 2d

> Cal. Rptr. 4th

Various rules and tables in the Bluebook provide other abbreviations:

> In the relation of, on behalf of, become: **ex rel**. (BB 10.2.1(b))

> Petition of, In the matter of, In re the Will of, In re the Estate of, become: **In re** (BB 10.2.1(b))

Abbreviate company, party, and other names in case styles according to BB Table T.6:

> Consolidated becomes Consol.

Enterprise becomes Enter.

Industry, industries, industrial become Indus.

South is S.

East is E.

Court names are abbreviated according to BB Table T.7. [Note the spacing]:

Appellate Division is App. Div.

Commonwealth Court is Commw. Ct.

Superior Court is Super. Ct.

Judicial Panel on Multidistrict Litigation is J.P.M.L.

Case history terms' abbreviations and non-abbreviations are found in BB Table T.8. Guess what the following abbreviations refer to:

aff'd

rev'd

cert. denied

rev'd on other grounds

There also are official non-abbreviations, as follows:

appeal denied

vacated

modifying

mandamus denied

Follow the rules for state's abbreviations and non-abbreviations in BB Table T.10. The Bluebook rarely uses the U.S. Postal Service abbreviation. For example:

Ala.

Del.

Miss.

N.M.

But see

    Alaska

    Iowa

    Idaho

    Ohio

    Utah

Abbreviate other terms according to Bluebook standard abbreviations in BB Tables T.6-T.16.

V.   CITATION FORMS FOR CASES (BB 10.9 and B4.2)

Each case citation must tell four pieces of information: (1) the case name; (2) where you find the case; (3) the court; (4) the year of the case. But this information may be conveyed in as many as nine components:

    (1) Case name (or style)

    (2) Reporter volume

    (3) Reporter abbreviation

    (4) First page of case

    (5) Jump cite (Pinpoint cite or Pin cite) page

    (6) Court abbreviation

    (7) Date of opinion

    (8) Subsequent history designation

    (9) Subsequent history citation

Here is an example (the first as it might appear in a legal document, the second broken down to label the nine components listed above):

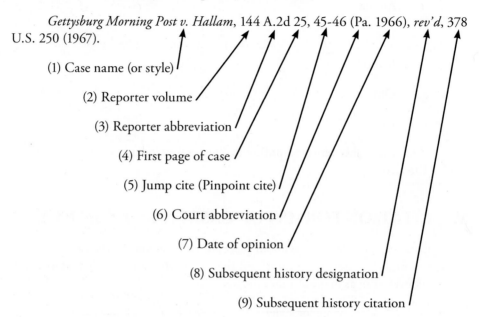

Gettysburg Morning Post v. Hallam, 144 A.2d 25, 45-46 (Pa. 1966), *rev'd*, 378 U.S. 250 (1967).

(1) Case name (or style)

(2) Reporter volume

(3) Reporter abbreviation

(4) First page of case

(5) Jump cite (Pinpoint cite)

(6) Court abbreviation

(7) Date of opinion

(8) Subsequent history designation

(9) Subsequent history citation

If you are referring to a particular part of the case (and whenever possible you should be referring to a particular part of the case), you must provide a **jump cite** (also known as a **pinpoint cite** or **pin cite**) that refers the reader to the specific page or pages of the opinion that support your proposition. To create a jump cite, put a comma after the page number where the case begins and then cite the page(s) where the material appears. More than one page can be referenced. If the material is on separate pages, cite them separately: 23, 24, 29, 35. If the material carries over from one page to another, indicate this in this way: 23-24, 35-37. If the second page number is a three or four digit number, reduce it to a two digit number, unless it follows a two digit number: 137-38, 205-06, 1078-79, 99-101. The following forms are all **correct**:

Presley v. Jackson, 833 S.W.2d 222, 225 (Tenn. 1996).

Presley v. Jackson, 833 S.W.2d 222, 226-27 (Tenn. 1996).

Presley v. Jackson, 833 S.W.2d 222, 225-26, 228, 230 (Tenn. 1996).

If you are referring to material on the first page of a case, you must repeat the first page number:

Presley v. Jackson, 833 S.W.2d 222, 222 (Tenn. 1996).

The court codes for each United States jurisdiction are listed in BB Table T.1. Study these well, and **note the spacing** of these codes. The codes for foreign jurisdictions are in BB Table T.2.

If the court that wrote the opinion is obvious from one of the reporters you are citing (for example, a reporter with the state's initials is presumed to report the cases of the highest court in the state; a reporter with the state's initials and "App." added on is presumed to report the decisions of the state's intermediate level appellate court), then you should not put the court designation in the parentheses with the year. The following forms are **correct**:

> *Lincoln v. Douglass*, 234 N.Y.2d 245, 247, 456 N.E.2d 234, 236, 565 N.Y.S.2d 238, 239 (1965).

> **[Reader presumes from the N.Y. reporter citation that the case is from the N.Y. Court of Appeals, the highest court in New York].**

> *Yousefi v. Seuss*, 345 Ill. App. 2d 235, 237 (5th Dist. 1989).

> **[Reader presumes from the Ill. App. citation that the case is from the Illinois Appellate Court, the intermediate level appellate court in Illinois].**

Sometimes an official reporter with the state's initials reports more than just the highest court's cases. If so, you must supply additional information to correct the reader's erroneous presumption, but only as much as is necessary to identify the court:

> *Vidal v. McCarthy*, 665 Idaho 456, 458 (Ct. App. 1st Dist. 1987).

> **Not** *Vidal v. McCarthy*, 665 Idaho 456, 458 (Idaho Ct. App. 1st Dist. 1987).

Note: The 1st Dist. in the parentheses in the example above is an example of a district or division identifier that is used if the case you are citing has the potential to be controlling authority. You use it to show the reader whether or not the case actually is of the proper district or circuit to be controlling. The Bluebook tells you to include reference to the district, department, or division of an intermediate level appellate court if the information is "of particular relevance." (*See* BB 10.4, p. 98.) We interpret "of particular relevance" to mean controlling or not controlling. In the example above, the lawsuit would have been governed by Idaho law, and filed somewhere in Idaho, so that a certain district of the Idaho Court of Appeals would be controlling. If there is no way that the case you are citing is controlling (for example, if the case you are citing is not an Idaho case), you do not use the district or division identifier.

If you are preparing a document (pleading, motion, memorandum) that will be filed with a state court and you are citing a case from a state court in the same state where you are litigating, you must consult the local rules of the court to determine if the local rules require you to provide a fifth piece of information: a parallel citation to the state's official reporter, if any. This *only* applies to documents that will be filed with the court, and *only* if the local rules of the court require you to provide a parallel citation. It does not apply to office memoranda even if you are writing a memo and you know that your case has been filed in a certain state court, and you are about to cite a case from a court of the same state.

Examples of this for the states of Illinois and New York, are shown below:

Illinois:

Supreme Court: *Townsend v. Plant*, 222 Ill. 2d 333, 444 N.E.2d 555 (1990).

[the form to use if you are writing a document that will be filed in a court in Illinois whose local rules require you to provide a parallel citation]

Townsend v. Plant, 444 N.E.2d 555 (Ill. 1990).

[the form to use if you are not writing a document that will be filed in a court in Illinois, or if the local rules do not require you to provide a parallel citation]

Appeals Court: *Proust v. Morrison*, 322 Ill. App. 3d 554, 677 N.E.2d 776 (1st Dist. 1988).

[form for an Illinois court if the local rules require you to provide a parallel citation]

Proust v. Morrison, 677 N.E.2d 776 (Ill. App. Ct. 1st Dist. 1988).

[form other than to an Illinois court or if the local rules do not require you to provide a parallel citation]

New York: *(especially note the spacing here):*

Court of Appeals: *Van Halen v. Death Row Records*, 522 N.Y.2d 333, 454 N.E.2d 545, 778 N.Y.S.2d 889 (1990).

[if you are writing to a court in N.Y. and if the local rules require you to provide a parallel citation. Note the two parallel citations]

Van Halen v. Death Row Records, 454 N.E.2d 545 (N.Y. 1990).

[if you are not writing to a court in N.Y. or if the local rules do not require you to provide a parallel citation]

If you are citing to a Court of Appeals case before 1848, note that the name of the highest court may not have been the Court of Appeals—check out BB at p.254, regarding the New York Court for the Correction of Errors, Supreme Court of Judicature, and Court of Chancery.

S. Ct, App. Div.: *Cash v. Sun Records*, 822 A.D.2d 554, 877 N.Y.S.2d 886 (1st Dep't 1988).

[to N.Y. court whose local rules require parallel citations]

Cash v. Sun Records, 877 N.Y.S.2d 886 (App. Div. 1st Dep't 1988).

[other than to N.Y. court or if the local rules do not require you to provide a parallel citation]

Trial courts: *Fisch v. Motown Records*, 677 Misc. 2d 668, 677 N.Y.S.2d 887 (Sup. Ct. Queens County 1988).

[Writing to a N.Y. court whose local rules require a parallel citation. This is a cite to a Supreme Court case. You are identifying the specific court in the parentheses, because it is "of particular relevance" to the reader. In a multi-level trial court system like New York's, it is relevant to show what level of court is cited and what county it is from because it may affect the persuasive value of the opinion. BB 10.4, p. 98.]

In re Sorenson, 344 Misc. 2d 853, 456 N.Y.S.2d 891 (Sur. Ct. Duchess County 1975).

[to a N.Y. court requiring parallel citations, citing a Surrogate's court case]

Fisch v. Motown Records, 677 N.Y.S.2d 887 (Sup. Ct. Queens County 1988).

[not writing to N.Y. court or if the local rules do not require you to provide a parallel citation]

VI. SUBSEQUENT HISTORY

Subsequent history codes must be used if there is relevant subsequent history to a case (for example, *appeal dismissed, aff'd, rev'd on other grounds, mandamus denied, etc.* - BB Table T.8). Example:

Rogers v. Hammerstein, 388 F.2d 345, 366 (2d Cir. 1958), *aff'd*, 354 U.S. 578 (1959).

The denial of a writ of certiorari (cert. denied) or the denial of other discretionary appeals should not be included under BB 10.7.1 unless the denial occurred less than two years ago or if "the denial is particularly relevant."

A citation that has no subsequent history information represents that there have been no relevant legal proceedings in the case occurring after the cited opinion.

If the year of the original opinion is the same as the year of the subsequent opinion(s), you only put the year in parentheses after the last citation. In the following example, all of these opinions would be from 1996:

> *Apple Computer, Inc. v. Gates*, 789 P.2d 876, 878 (Wash. Ct. App. 1st Dist.), *reh'g denied*, 791 P.2d 345 (Wash. Ct. App. 1st Dist.), *appeal dismissed*, 792 P.2d 579 (Wash. 1996).

VII. PARENTHETICALS (BB 10.6)

Parentheticals are used to provide useful explanatory information that will help the reader understand the significance of a case or the lack thereof. For example, parentheticals can be used for providing some details of the facts that show why you are citing it, or some clarification of the holding if this might not be clear from what preceded the citation, or to clear up a possible misconception about the case not obvious from a naked cite; for example, "Hey reader, this was a plurality opinion, not a majority opinion." Examples:

> *Jones v. Clinton*, 156 F.3d 678, 681 (8th Cir. 1999) (court indicated that defendant lied).

> *Marshall v. Brennan*, 477 U.S. 345 (1969) (per curiam).

Punctuation and complete sentences are usually avoided in parentheticals in order to save space. An exception exists if you actually quote a whole phrase or sentence from the case. Compare this example with the first example above:

> *Jones v. Clinton*, 156 F.3d 678, 681 (8th Cir. 1999) ("We find that the defendant lied to the country.").

If you are citing non-majority opinions, they are noted with their author:

> *Moller v. Texas Horn Co.*, 357 Ark. 456, 468 (1948) (Simpson, J., dissenting).

Multiple parentheticals are possible. Please separate each parenthetical with a space:

> *Marshall v. Brennan*, 477 U.S. 345, 349 (1969) (per curiam) (noting that the "clear and convincing evidence" standard applied).

VIII. SHORT FORMS FOR CASES (BB 10.9 and B4.2)

The long form of a citation need only be given once in any document; in fact, it is bad form to present it more than once. People will think you are citing a different case and got the citation wrong. In addition to the form used for all authorities (*id.*), with cases, you should use the plaintiff's name (or a short recognizable part of the name if the name is long, as in the case of a corporation) along with the volume-reporter-page number, or one of the other approved forms listed below when you are doing a repeat cite in a situation where *id.* cannot be used:

Full cite:	*Alexander v. Katrina*, 432 S.W.2d 356 (Mo. 1988).
Proper short forms:	*Alexander*, 432 S.W.2d at 358-59.
	In *Alexander*, the court dismissed the suit. 432 S.W.2d at 358-59.
Full cite:	*Speedy Drydock and Transfer Co., Inc. v. Bosley*, 517 S.W.2d 425 (Mo. Ct. App. E. Dist. 1978).
Proper short forms:	*Speedy Drydock*, 517 S.W.2d at 426.
	Speedy Drydock is the only case to apply the cruel and unusual standard. 517 S.W.2d at 426.

The following forms all are ***incorrect***:

Alexander at 358.

Alexander, at 358.

Alexander, 432 S.W.2d 358.

Alexander, 432 S.W.2d 356, at 358.

Alexander, 432 S.W.2d 356 at 358.

Alexander, *id.* at 358.

[It would be fairly easy to come up with several other ***incorrect*** short forms, variations on the themes shown above, because the Bluebook *only* allows the two proper short forms that we have shown above. Every other short form is *wrong*.]

If the plaintiff's name is too common (or shows up too many times in cases you are going to cite), use the defendant's name instead:

United States v. Calandra should be shortened to *Calandra*

Smith v. Netanyahu should be *Netanyahu*

Commissioner v. Mitchell should be *Mitchell*

Shalala v. Harris should be *Harris* [This would be the case if Donna Shalala is the Commissioner of Health and Human Services, and so is a plaintiff in 9 out of the 10 cases you are citing in your Social Security case.]

IX. CITATION FORMS FOR OTHER AUTHORITIES

STATUTES AND CODES

The Bluebook devotes a whole chapter to the topic of citing statutes (BB 12), but a lot of that is devoted to obscure citation forms that do not come up much in practice. The typical citation to a statute contains: (1) the title or volume number where the statute appears; (2) the abbreviated name of the code; (3) the section number of the statute; (4) the year the code was published (not the year the statute was enacted or became effective).

Some state statutes put the code name first, then the volume and section number. You should follow whatever order is listed in BB Table T.1.

When you are citing a statutory section, use the official version of the statute. Do not cite the annotated or other unofficial versions. Of course, if you are citing some commentary or notes or committee reports or interpretative information on the statute that is not found in the official version, certainly cite to the annotated version or wherever the material appears.

If you never learned how to do a § sign on your computer, write "sec." instead. For example, Mo. Rev. Stat. sec. 400.2-201 (1986). If a ¶ symbol is involved, and you cannot make the ¶ symbol, write "para." instead. More than one section is expressed by §§ or "secs." (*See* BB 12.9(b) and 6.2(c) for additional information on the use of the word "section" versus the section sign "§.") More than one paragraph is expressed by ¶¶ or "paras."

You are free to use the official or the popular name of the statute in your citation sentence or clause:

Securities Act of 1933, 15 U.S.C. §§ 77a-77aa (1994).

Labor Management Relations (Taft-Hartley) Act § 301(a), 29 U.S.C. § 185(a) (1988).

Note the spacing in the following examples—the § sign stands for the word section so there is a single space before and after the § sign.

Federal:

Official: 30 U.S.C. § 523 (1988).　　**Not:** 30 U.S.C. §523 (1988).

Annotated: 30 U.S.C.A. § 523 (West 1995).

Illinois (does not use § symbol):

Official: 510 Ill. Comp. Stat. 5/16 (1996). Not: 510 Ill. Comp. Stat. § 5/16 (1996).

Annotated: 510 Ill. Comp. Stat. Ann. 5/16 (West 1995).

New York:

The annotated versions of the statutes published by McKinney and Consolidated Laws Service are official. A third, unannotated form published by Gould also is official; go figure that New York would be so lax. The form of the citation is stranger still:

N.Y. [subject matter abbrev.] Law § x (publisher 19xx).

As in: N.Y. Gen. Constr. Law § 456 (Gould 1989).

N.Y. Mun. Home Rule Law § 77(a) (Consol. 1990).

N.Y. C.P.L.R. 8209 (McKinney 1991). [Note the lack of a section symbol in the C.P.L.R. cite—Bluebook Table T.1, p. 255 tells you to leave it out.]

CONSTITUTIONS

Under BB 11, a constitution is cited by the abbreviated name of the country or state followed by the word "Const.," followed by the abbreviated name of the section, article, or amendment, and none of it is underlined or italicized. Note, too, where the commas do and do not appear in these citation forms:

U.S. Const. amend IV.

U.S. Const. art. I, § 8, cl. 8

Ariz. Const. art. 2, § 6.

RULES

Rules of procedure and evidence are abbreviated as shown in BB 12.9.3 and are not underlined:

Fed. R. Evid. 401.

Fed. R. Civ. P. 23.

Fed. R. App. P. 4(a).

Under BB 14.2, administrative rules and regulations are cited to the Code of Federal Regulations (CFR), if possible, and to the Federal Register or other source if not found in CFR. A typical citation contains: (1) the volume number; (2) the abbreviation C.F.R.; (3) the section number; (4) the year of publication of the most recent edition of the C.F.R.

28 C.F.R. § 637.7 (1990).

You may include the name of the regulation:

Barge Overnight Locking Regulations, 85 C.F.R. § 251.1 (1990).

RESTATEMENTS, TREATISES, AND OTHER BOOKS

Bluepages Rule B5.1.3 and BB 12.9.5 provide that restatements are not underlined, so you would cite them as:

Restatement (Second) of Contracts § 90 (1981)

Restatement (Third) of Torts: Products Liability § 2 cmt. d (1998).

Restatement of Prop.: Servitudes § 453 cmt. b, illus. 1 (1944).

Under Bluepages Rule B8 and BB 15, other books and treatises are to be cited with: (1) volume number (if any); (2) author's or authors' full name(s), followed by a comma; (3) title of the book (underlined or italicized); (4) page(s) or section number(s) that you are citing; (5) parentheses with edition number (if any); and (6) year of publication. For example:

2 Michael D. Murray, *Federal Practice as I Practice It* § 10.2, at 44 (4th ed. 1999).

E. Allen Farnsworth & Willis M. Reese, *Contracts* 345, 346-48 (110th ed. 2000).

LAW REVIEW ARTICLES

Under B9 and BB 16, the form for citing law review articles is: (1) author's full name, followed by a comma; (2) the title of the article (underlined or italicized), followed by a comma; (3) the volume number of the law review; (4) the abbreviated name of the law review (check BB Table T.13 for spacing and abbreviations); (5) page number where the article appears, comma, followed by the page(s) you are citing; and (6) year of publication. If the material to which you are citing appears within a footnote on a certain page, then in the citation itself place the page number and note number in the form "n.#" as in "n.35." For example:

For example:

> Christy H. DeSanctis, *The Citation Games*, 99 Colum. L. Rev. 23, 29 n.75 (1999).

This cites to page 29 of Professor DeSanctis's article where the material appears in footnote 75 on that page.

Preparing a Case Brief or Case Analysis for Class

The decades-old tradition of teaching first year classes via the "case method" (*i.e.*, closely scrutinizing judicial opinions) remains in force today. To prepare for the intensity of the often-deployed Socratic Method, you are well-advised to "brief" assigned cases in advance of class. Even if upper-level students tell you that this practice is unnecessary, our sincere advice is to make this decision for yourself—and make it after completing several weeks of class preparation and classroom experience.

Yes, case briefing is time consuming, but its benefits outweigh its costs. The process also gets much easier with practice. We—like most of your 1L professors— encourage you to give it a chance, certainly until you are used to the expectations in each class and are more comfortable with case analysis, and hopefully well beyond that.

Why do we care so much about cases?

The Common Law tradition in the United States (and other British-influenced countries) allows courts to make binding law through the process of interpreting, and sometimes modifying or reversing, legal rules from prior sources and then applying newly-crafted rules to the case at hand. The result is a growing body of case **precedent** that lawyers and judges use to evaluate and determine the outcome of new cases. The related doctrine of ***stare decisis*** roughly translates to "looking to the decisions" of the past for aid in resolving the disputes of the present. Throughout much of the history of England, this process of advancing the law through a series of court decisions was more important than the passage of laws by Parliament or royal decree. Especially in the bedrock ("common law") subjects (torts, contracts, and property), we still discuss the law and its development primarily by reference to case law.

What kinds of things are you looking for in the cases?

Precedent can be **binding** (or **controlling**) on future courts, or it can merely be persuasive. A controlling case presumably dictates the actions of courts bound by it. *I.e.*, courts must handle a legal matter in the same way as in the precedent case. A persuasive opinion, in contrast, may be used to persuade a court that it should do things the same way as a prior case, even though it is not bound to do so.

A decision is binding only on cases that involve the same type of situation and similar facts as those of the precedent case. Therefore, the **facts** (the circumstances and events that resulted in the lawsuit) and the **issues** (the individual legal questions addressed) in each case are extremely important.

Also important is the **procedural history** of a case. This term refers to the experience of the case in the judicial system after it was filed. You should understand both the stage the case was in when the opinion was issued as well as how the case arrived at the court issuing it.

For example, is the court looking at the case before or after trial? Is a particular type of motion involved, or is the case on appeal? If on appeal, how many steps or stages have passed: is the case in the court of last resort in the particular jurisdiction? (*See* Chapter 3 for more information on these topics). This information is important; different types of opinions carry different weights. A ruling in a case from the trial court issued before trial has a different effect on future cases than a ruling from the court of last resort after a full jury trial occurred in the case below.

The ultimate **judgment** rendered on each issue (who won) involved in a case likewise is important because the more integral a discussion is to the judgment, the more significant it is in the long term.

Along these lines, you should know that only the **holding** of the case is controlling on future cases.

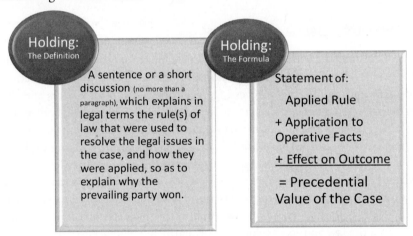

The holding is more than just the yes or no answer to a legal question. It is a sentence or short discussion explaining how the issue was answered. The holding explains the rule(s) that applied to resolve the issue in the case. A complete understanding of the holding also entails some discussion of the operative (**legally significant**) facts—those essential to the decision reached.

If part of the discussion has no bearing on the outcome of the case but, rather, indicates what would or should be the law in different or future circumstances, that material is called dicta. While not binding on future courts in future cases, **dicta** is important for predicting how a court would handle a future case where the facts and issues were as discussed. Dicta can be valuable **persuasive** authority. (Chapters 4 and 5 discuss these concepts in more detail.)

Dicta is not an easy concept to grasp; it can be difficult to locate and distinguish from the holding. Sometimes the line between them is tough to draw. In the beginning, do not expect to get every aspect of your case brief correct every time. Consider the following definition:

DICTA - The Definition

What is Dicta?

Dicta is anything in a case (any statement about the law, legal analysis, discussion of an element or factor) that is unnecessary to the outcome of the case. If the discussion of the law you are considering has no impact on the outcome of the case (the decision of the court as to who won and lost and why), then it is dicta.

DICTA - The Formula

Factors Establishing Dicta:

• Did the court make its decision halfway through the case, and announce it, but went on to discuss several elements, items, or factors anyway? If so, the items discussed after the court announced its decision are probably dicta.

• Did the court say that it was not reaching certain issues? This is a dead giveaway that any discussion of these issues is dicta.

• Did the court predict an outcome for a future case if the facts or circumstances were different? That kind of prediction is dicta.

• If you simply dropped the issue or the discussion of the issue from the case—removed every mention of it— would it still be possible to:

a. Discern why the prevailing party prevailed?
b. State the factors, policies and considerations that brought about the decision?
c. Explain the rule(s) or element(s) that were analyzed and applied to determine the outcome?
d. State the facts that the court found to be important to the decision?

If you answer YES to a, b, c, and d, you have dicta.

Why brief a case?

Case briefing forces you to engage in active learning, whereas merely reading a case (even with several highlighters in hand) constitutes only passive learning. You learn more and *retain more* when you step back from reading, determine the answers to the questions that a case brief entails, and write or type that information into a separate document or outline. You perform a level of analysis that merely reading does not achieve. In addition, case briefs can serve a very practical purpose: they give you something to rely on when you are called on in class (easier to read in the heat of the moment than the multi-colored, highlighted pages of your casebook).

What should a "case brief" include?

There is no magic formula or mandatory structure for a case brief, and your goal might be different for different classes or professors. The purpose is to capture the key pieces of information from the cases you read in a format that makes sense to you.

Presumably you will want to note the following key details:

1. the **name (or caption)** of the case;

2. the **identity of the parties;**

3. any significant **factual history;**

4. the **legal issues** raised;

5. the **court level and jurisdiction** (state or federal? trial, intermediate, last resort?);

6. the **procedural history** (how the case got there);

7. the **holding;**

8. and any other information that seems particularly noteworthy, memorable, or important (*e.g.*, the name of the **judge** or **votes in the majority;** the court's **rationale;** significant **dicta**).

What does it look like?

As for organization, that really is up to you. Below is a sample format that follows a logical structure; you can also ask your professors or upper-class friends for examples.

CASE BRIEF

Style of the Case:
Court:
Judge:
Facts:
Procedural History:
Issues:
Judgment:
Holding:
Discussion (and Dicta):

How long should a case brief be?

At first, your case briefs may consume a page or more. The longer and more complicated they are, however, the more likely you will tire of preparing them. Instead, aim to develop an efficient method that suits you (and the material). After several weeks, you will have a better sense of what to focus on for each class. Your case briefs in Civil Procedure, for example, may require more procedural history. In Contracts, perhaps the focus will be on certain factual details—the various discussions among the parties. Experiment a little with different formats and content before you give up the practice entirely.

APPENDIX B

Common Errors in Grammar and Punctuation

I. GRAMMAR

Lawyers are notorious for writing long-winded sentences replete with "legalese," including everything from antiquated expressions (such as "heretofore," and "aforementioned") to "throat-clearing" expressions ("it is obvious that" and "it is interesting to note that") to redundant words and phrases ("full and complete," "each and every," and "the reason is because"). In short, lawyers tend toward verbosity, using ten words to state what could be said in five. We could write an entire book about this tendency in legal writing but, fortunately, others beat us to it. We recommend that you purchase a good style manual early on in law school and keep it close at hand for the entirety of your career.

FYI

First Aid for Grammar

There are a number of excellent resources for grammar and usage help, many of which are self-help manuals. A few of the more popular and highly recommended ones are:

- Bryan A. Garner, The Redbook: *A Manual on Legal Style* (2d ed. 2006), and Bryan A. Garner, *Legal Writing in Plain English: A Text with Exercises* (2001). Bryan Garner is the current editor of *Black's Law Dictionary* and many other books on legal style. These two books are accessible, well organized resources on grammar, usage, and style for legal writing that will answer most of your questions. There are *Plain English* exercises on-line that you can try without buying the book (but no sample answers): http://press-pubs.uchicago.edu/garner/.

- Bryan Garner and Supreme Court Justice Antonin Scalia co-authored a book, *Making Your Case: The Art of Persuading Judges* (2008), at http://legalsolutions. thomsonreuters.com/law-products/Readers/Scalia-and-Garners-Making-Your-Case-The-Art-of-Persuading-Judges/p/100005899. The book is not only a type of style manual, but it is an entertaining read.

- Marc A. Grinker, *The Legal Writing Teaching Assistant: The Law Student's Guide to Good Writing* (1994), at http://www.kentlaw.edu/academics/lrw/grinker/LWTA. htm. This is a helpful introduction to grammar rules that come up often in legal writing. It has many examples and contains links to exercises (with answers!).

- Richard C. Wydick, *Plain English for Lawyers* (2005), at http://www.cap-press.com/ pdf/1476.pdf (table of contents). A short, easy-to-use manual that emphasizes plain English and covers common mistakes made by lawyers and law students.

For most people, learning grammar is as a much fun as learning citation. But the importance of good grammar cannot be overstated. Without it, you risk damaging your credibility before your audience has had time to process the substance of your writing. That is the best case scenario; the worst is that poor grammar actually risks *confusing* your reader to the point of her thinking that you meant the opposite of what you intended.

Instead of offering tips for style and usage, we have chosen to present some of the "most common" errors in grammar and punctuation. This information was compiled from our own students' writing and based on the results of a diagnostic exam we administered to a large group of 1Ls at a top-twenty law school.

A. Parallelism

Parallel structure requires that you use the same grammatical structure for things that are logically parallel.

- **Rule: Use parallel adjectives to describe parallel qualities.**

  Example: The plaintiff was disoriented, confused, and agitated.

  Not: The plaintiff was disoriented, confused, and walking down the street.

- **Rule: Use parallel structure in lists.**

  Example: The defendant shoved the gun into the cabinet, jumped out the window, and hurried down the street.

  Not: The defendant shoved the gun into the cabinet, jumped out the window, and was running down the street.

- **Rule: Use parallel structure to compare or contrast cases.**

  Example: In *Smith*, the court found that the defendant's agitated state should not be considered where he passed a drug test. In contrast, in *Jones*, the court found that the defendant's agitated state should be considered where he passed a drug test.

  Not: In *Smith*, the court found that the defendant's agitated state was evidence of his drug use. In contrast, in *Jones*, the court found that the defendant's disposition was irrelevant.

- **Rule: Use parallel structure to add emphasis.**

  Example: The defendant failed to show up at his probation meeting, failed to appear at his hearing, and failed to obtain employment as condition of his probation.

Not: The defendant failed to show up at his probation meeting, did not appear for his hearing, and is refusing to obtain employment as condition of his probation.

B. Word choice

Word choice is of paramount importance because every word counts in legal writing. Misusing words, moreover, can detract from the credibility and validity of your legal analysis.

- **Rule: Be careful with use of legal terms, or terms of art, because incorrect usage can damage your reputation as a legal writer.**

   Example: The *Marbury Court held* that judicial review is . . . .

   Not: The *Marbury Court found* that judicial review is . . . .

Note: Juries make findings of facts, courts do not unless the courts are holding a bench trial (non-jury trial). Courts make holdings; holdings are also known as rules of law. Other words to describe what courts do: conclude, determine, decide.

- **Rule: Avoid unnecessary modifiers (adverbs, adjectives, etc.).**

   Example: An alcoholic father

   Not: A habitually alcoholic father

- **Rule: Use pronouns at your own risk; be absolutely, unequivocally, categorically sure that it is clear to what or whom the pronoun refers.**

   Example: Christopher and Paulie disagreed about whether Paulie should kill the restaurant owner.

   Not: Christopher and Paulie disagreed about whether he should kill the restaurant owner.

- **Rule: Make sure each "this" is unambiguous.**

   Example: This ruling is a miscarriage of justice.

   Not: This is a miscarriage of justice.

- **Rule: That vs. Which**

Use "which" when the modifier is a completely separate clause.

> *Example:* Your car, which was still in the lot at midnight, was towed.

Otherwise, use "that" (*i.e.,* when there is no comma in the sentence).

> *Example:* All cars that remain in the lot after 10 p.m. will be towed.

- **Rule: Since vs. Because**

"Since" refers to a relationship in time.

> *Example:* It has been a while since I've seen you.

"Because" denotes an explanation (one event or thing is the cause of something else).

> *Example:* It has been a while since I've seen you because I don't like you.

> *Not:* It has been a while since I've seen you since I don't like you.

C. Dangling modifiers

A dangling modifier is a phrase that does not modify any word or words in a sentence. To avoid this problem, always make sure the subject of the verb in the modifying phrase is included in the remaining portion of the sentence.

> *Example:* Upon reviewing the exams, the results exceeded expectations.

> *Revised:* Upon reviewing the exams, the professor realized that the results exceeded her expectations.

D. Misplaced modifiers

A misplaced modifier modifies a subject other than the subject of the word or phrase that most closely follows it. To avoid this problem, place the modifying word or phrase next to the modified word.

> *Example:* The robber was described as a tall man with a black moustache weighing 150 pounds.

> *Revised:* The robber was described as a six-foot-tall man weighing 150 pounds with a black moustache. ("150 pounds" describes the man, not the moustache.)

"Only" is a frequently misplaced modifier.

Example: I only run in the spring.

Note: This is confusing because it is not clear if the subject runs only during the three months of the Spring season or if the subject only runs instead of walking, driving, etc. during this time.

Revised: I run only in the spring.

E. Active vs. passive voice

The passive voice consists of a "be"-verb (e.g., are, is, am), or a form of "get," combined with the past participle of a verb.

Examples:

Active: The 1L pulled his rolly-bag up the stairs and clogged traffic.

Passive: The rolly-bag was pulled up the stairs by the 1L.

Note: This is confusing because we do not know who pulled the bag—the 1L or someone else who pulled the bag past the 1L?

Even worse: The rolly-bag was pulled up the stairs and traffic was clogged.

Note: This is confusing because we do not know who pulled the bag or who or what clogged the traffic, nor do we know if there was a connection between the two events.

Active: Betty ignored Bob after "hanging out" with him at the bar last Thursday, but only because she forgot what he looked like.

Passive: Bob was ignored after "hanging out" at the bar with Betty last Thursday, but only because his looks were forgotten.

Note: Did everyone ignore Bob or just Betty? Were his looks forgotten by everyone or just Betty?

If after reading the sentence, the specific actor in the sentence is not clear, you probably used the passive voice. We suggest reviewing your paper specifically to change passive voice into active voice.

There are a few instances where passive voice, in moderation, is acceptable. These instances are limited to where the actor is unknown, unimportant, or intentionally concealed; and where the emphasis is on the recipient of the action instead of the actor. However, generally avoid using passive voice.

II. PUNCTUATION

Punctuation errors can be common even among the most polished writers, in part because we don't mark differences among punctuation marks in speaking. In other words, we "pause" in speaking where we might use a comma, period, or a semicolon, and nothing about our mastery of spoken English indicates which of these marks is appropriate in writing. Moreover, some punctuation marks—including ellipses and, often, colons—are not revealed at all in speech. As writers transcribe thoughts into written words, they may have to think twice about proper punctuation, or they may not use much punctuation at all at first-draft stage. Proper punctuation may thus be a necessary focus at the editing and polishing stage.

A. Comma usage

1. Commas and independent clauses

- **Rule: Use a comma before a coordinating conjunction joining two main, or independent clauses. (An independent clause is one that can stand on its own as a sentence.).**

    Example: The study group ordered pizza, and the slackers went out for a beer.

- **Rule: Do not use a comma when there is just one subject for the two clauses.**

    Example: The study group ordered pizza and went out for a beer.

2. Commas in a series

- **Rule: Place a comma at the end of each item listed, including the item listed immediately before the *and*. Adding the comma before *and* avoids any possible confusion about how many items are listed.**

    Example: Bring your pencils, pens, and paper to the exam.

    Example: Your writing assignments are due in October, November, and March.

3. Commas in dates

- **Rule: When referencing a specific date including the month, day, and year, place a comma between the day and year and another between the year and the rest of the sentence.**

  Example: We enjoyed the August 18, 2004, legal writing presentation immensely.

- **Rule: However, when referencing only the month and year, no comma after the year is necessary.**

  Example: The November 2000 election inspired tremendous controversy.

B. Quotation marks

1. Quotation marks with other punctuation marks

- **Rule: Place periods and commas inside closing quotation marks.**

  Examples: "Janice said to put the gun in the cabinet." "Put the gun in the cabinet," she testified.

- **Rule: Place semicolons and colons *outside* the quotation marks.**

  Example: Her three favorite expressions were: (1) "hakuna matata"; (2) "don't worry be happy"; and (3) "carpe diem."

- **Rule: Question marks or exclamation marks can go inside or outside the quotation marks, depending on whether it is part of the quotation.**

  Examples:

  "Put the gun in the cabinet!"

  I can't believe that she said, "You are a terrible shooter"!

  She asked me, "Where is the gun?"

  Did she say, "The gun is in the cabinet"?

Note: In the third example that the quotation itself is a question, whereas in the fourth example, the quotation is part of the question.

2. Single quotation marks

- **Rule: Use single quotation marks only for quotes within other quotes.**

    Example: The plaintiff testified, "Mark told me to 'hide the gun in the cabinet.'"

C. Ellipsis dots . . . in writing

Ellipsis dots are used in legal writing in two major ways: to indicate that words in a sentence or paragraph have been omitted or, when quoting legal passages, to eliminate unnecessary or repetitive language.

- **Rule regarding use of Three dots: Use three ellipsis dots to indicate the omission of one or more words inside a quotation. Be sure to press the space bar between each dot.**

    Example —Without Ellipsis

    "Law school students have been known to fall asleep during class because of lack of sleep and malnutrition."

    With Ellipsis

    "Law school students have been known to fall asleep . . . because of lack of sleep and malnutrition."

- **Rule regarding use of Four dots: Use four dots to indicate the omission of (a) content at the end of a sentence, (b) content after a completed sentence when the quotation continues, (c) content at the end of the sentence when the quotation continues, and (d) a complete paragraph.**

    Example—Without Ellipsis

    "Law school students have been known to fall asleep during class because of lack of sleep and malnutrition. In addition, they occasionally snore."

    With Ellipsis

- **Content at the end of a sentence.**

    Example:

    "Law school students have been known to fall asleep during class . . ."

- **Content after a completed sentence when the quotation continues.**

  Example:

  > "Law school students have been known to fall asleep during class . . . . In addition, they occasionally snore."

- **Content at the end of the sentence when the quotation continues.**

  Example:

  > "Law school students have been known to fall asleep during class because of lack of sleep and malnutrition. . . . [T]hey occasionally snore."

- **Rule: Four Dots are needed to show the deletion of a complete paragraph.**

  Example:

  > Section 8. The Congress shall have the Power to lay and collected Taxes, Duties, Imposts and Excises, to pay the Debts and provide for the common Defence and general Welfare of the United States; but all Duties, Imposts and Excises shall be uniform throughout the United States;
  >
  > . . . .
  >
  > To make all Laws which shall be necessary and proper for carrying into Execution the foregoing Powers, and all other Powers vested by this Constitution in the Government of the United States, or in any Department or Officer thereof.

- **Rule: It is never appropriate in legal writing to begin a quotation with an ellipsis. A bracketed capital letter indicates that something has been omitted.**

  Example: "[S]tudents have been known to fall asleep during class because of lack of sleep and malnutrition."

D. Colons

Proper use of the colon is extremely important in legal writing. It helps lead the reader down a chain of reasoning and serves as an arrow or pointing finger to the second clause.

Note: *Make sure you know the difference between use of a colon and use of a semi-colon (see below).*

There are a few specific rules you should remember when using colons.

- **Rule: Use a colon to introduce a quotation, list, or statement (*e.g.,* a block quote or categorical list).**

Note: *It may be helpful to use a colon when listing the elements of a rule; however, remember to use a semicolon to separate each particular element of the rule.*

> ***Example:*** There are 3 elements of a valid contract: (1) offer; (2) acceptance; and (3) consideration.

- **Rule: Do not use a colon directly after a verb when introducing a list.**

> ***Example:*** Your knapsack should include the following: a knife, a piece of wood, and a slingshot.

> ***Not:*** Your knapsack should include: a knife, a piece of wood, and slingshot.

- **Rule: Use a colon to join two independent clauses with a colon if the second interprets or amplifies the first.**

> ***Example:*** Things got worse in a hurry: our co-defendant turned state's evidence.

Note: *A semicolon can also be used in the above example; but remember, a colon emphasizes the second phrase, which can be extremely helpful in legal writing.*

E. Semi-colons

Legal writing usually requires using semi-colons on two occasions.

- **Rule: Semi-colons separate two independent clauses. Independent clauses are statements that could stand alone or can be combined using a conjunction, an adverb, or nothing at all. When two or more independent clauses are joined by an adverb or by nothing, use of a semicolon is appropriate (whereas a conjunction serves the same purpose as a semicolon and is preceded only by a comma).**

Examples:

Adverb: "Law school barely relates to legal practice; nonetheless, most students tend to work too hard and too long."

Note: Other common adverbs include: accordingly, also, besides, consequently, further, furthermore, hence, however, indeed, instead, later, likewise, meanwhile, moreover, nevertheless, now, still, then, therefore, thus.

No Connector: "One L's think the first year of school is the hardest; the second year will disabuse them of that notion."

Conjunction: "One L's may appear tired and overwhelmed, but they are still learning time management."

- **Rule: Semi-colons are used to separate elements in a series when the individual elements are complex or contain internal commas. This most commonly occurs in a statute or a contract.**

  Example: "As commonly defined for the charge of murder, 'malice' means the specific intent to kill; the specific intent to inflict serious bodily harm; the specific intent to commit a felony; or reckless indifference to human life."

TAKE NOTE!

English as a Foreign Legal Language

If you need additional assistance with English grammar and usage, and especially if English is not your first language, then consider this list of grammar and usage ESL resources on the Internet:

- The Writing Lab & The OWL, Purdue University, Online Writing Lab, https://owl.english.purdue.edu/owl/resource/678/01/

- The Internet TESL, Journal Activities for ESL Students, http://a4esl.org/

- Language Dynamics, Online English Grammar Book, http://www.englishpage.com/grammar/index.html

- Charles Kelly and Lawrence Kelly, A Website for Studying English as a Second Language, http://www.manythings.org

Appendix C

Preparing For and Taking Exams

This Appendix discusses exam-preparation and exam-taking strategies, but it is limited for two reasons: First, someone has beaten us to the task and written an excellent (and quite comprehensive) book on the complex world of law school exam-taking: *Getting to Maybe: How to Excel on Law School Exams*, by Richard Michael Fischl and Jeremy Paul. Second, you must **always keep in mind that the #1 source for information on exam-taking is your professor in each course**. Different professors have different advice and preferences—such as whether to follow IRAC at all. If your professors do not discuss their expectations on exams (in particular, on essay exams where it will matter how you write and organize your answers), ask them.

I.   OUTLINING and OUTLINES

A. What is "outlining"?

Outlining simply means pulling together the material assigned and covered in a class into an organized structure, typically in outline form. An outline is a "digested" compilation of the material that came thick and fast during the semester. You will want to lay out the big picture issues, the policies, and perform a synthesis of the cases and other sources of the law assigned and discussed in class to have an organized capsule summary of the law on a given topic.

In thinking about how to approach your outline, seriously consider the course syllabus. That document often provides considerable insight in how your professor sees the material hanging together and is a great place to begin the outlining process.

B. Why outline?

As we noted in connection with case briefing, the discipline of outlining forces you to tackle the material in an active way—reviewing, analyzing, processing, and synthesizing it into a cohesive summary of the law on the topic.

Merely reading the material, even reading it twice, is not enough. You have to try to make something out of it—make important connections; think about the big picture issues and the policies at work; think about how the holding of one case adds to the holding of previous cases, or modifies, expands, limits the rules and legal standards learned in other cases. Reading alone is a passive activity, whereas outlining engages the mind in an active way. As you no doubt will learn in your legal writing class, writing down what you know about a topic exposes your thoughts and your understanding. If your outline looks like a mess, your thinking in an area also may need cleaning up. Because outlining aids in learning and memorizing the law in the area in a way that simply reading and rereading the material does not, outlining is especially important on closed book exams!

FOOD FOR THOUGHT

There is an analogy to be made between our advice on outlining and our advice in Chapter 8, where we suggested that you read your memo aloud to catch typos. Reading and reciting are two different acts. The latter is a more active practice that forces you to stop and read each word aloud. Preparing an outline is an active practice that works a similar effect. It forces you to perform some analysis, to actually make sense of and organize the material you have read and reviewed in the semester. The act of writing the outline down also helps you to memorize the material.

Author Murray has often found that when you are learning lines for a theatrical production, the active practice of writing out your lines and running your lines with other actors beats the passive reading and rereading of the lines for memorization. Author DeSanctis does not do theatre; however, she agrees with this advice and uses it when giving any speech or presentation.

Finally, remember that the course material was not chosen at random. Rather, it was most likely presented in a way that exemplifies both the current state of the law and the development of the law in an area. Outlining will help you grasp both current legal rules and, as well, why and how they developed that way.

C. What about other people's outlines or commercial outlines?

For all the reasons above, *there is no substitute for making your own outlines.* Reading and rereading someone else's outline is not going to force you to think critically and synthesize and digest the material. Rather, making the outline—the process itself—is where the most learning takes place.

If you never read the material in the first place, you are going to run into some difficulties at the outlining stage, and no supplemental source is going to get you where you need to be. Of course, you always want to read as much as you can. If you thereafter need to supplement what you read, you might turn to a commercial outline or another student's outline. In addition, comparing your outline to the outlines of others can expose areas that you glossed over or misconstrued and areas that you may need to reexamine.

Commercial outlines can be less useful. They were written by someone who did not attend your classes, most likely did not have your professor, did not necessarily look at the material you were supposed to read, and may explain the law in terms that your professor did not use. Thus, be wary. That said, the leading commercial outlines may have been written for the textbook you were assigned, and that is a point in their favor. And you certainly can use a commercial outline to make sure your outline of the law looks correct and makes sense.

II. TAKING EXAMS

A. Closed book vs. open book

A closed book exam requires you to take the test without the benefit of your notes, the casebook, your outline, other outlines, flash cards, prayer cards, tarot cards, etc.—so you must have learned the material ahead of time. As mentioned above, having read, digested, and outlined the course material is a big step toward that goal. The bar exam is a closed-book exam covering many, many subject areas; so at some point you will be exposed to the concept even if you never face such an exam in law school.

TAKE NOTE!

The rules on what you can bring to an open book exam differ from class to class and from professor to professor. Learn them ahead of time, not on the morning of the exam when the proctor wrenches that commercial outline out of your clutching hands

Though it sounds less scary, do not rejoice in the open book exam. Often they are more difficult and more detailed precisely because they are open book. Even with everything you want in front of you, it can be challenging to put your hands on it in an exam setting unless you have read, digested, and—you guessed it—outlined the material in advance. Flipping to the correct section of your own outline is much faster that trying to find the material in your notes, the casebook, a 200-page commercial outline or even someone else's outline that you did not create.

B. Types of questions

1. Issue-spotting

"Issue-spotting" is a common term for what most law school exams require you to do. You are presented with a fact pattern—often recounting a series of wildly coincidental and sometimes fantastical events—and your goal is to parse through it looking for the types of claims that the various characters may bring against each other. Really what you are looking for are the potential **legal issues** implicated by the fact pattern. After you identify (or "spot") each issue, you will be tasked with articulating the rule(s) or standard(s) governing that issue, and then—importantly—*applying the most relevant facts from the question* to generate a conclusion. This should sound familiar to you because it is basically the same process you've been perfecting in your legal writing class.

Example:

Mr. Jones, a resident of Blackacre, the largest city in the State of Euphoria, was standing on the platform of the Blackacre Transportation Company's downtown subway station at rush hour. The trains were packed, and employees of the transportation company were present on the platform and helping to shove passengers into the over-packed subway cars. One such employee, Mrs. Smith, noticed a passenger standing on the platform near the front of the train. This passenger looked very ill and appeared to be having a mild seizure. The passenger swayed back and forth, and Smith thought she was in danger of toppling into the path of the train that was preparing to depart. Smith jumped and ran to aid of the swooning passenger. In her zeal, she knocked over a trash can that rolled into a small freestanding billboard for Breathless cigarettes, which caused the billboard to topple over onto Mr. Jones's head and knocking him unconscious. Mr. Jones suffered severe lacerations requiring 100 stitches and much pain and discomfort.

Discuss Mr. Jones' ability to recover for his injuries from Mrs. Smith and Blackacre Transportation Companies.

In this example, you would want to discuss issues of negligence, including the duty of care of a common carrier, whether that duty applies to someone on the platform, whether the duty was violated by the Transportation Co. or its agent Mrs. Smith, whether there was causation of Mr. Jones' injuries; issues regarding responsibility for the actions of an employee which involves issues of agency and *respondeat superior* liability (if those were covered in class); and "Good Samaritan" liability to the extent it might change the outcome of the above analysis.

Points generally are awarded for correctly identifying all the issues implicated in the facts, for spelling out the rules and legal standards that apply, and for performing a logical, plausible application of the law to the facts. Additional points may be awarded for exploring alternative outcomes based on different theories of the law, or based on facts that are not discussed in the fact pattern but would impact the outcome if they were present. Because all of this must be done in a very limited period of time, we recommend that you analyze your issues using a simple IRAC (Issue, Rule, Application, Conclusion) format, rather than the more sophisticated TREAT format.

PRACTICE POINTER

IRAC on Exams

The simple IRAC formulation can work well on exams when you have only three or four hours to address and answer several questions in essay form. The more thorough TREAT formulation is better for legal writing *in practice*, not necessarily on law school exams. Crafting a strong Thesis, for example, is not necessarily going to get you any more points on your exam than simply stating "The first issue is X." As always, listen first and foremost to your professor's advice on exam-taking tips.

You should identify and work through each issue as thoroughly as you can. Lay out rules and interpretive rules, do analogical and converse analogical reasoning, and perform counteranalysis (identifying and working through an opponent's (or Devil's advocate's) perspective on a problem)—but do not expect to have the time to work up complex inductive principles through explanatory synthesis in a three or four hour exam period.

If you have read and digested the law ahead of time, you will tend to spot more issues, and you generally will come up with the correct rules and legal principles to apply. If you have not, you will probably miss issues, apply the wrong law, or on an open book exam, you will be scrambling to find a case or a Restatement provision that covers the issues you think are there.

2. Big picture, policy questions

Essay questions also may ask you to explain why the law is the way it is today, or why it developed in a certain way, or the reasons for establishing the law as X or Y. These questions require that you demonstrate a broader grasp of the "meaning" of the law by revealing your understanding of the big issues and policies implicated by a topic or issue.

Examples:

Discuss the pros and cons of the "Good Samaritan" rule that modifies the rules on liability for negligence.

Discuss the reasons for and against the comparative negligence rule and the contributory negligence rule.

Points are awarded for discussing the policies, the pros and cons of these big picture issues, and doing so in a thoughtful, well organized way.

3. Information seeking—short answer

These are the "you know it or you don't" question. On an open book exam, you will know when others have reached this section because they will start madly flipping through the pages of whatever is allowed to be brought into the exam.

Examples:

A legislative enactment that allows a state to exert its jurisdiction over nonresidents is called: _____

The U.S. Supreme Court case that said you can only exert jurisdictional power over someone if they are physically present in the jurisdiction is:

The doctrine of tort law (expressed in a Latin phrase) covering an employer's liability for the actions of its employees, servants and agents is:_____

_____

The elements of a claim for promissory estoppel are: _____

_____

4. Multiple choice (multiple guess)

The prepared student (or the optimist) will call these kinds of questions multiple choice. The unprepared (or the pessimist) will call them multiple guess. You almost certainly have been exposed to this type of exam question in your life as a student before coming to law school.

Examples:

The person bringing an appeal can properly be referred to as the: (a) plaintiff; (b) defendant; (c) appellant; (d) appellee.

The party who prevailed in *Siewerth v. Charleston* was: (a) Roy Siewerth; (b) Robert Siewerth; (c) June Charleston; (d) Ruben Charleston.

In promissory estoppel, the claimant's reasonable and foreseeable reliance on a definite promise, to her detriment, can replace the element of consideration in the typical breach of contract case—True or False?

C. Time management

Exam taking not only tests your knowledge of a subject matter and skills as a lawyer but also your ability to manage time. Look for clues (direct or indirect) as to how much of your time to spend on a given question or section of questions. Occasionally the professor is nice enough to spell out the time or the percentage that each question or section is worth (*e.g.*, she may state, "spend no more than 45 minutes on each question"—meaning each question is weighted equally; or she may state, "question 1 (35%), question 2 (20%) . . . ." etc., so that you can allocate your time accordingly). Spending two hours on one of six equally weighted questions and fifteen minutes on each of the other five likely will cost you in your overall grade on the exam.

Our advice is:

Plan ahead—actually put a watch in front of you and when the allotted time is gone, wrap up quickly or simply leave your answer and move on to the next question.

Leave a space at the end of a "not so finished answer" and come back to if you finish the other questions early (Of course, you can only do so if the computer program you use to take the exam permits you to go back (some don't) or you are writing the exam longhand, the "old fashioned way").

Try to leave ten minutes at the end to read all of your answers and correct the obvious typos, complete your incomplete sentences and thoughts, and clarify the messiest areas.

One technique that may work for you (and again assuming that your exam software accommodates it) is to take some time at the outset of the exam to outline the answers to each of the major essay questions. Though you obviously will then go back and write out longer answers, if you get into a time crunch, at least you will have documented some of what you know and understand about a question—the issues you spotted, the rules and standards that apply, and so on. You may rack up additional points this way, even in the face of an otherwise incomplete answer.

Briefly outlining the answers at the outset also may help you get your bearings—and determine where and how you need to spend the most time. As well, taking this time often will help you produce better organized answers.

Index